THE CAMBRI
TWENTIETH-CENTI

MW00777698

In Russian history, the twentieth
ical transformations – changes in social systems, political regimes, and economic structures. A number of distinctive literary schools emerged, each with their own voice, specific artistic character, and ideological background. As a single-volume compendium, the *Cambridge Companion to Twentieth-Century Russian Literature* provides a new perspective on Russian literary and cultural development, as it unifies both émigré literature and literature written in Russia. This volume concentrates on broad, complex, and diverse sources – from Symbolism and revolutionary avant-garde writings to Stalinist, post-Stalinist, and post-Soviet prose, poetry, drama, and émigré literature, with forays into film, theatre, and literary policies, institutions, and theories. The contributors present recent scholarship on the historical and cultural contexts of twentieth-century literary development, and situate the most influential individual authors within these contexts: among them Boris Pasternak, Alexander Solzhenitsyn, Joseph Brodsky, Osip Mandelshtam, Mikhail Bulgakov, and Anna Akhmatova.

EVGENY DOBRENKO is Professor of Russian at the University of Sheffield.

MARINA BALINA is Isaac Funk Professor of Russian Studies at the Illinois Wesleyan University.

A complete list of books in the series is at the back of this book.

THE CAMBRIDGE COMPANION TO

TWENTIETH-CENTURY RUSSIAN LITERATURE

EDITED BY

EVGENY DOBRENKO AND MARINA BALINA

CAMBRIDGE
UNIVERSITY PRESS

CAMBRIDGE UNIVERSITY PRESS
Cambridge, New York, Melbourne, Madrid, Cape Town,
Singapore, São Paulo, Delhi, Tokyo, Mexico City

Cambridge University Press
The Edinburgh Building, Cambridge CB2 8RU, UK

Published in the United States of America by Cambridge University Press, New York

www.cambridge.org
Information on this title: www.cambridge.org/9780521698047

First published 2011

Printed in the United Kingdom at the University Press, Cambridge

A catalogue record for this publication is available from the British Library

Library of Congress Cataloguing in Publication data
The Cambridge companion to twentieth-century Russian literature / edited by Evgeny
Dobrenko, Marina Balina.
p.   cm. – (Cambridge companions to literature)
Includes bibliographical references and index.
ISBN 978-0-521-87535-6 (hardback)
1. Russian literature – 20th century – History and criticism.   I. Dobrenko, E. A. (Evgenii
Aleksandrovich)   II. Balina, Marina.   III. Title.   IV. Series.
PG3017.C36   2011
891.7'09004 – dc22   2010043700

ISBN 978-0-521-87535-6 Hardback
ISBN 978-0-521-69804-7 Paperback

CONTENTS

CONTENTS

CONTRIBUTORS

MARINA BALINA, Illinois Wesleyan University

DAVID BETHEA, University of Wisconsin, Madison and University of Oxford

BIRGIT BEUMERS, University of Bristol

NIKOLAI BOGOMOLOV, Moscow State University

PHILIP ROSS BULLOCK, University of Oxford

KATERINA CLARK, Yale University

EVGENY DOBRENKO, University of Sheffield

CARYL EMERSON, Princeton University

SIGGY FRANK, University of Nottingham

BORIS GASPAROV, Columbia University

JULIAN GRAFFY, University College London

ANDREW KAHN, University of Oxford

MARK LIPOVETSKY, University of Colorado, Boulder

STEPHANIE SANDLER, Harvard University

BORIS WOLFSON, Amherst College

MARIA ZALAMBANI, University of Bologna, Forlì

ACKNOWLEDGEMENTS

First and foremost, we wish to express our heartfelt gratitude to our contributors for their enthusiasm and skill, and their support of our collective efforts in completing this project. We gratefully acknowledge the help of Jesse Savage: his skilful translations and his invaluable and unstinting help with various aspects of this manuscript's preparation deserve special recognition. We want to express a special thanks to our copy-editor at Cambridge University Press, Barbara Docherty, whose investment of time and energy went far beyond her call of duty. Our wholehearted thanks goes to Lauren Nelson for her assistance with this project. We would also like to thank the Isaac Funk Foundation at the Illinois Wesleyan University and the Faculty of Arts and Humanities at the University of Sheffield for providing financial assistance for this project. Finally, we are grateful to Linda Bree, Maartje Scheltens, and Christina Sarigiannidou, our editors at Cambridge University Press, for their support, confidence, and patience during the completion of this volume.

NOTE ON NAMES

Every time that a writer discusses some aspect of a people who use a different writing system, the same problem arises: 'How do I spell the names?' To take just one Russian name, the 'romanized' spellings Juri, Jurij, Yuri, Yury, Iurii, and even Uri, might all represent (and most have represented) the name Юрий. In this collection, the editors have chosen to (mostly) follow the Library of Congress system for romanizing Cyrillic names, as it is widely used by the libraries and booksellers of Great Britain, Australia, and North America, with very few exceptions. We have upper-cased only the first letter of digraphs of that system (Ia, Iu, and Ts instead of IA, IU, and TS) when they are upper-case in Russian, and have not used the ligatures that join any such digraphs. Within the text of the articles (but not within note sources and Further reading), we have omitted the primes (′ and ″) used to represent the Russian 'soft sign' ь and 'hard sign' ъ, and have romanized both 'short i' й and 'i' и as *i*. All surnames ending in –skii are simplified to –sky, and first names are omitted for (Fedor Mikhailovich) Dostoevsky and (Lev Davidovich) Trotsky. The first name Aleksandr is spelled Alexander, and omitted for (Alexander Sergeevich) Pushkin; forenames are also omitted for (Anton Pavlovich) Chekhov. The surname of Vladimir (Vladimirovich) Maiakovsky is further slightly altered to 'Mayakovsky', and that of Andrei Belyi to 'Bely'. The poet Iosif Aleksandrovich Brodsky is probably as well known for publication in English, so herein he is called Joseph Brodsky. Maksim (Aleksei Maksimovich) Gor′kii is called 'Maxim Gorky'. For notes and Further reading, 'Evgeny' (not 'Evgenii') will be used as the co-editor's forename, whether the source is in Russian or in English; similarly, the German critic/theorist Hans Günther will be so called also for Russian publications cyrillicizing his name as 'Khans Giunter'. Within the body of notes, the names are spelled as they occur on the source. Any significant variations that arise on sources are accommodated by cross-references in the index.

CHRONOLOGY

1893	Merezhkovsky, *On the Reasons for the Decline and on New Trends in Contemporary Russian Literature.*
1894–1917	Reign of Nicholas II, the last tsar of Russia.
1896	Chekhov, *The Seagull.*
1898	Publishing house *Knowledge* and magazine *The World of Art* are founded.
1899	Tolstoy, *Resurrection*
1901	Chekhov, *Three Sisters.*
1902	Gorky, *The Lower Depths.*
1903	Balmont, *Let Us Be like the Sun.*
	Chekhov, *The Cherry Orchard.*
1904–1905	Russo-Japanese War, ending in Russia's defeat.
1904	Journal *Scales* is founded.
	Chekhov (b. 1861) dies.
	Tolstoy, *Hadji Murat.*
	Bely, *Gold in Azure.*
	Blok, *Verses on a Beautiful Lady.*
1905–1907	First Russian Revolution leads to a semiconstitutional regime.
1905	Lenin's article, 'Party Organization and Party Literature'
1906	Journal *The Golden Fleece* is founded.
	Gorky, *Mother.*
	Merezhkovsky, *A Prophet of the Russian Revolution* and *The Coming Boor.*
1907	Artsybashev, *Sanin.*
	Briusov, *The Fiery Angel.*
	Remizov, *The Pound.*
	Sologub, *The Petty Demon.*
1909	Musaget Publishing House and journal *Apollon* are founded.
	Miscellany *Landmarks.*
1910	Tolstoy (b. 1828) dies.
	Blok, *Retribution.*
	Bunin, *The Village.*

1911	The Poet's Guild (*Tsekh poetov*) is founded.
	Bunin, *Sukhodol*.
1912	Manifesto *A Slap in the Face of Public Taste*.
	Akhmatova, *Evening*.
	Rozanov, *Solitaria*.
1913	The literary groups *Mezzanine of Poetry* and *Centrifuge* are founded.
	Bely, *Petersburg*.
	Gumilev, *Acmeism and the Precepts of Symbolism*.
	Kruchenykh and Khlebnikov, opera *Victory over the Sun*.
	Mandelshtam, *The Stone* and *The Morning of Acmeism*.
1914–1918	First World War.
1914	Akhmatova, *Rosary*.
	Sologub, *The Created Legend*.
	Shklovsky, *Resurrection of the Word*.
1915	OPOIaZ is founded.
	Bunin, *The Gentleman from San Francisco*.
	Rozanov, *Fallen Leaves*.
	Mayakovsky, *The Backbone Flute*.
1917	The February Revolution. Abdication of Nicholas II. The October Revolution establishes Soviet power.
	Proletkult is founded.
	Shklovsky, *Art as Device*.
1918–1921	Civil War.
1918	Blok, *The Twelve*, *The Scythians*, and *Intelligentsia and Revolution*.
	Gastev, *The Poetry of the Working-Class Attack*.
	Gorky, *Untimely Thoughts*.
	Mayakovsky, *Mystery-Bouffe*.
	Rozanov, *The Apocalypse of Our Time*.
1919	The State Publishing House (*Gosizdat*) is established.
	Mayakovsky, *150,000,000*.
1920	*The Smithy* literary group and the All-Russian Association of Proletarian Writers (VAPP) are founded.
	Zamiatin, *We*.
1921–1928	Era of the New Economic Policy (NEP).
1921	*Serapion Brothers* literary group emerges.
	Blok, *On the Poet's Calling*.
	Blok (b. 1880) dies.
	Gumilev executed for his alleged participation in an anti-Soviet conspiracy.
	Ivanov, *Armoured Train No. 14–69*.
	Journals *Red Virgin Soil* and *Press and Revolution* are founded.
	Aleksei Tolstoi, *Sisters*.
	Tsvetaeva, *Mileposts* and *The Swans' Demesne*.

1922   FEKS group publish manifesto of *Eccentrism*
Glavlit, the censorship authority, is established. Soviet government decides to deport over 160 intellectuals.
LEF, Young Guard and *October* literary groups are founded.
Akhmatova, *Anno Domini.*
Khlebnikov, *Zangezi.*
Khodasevich, *The Heavy Lyre.*
Libedinsky, *The Week.*
Mandelshtam, *Tristia.*
Pasternak, *My Sister Life.*
Pilniak, *The Naked Year.*
Tikhonov, *The Horde* and *Mead.*
Zoshchenko, *Tales of Nazar Ilich, Mr. Sinebriukhov.*

1923   *Pereval* literary group is founded.
Journal *On Guard* is founded.
Babel, *The Odessa Tales.*
Furmanov, *Chapaev.*
Mandelshtam, *The Noise of Time.*
Mayakovsky, *About That.*

1924   Journals *October* and *The Star* are founded.
Trotsky, *Literature and Revolution.*
Bulgakov, *White Guard.*
Fedin, *Cities and Years.*
Leonov, *Badgers.*
Seifullina, *Virineia.*
Serafimovich, *The Iron Flood.*
Tsvetaeva, *Poem of the End* and *Poem of the Mountain.*

1925   Journal *The New World* is founded.
Central Committee's Resolution *On the Policy of the Party in the Sphere of Artistic Literature.*
Babel, *Red Cavalry.*
Bulgakov, *The Days of the Turbins.*
Erdman, *The Mandate.*
Esenin, *The Black Man.* Suicide of Esenin (b. 1895).
Gladkov, *Cement.*
Trenev, *Liubov Yarovaia.*
Shklovsky, *On the Theory of Prose.*

1926   Journal *On Literary Guard* is founded.
Nabokov, *Mashenka.*
Pilniak, *The Tale of the Unextinguished Moon.*
Shmelev, *The Sun of the Dead.*
Vesely, *Russia Washed in Blood.*

1927	Fadeev, *The Rout.*
	Leonov, *The Thief.*
	Mayakovsky, *Very Good!*
	Olesha, *Envy.*
	OBERIU poets' group founded
1928	The 'Cultural Revolution' begins.
	First All-Union Party Conference on Cinema
	Gorky returns to the Soviet Union.
	Erdman, *The Suicide.*
	Ilf and Petrov, *Twelve Chairs.*
	Mayakovsky, *The Bedbug.*
	Panferov, *Bruski.*
	Vaginov, *The Goat Song.*
	Propp, *Morphology of the Folktale.*
1929	Stalin's fiftieth birthday; the beginning of the 'Stalin Cult'.
	Attacks on Bulgakov, Pilniak, and Zamiatin.
	Kuzmin, *The Trout Breaks the Ice.*
	Mayakovsky, *The Bathhouse.*
	Platonov, *Chevengur.*
	Zabolotsky, *Scrolls.*
	Bakhtin, *Problems of Dostoevsky's Poetics.*
	Tynianov, *Archaizers and Innovators.*
1930	Journal *The Banner* is founded.
	Mayakovsky, *At the Top of My Voice.* Suicide of Mayakovsky (b. 1893).
	Nabokov, *Luzhin's Defence.*
	Platonov, *The Foundation Pit.*
1931	End of the 'Cultural Revolution'. Beginning of the 'Great Retreat'.
	Afinogenov, *Fear.*
	Ilf and Petrov, *The Golden Calf.*
	Shaginian, *Hydrocentral.*
1932	Dissolution of RAPP and other proletarian artists' associations.
	Socialist Realism proclaimed.
	Pasternak, *Second Birth.*
	Kataev, *Time, Forward!*
	Sholokhov, *Virgin Soil Upturned.*
1933	Gorky Literary Institute is established.
	Journal *The Literary Critic* is founded.
	Bunin wins the Nobel Prize for Literature.
	Makarenko, *Pedagogical Poem.*
	Shmelev, *The Summer of the Lord.*
	Vishnevsky, *Optimistic Tragedy.*
1934	First Congress of the Union of Soviet Writers, which effectively established the Union.

	Ostrovsky, *How the Steel Was Tempered.*
	Evgenii Shvarts, *The Naked King.*
1935	Nabokov, *Invitation to a Beheading.*
	Pogodin, *Aristocrats.*
	Zoshchenko, *The Blue Book.*
1936	Anti-Formalist campaign.
	Gorky (b. 1868) dies.
	Tvardovsky, *The Land of Muravia.*
1937	Height of the Great Terror.
	Execution of Kliuev by NKVD.
	Mandelshtam, *Lines on the Unknown Soldier.*
	Nabokov, *The Gift.*
1938	Arbuzov, *Tania.*
1939	Kharms, *The Accidents* and *The Old Woman.*
1940	Akhmatova, *Poem without a Hero* and *Requiem.*
	Bulgakov, *The Master and Margarita.*
	Chukovskaia, *Sofia Petrovna.*
	Sholokhov, *Quiet Flows the Don.*
	Aleksei Tolstoi, *Peter the First.*
1941–1945	The Great Patriotic War.
1941	Simonov, *Wait for Me.*
	Suicide of Tsvetaeva (b. 1892).
1942	Journal *New Review* is founded in New York.
	Leonov, *Invasion.*
1943	Antokolsky, *A Son.*
	Bunin, *Dark Alleys.*
	Gorbatov, *The Unvanquished.*
1944	Kaverin, *Two Captains.*
1945	Fadeev, *The Young Guard.*
	Panova, *Fellow Travellers.*
	Tvardovsky, *Vasily Terkin.*
1946	Attacks on Zoshchenko and Akhmatova; beginning of *zhdanovshchina.*
	Nekrasov, *In the Trenches of Stalingrad.*
	Polevoi, *Story of a Real Man.*
1949	Anti-cosmopolitanism campaign.
1952	Bunin, *The Life of Arseniev.*
1953	Stalin dies and is succeeded by Malenkov.
	Leonov, *The Russian Forest.*
	Soloukhin, *Vladimir Country Roads.*
	Pomerantsev, *On Sincerity in Literature.*
1954	Ehrenburg, *The Thaw.*
	Prishvin, *The Chain of Kashchei.*

1955	Journal *Youth* is founded.
	Paustovsky, *The Golden Rose.*
1956	Twentieth Congress of the Communist Party. Khrushchev's 'Secret Speech'.
	Suicide of Fadeev (b. 1901).
	Dudintsev, *Not by Bread Alone.*
	Iashin, *Levers.*
	Tendriakov, *Tight Knot.*
1957	Journal *Problems of Literature* is founded.
	Boris Pasternak, *Doctor Zhivago.*
1958	Pasternak wins the Nobel Prize for Literature.
	Campaign against Pasternak.
1959	Arbuzov, *An Irkutsk Story.*
	Voznesensky, *The Masters.*
	Siniavsky (Abram Tertz), *Fantastic Tales.*
1960	Pasternak (b. 1890) dies.
	Grossman *Life and Fate.*
	Tvardovsky, *Distance beyond Distance.*
1961	Height of de-Stalinization. Stalin's body is removed from the Lenin Mausoleum.
	Miscellany *Pages from Tarusa.*
	Aksyonov, *Ticket to the Stars.*
	Evtushenko, *Babii Iar.*
1962	Evtushenko, *Heirs of Stalin.*
	Solzhenitsyn, *One Day in the Life of Ivan Denisovich.*
	Voznesensky, *The Triangle Pear.*
1963	Shukshin, *Rural People.*
	Solzhenitsyn, *Matryona's House.*
	Voinovich, *I Want to be Honest.*
1964	Khrushchev's fall.
	Brodsky trial.
	Zalygin, *On the Irtysh.*
1965	Sholokhov wins the Nobel Prize for Literature.
	Ehrenburg, *People, Years, Life.*
	Evtushenko, *Bratsk Hydroelectric Plant.*
1966	Trial of Siniavsky and Daniel.
	Akhmatova (b. 1889) dies.
	Aitmatov, *Farewell, Gulsary.*
	Belov, *That's How Things are Done.*
	Kataev, *The Holy Well.*
1967	Ehrenburg (b. 1891) dies.
	Kataev, *The Grass of Oblivion.*
	Vampilov, *Duck-Hunting.*

1968 Soviet suppression of the 'Prague Spring'.
     Astafev, *The Last Tribute*.
     Belov, *The Carpenters' Tales*.
     Solzhenitsyn, *Cancer Ward*.
     Tvardovsky, *By the Right of Memory*.
1969 Bondarev, *The Hot Snow*.
     Bykov, *Krugliansky Bridge*.
     Venedikt Erofeev, *Moscow to the End of the Line*.
     Solzhenitsyn, *The First Circle*.
     Trifonov, *The Exchange*.
1970 Solzhenitsyn wins the Nobel Prize for Literature.
     Aitmatov, *The White Steamship*.
     Bitov, *Pushkin House*.
     Bykov, *Sotnikov*.
     Rasputin, *The Final Stage*.
1971 Simonov, *The Living and the Dead*.
     Vladimov, *Faithful Ruslan*.
1973 Iskander, *Sandro from Chegem*.
     Shalamov, *Kolyma Tales*.
     Shukshin, *Characters*.
     Sasha Sokolov, *School for Fools*.
1974 Journal *Kontinent* is founded.
     Solzhenitsyn is arrested and expelled from the Soviet Union.
     Solzhenitsyn, *The Gulag Archipelago*.
1975 Aksyonov, *The Burn*.
     Astafev, *Tsar-Fish*.
     Siniavsky, *Strolls With Pushkin*.
     Voinovich, *The Life and Extraordinary Adventures of the Soldier Ivan Chonkin*.
1976 Gelman, *Minutes of a Meeting*.
     Rasputin, *Farewell to Matyora*.
     Rubinshtein, *The Catalogue of Comedic Innovations*.
     Trifonov, *The House on the Embankment*.
     Zinovev, *Yawning Heights*.
1977 Brodsky, *The End of a Beautiful Epoch* and *A Part of Speech*.
     Nabokov (b. 1899) dies.
1978 Andrei Bely Prize is established by underground writers.
     Kataev, *My Diamond Wreath*.
     Trifonov, *The Old Man*.
1979 *Metropol* affair.
     Limonov, *This is Me, Eddie*.
     Okudzhava, *Journey of Dilettantes*.
1980 Vysotsky (b. 1938) dies.
     Dovlatov, *A Solo on an Underwood*.

Evgenii Kharitonov, *Under House Arrest.*
Petrushevskaia, *Three Girls in Blue.*
Prigov, *The Apotheosis of Militsaner* and *Tears of the Heraldic Soul.*
Sasha Sokolov, *Between a Dog and a Wolf.*

1981   Trifonov (b. 1925) dies.
Aitmatov, *The Day Lasts More Than a Hundred Years.*
Gorenstein, *The Psalm.*
Krivulin, *Poems.*

1982   Brezhnev dies and is succeeded by Andropov.
Shalamov (b. 1907) dies.
Yuz Aleshkovsky, *A Little Blue Kerchief.*
Dovlatov, *Zone.*
Sadur, *The Weird Peasant Woman* and *The Trapped Swallow.*
Sorokin, *The Norm* and *The Queue.*

1983   Prigov, *The Image of Reagan in Soviet Literature.*

1984   Andropov dies and is succeeded by Chernenko.
Brodsky, *Urania.*
Rubinshtein, *The Six-Winged Seraph.*
Sorokin, *The Thirtieth Love of Marina.*

1985–1991   Gorbachev's *glasnost'* and *perestroika.*

1985   Chernenko dies and is succeeded by Gorbachev.
Elena Shvarts, *Dancing David.*
Sasha Sokolov, *Palisandriia.*

1986   Aitmatov, *The Execution Block.*

1987   Brodsky wins the Nobel Prize for Literature.
Dudintsev, *White Robes.*
Viktor Erofeev, *Russian Beauty.*
Granin, *Bison.*
Rybakov, *The Children of Arbat.*
Elena Shvarts, *The Works and Days of Lavinia.*
Tolstaia, *On the Golden Porch.*

1988   Petrushevskaia, *Our Circle* and *Immortal Love.*

1989   Evgenii Popov, *The Soul of the Patriot, or Various Messages to Ferfichkin.*

1990   Dovlatov (b. 1941) dies.
Palei, *Cabiria from the Obvodnoi Canal.*

1991   Yeltsin elected President of Russian Federation (re-elected 1996).
Attempted coup against Gorbachev fails.
Gorbachev resigns as President of the Soviet Union. Soviet Union collapses.
Russian Booker Prize is established.
Petrushevskaia, *The Time: Night.*
Vasilenko, *Shamara.*

1992	Journal *New Literary Review* is founded.
	Narbikova, *In the Here and There.*
	Pelevin, *Omon Ra.*
1993	Pelevin, *The Life of Insects.*
	Prigov, *Fifty Drops of Blood.*
	Rubinshtein, *The Problems of Literature.*
1994	Limonov founds National-Bolshevik Party.
	Solzhenitsyn returns to Russia.
	Astafev, *The Cursed and the Slain.*
	Mark Kharitonov, *Lines of Fate.*
	Kibirov, *The Sentiments.*
	Prigov, *Stalinskoe.*
	Rubinshtein, *I Am Here.*
	Sadur, *Witch's Tears.*
	Sorokin, *Roman* and *Hearts of the Four.*
	Vladimov, *The General and His Army.*
1995	The Anti-Booker Prize established.
	Kibirov, *When Lenin Was a Little One.*
	Makanin, *The Prisoner from the Caucasus.*
	Parshchikov, *Cyrillic Light.*
1996	Brodsky (b. 1940) dies.
	Gandlevsky, *The Trepanation of the Skull.*
	Pelevin, *Chapaev and Void.*
1997	Apollon Grigoriev Prize established.
	Solzhenitsyn Prize established.
	Tolstaia, *Love Me – Love Me Not.*
1998	Grishkovets, *How I Ate a Dog.*
	Makanin, *Underground, or The Hero of Our Time.*
	Sorokin, *Blue Lard.*
1999	Pelevin, *Generation P.*
2000	Putin elected President (re-elected 2004).
	National Bestseller prize established.
	Tolstaia, *Slynx.*
	Ulitskaia, *Kukotsky's Case.*
	Vasilenko, *A Little Fool.*
2001	Prokhanov, *Mister Hexogen.*
	Solzhenitsyn, *Two Hundred Years Together.*
	Sorokin, *Feast.*
2002	Attacks of the pro-Putin youth group 'Moving Together' against Sorokin and Pelevin.
	Sharov, *The Resurrection of Lazarus.*
2003	Dmitrii Bykov, *Orthography.*
2005	Literary Prize 'The Poet' is established.
	Shishkin, *Venus' Hair.*

2006   Literary Prize 'The Big Book' established.
Bykov, *ZhD* (Jewhad).
Pelevin, *Empire V.*
Sorokin, *The Day of the Oprichnik.*
Ulitskaia, *Daniel Stein, a Translator.*

PREFACE

This volume is the first in the series of Cambridge companions to literature to be devoted to post-classical Russian literature. Individual twentieth-century Russian literary works enjoy great popularity with English-speaking audiences: readers have gained access to and familiarity with these works through comprehensive translations, literary and film adaptations, and a number of surveys and monographs. This familiarity with individual exemplars has increased the public's awareness of lesser-known works, and has consequently led to a need for a more complete understanding of the cultural contexts of post-classical Russian literature.

In previous decades, scholars in the former Soviet Union were accustomed to compiling a quite different history of twentieth-century Russian literature from that produced by their counterparts in the West, since each group based its history on a different body of literary texts. In the Soviet Union, major literary works written at the turn of the century and in the 1920s were taken out of circulation, much like those produced at various times by dissident and émigré writers, which were forbidden and therefore never published. In the West, however, all literature created by Soviet literati was considered tantamount to co-opted officialdom. Both groups of scholars used an ideological standard – opposite though their standards were – as a basis for judgements concerning the value of these literary works. Moreover, both Soviet and Western scholars were stymied by the inaccessibility of Soviet archives, and were thus forced to work with a limited number of literary texts. The twofold situation of restricted access and ideological axe-grinding was improved only very recently, with the collapse of the Soviet Union and the publication of previously unknown sources. Finally, readers and scholars in both Russia and the West were able to see twentieth-century Russian literature as a united body of works in all its fullness.

A new, revisionist post-Soviet spirit now suffuses approaches to this subject at all levels, from the production of new editions and new biographical studies to the construction of new interpretive readings. Both mature and

PREFACE

younger generations of scholars in Russia and in the West are seizing the opportunity to 'modernize' twentieth-century Russian literature studies. The past two decades have seen major developments in the way this literature is approached and understood.

The twentieth century was perhaps the most turbulent time in all of modern European history. In Russian history, this 'age of extremes' was a century of unprecedented, radical transformations – changes in social systems, political regimes, and economic structures – which occurred in unimaginable leaps and retreats. For Russia, whose political culture had long been based on authoritarianism and, consequently, on an acute lack of political freedoms, these changes were particularly dramatic. Contributing to this was the historically developed literary centrism of Russian culture: literature here had always been something more than simply literature in the Western sense, and had also played the role of political tribune, the repository of national self-awareness, and a sort of discussion club that provided an outlet for the need to appraise the country's history in terms of ethics (or of what Russian classical tradition called a 'moral verdict') and to reflect philosophically upon its past, present, and future. Thus these changes profoundly altered the very processes by which culture – and, of course, literature – functioned: more than once in the twentieth century, the very content and style of literary production changed radically, as did the makeup of those producing and consuming literature and the scope and functions of literary institutions.

The development of Russian literature in the twentieth century presents an extraordinarily motley picture. It is not even a question of changing styles or trends, but rather of distinct cultural ecosystems. Although each of them did in fact have roots in the preceding sociocultural situations, they were practically autonomous. Russian Symbolism, for example, was the product of the search for new means of artistic expressiveness and of the rejection of the overburdened ideology and psychologism of Russian classical realism; Futurism can be viewed as an abrupt radicalization of the idea of the autonomy of art that lay at the heart of the Symbolist aesthetic; from this perspective, one could define Socialist Realism (as Boris Groys does) as 'the avant-garde, Stalin-style' and, simultaneously, as a return to a pre-avant-garde aesthetic; similarly, one could consider post-Stalinist literature to be a return to the traditions of revolutionary culture that had been abolished in Stalinism; finally, one might conceive of post-Soviet literature as a heterogeneous cultural model open to practically all of the preceding artistic practices (this aesthetic omnivorousness allows us to investigate this literature in the postmodernist paradigm). At the same time, each of these aesthetic schools that successively replaced each other possessed an autonomy that was by no means simply chronological. Each was shaped in a deeply engaged polemic

xxii

with the foregoing one, and could only consolidate itself on the ruined foundations of the preceding tradition: Symbolism destroyed psychological Realism; Futurism rejected both Symbolism and the Realism that had preceded it; likewise, Socialist Realism rejected both its predecessors (and, in fact, Realism as well); post-Soviet literature, begotten as a freakish hybrid of practically all of the preceding traditions, grounds itself upon a principled distance from all of them and often in ironic superiority over them.

Although all of these cultural ecosystems did in fact have certain features of resemblance to the styles and artistic trends that were developing in parallel in other European cultures, each differed in its profound uniqueness. The ties of the Russian Silver Age to French Symbolism, for example, are obvious, as are those between the Russian avant-garde and Italian Futurism and German Dadaism; Stalinist 'Socialist Realist art' has much in common with the art of fascist Italy or Nazi Germany; the parallels between the culture of the post-Stalinist 'Thaw' and the general tendencies of 1960s European culture are obvious, as are those between the tendencies of post-Soviet Russian literature and Western postmodernism. Nonetheless, the distinctiveness of each of these literatures cannot be doubted: Russian avant-garde literature was a deeply innovative phenomenon; the Stalinist model of the functioning of culture was, for better or worse, in many respects unprecedented; and, because of the very specifics of all the changes in artistic trends in Russian literature over the twentieth century, 'Russian postmodernism' is totally unique.

A final point to note about these cultural ecosystems is that, although each had a dimension that pervaded *all of* culture, each led to a break with previous *literary* conventions *per se* as it created new ones differing markedly from the preceding conventions – whether it was a system of literary genres or of narrative models, a new type of plot or hero, systems of expressive devices or indeed of literary institutions, or even a new type of reader sensitivity.

Revealing these peculiarities of twentieth-century Russian literature is exactly what the chapters comprising this book aim to do. We speak of a single twentieth-century Russian literature, including the literature of the Silver Age, the revolutionary avant-garde, the Stalinist era, the post-Stalinist and post-Soviet eras, and, finally, that of émigrés. Nonetheless, there are at times such distinctions where it probably would not be a mistake to say that we are talking about *literatures*, in the plural. These literatures are so different that it seems as if, apart from the Russian language, nothing unites them. But this, too, is probably not completely true: even the literary language was often completely incomprehensible to the reader of the preceding culture. The language of Symbolism and Acmeism, for example, saturated with cultural allusions, or Khlebnikov's 'trans-rational' language, was already completely incomprehensible to the new readers of the early 1930s – yesterday's peasants, who found themselves in an urban culture so new to them, into which Stalin's industrialization and collectivization had thrown them. But the language of Soviet officialese, too, or even the everday Soviet language developed in the new culture – the language of Zoshchenko's characters in the 1920s or of Galich's in the 1970s – also remains opaque to the uninitiated. The story is told that, at one of Galich's concerts in Paris, an old emigrant woman turned to the person sitting beside her and asked, 'Excuse me, but do you know what language he's singing in?'

In a word, the literary schools that replaced each other in turn were so different, the metamorphoses so profound and radical, and the social contexts of literary production and consumption each time so distinctive, that the book here presented to the reader might well be properly called The Companion to Twentieth-Century Russian *Literatures*.

Evgeny Dobrenko and Marina Balina

I

BORIS GASPAROV

Poetry of the Silver Age

The moniker 'Silver Age' refers to the epoch of early and high modernism in Russian culture, which began around the mid-1890s and was put to a rather abrupt end by the October 1917 Revolution. While the most fundamental feature of this time period is marked by its idealist philosophical revolution – a trend Russia shared with other European cultures – its most spectacular manifestation on the Russian scene undoubtedly belonged to poetry and art. In less than a quarter of a century, Russia produced a remarkable constellation of poets, quite a few of whom (Alexander Blok, Mikhail Kuzmin, Osip Mandelshtam, Anna Akhmatova, Boris Pasternak, Marina Tsvetaeva, Velimir Khlebnikov, Vladimir Mayakovsky) stood at the world-wide cutting edge of the poetic culture of their time. The very feeling of the era seemed to be saturated with poetry: even those authors whose main talent and achievements lay in the domain of prose – such as Andrei Bely, Dmitrii Merezhkovsky, Zinaida Gippius, Fedor Sologub, and Ivan Bunin – made significant contributions to the poetic landscape of the time as well.

The flowery name of the age was probably indigenous to the epoch itself, although it never surfaced in documents of the time, perhaps because it was just too obvious to be mentioned. It lay dormant in the collective memory for almost half a century, until it surfaced almost simultaneously in two venues – in the title of critic Sergei Makovsky's memoirs, *On the Parnassus of the Silver Age* (Munich, 1962), and in a line in Akhmatova's 'Poem without a Hero' (first published in 1965) which mentions 'the silver moon hovering brightly over the Silver Age'.[1]

By virtue of its name, the era claimed a special relationship with the 'Golden Age' of Russian poetry, that is to say, of Pushkin and the Pleiades of his contemporaries from the 1810s to the 1830s. This reference implied a kinship between the two ages – a connection established circuitously around the epoch of 'positivism' and realism (that is, the second half of the nineteenth century), now a target of sharp critique by adepts of neo-Kantian and idealist philosophy, and modernist aesthetics. The Silver Age symbolically bowed down to its hallowed predecessor, a gesture in which a nostalgia for the unsurpassable harmony of the past was underlain by the awareness of the superior emotional energy and intellectual maturity of the modern. Against the backdrop of the Golden Age's absolute 'harmony', the new age cast itself as cursed with self-reflection, torn apart by contradicting passions, willing to go to any length in exploring the heights of the sublime and the depths of vice, while simultaneously exalted and desperate about its own wretchedness. In many respects, this attitude was reminiscent of how the champions of 'sentimental' or 'Romantic' poetry (as defined by Friedrich Schiller and Friedrich Schlegel) had viewed their optimistically 'naive' predecessors of the previous century. The neo-Romantic undertones of the Silver Age stood, once again, in sharp contrast to the age of realism, and in firm defiance of it.

Another association ushered in by the epoch's name was that with the Roman Silver Age of Petronius and Nero, an allusion encouraging apocalyptic prophecies and eschatological expectations. The Silver Age perceived itself as a fragile flower doomed to fade quickly, due to both its delicate beauty and poisonous corruptness.

Despite the powerful overall image with which the Silver Age went down in history, it was also an epoch of rapidly evolving and diverse trends. Its major watershed appeared around the year 1910, which divided the Silver Age into two seemingly disconnected yet related stages: 'Symbolism' and 'post-Symbolism' (or 'avant-garde'). The latter in its turn took a bifurcated path due to the rivalry between the two dominant schools of the 'Acmeists' and the 'Futurists', which had little in common with each other, but which nevertheless adopted and transformed, each in its own way, the Symbolist heritage.

Symbolism

The term 'Symbolism' served as an umbrella name for a variety of aesthetic phenomena emerging at the turn of the twentieth century in Russia whose overt differences were sometimes more apparent than their essential affinities. The most obvious internal distinction derives from the two subsequent waves of the movement – the so-called 'elder' and 'younger' Symbolists.

The emergence of the 'elder' stage was marked by Merezhkovsky's collection of poems programmatically titled *Symbols* (1893). As a poet, Merezhkovsky was soon overshadowed by Valerii Briusov and Konstantin Balmont, but he remained the movement's principal ideologue throughout the 1890s and early 1900s. The next wave arrived at the turn of the new century, with Andrei Bely and Viacheslav Ivanov emerging as its leading theoreticians and Alexander Blok and Ivanov representing its main poetic achievement. Another major figure of the time was Mikhail Kuzmin, who for many years remained one of the epoch's defining forces while staying aloof from all literary parties.

The philosophical, aesthetic, and psychological foundations of the movement were embodied in three towering figures of the preceding century: Charles Baudelaire, Friedrich Nietzsche, and Richard Wagner. The central concept of the symbol had as its primary source Baudelaire's programmatic poem 'Correspondences' (1857), which described the world as a 'forest of symbols', palpitating with allusions like animated columns in the temple of nature and casting 'familiar glances' at man as he traverses this enchanted forest. The symbols flutter with metamorphoses, showing themselves in a variety of appearances – as colours, sounds, odours – whose suggestive and elusive resemblances (or 'correspondences') carry the promise of an ultimate wholeness of the transcendent realm of the spirit, which finds in them fragmented and scattered representations.[2]

In the Symbolists' view, any particular phenomenon appears to be wrapped in a web of associations, no matter how tenuous or contradictory, which spreads into infinity. Whenever the subject of Symbolist poetic consciousness sees the colour red, it brings home the ideas of blood, passion, murder, lecherousness – but, also, of stained-glass windows in a cathedral, making sanctity and vice, confessional awe and violent frenzy all fuse into a contradictory synthesis. The red lanterns at the church altar merge with the red lanterns of the house of ill repute, portending the advent of a heavenly female figure – who may well turn out to be a prostitute (Blok, 'Whenever I enter dark temples').[3] An echo of a shepherd's horn heard in the mountains carries a momentous revelation that the human body, like a musical instrument, exists not for its own sake but as a means for spreading echoes into the infinite (Ivanov, 'The Alpine horn'[4]).

The lyrical subject of Symbolist poetry readily forfeits his quotidian existence in pursuit of such transcendent moments. He plunges himself into the depths of vice and lowliness for a chance to discern in them glimpses of the sublime. In doing so, the subject cuts simultaneously a demonic and Christ-like figure – experiencing satanic joy amidst infernal orgies but at the same time feeling crucified by his passions. He revels in the vision of the world – and himself – being overtaken by chaos and violence while ardently prophesying, from the brink of extinction, the new 'dawns' looming beyond the annihilating apocalypse (Briusov, 'Where are you, future Huns?'[5]).

Among the most characteristic features of Symbolist culture is its urbane, cosmopolitan character. Symbolism is about opening horizons, reaching out to the most remote places and, ultimately, to the unreachable. It encourages one to challenge the frontiers of one's culture, and even one's native language. While Rainer Maria Rilke made a Russian Orthodox monk the poetic voice of his early *Book of Monastic Life*, Ivanov's subjects felt at home in Renaissance Italy and ancient Greece. A fashionable trait of the time was to give an exotic (mostly Latin) name to a poem or a book of poems (Ivanov's *Cor ardens*, Briusov's *Stephanos* and *Tertia vigilia*, Alexander Dobroliubov's *Natura naturans et natura naturata*). The urban landscape's dense cohabitation of diverse phenomena, restless commotion, and sharp social contrasts presented a fertile ground for hunting down symbolic correspondences, while its stark pictures of vice and social injustice portend apocalyptic catastrophes, with hordes of the disenfranchised threatening to engulf the city's dubious splendour. Frenzied urban scenes became a 'trademark', particularly for Briusov and Blok.

At the beginning of the movement in Russia, the early adepts of the new school adopted 'Symbolists' as their name; the public and critics in the 1890s, however, preferred to call them 'decadents'. Indeed, it seems fair to say that in the 1890s the 'decadent' side of the nascent movement was more tangible than the 'symbolist' one. The 'elder Symbolists' proved more successful in making gestures of defiance toward the conventional bourgeois moral order and utilitarian aesthetics than in articulating aesthetic and philosophical principles of their own. While the example of the French Symbolists and the Russian 'metaphysical' poets (Fedor Tiutchev, for example) was eagerly adopted, their influence was initially more atmospheric and stylistic than intellectual. But the 'decadent' aspect, which involved self-aggrandizement, defiant extravagance, and demonic posturing, was plainly visible even to those who were unfamiliar with the intricacies of modernist aesthetics.

The foremost example of this early 'atmospheric' Symbolism can be found in the poetry of Balmont. Unlike Baudelaire or Tiutchev, Balmont does not strive to plumb the transcendent meaning of images of nature and human life that come his way. As far as themes and motifs of his poetry and its metrical and strophic repertory are concerned, Balmont appears more closely related to his immediate predecessors in the 'twilight' epoch of the 1880s, such as Semen Nadson or Iakov Polonsky. Traditional images in his poetry are wrapped in a dense web of paronomastic associations, out of which the meaning arises via glossolalia.

Balmont reached the Symbolist vision on the most elementary and most elemental level. While the other Symbolist poets mostly shied away from his visceral glossolalia, his influence on certain leading figures of the post-Symbolist decade (notably Khlebnikov and Pasternak) was palpable.

Similarly, Briusov's pursuit of the trans-empirical progressed on more an emotional than a metaphysical level. He sought to pierce the surface of the ordinary by striving toward the exotic and the extreme; he preferred introducing rarefied colours ('Lilac hands over a pale yellow wall'; 'Invisible hands embroider over the blue atlas with yellow silk') to exploring the symbolic values of ordinary ones. Briusov's subject appears more interested in grasping 'moments' (*migi*) of transcendent vision than in representational phenomena that might trigger them. In a characteristic fit of defiant egocentrism, Briusov's poetic subject professes his hatred to 'ignominious' nature, declaring that 'only the realm of the dream is eternal'[6] ('There is something ignominious in nature's might'). Briusov revelled in provoking shock, bewilderment, and outrage, a posture emblematically represented by his most notorious one-line poem: 'Oh, cover your pale legs!'[7] (He added insult to injury by suggesting privately that what he meant in this monostich was not a daring erotic scene, as many guessed, but the sight of the crucifix.)

The early stage of Symbolism made the idea of 'art for art's sake' its profession of faith, maintaining it against populist tastes, utilitarianism, and (as part of the same 'package') conventional morality. In terms of poetic practices proper, this attitude catalysed the development of sophisticated and esoteric poetic forms and patterns of versification. This trend was particularly tangible in Briusov, and later in Ivanov, who embraced technically demanding genres (such as the 'wreath of sonnets') and rare metrical and strophic forms (i.e. the trochaic heptameter in 'The Pale Horse'). The result was a paradoxical double allegiance among Russian Symbolists to the two competing schools of French poetry, the Symbolists and the Parnassians (the latter led by Théophile Gautier). In particular, Briusov's poetic style combined the neoclassically chiselled poetic form with emotional hyperbolism and graphic extremism of images and situations. In the 1900s, this trend was maintained by Blok, whose poetic diction had a distinct 'Pushkinian' ring to it, making the expressionist eruptions of his imagery all the more striking. It was perhaps this 'Parnassian' inclination that hindered Russian Symbolists from bolder experiments with versification; examples of irregular metre or free verse were rare. The explosive combination of two contradictory elements of poetic discourse retained its spell into the epoch of the Russian avant-garde, whose foremost representatives (such as Pasternak, Akhmatova, and Mandelshtam) remained loyal to classical (though occasionally slightly modified) metres.

Unlike the predominantly decorative and rhetorical postures of the 'decadents', the next generation's concerns remained primarily in the metaphysical and ideological spheres. While retaining the cosmopolitan aesthetic orientation of their predecessors, the younger Symbolists became ardent champions of a mystical 'Russian mission'. The generation of the 1900s defied the quotidian routine – but not in a decadent gesture, rather in the spirit of a Nietzschean critique of conventional morality that was perceived as a vehicle for the radical spiritual transformation of life. This plunge into the depths of demonic chaos is carried out in the name of a Dionysian challenge to the smug Apollonian veneer of civilization. Ivanov hailed Dionysus as the 'Slavic god' (citing his ostensible Thracian origin), viewing his confrontation with the indigenously Hellenic Apollo as a prototype of the challenge to Western rationalism by proponents of the 'Russian idea' like Dostoevsky and Vladimir Solovev. Russia's unique position between the worlds of Western rationalist modernity and Eastern primordial chaos portend its destiny to become the playground of apocalyptic catastrophe and renewal. In suicidal exaltation, the Symbolists revelled in a vision of rising hordes of 'Scythians' or 'Mongols' bringing a bloody renewal to the aging world – even if this renewal meant the annihilation of its prophetic champions. The atmosphere of mystical exaltation, frenzied self-abandonment, and catastrophic prophetic visions – typical of the 1900s – was subsequently amplified by shattering political events: the Russo-Japanese war, the Revolution of 1905, and ultimately, the First World War and the Bolshevik Revolution. In the 1910s, this mood found a particularly powerful expression in Bely's novel *Petersburg* and Blok's poems *The Scythians* and *The Twelve*.

Ivanov's enormous influence throughout the 1900s can be explained, besides merely by his personal charisma, by the fact that his poetry was entirely driven by the philosophical ideas and messianic aspirations of the time. There is something almost didactic in the persistence with which Ivanov's poetic subject points toward the symbolic reverberations of every phenomenon that comes his way. The phenomena themselves tend to be of a rather generic nature: a sudden change of light, a sound, a fleeting shape. The very 'tedium' of their impoverished features highlights the infinite richness of echoes they evoke ('Taedium phenomeni').[8] Sometimes, the symbol-building process does not need any empirical trigger at all. In the poem 'Eros pierced me with the rays of his arrows',[9] the familiar associative cluster of redness, passion, blood, fire, and suffering goes straight to secondary images, over the head of empirical reality: Eros' piercing arrow evokes the execution of Saint Sebastian, the 'bunch' of arrows turns into a bunch of brushwood thrown onto a pyre; both execution scenes – the arrows and the fire – are symbolically represented with 'piercing' rays of the sunset, whose redness is replicated in 'springs' of blood trickling over the subject's body (a hint at ejaculation, making the symbiosis of erotic passion and the execution complete). The hermetic density of the poem's imagery is as striking as the absence of any non-generic life detail, and is further underscored by the abundance of lofty cultural references. Ivanov's somewhat abstract other-worldliness is reflected in his language, saturated with heavy Church Slavonicisms, many of his own coinage; from the pen of Ivanov, an accomplished classicist, the Russian language itself turns into a hint at (or a recollection of) Church Slavonic and Greek.

Blok, on the other hand, manifested an ability to convey mystical meaning through sharp detail in which an other-worldly subtext did not obfuscate its empirical palpability; on the contrary, it is the vividness of the physical world that makes the sense of the metaphysical so acute. Discovery of the 'false infinity' of the material world is triggered by a casual glance at a city landscape, perpetual in its banality: 'A night. A street. A lantern. A pharmacy. Senseless and dim light. You may live another quarter of a century – everything would be the same; there is no escape.'[10] The predicament of modernity, which brought itself to the brink of extinction by challenging God's creation, reveals itself at an aviation show, at the moment an airplane precipitates to the ground: the impassioned monologue addressed to the 'wingless, soulless and faceless bird of steel' is punctuated by an anapaestic rhythm – an echo of a cheap waltz played at the show, to which music the 'bird' performs its fatal circling in the air ('In an uncertain, precarious flight').

Perhaps the most powerful influence that triggered the younger Symbolists' movement was the philosophy of Vladimir Solovev: his critique of the rationalism of Western philosophical tradition (of which the much-despised 'positivism' was only one particular instance), his idea of love and the eternal feminine as a metaphysical concept and, finally, his invocation of 'Pan-Mongolianism' – the new wave of barbarians coming from the East to destroy, and thus renew, the aging Rome of modern civilization. One of the epicentral images of Blok's poetry – the 'Fair Lady' (*Prekrasnaia Dama*) – clearly stemmed from Solovev's concept of the feminine. The Lady's lofty image lurks in the figure of 'The Unknown Woman' (*Neznakomka*) spotted in crowds.

The most striking poem representing this thematic domain is the famous 'The Unknown Woman'. Its subject finds himself in a low-life restaurant, amidst 'drunkards with eyes of rabbits' proclaiming their trite toast, 'In vino veritas'.[11] It is a world of unbearable vulgarities, from which the subject escapes in the company of his only friend – a glass of wine. Suddenly, a virginal figure, clad in silk, appears at the scene, slowly moving amidst all the clatter. The fluttering ostrich feathers of her hat evoke the vision of an 'enchanted shore', on which her blue eyes (hidden behind a veil) blossom like flowers. Apparently, the subject is not totally oblivious to the dubious side of this vision – it is hard to imagine a lonely woman coming to such a place being anything other than a prostitute who has come there in search of clients. No one but he could divine the mystical side of her appearance;

realizing that he owes the secret treasure of his revelation to 'the monster of drunkenness', the poem's hero is now ready to concede that in wine there is, indeed, truth.

The unbearable suspense of eager expectations of the Lady's advent, as well as fears about the character she may choose for her incarnation in the world, permeate Blok's poetry of the 1900s. His earlier book, *Verses on a Beautiful Lady*, is palpable with these dualities; years later he plunged into the depths of despair and dejection, a state that reached its climax in the book entitled *Terrible World*. As Bely suggested in his *Memories of Alexander Blok* (published after Blok's death), Blok in the 1910s found his 'Sublime Lady' in the image of Russia. Blok's late poetic cycle, *On the Field of Kulikovo* (1913), dedicated to one of the defining moments in Russia's history (its first major victory over the Tartars in 1380, after a century and a half of subjugation), seems to substantiate this idea. In this vein, Blok's two long poems of 1918, *The Twelve* and *The Scythians*, can be seen as revealing the other side of the duality that for Blok was inalienable from the idea of the Fair Lady. In these poems, written in the wake of the Revolution, Blok's Russia, like his Unknown One of the 1900s, assumes features that are simultaneously sublime and lowly, redemptive and horrifying.

One thing that was rare among Symbolist poets of both generations was irony. Their lofty visions and their satanic ravings proceeded alike, in a mode of unqualified eagerness. Although Blok's *The Fair Show Booth* caricatured clichés of Symbolist images and postures so relentlessly that even his close associates felt embarrassed, Blok's own self-annihilating sarcasm was as remote from irony proper as were outbursts of Symbolist megalomania; it contributed to the vision of a world precariously balancing between the sublime and the ridiculous.

In the overheated world of the 1900s, Kuzmin and his poetry stood out as a single but remarkable exception in this regard. Kuzmin maintained close personal and artistic relationships with some of the leading figures of the epoch (notably Ivanov), yet his art stood in a class of its own. In Kuzmin's poetry, every phenomenon encountered acquires a mode of elegant stylization touched with mild irony. A weekend trip to the countryside in the summer ('Where can I find words to describe the stroll, a Chablis on ice, a freshly toasted loaf of bread, and the sweet agate of ripe cherries?'),[12] a morning after a night of love ('They washed, they got dressed'), a train taking the subject from 'northern frenzies' to 'the land of Goldoni', with its simple and serene joys ('It is a joy to fly away in a fast train') – every scene turns into a tableau recalling Watteau or Fragonard: straightforward and ingenious, innocently naive and daring, serene and evocative, unabashedly artificial and rich with perceptive observations. Kuzmin's world is a radiant literary Arcadia, yet – as befits the original Arcadia, in contradistinction to its sterile neo-classical representations – it is palpable with physical sensations.

Acmeism

1910 was dubbed as the year of the decisive 'crisis of Symbolism' by its protagonists. In the foreword to his poem *The Retribution*, written in the wake of the Revolution (1918), Blok cast a retrospective glance at the 'crisis' alongside varied events of the same year – from Tolstoy's death to the proliferation of mid-air catastrophes that marked the dawn of the aviation era, to the sudden popularity of circus wrestling contests (a reminiscence of the late Roman empire) – putting them together in a paradigm rife with eschatological symbolism. The immediate cause of the crisis was a polemical exchange between Briusov, Blok, and Ivanov concerning the essence and the goals of the movement, which highlighted sharp disagreements among its leading proponents. Perhaps a more substantial sign of the impending crisis was the establishment in 1909 of a new journal, *Apollon* (*Apollo*) (under Makovsky's editorship): originally believed to be another publishing vehicle of Symbolism, it in fact quickly turned into a stronghold of a nascent school of poetry whose very first steps were marked by a pointed criticism of Symbolist theories and poetic practices.

Nikolai Gumilev, a poet with considerable Symbolist credentials by that time and a close friend of Ivanov, emerged as the leader of a small group of younger poets, among them Anna Akhmatova (his ex-wife) and Mandelshtam, which challenged the very foundation of the Symbolist heritage. Adepts of the new trend initially gave it the name 'Adamism' (signifying a return to the directness of meaning with which Adam had originally bestowed names on all the phenomena around him). The name the new school eventually settled upon, 'Acmeism', was suggested (with a hint of irony) by Ivanov; by virtue of its etymology (from Greek *akme* 'frontier, cutting edge, the foremost state') it alluded to the Acmeists' allegiance to the 'upper crust' of meaning, in contradistinction to the Symbolists' metaphysical depths. The group defined itself in a series of influential programmatic articles, in particular Gumilev's 'The Heritage of Symbolism and Acmeism' and Mandelshtam's 'The Morning of Acmeism' (a subtle contrast to the Symbolists' 'dawns'). Kuzmin's programmatic essay, pointedly titled 'About Beautiful Clarity' (published in *Apollo* in 1910), with its critique of irrationality and intemperance as 'barbaric' qualities, had a catalysing effect on the new school.

The emergence of Acmeism coincided with anti-Symbolist and anti-expressionist trends in European art and poetry. One can see significant parallels between Acmeists and Anglo-American Imagists, Rilke's evolution away from his early Symbolist style in the 1910s (*Neue Gedichte*), and the poetry of Guillaume Apollinaire. Acmeists accused their Symbolist predecessors and mentors of losing sight of direct, substantial meanings while chasing symbolic correspondences – of not seeing 'trees' in the symbolic 'forest', as it were. Mandelshtam wrote that under the order of Symbolism, all phenomena lose their own footing, with each phenomenon existing solely by 'winking' at some other: the rose winks at the maiden while the maiden winks at the rose.[13] The proclaimed return to substances did not mean, however, that what Acmeists promoted was only direct, unmediated meanings. For them, 'tangible' meant grounded in culture. A word might resound with a multitude of meanings, provided that each of them could be placed in its authentic cultural 'home'.

Symbolist polysemy was based on the universal network of symbols, within which individual symbols could easily be transformed into each other. Acmeist polysemy arises from individual ideas or images resounding against each other due to the 'duration' of the global cultural tradition. A Symbolist poem deliberately blurs the contours of phenomena so that they do not obstruct the trans-experiential vision. An Acmeist poem builds a cultural 'home' under whose 'roof' different concepts, no matter how distanced in space and time, come together as 'cohabitants'. Mandelshtam's image of Homeric Greece as a world of domesticity, in which every household object becomes simultaneously an object of culture and art, stood in contrast to Ivanov's vision of Greece as the land shaken by the Dionysian challenge.

The titles of Mandelshtam's two books of poetry in the 1910s, *Stone* and *Tristia*, exemplify the two defining features of Acmeist imagery: its tangible nature and its cultural appeal. There is nothing 'mysterious' (in the Symbolist sense) in Mandelshtam's images, for all their density; they may be complex, but they are not vague.

The Acmeist appeal to diverse cultural chronotopes in an effort to 'bring them home' (a feature once formulated by Mandelshtam, according to his wife, as 'the yearning for world culture') made their poetry intensely intertextual. Another aspect of this effort to domesticate every cultural space involved the sharply outlined social and psychological parameters of any situation being described. While the former aspect of Acmeist poetics was particularly characteristic of Mandelshtam, the latter found the most notable expression in Akhmatova's early poetry.

Mandelshtam's poem about the solstice ('There are orioles in the woods, and the vowels' length, the sole measure in tonic verse')[14] is characteristic of his early style. In a seemingly baffling leap of meaning, the poem suggests that, 'only once in a year', the metrical 'duration' of Homer's hexameter (e.g. its long lines), with its watershed of a caesura in the middle (a pause after the third foot, created by an obligatory word division) replicates itself in nature, making the solstice day; it is a day of 'laborious durations', a day when the reed itself is too overcome with 'golden laziness' to yield the bliss of the whole note. This stunning array of disparate images (which looks even more bewildering because of the syntactically and metrically impeccable discourse) coalesces into a complex yet logical semantic design as soon as proper cultural homes for each image are noted. The word 'duration' recalls Henri Bergson's *durée* (the philosophical concept, introduced in 1907, referring to an uninterrupted evolution of all phenomena, understood as a continuum of incremental changes), while the 'lazy' languor of the reed evokes the oboe solo in Claude Debussy's symphonic poem (inspired by Stéphane Mallarmé), *Prélude à l'après-midi d'un faune* – alongside its ballet incarnation, with Vaclav Nijinsky in the title role. The intensity of French connections casts its shadow on the way Homer is presented in the poem. It should be noted that the French neo-classic version of Homeric hexameter was the so-called Alexandrine metre (twelve-syllable verse with a caesura in the middle), which in turn was imitated in Russian neo-classicism as iambic hexameter. A line of the Alexandrine or iambic hexameter can be perceived as emblematic of a year's time, with the twelve syllables standing for months and with the 'solstice' of the caesural pause in the middle. By virtue of these parallels, Homer and Homeric Greece reverberate with neoclassical and modernist, French–Russian reincarnations. The allusions 'Homer – Racine – Mallarmé – Debussy – Nijinsky' evolve and intertwine; their conflation signifies a synthesis of poetic prosody, music, and dance. This evolving continuity, a powerful exemplification of the Bergsonian 'duration', is joined by nature itself. The sense of the uninterrupted intertemporal and intercultural duration is highlighted by a momentary suspense; it stands in the midst of the unceasing time flow, like a solstice, a caesura, a whole note, or a neo-classically static ballet tableau.

What Mandelshtam achieves in simultaneity, within the dense space of a single poem, Akhmatova does in contiguity, by the implied juxtaposition of different poems, each presenting a sharply outlined poetic picture. Akhmatova's poetic subject is placed in an astonishingly diverse variety of situations and roles. In one poem, she is a young woman on a first date with her would-be lover in a restaurant ('Music in the park was ringing with such an inexpressible grief'); in another, she is the wife of a peasant or merchant who punishes her by whipping, presumably for adultery ('My husband whipped me with his folded ornate belt'); in yet another, she is a sly young girl, teasingly employing feigned modesty in response to her partner ('I will not drink wine with you, because you are a naughty boy').

She bears a child from a 'grey-eyed king' whom her secretly jealous husband (perhaps his vassal) has killed during a hunt; in yet other instances, she is an experienced, disenchanted woman who feels pity at the sight of a 'boy' tormented by love ('The boy said to me: it is so painful!'), or an abandoned lover who tries to hide her pain by a dignified or defiant posture – and so forth. The constant features of Akhmatova's heroine, who hides behind these kaleidoscopic outward appearances, owe themselves to her existential grief and to her gift of mercilessly sharp furtive observations.

In many respects, the Acmeists were indebted to the fundamental achievements of Symbolism, despite their vocal criticism of the Symbolists. Their efforts to make every image reverberate in space and time continued the Symbolist strategy, despite the disagreement about the means for achieving this goal; it can be said that Acmeism turned Symbolist mystical 'echoes' into more palpable 'resonances'. Unlike the Futurists, their more aggressive fellow-travellers in the post-Symbolist epoch, Acmeists mapped the road from early modernism toward the avant-garde as that of transition, not revolution. But this did not make the Acmeist poetic message any less forward-looking: in their restrained way, Acmeists expressed the spirit of the 1910s, a time on the verge of explosion, as penetratingly as any of their expressionist contemporaries.

Futurism

In the latter half of the first decade of the twentieth century, a small group of young men coalesced around the magnetic personality of Viktor (or, as he called himself in an archaic Slavonicized fashion, Velimir) Khlebnikov, whose first poetic efforts proved baffling even to a public used to 'decadent' eccentricities. The group called itself 'Hilaea' (after the name of an estate in the Ukraine where they spent time together), and later *budetliane* 'futureniks', another pseudo-archaic neologism. Yet hostile critics insisted on calling them 'futurists', a name that pegged them as imitators of the Italian–French Futurists. No matter how vehemently the 'futureniks' tried to shed this label (pointing to their disdain for the 'bourgeois' shallowness of Filippo Tommaso Marinetti's ideas), the name stuck. In any event, by the early 1910s Russian Futurists had established themselves on the literary scene. Their advent was marked by the publication of a collective volume under the characteristic title *A Slap in the Face of Public Taste* (1912), followed by another, fancifully entitled *A Trap for Judges* (1913). Vladimir Mayakovsky and Aleksei Kruchenykh emerged alongside Khlebnikov as the group's leading poets. Most of the leading avant-garde painters, such as Mikhail Larionov, Natalia Goncharova, Kazimir Malevich, and Olga Rozanova, were closely associated with the group, which also included amateur musicians and anti-establishment critics (among them, the then seventeen-year-old Roman Jakobson). In 1913, the Futurists created two widely publicized stage productions: the tragedy in verse *Vladimir Mayakovsky* (with the poet in the title role), and Kruchenykh's opera *Victory over the Sun* (for which Mikhail Matiushin wrote the music and Malevich did the scenery).

The most immediately striking feature of the new movement was its vigorous attacks against establishment culture and, ultimately, against all conventions and established ways of life. Their numerous opponents liked to refer to them as 'savages' and as adepts of an 'animalistic Nietzscheanism'. The Futurists responded in turn by calling for 'Pushkin, Tolstoy, Dostoevsky etc. etc.' to be 'dropped from the steamship of modernity' (*A Slap . . .*),[15] or by suggesting that there is more poetry in a laundry bill than in all of *Eugene Onegin* (Kruchenykh, *Secret Vices of the Academicians*). Parodying the Symbolists' and Acmeists' penchant for sublime cultural references, *Victory over the Sun* featured 'Nero and Caligula in one shape', whose damaged statue appears in a chariot, singing nonsensical yet vaguely ominous couplets: '*Kiuli surn der*/Drove without luggage/Last Thursday/Burn tear what I didn't bake through.'[16] Mayakovsky, in his capacity as the hero of his tragedy, urged the abandonment of all vestiges of everyday life: 'Leave your apartments. Come out to stroke dry black cats!'[17] (Stroking a dry black cat would produce electricity – a symbol of modernity, incompatible with the quotidian world of 'apartments' – much in the same way that 'Pushkin, Tolstoy, Dostoevsky, etc. etc.' were unfit for the 'steamship of modernity'.) According to Mayakovsky, the four parts of his 'tetraptych' *A Cloud in Trousers* (1915) constituted four 'shouts': 'Down with your love, down with your state, down with your art, down with your religion!'[18]

As if defying the civilization of printing, the Futurists issued hundreds, if not thousands, of handmade books – each one unique, if only slightly distinguished, from many others. Made from sheets of cheap paper crudely bound together and covered with Kruchenykh's careless scribbling and Larionov's doodles, and bearing provocative or inscrutable titles, the books in fact offered, with deliberate crudeness, a message of variety and of the resemblance of phenomena that was no less powerful than Symbolist 'correspondences'.

For all the differences between the 'wild' Futurists and the culture-oriented Acmeists, these groups shared one feature of 'family resemblance' that opposed them to Symbolism: their mutual distaste for metaphysical vagueness and the embrace of a tangible, sculptured meaning. If for Acmeists the word 'tangible' meant grounded in a cultural context, for Futurists the word had simply its literal meaning. Futurists proclaimed the principle of the 'word as such' – the word liberated from any ideological and cultural vestiges by being stripped down to its bare 'physicality'. Considering a word (or, in Mayakovsky's case, an image) as a 'thing' having physical texture and shape meant that one could deal with it the same way one deals with material objects. A word could be reshaped, dismembered, glued to a splinter of another word, even ground into the 'dust' of its phonic elements. A 'dislocation' (*sdvig*) of conventional language stripped it from the automatic, unthinking usage to which it was subjected in everyday life; the disfigurement of a word meant its 'resurrection', from deadly routine, to new life. ('Resurrection of the Word' was the title of the groundbreaking 1914 essay by Viktor Shklovsky, the principal theoretician of the movement.)[19] Likewise, Futurist attacks on the routine of quotidian life and civilization meant its renewal through vandalism. Futurists took the Symbolist call for hordes of 'future Huns' literally, as it were, posing as the very hordes that had arrived long ago.

Each leading Futurist poet developed these general principles in his own way. Khlebnikov, the founder and spiritual leader of the movement, was driven by a vision of the ultimate unity of all meanings represented in words. In a rare instance of an explicit intertextual allusion, he spoke of 'a scale of would-be correspondences' out of which a 'face beyond dimensions' emerges. Khlebnikov's correspondences arose not from a metaphysical background but from words themselves, by virtue of similarities between their sonic (or written) shapes. A partial overlapping of the shapes of two words indicated, according to Khlebnikov, that the meanings of those words also have something in common, no matter how far apart they might stand in everyday consciousness. Noting that *chashka* 'cup' and *cherep* 'skull' share an initial sound, one could be compelled to search for a common feature of meaning hidden behind this similarity (in this case, it turned out to be the idea of the object as a 'vessel' ostensibly shared by both words). Like Balmont, Khlebnikov relied on paronomasia (i.e. the technique of juxtaposing semantically disparate words by virtue of partial coincidences between their phonetic features), but he used it in a more aggressive mode; far from being satisfied with existing paronomasias, Khlebnikov sought to expand them by altering the sound shape of words to achieve new effects of meaning. Changing the initial consonant in the word *dvoriane* 'gentry' (derived from *dvor* 'court') yielded *tvoriane* – a neologism that could be construed to have an etymological link to *tvor* (itself a neologism – a noun derived from *tvorit´* 'create'). Thus, since the meaning of *dvoriane* is 'aristocracy of the court', the meaning of the new-born word *tvoriane* had to be 'aristocracy of creativity'.

Khlebnikov's fight against conventions was targeted primarily at the established language. He found the existing state of any language unsatisfactory because of numerous derivational 'gaps' between words and, as a consequence, between meanings they can express. Khlebnikov envisioned a messianic task of filling in all such 'gaps' by creating neologisms that would realize all derivational possibilities, making the whole vocabulary into a web of uninterrupted derivational connections. Khlebnikov's poem 'Incantation by Laughter' exemplified this principle, building on all the conceivable and inconceivable derivational transformations of the single word *smekh* 'laughter'. This technique resulted in poetry that exuded an elemental energy – simultaneously inarticulate and suggestive, clumsy and dense.

Kruchenykh's experiments with verbal 'material' were as daring as Khlebnikov's, albeit of a different nature. They relied more on the expressive qualities of speech sounds than on derivational patterns. His trademark was crudely expressive, arbitrary sound combinations that posed as 'words'. Kruchenykh's famous nonsense distich '*Dyr byl shchyl./Ubeshchur*' became emblematic of Futurist 'trans-reasonable' (*zaumnaia*) poetry – a verbal analogy of abstract painting. Kruchenykh argued that the 'melodiousness' of Pushkin's verse made it devoid of a vivid expressiveness, hence his preference for a laundry bill that featured a less 'polished' sound palette; to his ear, everything in *Eugene Onegin* sounded like a monotonous 'narcoleptic wheeze'.

A few years prior to the emergence of the Dada, Kruchenykh showed a very similar combination of hilarious, almost childish bantering and subliminal messianic fervour. His most outrageous pronouncements always had a playful ring to them. His books of poetry, appearing under titles such as *Hair Lotion*, *The Piglets*, etc., were filled with provocative parodies of banalities of popular aesthetic tastes and social sentiments. For instance, the poem with a mock-epic title 'Russia' (*Rus'*) makes an outrage out of clichés of sentimental patriotism (a feat demanding more than a little courage in the years of the First World War): 'Wallowing in labour and swinishness,/You are growing, our beloved, our strong one,/Like that maiden who saved herself/By digging herself up to the waist in manure.'[20]

Although Mayakovsky showed considerable inventiveness in producing occasional neologisms, his treatment of language was not nearly as radical as that of Khlebnikov and Kruchenykh. His strategy of futurist 'displacements' was targeted primarily at images rather than words, and one of the most characteristic features of his style was the sharply visual nature of his poetic imagery. The striking vividness of his images cast them as palpable 'things' that could be subjected to violent manipulations. The landscape of Mayakovsky's poems recalls a cubist collage: images penetrate and pile upon one another, producing violent clashes in which they become severely deformed. Rain clouds over the industrial skyline of St Petersburg suburbs assume the shape of the pouting lips of a crying baby into whose mouth someone has violently 'stuck' a stone 'pacifier' – a factory chimney ('Something about Petersburg'). Evening is depicted through a scene of momentary vice and lecherousness: a bald lantern voluptuously peels a black stocking off the night's leg ('From one street to another').

Mayakovsky's urban landscape is invaded by a crowd whose image is totally dehumanized. The crowd condenses into an amorphous mass of congealed fat, on the surface of which occasional grotesque human fragments emerge – a piece of cabbage stuck in someone's beard, a thick layer of makeup on a woman's face; the outraged mob (apparently, after a performance) pushes forward, seeking to trample down the butterfly of the poet's heart with their dirty galoshes, while the poet responds to their assault by heartily spitting into their collective face ('In your face!'). The mob has lost the faculty of speech: from its collective mouth, with little corpses of decomposing words, only two words survive and thrive: 'slime' and 'borsch' ('The Cloud in Trousers').

Despite their much-advertised contempt for 'all those Briusovs, Balmonts, Bunins, etc. etc.', as *A Slap...* puts it, the Futurists inherited from Symbolism more than they would have liked to admit. The Futurists' faith in destroying/transcending the ugliness and cruelty of the world by dint of their creative will was derivative of the earlier part of the Silver Age. What Futurists accomplished with that legacy was to reduce it to a crude literalism. The Symbolists' vacillation between the lowly and the sublime was turned into shocking exhibitions of the utmost vulgarity; lofty visions of unspecified hordes destined to destroy and renew the civilization gave place to very concrete, animal-like crowds roaming in the streets. Above all, the Symbolists' ethereal correspondences were now manifested in words and images undergoing violent collisions, from which they emerged grotesquely disfigured.

In his autobiography, written in 1931, soon after Mayakovsky's suicide, Pasternak recalled their first meeting in the mid-1910s.[21] At that time, Pasternak, a late starter, was only beginning to search for his poetic identity. He joined the group 'Centrifuge', whose obvious aesthetic kinship to the Futurists made it struggle to assert its own identity. As he later described it, Pasternak's encounter with Mayakovsky revealed to him that Mayakovsky had already accomplished everything to which he had aspired, a discovery that compelled Pasternak to 'reinvent' his poetic self.[22] This inner creative process eventually yielded three closely interconnected books of poetry whose appearance from 1916 to 1923 propelled Pasternak to the forefront of poetic culture of the time: *Over the Barriers*, *My Sister Life*, and *Themes and Variations*.

Whether true or not, Pasternak's autobiography portrays his relationship with Mayakovsky by highlighting both their close kinship and antipodal differences. Like Mayakovsky, Pasternak created vivid visual images, making them merge in a cubist-like collage; sometimes, especially in his early poetry, their collisions take a violent turn: in the far North, the pink sun is violently dragged over ice, like a salmon caught by a polar bear ('The ice-drifting'); a winter's day is damaged beyond repair by the dusk, making futile all desperate attempts of street lanterns to mend it ('A winter night').

The difference between the two poets lay in the character of their respective poetic subjects and their relationships to the world. Mayakovsky represented perhaps the most egocentric poetic self in an epoch that was not short on egocentrism and megalomania. He transformed everything in the world into sensations (mostly painful or violent) of his hypersensitive, charismatic creative self. Pasternak, on the contrary, positions himself as a 'weak subject', one whose integrity is easily overwhelmed and eroded by invading impressions. Pasternak's aesthetic position went against the grain of an epoch that by and large focused on the subject's stance *vis-à-vis* the world: in his own formulation, 'Modern art has imagined itself to be a fountain, while in fact it is a sponge'.[23] The metaphor is further developed in an image of poetry as a sponge left out on a wet bench in a park in April: having swelled with the images it has absorbed, it is then squeezed out over a 'thirsty' sheet of paper ('Spring'). Mayakovsky feels the poet's soul being invaded by the crowd in dirty galoshes; Pasternak's poetic soul carries a warning sign: 'Fresh paint' – which, however, does not save it from getting chaotic imprints of 'legs, cheeks, arms, lips, and eyes' ('Don't touch: fresh paint').

While Mayakovsky's subject fights back ferociously and desperately, Pasternak's subject stays passive, mesmerized and overwhelmed by the grandiose commotion of phenomena. The active role is assumed by the phenomena themselves. An excursion to city suburbs reveals a world 'conceived by the forest, instilled in the mind of a glade, poured down on us from the clouds' ('The Vorobyevo Hills'); the end of the summer season is commemorated with farewell photos of the summer house taken by the thunderstorm overnight, with the help of blinding flashes ('The thunderstorm, momentary forever'). The animated commotion of the world makes even the slightest events into signs of the grandiose unity of being: when one is sitting in a suburb train, reading the timetable, it appears 'more grandiose than Holy Scripture' ('My Sister Life', the title poem of the book).

Pasternak's poetry emerges as if on its own, from a mixture and merger of phenomena that stream toward his poetic self. In one poem, he describes his creative process as a culinary recipe: 'ground over the pavements, with equal proportion of sun and windowpanes' ('About these verses'). The cubist character of this poetic picture is unmistakable: the spring sun is scattered among reflections in windowpanes and on the wet asphalt. Yet this fancy picture is not the subject's wilful creation: on the contrary, his duty is only to follow strictly, in his poetic 'cooking', the recipe dictated by the spring surroundings.

Pasternak's books of the late 1910s and early 1920s can be seen as emblematic of the end of the epoch. The keen interest in the nature of the relationship between the world and the subjective self, between 'poetry' and 'life', clearly continued the fundamental metaphysical concerns of the Silver Age. Yet this relationship itself appears to have been reversed. Coming on the heels of so many 'victories' of the subject over the world around him – from Symbolist visionary conquests of the world to the Futurist 'victory over the sun' – Pasternak's poetry showed a submission of the self to the tremendous dynamic force of the world, obediently taking from it clues to all 'metaphysical' problems. The fate of the world would no longer be shaped by a larger-than-life creative self; rather, it is in the hands of a local railroad's timetable, or a wet bench in a park, or a grove in suburban woods.

In its overt content, Pasternak's early poetry was singularly 'apolitical'; it showed not the slightest hint of the tumultuous times during which it was written. Looking out from the window, his subject asked children playing in the yard, with a naiveté that was more striking than all the spitting and slaps in the public's face: 'My dears, what millennium is it out there?' Yet in its own way, Pasternak's poetry recorded the new humility of the creative self in the face of overwhelming elements of history whose eruption signified the end of the epoch.

NOTES

1 Akhmatova, Anna, *The Word that Causes Death's Defeat: Poems of Memory*, trans., with introductory biography, critical essay and commentary Nancy K. Anderson (New Haven, CT: Yale University Press, 2004), pp. 148–181.
2 *Selected Poems by Charles Baudelaire*, trans. Geoffrey Wagner (New York: Grove Press, 1974), p. 87.
3 Blok, Alexander, *Sobranie sochinenii v 6-ti tomakh*, T.I (Moscow: Pravda, 1971), p. 168. For Blok's poems in English, see *The Twelve, and Other Poems*, trans. Peter France and Jon Stallworthy (New York: Oxford University Press, 1970).
4 Ivanov, Viacheslav, *Sobranie sochinenii v 4-kh tomakh*, T.1 (Brussels: Foyer Oriental Chrétien, 1974), p. 606.
5 Briusov, Valery, 'The Future Huns' in *Modern Russian Poetry: An Anthology*, trans. Babette Deutsch and Avrahm Yarmolinsky (New York: Harcourt, Brace & Company, 1921), p. 90.

6 Briusov, Valery, *Sobranie sochinenii v 7-i tomakh*, ed. P. Antakolskii, T.I (Moscow: Khudozhestvennaia literatura, 1973), p. 113.

7 Briusov, V.Ya, 'Oh, do cover your pale legs' in *Modern Russian Poetry: An Anthology*, trans. Babette Deutsch and Avrahm Yarmolinsky (New York: Harcourt, Brace & Company, 1921), p. 88.

8 Ivanov, Viacheslav, *Sobranie sochinenii v 4-kh tomakh*, T.II: *Cor ardens, Kniga Pervaia* (Brussels: Foyer Oriental Chrétien, 1974), p. 305.

9 Ivanov, *ibid.*, *Cor ardens, Kniga Vtoraia*, p. 383.

10 Alexander Blok, *Sobranie sochinenii v 6-ti tomakh*, T.I (Moscow: Pravda, 1971), p. 24. For Blok's poetry in English, see *The Twelve, and Other Poems*, trans. Peter France and Jon Stallworthy (New York: Oxford University Press, 1970).

11 Blok, *ibid.*, T.II, p. 158. For this poem in English, see *Modern Russian Poetry: An Anthology*, trans. Babette Deutsch and Avrahm Yarmolinsky (New York: Harcourt, Brace & Company, 1921), p. 121.

12 Kuz′min, Mikhail, *Stikhotvoreniia*, ed. N.A. Bogomolova (St Petersburg: Akademicheskii proekt, 2000), p. 26. Kuzmin's poetry can be found in English in an electronic version translated by John Barnstead at the Kuzmin Collection, 1999), Dalhousie University Electronic Text Centre at www.dal.ca/kuzmin/toc_e.html.

13 Mandelshtam, O.E., 'O prirode slova' in his *Sobranie sochinenii v 4-kh tomakh*, T.II (Moscow: TERRA, 1991), p. 254. For an English translation, see *Mandelstam: The Complete Critical Prose and Letters*, ed. Jane Gary Harris (Ann Arbor, MI: Ardis, 1979).

14 Mandelshtam, *ibid.*, p. 38.

15 'A Slap in the Face of Public Taste' in *Russian Formalism: A Collection of Articles and Texts in Translation*, ed. Stephen Bonn and John E. Bowlt (Edinburgh: Scottish Academic Press, 1973), p. 27.

16 Kruchenykh, A.E., A. *Victory Over the Sun*, ed. Patricia Railing, trans. Evgeny Steiner (London: Artists. Bookworks, 2009).

17 Maiakovskii, V., 'Vladimir Maiakovskii' in his *Sobranie sochinenii v 8-mi tomakh*, T.I (Moscow: Pravda, 1968), pp. 99–120. For Mayakovsky's poems in English, see Mayakovsky, Vladimir, *Listen: Early Poems 1913–1918*, trans. Maria Enzensburg (London: Redstone, 1987).

18 Maiakovskii, 'Oblako v shtanakh', *ibid.*, pp. 36–57.

19 Shklovsky, Viktor, 'Resurrection of the Word' in *Russian Formalism: A Collection of Articles and Texts in Translation*, ed. Stephen Bonn and John E. Bowlt (Edinburgh: Scottish Academic Press, 1973), pp. 41–47.

20 Kruchenykh, A.E., *Izbrannoe*, ed. Vladimir Markov (Munich: Wilhelm Fink Verlag, 1973), p. 40.

21 Pasternak, B.L., 'Okhrannaia gramota' in his *Sobranie sochinenii v 5-ti tomakh*, T.IV (Moscow: Khudozhestvennaia literatura, 1989), p. 215. See in English: *Safe Conduct: An Early Autobiography and Other Writings*, trans. Alec Brown and Lydia Pasternak-Slater (New York: New Directions, 1958).

22 Pasternak, 'Liudi i polozheniia', *ibid.*, pp. 333–334. See in English *I Remember: A Sketch for an Autobiography*, trans. David Magarshak (New York: Pantheon, 1959).

23 Pasternak, 'Neskol′ko polozhenii', *ibid.*, p. 367.

FURTHER READING

Anthologies

Unless otherwise specified, poetry of the authors discussed in this chapter may be found in English translation in the following anthologies:

Poetry of the Silver Age: The Various Voices of Russian Modernism, ed. Victor Terras, trans. Alexander Landman, and preface by Horst-Jürgen Gerigk (Dresden: Dresden University Press, 1998).

Russian Poetry, the Modern Period, ed. John Glad and Daniel Weissbort (Iowa City, IA: University of Iowa Press, 1978).

Twentieth Century Russian Poetry: Silver and Steel: An Anthology, introd. Yevgeny Yevtuschenko, ed. Albert Todd and Max Hayward, with Daniel Weissbort (New York: Doubleday, 1993).

Secondary sources

Barnes, Christopher, *Boris Pasternak: A Literary Biography*, vol. 1 (Cambridge: Cambridge University Press, 1989).

Cavanagh, Clare, *Osip Mandelstam and the Modernist Creation of Tradition* (Princeton, NJ: Princeton University Press, 1995).

Doherty, Justin, *The Acmeist Movement in Russian Poetry: Culture and the Word* (Oxford: Clarendon Press, 1995).

Fleishman, Lazar, *Boris Pasternak: The Poet and His Politics* (Cambridge, MA: Harvard University Press, 1990).

Freidin, Gregory, *The Coat of Many Colors: Osip Mandelstam and His Mythologies of Self-Presentation* (Berkeley, CA: University of California Press, 1987).

Gasparov, Boris, Hughes, Robert, and Paperno, Irina, eds., *Cultural Mythologies of Russian Modernism: From the Golden Age to the Silver Age* (Berkeley, CA: University of California Press, 1992).

Grossman, Joan Delaney, *Valery Briusov and the Riddle of Russian Decadence* (Berkeley, CA: University of California Press, 1985).

Grossman, Joan Delaney and Paperno, Irina, eds., *Creating Life: The Aesthetic Utopia of Russian Modernism* (Berkeley: University of California Press, 1994).

Malmstad, John E. and Bogomolov, Nikolai, *Mikhail Kuzmin: A Life in Art* (Cambridge, MA: Harvard University Press, 1999).

Markov, Vladimir, *Russian Futurism: A History* (London: MacGibbon & Kee, 1969).

Matich, Olga, *Erotic Utopia: The Decadent Imagination in Russia's fin-de-siècle* (Madison, WI: University of Wisconsin Press, 2005).

Pyman, Avril, *A History of Russian Symbolism* (Cambridge: Cambridge University Press, 1994).

Rylkova, Galina, *The Archeology of Anxiety: The Russian Silver Age and its Legacy* (Pittsburgh, PA: Pittsburgh University Press, 2007).

2

NIKOLAI BOGOMOLOV*

Prose between Symbolism
and Realism

The great Russian prose of the mid-nineteenth century and the years following by no means ceased to exist toward the century's last decade. Tolstoy
(1828–1910) and Nikolai Leskov (1831–1895) were still writing, and the
talent of Chekhov (1860–1904) was revealing itself more and more clearly.
These three names alone were enough to create a real, extensive literature.
But alongside this, the very essence of Russian literature at the time, the
influence of Western (most of all French) literature, and the general state of
fin-de-siècle society, all burst forth in various attempts to search for something new that was still difficult to put into words. With time, this new thing
would be identified with modernism, and, more specifically, with symbolism,
although it was far from being so well defined in its origins.

In 1892, the twenty-seven-year-old poet Dmitrii Merezhkovsky (1865–
1941) delivered a lecture in Petersburg. The name of the lecture, which
would thenceforth for many years be mentioned (indeed, even now it is often
mentioned) by everyone who undertook to write about later-nineteenth-
century Russian literature and about Russian literature in the first third of the
twentieth century, was 'On the Reasons of the Decline and on New Trends
in Contemporary Russian Literature' (O prichinakh upadka i o novykh
techeniiakh sovremennoi russkoi literatury). A printed version of this lecture
appeared in 1893, and many researchers take this date as the beginning of
the existence of Russian symbolism. But on re-reading this lecture today,
one finds it hard to agree with that date.

Of course, the reason for this conclusion was to be found in the author's
own words: 'The three main elements of the new art are: *mystic content*,
symbols, and the expansion of artistic impressionability.'[1] In fact, the words
spoken here are the ones that later became the basis of all of symbolism. But
they meant something completely different.

What stands out most of all is that Merezhkovsky understood the word
'symbol' itself differently than those who are usually considered first-rate
theorists. And 'mystic content' for him is obviously found not only in sacral

texts or in the discoveries of visionaries, but also in the works of Ernest Renan (1823–1892), Thomas Carlyle (1795–1881), and Herbert Spencer (1820–1903) – those whom we could quite justifiably call thinkers of a positivist bent. And Merezhkovsky calls Ivan Turgenev (1818–1883), Ivan Goncharov (1812–1891), Dostoevsky (1821–1881), and Tolstoy the founders of the new art (and in Western literature, Gustave Flaubert [1821–1880], Guy de Maupassant [1850–1893], and Henrik Ibsen [1828–1906]) – that is to say, those who in the traditional history of literature would more likely be associated with realism. Among the new prose writers, either still living then or recently having died, he undoubtedly would have named only Vsevolod Garshin (1855–1888) and Chekhov, who are also realists in today's classification.

We must remember, of course, that around 1892 the 'new prose' had still not yet taken shape: neither Merezhkovsky himself, nor his wife, Zinaida Gippius (1869–1945), nor Fedor Sologub (1863–1927) had actually published a single work, and even Maxim Gorky (1868–1936) had only begun to appear in print (his first publication, in a provincial newspaper and unnoticed by all at the time, had appeared barely three months before Merezhkhovsky's lecture). But this is not the only issue. It is not by chance that Merezhkovsky's best books as a critic (*Timeless Fellow Travellers/Vechnye sputniki, Tolstoy and Dostoevsky/Tolstoy i Dostoevsky, Gogol and the Devil/Gogol' i chert, Lermontov, Poet of Superhumanity/ Lermontov, Poet sverkhchelovechestva,* and *Two Mysteries of Russian Poetry: Nekrasov and Tiutchev/Dve tainy russkoi poezii: Nekrasov i Tiutchev*) are dedicated not to his own time but rather to writers of the past. Evident in all these works is his desire to link inseparably the literature being created at the time with what had been done by all of world literature over the course of its many centuries of existence; and, of course, Merezhkovsky devoted special attention to his immediate predecessors, the nineteenth-century Russian writers.

In the 1890s, and later, at the beginning of the twentieth century, Russian literature was being re-read by new eyes. Gogol's fantasy, Lermontov's superhuman demonism, the baring of the human soul in Dostoevsky, and such like: these are the things that most attracted those creating the literature of the new era, and this attractiveness was mainly rooted in the fact that these writers (and others, of course) allowed readers to understand not only the times represented in these works but also the situation in their own era of revolutions and cataclysms. Even from the harmonious prose of Pushkin, the works that became more prominent than any others were 'The Queen of Spades', with its fantastic elements, and the lopsided *The Captain's Daughter*, which became a story about the Guide, mystically transformed into a peasant czar, and about a senseless and merciless Russian revolt.

Tolstoy, however, was needed least of all by later nineteenth- and early twentieth-century Russian prose. Perhaps this was because he was simultaneously perceived as both a writer of the past and as a contemporary ('The Kreutzer Sonata' and *Resurrection* were published in the 1890s, and 'Father Sergius', 'After the Ball', *Hadji Murat*, and *The Living Corpse* were published in the first decade of the 1900s), thus having the possibility of expressing his views on art and his attitude toward the phenomena of contemporary literature, and also as a 'teacher of life'. On the other hand, Dostoevsky's novels were not only read but also profoundly assimilated. This was facilitated by the fact that in a number of his works the mythological essence was partially evident. 'The Legend of the Grand Inquisitor', part of *The Brothers Karamazov*, not only became the object of special analysis by Vasilii Rozanov (1856–1919) but also became part of the very fabric of many works of Russian prose. It is hardly mere chance that an article of Viacheslav Ivanov (1866–1949), 'Dostoevsky and the Tragedy/Novel' ('Dostoevsky i roman-tragediia'), anticipating Bakhtin's reading of Dostoevsky, appeared as early as the 'teens of the twentieth century. Finally, the significance of Gogol's work was extraordinarily huge, especially for the prose of Andrei Bely (pseud. of Boris Bugaev, 1880–1934), who even wrote a special study entitled *The Master Craftsmanship of Gogol* (*Masterstvo Gogolia*).

It was no less important to understand, alongside all this, what had been rejected by the writers of the time that interests us here. Of the authors named by Merezhkovsky, the influence of Goncharov was almost undetectable (possibly because readers and critics understood his creative work too one-sidedly), and the impact of Turgenev's once extremely influential prose was constantly receding. Very few remembered Leskov (only in the 1920s was he again mentioned as an artistically influential author) and Saltykov-Shchedrin, and the prose of Pushkin and Lermontov already seemed to be too far in the past.

Beginning with the 1890s, Russian prose was predominantly preoccupied with overcoming the naturalist tendencies that had developed primarily in French literature (which had traditionally been well known in Russia) but which had had a serious effect on Russian literature as well. The path of maximal rootedness in the reality of one's own time did not seem too promising: even Chekhov's prose was interpreted as humour of not too high a style, or as 'boring stories'. Contemporaries found it difficult to detect the symbolist meaning that is now patently obvious in many of his stories. To all appearances, this was tied to the fact that the reader (and even the critic) could not easily discern such symbolism, well hidden as it was in the artistic fabric (as if 'ashamed of itself'). This is why, in the earliest times, authors themselves would suggest to readers the possibility – even the necessity – of reading their works on at least two levels.

One of the clearest examples of this kind of authorial behaviour was in Maxim Gorky's prose of the 1890s. This prose quite distinctly separates into several apparently isolated groups. First, there are the 'romantic works' – 'Makar Chudra' (1892), 'Old Woman Izergil' (1895), 'The Maiden and Death' (pub. 1917), and 'Song of a Falcon' (1895, 1898); the second group comprises works about 'down-and-outs' – 'Chelkash' (1895), 'Mal'va' (1897), 'Konovalov' (1897), and 'Twenty-Six and One' (1899); the third and final group is composed of works rooted in contemporary reality, with a powerful artistic and analytical origin, the best example of which is *Foma Gordeev* (1899). Stalin's inscription on a copy of the poem 'The Maiden and Death' became a curious formula for contemplating works in the first group: 'This thing is more powerful than Goethe's *Faust (love conquers death)*.'[2] Artistically unconvincing and stilted, these works are allegories, obviously intended for an ostensibly symbolic reading of the whole text. Gorky's 'down-and-outs' are no more convincing, especially if one attempts to confer on them an awareness of the type that found expression in Nietzsche's prose. If it *is* Nietzsche, then it is very vulgarized and has almost no connection to the real philosopher and writer. Only where Gorky successfully avoids the allegorical principle and sham philosophizing can he create a work that compels readers not only to endure the slogans and declarations that are proclaimed in the poems, short stories, and sketches of the first two groups, but also to grasp the artistic world created in his best prose.

Plainly, Gorky's turn to dramaturgy garnered him a great deal as an artist: here, the weakened degree to which the author could interfere in the text allowed directors and actors to depart from the prescriptiveness in the delineation of the characters. The character 'Nil' in the play *The Philistines* (1902), for example, could be interpreted both as a proletarian who will be faced with directing Russia toward a bright future (not for nothing is he a machinist by profession) and as a narrow-minded, brutal, and ungrateful person under whose authority one would dread to fall. Luka and Satin, characters in *The Lower Depths* (1902), could similarly be interpreted as completely different individuals, each having his own different value system. Even in his later work, Gorky at times torturously departed from his authorial dictate, from his striving to present his own viewpoint as the only true one. Ending up on this path were both painful failures (the novel *Mother*, 1905), which were, unfortunately, sometimes canonized by Bolshevik criticism, and serious successes (the novel *Okurov Town*, 1909, or the first two parts of the autobiographical trilogy, *Childhood*, 1913 and *In the World*, 1916; the third part, *My Universities*, was not finished until the 1920s). Only as the 'teens drew to a close did Gorky's skill become significantly more stable, when he had assimilated many lessons from his contemporaries.

Gorky's close companion-in-arms, Leonid Andreev (1871–1919), to a certain extent followed the same path that Gorky, albeit with somewhat different priorities. The romanticism of early Gorky was alien to Andreev, but in many cases he quite freely resorted to a too-obvious symbolization intended for the comprehension level of the most undemanding readers. This is seen with particular clarity in his famous play, *The Life of Man* (*Zhizn´ cheloveka*, 1907), wherein even a special character appears, 'someone in gray' (the name quickly became famous), who delivers rhetorical tirades intended to sum up the meaning of what is taking place onstage.

Yet another difference between Gorky and Andreev was that they came to literature at different times. Gorky began to appear in print in 1892, but Andreev's first stories to be noticed by readers were from 1898, a time when symbolism had already become part of Russian literature and its influence was impossible to ignore. Sensitive to the aspirations of the new artistic schools, Andreev strove in his work to combine an interest in solving the urgent problems of the times with attempts to penetrate the psychologies of both the individual and the masses. His prose could be likened to the Expressionists' paintings, with bold strokes, bright colours, and the desire to awaken in the viewer (for Andreev, in the reader) clearly and unambiguously expressed feelings – compassion, anger, and the aspiration toward open action. However, the desire to shock the reader, to put him face to face with the existential situations that were easily imagined in the Russia of the first twentieth-century decade (as in the stories 'The Abyss' [Bezdna, 1902], 'The Tale of the Seven Who Were Hanged' [Rasskaz o semi poveshennykh, 1908], 'The Life of Vasilii Fiveisky' [Zhizn´ Vasiliia Fiveiskogo, 1904], 'Red Laughter' [Krasnyi smekh, 1904], and others), not uncommonly degenerated into an incompletely thought-out overall logical structure, so that any attempt to find a rational relationship to the next story reveals each work's imperfections of construction. Tolstoy's pithy phrase concerning 'Red Laughter' – 'It's scary, but I'm not afraid' – very acutely highlighted the significant peculiarity of Andreev's creative work.

Andreev's prose was especially influential during the Russo-Japanese war and the first Russian revolution of 1905–1907, when his contemporaries hungered more for garishly recorded situations and problems and cared less about artistic perfection (or imperfection). But with a change in historical reality, it became clear that for the people of the new generations who did not know these problems, or even for those who knew them in a very slightly different environment, they would, as it were, cease to exist. Incredibly popular in the first decade of the 1900s, Andreev lost his appeal in the next decade, becoming in time not a classic author of Russian literature but rather a background figure in it.

The writers connected to Russian symbolism had significantly more reasons to become classic authors. The prose works of Sologub and Bely and, for a while, those of Merezhkovsky, Gippius, Aleksei Remizov (1877–1957), and Valerii Briusov (1873–1924), all became noted phenomena in Russian prose. All these writers tested different ways of developing their talent, and the results turned out to be just as varied.

We are inclined to believe that the history of Russian Symbolism did not in fact begin with the Merezhkovsky lecture that served as the starting point in our discussion, but from approximately the year 1896. By this time, the trend had accumulated a sufficiently solid reserve of books by various authors who had openly stood under the banner of the 'new art' that many at the time were calling decadence. For the most part, these were collections of poetry: Merezhkovsky, Briusov, Konstantin Balmont (1867–1942), and Alexander Dobroliubov (1876–1945?) were well known as poets. But at the same time, Gippius, Sologub, and Merezhkovsky had already garnered some distinction as prose authors. It is traditionally assumed that symbolism was a primarily poetic trend. But it is in fact clear that prose was no less important to its founders.

What did Russian Symbolism offer in the area of prose to those who did not disdain it as 1896 drew to a close? There were two novels, Merezhkovsky's *The Outcast* (*Otverzhennyi*, 1895, later called *Death of the Gods: Julian the Apostate* [*Smert' bogov: Iulian Otstupnik*]), and Sologub's *Bad Dreams* (*Tiazhelye sny*, 1895); there were also two collections of short stories and poems, Gippius' *New People* (*Novye liudi*, 1896) and Sologub's *Shadows* (*Teni*, 1896). From these very first efforts one could imagine, albeit distantly, the direction of further movement.

Gippius followed the simplest path, one that had been tested more than once. Her prose was completely traditional, but her characters were untraditional. In her most significant early short stories, the characters constantly end up in situations that force them to make a choice between their own desires, which are determined by egotistical motives, and the possible tragedy of someone else's life. The pointed title of her book *New People* by no means implied that Gippius accepted and unconditionally approved of the rise of this type of person – the 'no limits' individualist or 'superman' in the vulgarized concept that was characteristic of the era. The existence of such people was for her the evidence of a new and changed lifestyle, but her appraisals of this state of affairs were completely unequivocal. Gippius did not accept the model of the 'decadent' as she understood it. And despite any experiments she may have made, she was not, strictly speaking, on an artistic quest. It is probably for just this reason that her prose was forgotten somewhat earlier than her poetry was, and that the attempt to revive it at the end of the twentieth century failed.

The pursuits of Merezhkovsky and Sologub were significantly more substantial. Merezhkovsky's still-isolated novel (which in time became the first part of the trilogy 'Christ and the Antichrist' ['Khristos i Antikhrist']) was outwardly reminiscent of the traditional historical novels well known in both Russia and in other countries. Sologub's *Bad Dreams* could quite possibly be considered a naturalistic novel based on life in a Russian province in the 1880s or 1890s, but entangled in a criminalistic chronicle. And, in fact, Merezhkovsky's novel was based on the painstaking investigations of its thoroughly and well-roundedly educated author (for the second novel of the trilogy, *The Risen Gods: Leonardo da Vinci* [*Vosskresshie bogi: Leonardo da Vinchi*], which appeared in 1900, he made a special trip to Italy). Sologub's novel straightforwardly includes his own impressions and the stories about acquaintances and life in the province, and even the unnamed little town is recognizable. But this is only the first level of narrative. In parallel to it, a completely different life unfolds, one that is transparent (as with Sologub) or historiosophically interpreted (as with Merezhkovsky).

The real and the imagined, the things recorded by historians and those unknown to them – this mix constitutes the essence of the first symbolist novels. At the same time, it is often quite difficult to separate these things from each other. With Merezhkovsky, it is true, the general idea is incomparably easier to grasp, and it is no accident that his formula of universal historical development – the struggle between Christ and Antichrist, like between primeval principles, in which first one and then the other wins temporary victories – rather quickly became a commonplace for even the most unrefined mind. *Bad Dreams*, which did not enjoy particular success (partially owing to censors' and editors' cuts in the earlier editions), was in this respect more perfected, since in it the coupling of the two realities seemed more natural and less declarative. Even more successful, due to being large-scale in a smaller space, was the short story 'Shadows', which gave its name to Sologub's first separately published book (the story was subsequently renamed 'Light and Shadows'). On the one hand, it was a completely naturalistic narrative about the descent of two people, a mother and son, into madness and, on the other, a set of responses in a philosophical dialogue with Plato and Nietszche. Not by chance did this short story evoke such unanimous approval, not only among figures of the 'new art' but also simply among sensitive readers, who were able to appreciate the two-dimensional nature of the story.[3]

Sologub's novel *The Petty Demon* (written in 1892, partially published in 1905, and completely in 1907) should be acknowledged as the most successful experiment in this sort of artistic comprehension of the world. In this novel, as in *Bad Dreams*, the action takes place in a provincial city; the plot is constructed around a few episodes from a criminal or half-criminal chronicle; the naturalistically portrayed details and situations suddenly plunge into an abyss of the absurd and the fantastic. However, as distinct from the preceding examples, *The Petty Demon* was written by a master craftsman who was already quite a bit more self-assured, and for whom any word would become essential. In it, we can already see not just hints of the famous philosophical ideas, but also attempts to create an aestheticized utopia of one's own.

On the one hand, *The Petty Demon* is founded upon the traditions of Russian literature. Sologub does not hide the fact that his teachers were Pushkin, Lermontov, Gogol, and Dostoevsky. The title of the novel very quickly became linked to Lermontov's poem 'A Tale for Children'; even in the foreword, we find obvious references to Lermontov's *A Hero of Our Time* and to Gogol's *The Inspector General*; the constantly reappearing Princess Volchanskaia recalls the old princess from Puskhin's *Queen of Spades*; and situations from Dostoevsky clearly permeate the whole fabric of the novel. In it, no doubt, there are more subtle threads that connect the text with the nineteenth-century Russian classics – but there are plenty of quite obvious ones as well. The method of delineating the main character through encounters with his co-workers, neighbours, and the women and children dependent upon him is also quite traditional, obliging one to perceive the novel as a continuation of what Russian realism had already achieved. However, the unexpected revelations of Peredonov's awakened consciousness bear testimony to the fact that he is gradually transgressing the boundary of 'normality'. He needs not only his taunts of the helpless children but also his patently perverted enjoyment of their sufferings. The resultant scandals gradually become unbelievable, and this is not a simple amplification of, as it were, the natural course of events, but rather a transformation of these events into something extreme. From a severe and gloomy man, but one who still fits within the framework of ordinary life, Peredonov is step by step transformed into a madman, dangerous to society. But the problem is that his madness is unnoticed, and is perceived to be the norm. Peredonov's absurd accusations not only go unrebuffed but are even intensified by the people whom he visits, demanding that the children be punished; guests take pleasure in helping destroy the apartment; and neither the eyes poked out of the playing cards nor the shaved-down cat evoke the faintest surprise.

It is not by chance that the fantastic Nedotykomka, which reveals itself to Peredonov in his half-delirious visions and brings misfortune, now and then turns up among other people, even in a church. It extends the connecting thread between Peredonov and the other inhabitants of the city – but not just those of this city. The visiting writers Sharik and Sergei Turgenev (Sologub cut the scenes with these characters from the text, but later had them published separately) react just as calmly, and even sympathetically, to Peredonov's diseased fantasies; for them, he is just a part of a completely ordinary world. The only thing that can disrupt Peredonov's harmony with the world surrounding him is crime. The murder of Volodin (in the final scene of *The Petty Demon*, recalling the ending of Dostoevsky's *The Idiot*) not only concludes the novel but also destroys Peredonov as a human being. The text reveals his abrupt transformation: just previously in an extremely excited and active state, he 'sat downcast and mumbled something disjointed and meaningless'. The end of the novel becomes the end of its main character, but by no means an end to the dreadful life of the society that surrounds him and that of the city and the country.

On the other hand, no less important to the novel are the episodes with Sasha Pylnikov and the Rutilov sisters, which in any ordinary reader's reading recede to the background owing to their aesthetic obsolescence. But for Sologub they were full of real and extremely important content: to the abnormal harmony between Peredonov and the city, he contrasted the beautiful as it seemed to him. Erotic tension without 'disgusting achievements'; the atmosphere connected to flowers, scents, costumes, and sweets in which the quite young boy found himself; the alluring possibility of perceiving this boy as a Platonic androgyne – all this, it would seem, can create a palpable counterbalance to the world's ugliness. But Sasha's appearance in a geisha costume at the masquerade causes a stunning scandal that culminates in a conflagration. This utopia as well is destroyed, incapable of being realized.

Aleksei Remizov followed a path similar to Sologub's in his early creative work. He was also attracted to unhealthy fracturings of the human psyche and to portrayal of a frightening environment into which a helpless person is cast. The famous formulation from perhaps Remizov's best story, 'Sisters of the Cross' ('Krestovye sestry', 1910) – 'Man is a dullard to man' – might also well define the characteristics of Sologub's works. Just as Sologub did, Remizov tried to construct an alternative to a grim reality. The difference was that Remizov saw the alternative elsewhere – in folklore (fairy tales, popular demonology, and stylizations of varying sorts of ancient texts). The resulting balance turned out to be too precarious, however, and Remizov was obliged to try and steady it with varying sorts of playful behaviour.[4]

Other possibilities for symbolist prose were demonstrated by Briusov and Bely. They first achieved fame as poets, and only with time did they begin to publish outstanding prose works. For Briusov, one of these was the novel *The Fiery Angel* (*Ognennyi angel*, 1907), and for Bely, his tale entitled *The Silver Dove* (*Serebrianyi golub´*, 1909) and the novel *Petersburg* (*Peterburg*, 1913).

On the surface, Briusov's novel is a historical narrative, but which has an expressive subtitle: ' . . . or, A true tale which tells about a devil that has more than once appeared to a certain girl in the form of a bright spirit and has tempted her to various sinful acts; about the ungodly activities of magic, alchemy, astrology, cabalism, and necromancy; about the trial of a certain girl, presided over by His Reverence the Archbishop of Trier; and also about meetings and interviews with the knight and thrice doctorate-holding Agrippa of Nettesheim and with Doctor Faustus, all written by a witness.' This subtitle at once indicates that the author's intention was to create a narrative, stylized after an old German text (the events in the novel take place in the first half of the sixteenth century), in which not only imaginary people play a part, but also real people, as well as famous characters from folklore and literature, like Doctor Faustus. This stylization was, of course, extremely relative, since no serious tradition of Russian translations of such texts existed. Briusov was obliged to resort to relativity: to create the illusion of the existence of an ancient manuscript, rendered by him, a Russian writer, from German into Russian. There are several studies that demonstrate how hard the author had to work to create a historically believable text. But this was only partly 'the main thing' for readers. Some of them were initiated into the details, and some of them surmised that this whole illusion of an ancient narrative was created not only to penetrate a tense moment in history, but also to convey the things that the author himself found so relevant to his immediate historical milieu.

The novel was connected most intimately to Briusov's personal life, to his relationship with the young writer Nina Petrovskaia and with Bely. Many people knew about this relationship, and an even greater number read Briusov's and Bely's poems that were devoted to events in it. But for the novel, to which Briusov attached a great significance, and which he wrote in obvious rivalry to the prose of Merezhkovsky and Sologub, the real-life story underwent several metamorphoses. These can roughly be divided into the following stages: the real-life rivalry of the lovers took on mythological connotations, such that the features of a 'bright spirit' were bestowed upon Bely but Briusov was a demon, without regard for the German story and mythology; then, this mythological interpretation was again projected onto life, and real-life relations began to be constructed in accordance with the myth; still later, the resultant living reality was transformed into a historical reality attached to a specific time and its events, as well as to the religious ideas and mystical practices of that time, and all of this was captured in the narrative. Quite naturally, the frequent refraction of the events through various prisms gave them a multitude of supplemental meanings. The original real-life story and personal relationships were sublimated, which is why the characters in the novel became more real than their real-life prototypes. In time, Nina Petrovskaia began to perceive herself as a contemporary embodiment of the novel's heroine, Renata, and Vladislav Khodasevich's (1886–1939) memoirs about her are in fact titled 'The End of Renata' ('Konets Renaty').

Nonetheless, *The Fiery Angel* is intentionally written in a somewhat dry style, with allusions to a number of historical events, as if the author were concerned exclusively with historical authenticity. And thanks to the collision, quite intense, of different levels of the narrative, the novel became attractive to readers.

This was partly tied also to the fact that, in general, stylization was a customary phenomenon in prose during the second half of the 1900–1910 decade. Appearing at about the same time as Briusov's novel were the stylizations of Mikhail Kuzmin (1872–1936), grounded in imitation of classical (and not only classical) prose; the short stories and novellas by Sergei Auslender (1886–1937) about Revolution-era France or else later-eighteenth- or early-nineteenth-century Russian life; and the works of Boris Sadovsky (1881–1952) that artfully imitated Russian prose from the first half of the nineteenth century. Nonetheless, none of these authors balked at portraying the present as well; the difference was that they did this more openly and less subliminally than did Briusov. Kuzmin's *The Little Cardboard House* (*Kartonnyi domik*, 1907) and *The Dual Confidant* (*Dvoinoi napersnik*, 1908) were on the whole classic *romans à clef*; but among the stylizations, too, were the kind that quite openly told stories of current events, simply changing the names of the characters to historical or pseudo-historical ones. This playing with narrative possibilities, which was tied to both stylization and revelation of private lives, was for a time received as something promising. This time, however, proved to be short.

The creative work of Bely from the period of around 1905 to 1916 or so should be recognized as exhibiting perhaps the highest achievements of the prose tied to symbolism. Before then, Bely had been publishing 'symphonies' and lyrical fragments that stood on a boundary between poetry and prose, and after the novel *Petersburg* came out, he turned to completely new forms of narrative which ought to be regarded in a quite completely different context. But *Petersburg* and *The Silver Dove* are connected to symbolism with the closest of ties.

And not only with Symbolism as such (that is, the method of artistic thought and vision), but with the evolution of Symbolism up to that time. Towards the end of the decade approaching 1910, the articles and speeches of Blok, Bely, and Viacheslav Ivanov had more and more distinctly declared the necessity of profound comprehension of Russia in all its peculiarities, a most important component of which was the mystical essence of the Russian peasantry that comprised the majority of the country's population. The events of the first Russian revolution demonstrated that the 'age-long silence' of this part of Russia was imaginary: it was ready to explode with 'unprecedented revolts'.

There had of course been people earlier among the symbolists who had seen the necessity of addressing the unpredictability of the people – for example, Dobroliubov, who had rejected literary work and become the founder of a remarkable sect of simple folk. But these were isolated episodes. In 1908 and 1909, the public speeches (Blok's 'The People and the Intelligentsia' ['Narod i intelligentsiia'], Ivanov's 'On the Russian Idea' ['O russkoi idee']), the articles based on them, Bely's 'Nekrasov-style' book of poetry, *Ashes* (*Pepel*, 1909), Ivanov's review of the same book, and the like, all bore witness to the shift of symbolism towards 'populism' (*narodnichestvo*) – as the language of the era called this. An indubitable component of this shift was *The Silver Dove*.

Bely himself wrote that his tale was oriented toward Gogol's stories. But Dostoevsky was no less significant to him (one of the chapters was called 'Demons' when it was published in a journal). These are the very same writers, it would seem, who were important to Sologub. But Bely emphasizes different aspects of creativity in one and the other: Gogol was taken foremost as an exemplar of construction and even of specific stylistic devices, but Dostoevsky as an anticipator of many themes. Ill-fated love, a web of conspiracy, the unexpectedly revealing mystical content of the most elemental things, the tragic opposition between the 'nobleman' and simple folk – all of this is easy to find in Dostoevsky. But in distinction from Dostoevsky, Bely is quite a bit more open in letting the reader see into his subtexts. Readers of *The Silver Dove* can rather easily observe the allegorical meanings, such as the geographical ones: the village called Tselebeevo is at the centre of the narrative space (the root 'tsel' ['whole'] hints at the completeness and integrity of this centre); west of it is the Gugolevo estate, owned by the Baroness Todrabe-Graben (the obviously German surname of the owner and the books on her shelves symbolize

'Westernness'); and to the east is the city of Likhov, the name of which comes from the word *likhoi* ('evil'). These allegorical images read unambiguously: the main character, Darialskii, left the 'West' (his old home) and rushed eastward (although attempting to escape from his destiny) – where he dies. This idea is intensified when we observe that in the centre of Tselebeevo there is a vast green meadow, representing all of Russia, and then it becomes clear why the first section is called '*Our* village'; only later would Bely create distance by entitling another part 'Inhabitants of Tselebeevo Village' – for the clever reader, this was enough of a hint.

But the only thing that is obviously insufficient is the assortment of allegorical meanings to understand the story. The story is connected to the generally symbolist conception of the world by a number of threads, from the names of the characters to literary and contextual references. In presenting the fundamental complications of the story allegorically, Bely expands and deepens it with practically infinite symbolic images, and it is understandable why he does this: the symbol differs from the allegory precisely in the endless assemblage of its meanings, which cannot be read unambiguously. And because of this, the attentive reader is denied a simplistic answer to the story's fundamental questions. Russia is not simply East or West, but rather one of the possibilities in the endless diversity of human cultures. Darialskii's fate is not simply determined by historical sin: it is besides a symbol of atonement. What happens with the characters is not so much fitted into even the fate of Russia as it is into the mystically comprehended condition of the world. But Bely does not do all of this directly and straightforwardly, but rather on a symbolic level, for the understanding of which one must feel the text simultaneously on several planes.

Of course, according to one of the original plans, *Petersburg* was supposed to be the second part of a trilogy called 'East or West' ('Vostok ili Zapad'), as a continuation of *The Silver Dove*. Ultimately, Bely rejected this idea but, in an artistic sense, the two texts are clearly interconnected. This is not in the plots, not in the characters, and not in the 'problematics' of the novel in the strict sense of this word. *Petersburg* is quite a bit more defined chronologically (October 1905), characterologically (we learn details about many of its characters that we do not know about anyone in *The Silver Dove*), and socially. The first of the novels has rather indistinct social characteristics, but in the second we are presented with types well known to readers: the classic bureaucrat (obviously projected onto the image of Karenin from Tolstoy's novel), his wife, the student son (endowed with many of the author's own features), and the mysterious terrorists about which much had been written in literature not long before (the clearest example being the account of the real life of the famous terrorist Boris Savinkov [1879–1925], published by him as *The Pale Horse* [*Kon´ bled*] under the pseudonym 'V. Ropshin'). But instead of a social/psychological novel, which we would be right to expect, we are again presented with (as with *The Silver Dove*) a symbolist novel, in which every character and every episode is exposed to a whole spectrum of meanings. Depending on the code that the reader or researcher applies to the text, it can be read as an adventure novel with elements of parody, as a description of a psychopathological incident that needs analysis through psychoanalytic methods, as a judgement on the Russia of the past that statesmen like Senator Ableukhov had led into a dead end, and as a study of revolutionary ideas. Nonetheless, it is obvious that each of these codes, even the most common ones like the occult, is insufficient. Bely had to simultaneously create recognizable images, seemingly familiar to every reader, and play a 'brain game', forcing the reader to experience tragic collisions and to parody them right then and there, to form an integral construct from the pieces of the split-up world in order to immediately destroy it again.

The endless sequence of symbolic meanings that almost every element of the novel possesses, from the tiny details of form up to global historicosophical problems, endlessly expands the artistic world of the novel, making it practically inexhaustible. This is of course a characteristic of any genuine work of art but, for the most part, it is revealed alongside the perception of what we might call its inner form. But Bely (and, after him, many other twentieth-century writers as well) pushes the reader to think that without this kind of relationship, reading makes no sense at all, is not appropriate to the design nor to the construct. It is hardly a coincidence that enthusiasts of the novel think that in all of world literature from the first half of the twentieth century, only James Joyce's *Ulysses* is comparable to *Petersburg*.

Nonetheless, the appearance of novels like this and the very tendency to write in this style evoked a backlash. In 1910, Kuzmin published the short story 'High Art', with the title in quotation marks, which signified the author's ironic attitude toward this concept: the main character of the story, who was a talented writer of simple, elegant short stories, at the instigation of his wife began to write complicated works full of symbols, lost his readers, and ultimately killed himself. In popular literature as well, after about 1905 and through the 'teens, the 'high art' of symbolist prose found acceptance with difficulty. The easiest part to assimilate and reproduce was the ideologems, but only the place of the complex problems, never reducible to a single meaning, occupied the attention of the momentary and often speculative 'questions'. A number of works during and after the 1905–1907 revolutions were devoted to the theme of revolutionary violence and the terrorism closely tied to it; the defeat of revolution and the decline of the social movement following it gave rise to a flood of novels and shorter works about the disillusionment of individuals and of all of society, the breakdown of former ties, the new solitude and the tragedies of particular people connected with it. The elitist philosophical concepts (primarily Nietzscheanism) that had earlier become popular, and the religious or quasi-religious probings, gave rise both to entire works and many pages within other books, that were, it appeared, in no way tied to them, which provoked critics and readers to talk about the lofty intellectualism of popular literature; and the formerly forbidden theme of eroticism in its different variants, including 'perverted' eroticism, came to the surface. Perhaps the most popular figure of this kind was the main character of Mikhail Artsybashev's (1878–1927) novel *Sanin* (written 1902–1903, but published in 1907): the incarnation of the vulgarly understood Nietzschean 'superman', the vulgarized individualist hero revealed in his amorous adventures and in the discussions surrounding them, which took place within the novel itself and which were continued by critics. The next step along the path of simplification and debasement of the 'new man' were the characters of Anatolii Kamensky's (1876–1941) short stories 'Leda' (1906) and 'The Four' ('Chetyre', 1907), which reduced complex problems down to an elementary hedonism and almost parodic actions, such as the appearance of the hostess in a high-society home before her guests completely naked, advocating in this way feminist (in the primitive masculine conceptions of them) stances.

In Russian prose, two opposite tendencies were created: on the one hand, prose became intellectually and artistically complex, giving rise to unique artistic worlds that were not subject to one-sided interpretation and, on the other, it was simplified, actively shaping the mythologems of mass consciousness but only outwardly responding to what was then called 'the needs of the times'.

A peculiar offshoot of popular literature was what might be called 'common sense literature'. This was primarily manifested in the humour genres, and with particular talent in the short stories of Arkadii Averchenko (1881–1925). These were most often based on a central character who has a simple, uncomplicated view of life, and when he confronts one cultural phenomenon or another that claims to create 'high art' (no matter whether this is in earnest or without any internal foundations at all), such significant imperfections are very quickly discovered in him that his right to an intelligent existence in culture comes into doubt. The irony that permeates this kind of prose became an essential component of the literary process of those times.

However, by no means did this destroy either popular literature or the rather more serious phenomena. In the space between the two tendencies that we have discussed, and also in the framework of the still-existing traditions of realism and naturalism, there were quite a few creative individuals (who have to this day retained their attractiveness to readers) that found a place. We have already mentioned the creative work of Andreev, who actively used allegory and other quasi-expressionist means to artistically embody his ideas. To some degree, the works of the first Russian Nobel Prize winner, Ivan Bunin (1870–1953), were similar to Andreev's – but at the same time, sharply distinct from them. The primary distinction between them is their means of expression: Andreev tended to expressionism, coarse strokes that were charged with expressing strong and definite feelings; but an inclination toward impressionism is more characteristic of Bunin.

The classic analysis of Bunin's short story, 'Light Breathing' ('Legkoe dykhanie'), done in the 1920s by psychologist Lev Vygotsky (1896–1934),[5] demonstrated that in its structure (and equally so in many others of Bunin's best short stories) there is a transformation of lowly everyday material into aesthetically perfect form. The story of the feckless life of a provincial school-girl, senselessly and tragically cut short, acquires on a symbolic level an almost universal character that combines the incidental and natural into a complex, simultaneously harmonious and tragic unity, which can only be comprehended within the framework of the artistic transformation of the material. All the elements of the story lead to this goal: the texture of vocabulary, the world of reality, the literary allusions, the artful arrange-ment of the basic narrative line with other parallel lines that sometimes are completed and sometimes not and thereby evoke in the reader an impres-sion of opening out into a supra-aesthetic reality. Thus the mechanism for engendering meaning in Bunin's best works is a complex system that pulls in both nineteenth-century literary traditions and the innovations tested by symbolism.

Another variation of literary development was associated with authors who had begun as traditional realists but who gradually assimilated the attainments of 'the new prose'. Among these authors, one of the most famous was Alexander Kuprin (1870–1938). Kuprin made his entrance into literature in the 1890s but, unlike the symbolists and Gorky, was almost completely disassociated from the ideological movements of his times. What is attractive in his best works is his skilled use of the figurative possibilities of language and style, or his ability to organically combine the ordinary and the symbolic in the narration. Nevertheless, Kuprin's overall level of crafts-manship is too fragmented to consider him a first-rate author in Russian literature.

One of the most striking writers of the generation that had already made its start in literature by the 'teens was Evgenii Zamiatin (1884–1937). In 1913 and 1914 he published, one right after the other, the two novels *A Provin-cial Tale* (*Uezdnoe*) and *Out in the Sticks* (*Na kulichkakh*), in which the realistic and the symbolic sources are fused in an absolutely natural way. For the authors we discussed earlier, these principles were felt to be potentialities; but for Zamiatin, they existed as a given. With an equal measure of freedom, he patterns his behaviour on the almost-Symbolist Remizov, or on Kuprin with his realistic background and, without skipping a beat, his ornamental prose transitions into an averaged-out literary style. At this time, he was already paving the way, apparently, for his post-October work, in which the 'little fairy tales' that have a spiteful irony reminiscent of Saltykov-Shchedrin and the allegorism characteristic of this genre live alongside clearly symbolist-oriented short stories like the famous 'Mamai' (1921) and 'The Cave' ('Peshchera', 1922), the stylistically dry and rationalistically pointed anti-utopia, as in his even more famous novel, *We* (*My*, 1921), and various forms of stylization based on popular speech. Like a professional painter, Zamiatin unerringly selects the right colour for the right spot, knowing in advance how it will work in one spot or another. This kind of relationship to a literary palette is possible only when already settled methods for artistic transformation of reality exist and only the choice of them depends on the writer. In this respect, Zamiatin is the culmination of the artistic quest on which Russian prose journeyed in the space between symbolism and traditional realism.

The attempt to find new artistic paths was also taken up by Vasilii Rozanov in his extraordinarily heterogeneous creative work. His first published work was a philosophical treatise; he published several books of essays; he won fame with his journalistic articles, which sometimes remained separate fragments and sometimes transformed into collections of articles with their own internal logic, devoted to several of the issues that were extraordinarily vital to Russia at the time. His various books about the church and its role in Russian life, about various interpretations of the erotic principle in contemporary reality, and about the 'Jewish question' (these writings were excoriated, often quite justly), all provoked a stormy polemic. But as a man of letters (in the true sense of the term) he created three books that were published one after the other: *Solitaria* (*Uedinennoe*), and the two 'baskets' of *Fallen Leaves* (*Opavshie list′ia*).

These books are arranged and published in such a way to create an illusion for the reader that the text arose spontaneously, that it is unpremeditated and completely intimate. They lack practically all the features that are characteristic of traditional prose: narrative, a unified plot and even unified subject matter, unity (or natural metamorphoses) of style, and invention as such. They consist of a number of fragments of varying length, from a single line to several pages, sometimes pinpointing the author's state of mind at some point or another, sometimes expressing his attitude toward current events, and sometimes analysing a particular aspect of a problem, most often from among those that traditionally interested the author. In all of this, the author's personality is strongly stylized as a figure that is in no way fictional but completely real. The author of the 'trilogy' is endowed with all the features of the journalist well known to all Russian readers, with his family problems, his real-life interests and passions, and friends and acquaintances ranging from nameless female students and fellow train passengers to litterateurs and society figures no less famous than himself. Nonetheless, he declares that the distance between the time a thought arises and it is formulated for the reader is reduced to a minimum: 'Any movement of my mind is accompanied by an *utterance*, and I try to *note down* any utterance right away. This is instinct.'[6]

Rozanov provides a 'label' for *Solitaria*: 'By all rights, almost a manuscript.' Above many entries, there are notes about the time, place, and circumstances in which they appeared; in *Fallen Leaves*, the photographs are intertwined so as to create the impression of their unity with the written text. Rozanov contrasts his own writing to the literature in print, but at the same time he cannot break free from its fetters. If the futurist poets rendered their works by 'self-writing', then Rozanov translates everything into the printed text; the impression of spontaneity is combined with an artificially constructed composition; the actual 'movements of the mind' often carry over into journalistic, historical, or philosophical reflection, the function of which is to say everything that was impossible to say in the pages of the newspaper or journal. And the end of Literature is at the same time transformed simply into one of its paths, one that had hitherto existed happily, although on the periphery of Russian letters.

Over a quarter of a century, as we have seen, Russian prose evolved quite significantly. However, the new historical reality that raged outside it, most of all in the 1917 revolutions and the subsequent events that shook Russia (or 'whirled it apart', as Remizov said), provided the impulse for the appearance of new authorial individualities that in turn gave birth to new possibilities in literature. One need only mention the names of Platonov and Nabokov, or Babel and Bulgakov, to understand what this means. But that period merits a separate study.

NOTES

* Translated from Russian by Jesse Savage.
1 Merezhkovsky, D. S., *Estetika i kritika* (Moscow: Iskusstvo, 1994), vol. 1, p. 174.
2 Stalin wrote this inscription on 11 October 1931. It was published in Gor′kii, Maksim, *Sobranie sochinenii v 30 t.*, vol. 1 (Moscow: Khudozhestvennaia literatura, 1949), as an insert between pp. 48 and 49.

3 For more detail, see: Pavlova, Margarita, *Pisatel'-inspektor. Fedor Sologub i F. K. Teternikov* (Moscow: Novoe literaturnoe obozrenie, 2007), pp. 188–190; Elsvort, Dzhon [J.D. Elsworth], 'O filosofskom osmyslenii rasskaza F. Sologuba "Svet i teni"', *Russkaia literatura*, no. 2 (2000), pp. 135–138.
4 See Obatnina, Elena, *Tsar′ Asyka i ego poddannye. Obez′ian′ia Velikaia i Vol′naia Palata A. M. Remizova v litsakh i dokumentakh* (St Petersburg: Ivan Limbakh, 2001).
5 Vygotskii, Lev S., *Psikhologiia iskusstva* (Moscow: Iskusstvo, 1986), pp. 183–204 (and many other editions of Vygotsky's work).
6 Rozanov, Vasilii, *Uedinennoe* (Moscow: Russkii put′, 2002), p. 118, emphasis in original.

FURTHER READING

Alexandrov, Vladimir, *Andrei Bely: The Major Symbolist Fiction* (Cambridge, MA: Harvard University Press, 1985).
Bedford, C. Harold, *The Seeker: D. S. Merezhkovsky* (Lawrence, KA: University Press of Kansas, 1975).
Crone, Anna Lisa, *Rozanov and the End of Literature: Polyphony and the Dissolution of Genre in Solitaria and Fallen Leaves* (Würzburg: Jal-Verlag, 1978).
Greene, Diana, *Insidious Intent: An Interpretation of Fedor Sologub's The Petty Demon* (Columbus, OH: Slavica Publishers, 1986).
Il′ev, Stepan, *Russkii simvolistskii roman. Aspekty poetiki* (Kiev: Lybid′, 1991).
Lavrov, A., *Andrei Bely v 1900 gody. Zhizn′ i literaturnaia deiatel′nost′* (Moscow: Novoe Literaturnoe Obozrenie, 1995).
Malmstad, John, ed., *Andrey Bely: Spirit of Symbolism* (Ithaca, NY: Cornell University Press, 1987).
Paperno, Irina and Grossman, Joan Delaney (eds.), *Creating Life: The Aesthetic Utopia of Russian Modernism* (Stanford, CA: Stanford University Press, 1994).
Slobin, Greta, *Remizov's Fiction, 1900–1921* (DeKalb, IL: Northern Illinois University Press, 1991).

3

ANDREW KAHN

Poetry of the Revolution

The creative response of Russian poets to the political, ideological, and cultural changes unleashed by the October Revolution is unprecedented in modern literature. Whether Symbolist or Futurist, traditional or avant-garde in style, poets greeted the October Revolution with astonishment at the course of events leading from February 1917 to the fall of the Provisional Government and establishment of the Bolshevik state. Like photographic snapshots, even the briefest lyrics written in the heat of the moment reflected the speed and chaos of upheaval. Poets across the entire political spectrum and across generations, from aging Symbolists to the leaders of the avant-garde, lent vocal support to the positive revolutionary ideals of political freedom, economic equality, and parliamentary democracy, and welcomed the abolition of autocratic privilege, the eradication of poverty, the release of political prisoners, and improvement of labour conditions for the proletariat. Their lyrics spoke to these issues and at times espoused class warfare as a means to these ends.

Since the 1905 Revolution, Alexander Blok (1880–1921) had anticipated a historical cataclysm that would purge Russia of its old structures and leave it ripe for renewal. The most famous of the younger Symbolists and cynosure of younger writers like Anna Akhmatova and Marina Tsvetaeva, Blok feared that a negative resolution of the tensions between the country's European and Asiatic heritages might leave Russia vulnerable to collapse.[1] In 1918, the spectacle of increasing violence inspired 'The Scythians', a poem that frames the conflict of brewing Civil War between the Reds and Whites as the playing out of the irreconcilable fissures in Russian history in which infinite waves of Mongolian hordes overwhelm Russia's European stock. Tsvetaeva commemorated her loyalty to the Whites in the poems of *The Swans' Demesne* (*Lebediny stan*, 1917–1921) and in exile would glorify the conflict in 'Perekop', her dramatic poem of 1929.

Never a Marxist, Blok initially applauded the Bolshevik cause, and then tempered his optimism as the Revolution collapsed into civil war. Blok's ambivalence to the events of late 1918 permeates his revolutionary masterpiece, *The Twelve* (*Dvenadtsat'*, 1918) with a greater ambivalence and complexity. Written in stanzaic and non-stanzaic verse patterns with mixed metres, the narrative follows a motley platoon of twelve raw Bolshevik recruits on patrol in Petrograd. During the course of their mission a quarrel erupts between Petka and Vanka, two soldiers who are in love with the harlot Katka, leading to her accidental death. *The Twelve* fuses a polyphonic narrative of upheaval at street level with the symbolic language of Blok's philosophy of history. Blok punctuates whole sections with onomatopoeic, non-verbal explosions of sound-effects in order to convey rifle fire, and class distinctions mark the speech of characters. Osip Mandelshtam, who saw the Revolution as 'the twilight of freedom', appreciated the poem as a 'monumental dramatic popular jingle' (*chastushka*). The exposition of the poem has a montage-like effect as the eye of the camera cuts from scene to scene. Amidst the confusion, only sparse historical details mark the cityscape as Petrograd, and the blizzard that rages has the archetypal quality of a cosmic storm.

The Twelve has produced contradictory interpretations of its political meaning, but few dispute Blok's success in evoking the chaos of revolutionary Petrograd, and the work remains a high point of Russian modernism. The poem represents the outcome of history as a dynamic of destruction exercised through the class warfare and revenge that the oppressed wreak on the former ruling classes. At the same time, the stories of Katka, Petka, and Vanka incorporate the motif of the love triangle familiar from puppet-theatre and the *commedia dell'arte* tradition of Harlequin and Columbine. The two plot-lines intersect at a symbolic level with hints that Katka, a *femme fatale* in the manner of Carmen or Goethe's Mignon, also represents Russia. By interweaving a love sub-plot with the main Revolutionary narrative, Blok also exposes a squalid aspect of the Revolution, where personal motivations and random violence can be pursued under the name of class warfare or revolutionary ideals. Pathos is evident from the very first section, where the forlorn figure of the 'bourgeois', the term explicitly associated with class warfare, is positioned between a wrecked past and an uncertain future. While the twelfth and final section of the poem caused immediate controversy and to this day remains enigmatic, most critical attention sees it as central to Blok's meaning. As the soldiers, an apostolic twelve, run amok, Christ crowned in roses appears 'unseen' behind a snowdrift. Religiously minded contemporaries regarded the transformation of Christ into a Bolshevik leader as blasphemous, while readers inclined to see it as an endorsement of the Revolution were troubled by its religious content, since the Orthodox Church and religion were targets of both satire and sanction by the new state.

Proletarian poets, the Neo-peasants, and national renewal

From its inception (and even shortly before) the Bolshevik regime acted as a cultural power by encouraging workers to see the Revolution as an opportunity to develop the talent of the proletariat in the arts. Clubs and circles proliferated as spaces where a workers' intelligentsia could nurture their own talent by attending musical performances, readings, lectures, screenings, and evening dances. By 1920, as Mark Steinberg has observed, the Moscow trade unions ran hundreds of clubs and libraries, and the creation of Proletkult (*Proletkul´t*) studios and organizations in factories and artels extended across provincial Russia, the Urals, and Siberia.[2] From November 1917, in part as a result of an initiative by Lunacharsky, the Proletkult was formed by local workers and activists in an attempt to co-ordinate the diffuse network of organizations that had sprung up locally with the aim of creating cultural work for the masses. The class origins of members lent social cohesion and a sense of purpose. While their trade-union origins differentiated these studios and workshops from the activities of the bourgeois elite, they were also open to older revolutionary activists who lent a sense of solidarity across generations. For the most part, proletarian poets lacked technique and sophistication, and while Blok at least initially had hopes of fostering the new talent that was emerging from the depths of Russia, he became disenchanted as the message of the proletarian poets turned increasingly hostile towards tradition. Mikhail Gerasimov summed up the group ethos when he said, 'We must construct our own culture. We must not leave Proletkult [since] it is an oasis where our class will be crystallized.'[3] The leaders of Proletkult, and most especially Alexander Bogdanov, took a hard line on both the ideology and purely proletarian quality of its art. This provoked the hostility of Lenin and Trotsky, both of whom felt that workers, whatever their raw talent, could only develop if they benefited from a traditional education and the mentoring of experts. In fact, not all proletarian poetic groups wished to heed the Proletkult line. A number of poets who gave importance to mastery of artistic form felt little sympathy for the industrial rhythms and dogmatism of Proletkult, and disagreed with Bogdanov's insistence that proletarian art be accessible to the masses. They opposed the leadership and broke off to form the group *The Smithy* (*Kuznitsa*), which included worker writers like Vladimir Kirillov, Egor Nechaev, and Gerasimov himself. By 1920 Lenin's disapproval led him to shut down Proletkult. But in any case the organization, very much the spontaneous product of the heady energy of the October Revolution, was incapable of overseeing the process of factionalization and splintering that persisted in Bolshevik culture in the 1920s.

After seceding from Proletkult, members of *Smithy* founded the All-Russian Association of Proletarian Writers (VAPP) in 1921. It would come to be renamed the Russian Association of Proletarian Writers (RAPP) in 1928. Their initial enthusiasm spurred them to publish a journal and organize public activities until disenchantment set in over the policies of the New Economic Policy (NEP) period. Former Proletkultists loyal to the Central Committee came together in 1925 in groups like *October* and *The Young Guard*, where under the umbrella of VAPP they clashed over different aesthetic policies and revolutionary tactics. The most radical, such as *October*, saw poetry as a tool for mobilizing society for fierce class warfare. During a period of turmoil, uncertainty, and national hope, they reinforced the positive message about economic and social progress coming from the top. Whatever their factional differences, these groups made class origins of paramount importance in promoting writers explicitly committed to a socialist message, and spoke for a broader section of the population, voicing the sentiments of working men and women as never before.

Most sympathetic to the Proletkult poets was Aleksei Gastev (1882–1939), a metal worker and syndicalist politically closer to the Social Democrats whose verse embodies the utopian aspirations of the proletarian intelligentsia and the art of mass creation. As a disciple of the English management theorist Frederick Taylor, and a follower of the nineteenth-century radical thinker Nikolai Chernyshevsky, Gastev believed that humans were fundamentally rational and craved complete order. He believed that the movements and functions of men and machines were becoming synchronized, and that before long the symbiosis would create a mechanized proletarian collective possessing 'explicit grandeur totally freed from anything intimate or lyrical'. Once this new order was established through the implementation of 'engineerism' (*inzhenerizm*), group identity with its standardized psychology would prevail over individual identity, and man's egotistical nature would be replaced by a world of harmony run like a machine. In a 1922 tribute, the Futurist poet Nikolai Aseev dubbed Gastev the 'Ovid of the miners and metal-workers' because the scale of industrialization and transformation envisaged by Gastev in the Soviet utopia was on a par with the cosmogony described at the beginning of the *Metamorphoses*. Gastev's collection *The Poetry of the Working-Class Attack* (*Poeziia rabochego udara*, 1918) contained fourteen works, in mixed forms of prose and verse, which deploy a rapid-fire short lines consistent with their function as praise of mechanization.

The message of the proletarian poets supported the stated aims of the regime, praising contemporary achievements and visionary hopes for the future. In 'The Iron Messiah' ('Zheleznyi messia', 1918), the sailor and revolutionary activist Vladimir Kirillov (1890–1943) elevated Lenin as a titan of the proletariat who, 'invincible and swift', acts like a 'flame that purges'. Here crowds and nature fall under the spell of the hero's amazing charisma:

> Where his powerful cry rings out
> The bowels of the earth reveal themselves,
> Mountains part before him in an instant
> The ends of the earth come together.[4]

In investing Lenin with his mythic status as the genius of historical change and social renewal, Kirillov creates a revolutionary saint, referring to him as a 'saviour' with an 'aura of divine mystery' who emerges from the proletarian landscape of Russia's factories and railway stations, illuminated by the 'rays of electric suns'.

While the proletarian poets voiced the belligerent aspiration of workers, others saw national renewal as a resurrection of a Russia best preserved in the peasantry. In the two years preceding the Revolution, Sergei Esenin (1895–1925), Sergei Klychkov, and Pavel Oreshin formed a group known as 'the neo-peasant movement' that lasted only until 1918. They were led by the gifted if controversial Nikolai Kliuev (1887–1937), a member of the Old Believer sect from Northern Russia, who had already made a name for himself in Moscow and St Petersburg as a poet of the common folk. Kliuev and Esenin rose zealously to the events of the Revolution and were joined by their own rural origins and commitment to the countryside. They opposed urban values, and scorned an intelligentsia that was aloof from the people. Their essentially Slavophile vision of Russia identified the peasantry as the source of Russia's own distinctive patriarchal culture, an ancient and static agrarian realm. As Kliuev wrote, 'The mind wants a Republic, the heart wants Mother Russia'. Esenin viewed the Revolution through a mystical lens as a cosmic and Biblical event. As Gordon McVay points out, there was always a politically 'unreal' element in Esenin's treatment, which we see in short poems like 'Advent' ('Prishestvie', 1917), 'Transformation' ('Preobrazhenie', 1917). In the longer 'The Dove of the Jordan' ('Iordan-skaia golubitsa', 1918) he hailed the arrival of a 'new sower', foretelling a paradise.[5] Written at the same time as *The Twelve*, Esenin's most celebrated revolutionary poem is 'Inoniya', dedicated to the prophet Jeremiah, in which he casts himself as the prophet 'Esenin Sergei'. Roused to see the Revolution as a Second Coming, he prophesies in blasphemous terms a pastoral Golden Age that will threaten the industrial might of America, and ends with a prayer to the Jesus of the 'new faith'.

At heart, Kliuev and Esenin were not political poets. In fact, Kliuev confessed in a letter of 1918 that he was not 'a revolutionary or a Bolshevik', and presciently acknowledged that 'in an age of proletarian culture people like me ought to perish'.[6] In *Literature and Revolution*, Trotsky classified Esenin as a 'fellow-traveller' (*poputchik*) whose art was at one with the revolution while not being an art of the Revolution. Both poets promoted a vision of Russia that was threatened first by the aggressive advance of proletarian art in the 1920s and then by industrialization in the 1930s. Esenin's narrative 'Sorokoust' (1920) recounts how the poet watched a horse race against a train (a 'steel horse') – and lose. In 'I'm the Last Poet of the Village' ('Ia poslednii poet derevni', 1919) Esenin, who dreamed of a rich peasant kingdom, dreads the 'black hand' of the Socialist Revolution that will disrupt timeless peasant ways. In 'Mysterious world, my ancient world' ('Tainstvennyi mir', 1922), he represents the conflict as a ferocious fight between a dying wolf cornered by predatory man.

Esenin enjoyed the limelight and affiliated himself with different literary groups, projecting the poetic personality of a peasant swagger and bohemian hooligan. Always a eulogist of the countryside, he moved closer in the 1920s to the more experimental Imaginists whose hostility to collective movements gave him more space than the neo-peasant poets for his individuality. All this put Esenin on a collision course with the authorities. While the Bolsheviks were wary of the Futurists, they disapproved even more strongly of the Imaginists and their philosophy of anarchy. Personal misery and alcoholism led to Esenin's suicide in 1925.

Kliuev, whose poetic persona was more meek and monk-like, produced some lines of bloodcurdling violence when he arrived in Petrograd early in 1918. He affirmed his enthusiasm for the Revolution in the 1919 collection 'The Bronze Whale' ('Mednyi kit'), which included political poems like 'Red Song' ('Krasnaia pesnia'), and his militant views characterize his 'Hymn to the Great Red Army' ('Gimn Velikoi Krasnoi Armii', 1918). In the idiom of Lenin's Red Terror, Kliuev preached rebellion across Russia, from Arkhangelsk to the Caucasus, hailed Bolsheviks as comrades (*tovarishchi*), wished peace to country dwellers, war on palaces, and gloated over the fat carcasses of merchants in anti-capitalist rhetoric typical of the moment. Poems like 'Comrade' ('Tovarishch') revel in the upheaval, while works like 'Song of the Sun-Bearer' ('Pesn′ solntsenostsa', 1917) treat the Revolution as a cosmic creative act of emancipation. The lyric poems in his collection celebrate violence and bloodshed, speaking of God's will as a 'machine gun', but this was not enough to appease the proletarian critics who excoriated his 'peasant mysticism'. From 1922 Kliuev's avowed disenchantment with the Revolution led him to reiterate his faith in his mystical–Christian vision of Russia and to attack all aspects of modernization, including the Bolshevik Revolution that threatened the culture of the peasantry. Stubborn in his beliefs, Kliuev eventually retreated from the city and lived in northern Russia until his execution by the NKVD in 1937.

Among the most prominent of writers of popular origin and populist in message is Demian Bednyi (1883–1945), who published more than forty poetic collections marked by extreme nationalism and loyalty to the regime, until his relations with Stalin soured. His poetic narrative 'About this land, about Freedom, about the Worker's Lot' ('Pro zemliu, pro voliu, pro rabochuiu doliu', 1917) shows the rapidity with which poets could turn current events into history and even modern myth. A gigantic overview of the rise of the Bolsheviks and the success of the October Revolution, the narrative poem was issued in a large print-run, with the Marxist slogan 'Proletariat of all nations, unite!' printed on the cover. A versatile manipulator of verse-form from the *chastushka* to the formal lament and peasant song, Bednyi captures the perspective of the peasant or soldier and makes his characters speak the uninhibited language of class warfare. The cycle puts forward a view of how Party activists fomented revolution in the countryside, and aims to demonstrate the social justice of the October Revolution by lampooning priests for greed, deriding the gentry as thieves for expropriating peasant wealth, and subjects the Mensheviks and SR leaders to ideological critique and accusations of a lack of leadership, since 'all our salvation lies in a strong power'. History, as recounted in the colloquial language of the peasants and soldiers who are its agents, unfolds before the reader's eyes, and the excitement of the narrative is a function of its uncertain outcome. Ordinary readers appreciated his chronicle of the heroism of the people, illustrated with vignettes showing the exploitation of the old order and the liberty promised in the new state. Scarcely any of the proletarian poets of the 1930s remain household names.

The 'third front', NEP, and Futurism

Once victory in the Civil War was achieved, culture became the 'third front' of revolutionary activity in the eyes of the Party. The establishment of NEP delayed the 'top-down' management of literature and the arts that would emerge in the early 1930s. Despite the strident advocacy of RAPP, poetry in the NEP period was pluralist, and proletarian writers faced vibrant (and superior) competition from groups like the Futurists and Imaginists.

Utopianism and Futurism were natural allies against the old order. Despite the whiff of political subversion that Futurism acquired thanks to the theatrical antics of its members, who saw themselves as cultural provocateurs, from its beginnings in 1913 its constituent groups had no organized political programme. Rather, their focus on formal structures, especially on the semantic interplay of sound-structures, verse-form, and images, created a shared commitment to art that defamiliarized the world, using aesthetic shock-tactics to enable the reader (and viewer, in the case of visual artists) to see reality afresh. Velimir Khlebnikov (1885–1922) was an original member of the group of Futurists that included the Burliuk brothers, Aleksei Kruchenykh, Elena Guro and, later, Vladimir Mayakovsky (1893–1930). Perhaps the most experimental of avant-garde poets, his lasting reputation rests on the verbal ingenuity and mystical quality of his trans-sense poetry (*zaum´*) in which linguistic associations override mimesis. But Khlebnikov also responded creatively to the Revolution with poetry attuned to its violence as well as its utopian promise. He regarded the Revolution as a transformation of the organic structure of the universe, and represented this restructuring in the narrative poem *Ladomir*, first published in 1923. Allusions to Russian history from the past, such as the rebel folk hero Stenka Razin, and to more recent turning points like the storming of the Winter Palace in St Petersburg, give a frame of reference to a surreal narrative in which the deity of the title, whose name combines the roots for 'harmony' (*lad*) and 'world' (*mir*), eliminates poverty and hardship by reducing that world to ash. In highly lyrical language, the poem describes a domain in which space is transfigured into a new dimension as a habitat for a people known as the 'future dwellers' (*budetliane*, coined from the future of the verb 'to be' in Russian) who know no alienation from their work, enjoy freedom, and even freedom from death. Amidst the conflation of the human and natural worlds, revolutionary tones occasionally ring out: 'So little have we lost,/By taking the path of rebellion,–/The representatives of the earthly sphere/Stride along a daring path.'[7]

Even at his most futuristic, Mayakovsky kept things far more down to earth than Khlebnikov. From 1917 until his suicide, Mayakovsky deployed his boundless talent across a spectrum of genres, from agit-prop jingles to futuristic epic, in speaking to both the public and to the regime.[8] Mayakovsky, too, aimed to rally support by referring to the fragility of the October Revolution, citing its enemies both at home and abroad. His 'Ode to the Revolution' appeals to industrial workers to throw their might behind Lenin and resist the opposition of mutinous sailors. At the end, he bestows a poetic blessing that drowns out the opponents' curses.

The October Revolution was Mayakovsky's greatest inspiration and subject, and the consequent mutations of the new state's agricultural, economic, and cultural policies could not fail to galvanize his imagination. The 'Order

No. 2 to the Army of Arts' ('Prikaz No. 2 armii iskusstv', 1921) was a manifesto to writers, musicians, painters, and dancers to forget and even spit on their 'rhymes, arias, rosy shrubs', all of which fared poorly when compared with the productivity of miners, carpenters, and oil workers in helping the state to advance. His call was not to abandon art, but rather to enjoin his fellow artists to create a 'new art, one that would help wrestle the republic from the mire'. [9] A declamatory poet with a booming voice given to titanic gestures and hyperbolical caricature and metaphor, Mayakovsky naturally saw the struggle to establish a new state and a new social order as a global battle: for him, the fundamental changes of revolution were political and, consequently, social. The fervent wish to defend the Revolution and extend its reach by extirpating bourgeois values on a global scale inspired the science-fiction fantasy of the narrative poem *150,000,000*, which Mayakovsky began in 1919 and completed in 1920, during the most difficult days of the Civil War. Lenin savaged *150,000,000* when asked to grant permission for its publication. The number in the title represents the population of the Soviet Union, whom he serves as spokesman. Written as a modern version of the *bylina*, a Russian folk epic, the story pits Ivan, a representative common man, against Woodrow Wilson, the champion and epitome of capitalism, based in Chicago and representative enemy of Russian communism. As in the *bylina*, Ivan works wonders against the well-armed Wilson and vanquishes the enemy. Recounted with Mayakovsky's typical satirical brilliance, the poem celebrates the Russian people as a fighting machine whose marshalled discipline foils the arch-capitalist Wilson's weaponry, and identifies the source of their strength in their belief in a new society rationally organized on sound economic principles:

> Instead of beliefs – we have electricity in our soul, steam.
> Instead of beggars – put in your pockets the wealth of all the worlds.
> Kill off the old.
> Turn their skulls into ashtrays.
> After wiping out the old
> In a fierce onslaught,
> Let us announce
> A myth for the whole world.
> Let us kick down the time-barrier,
> Let us kick up to the sky
> A thousand rainbows. [10]

Mayakovsky's message is at one with the new order, but he remained stylistically faithful to his avant-garde poetics, with syntax governed by his use of the 'ladder' verse-form, also employing a type of word-play based on distortions (or what the Futurists called 'swerves') of similar verbal roots. History as Mayakovsky told it in *150,000,000* was 'like the curve in the palm of your hand' (l. 1555), and therefore much harder to use for the Bolshevik purposes of nation-building.

Despite his unequivocal commitment to communism, Mayakovsky's futurist flamboyance won him little loyalty from the Bolshevik leadership. Party leaders were increasingly uncomfortable with avant-garde writing. While the imposition of conservative tastes was tentative in the early years of the NEP period and hardened only in 1927, the regime made clear its displeasure with literature not written for consumption by the proletariat, whose re-education would be a precondition for the creation of Communist society, as attested in the Politburo's 1925 resolution on literature. A host of Leninist initiatives, including action against Proletkult, the proletariazation of the Party and the formation of a new intelligentsia whose traditional (albeit 'bourgeois') tastes for the classics was acceptable, narrowed the scope of freedom for poets keen on applying Futurist means to Communist ends. In 1923 Mayakovsky and prominent Constructivist artists like Rodchenko and Exter joined forces in the Left Front of Art and founded the short-lived journal *LEF* in order to safeguard the achievements of the avant-garde for the revolutionary state. The serious assertion of their ideological faith in a platform that promoted the 'discovery of a Communist path for all varieties of art' was, if only in their eyes, compatible with their continued spirit of philological and poetic invention.

It would not be until 1934, when at the First Congress of the Union of Soviet Writers Zhdanov, speaking for Stalin, proclaimed Socialist Realism the official doctrine of Soviet art, that proletarian poetry would finally stifle creative diversity. A decade earlier, Lenin himself had shown far more enthusiasm for the classics, Trotsky had been withering about proletariat poetry, and Bukharin was convinced that the creation of high-quality Soviet literature depended on writers of genuine talent, whatever their class origins. But from the second half of the 1920s and into the early 1930s, VAPP, and then RAPP, fought doggedly against other literary groups to assert class origins over all other criteria as the basis of Soviet art.

The images used by proletarian poets are the portraits, flags, red banners, and the hammer and sickle, that decorate the actual landscape as symbols of the regime. Such uniformity stands in striking contrast to the individual voices and thematic diversity of works by a long list of other non-proletarian poets, including Mayakovsky and Pasternak, whose support for the Revolution was clear. Epic times demanded epic production, but there was a huge gap between the outlook and artistic approach of the two groups. A qualitative difference distinguishes masterpieces of Communist poetry from mere propaganda. One has only to contrast Mayakovsky's *Vladimir Ilich Lenin* (1924) which puts the man back in the myth, and pays tribute to his willpower and eloquence, with the two-dimensional figure of Alexander Bezymensky's *Vladimir Ilich Ulianov* (1926); or contrast Mayakovsky's *150,000,000*, and its cosmic comic-strip battle, with the proletarian poet Mikhail Gerasimov's narrative works. In *At the Front of Labour* (*Na fronte truda*), Gerasimov applies a new version of the pathetic fallacy. The speaker imbues nature with an industrial dynamic, its every movement comparable to a mechanical process: the sound of rain is like the ringing 'of a noisy tractor', the clouds 'put on steel cheeks/and pour live juices/on the front of fieldwork', and the wind is made of steel. Labour, newly emancipated in the Soviet state, will in co-operation with sympathetic nature build 'different palaces'. In *Elektropoema* (1922), the relationship between a power station and its technical workers is eroticized, with man and machine blending souls as man–machine.

Not all poets, however, felt comfortable, either immediately or in retrospect, with the idea of celebrating 1917. In general, Pasternak approached topical themes obliquely. His poetic narratives on revolutionary subjects fold complex questions into their dense poetic texture and avoid overt statements of ideology. It is not for nothing that a contemporary critic referred to his 'inharmoniousness with the era' ('nesozvuchnost′ epokhe'); and while Pasternak was for a time a member of *LEF* that was receptive to his modernist style, unlike Mayakovsky he never engaged in blatant agit-prop. Above all, contemporary events inspired a microscopic attentiveness to man's emotional and aesthetic relationship to the world. He measures the impact of history in new awareness of nature, and a miraculously fresh perspective on the world. *My Sister Life*, Pasternak's second (and perhaps most celebrated) collection, contains no explicit tributes to the October Revolution. Across the fifty poems, poetic subjectivity captures through intricate syntax, complex metaphors, and marvellous painterly and impressionistic effects a unique receptivity to the tenderness and yearning of love, to numerous manifestations of nature and weather, and to landscapes like the steppe. Yet behind the collection as a whole, with its dramatic thunderstorms and emotional outpourings, there is such a sense of rebirth that contemporaries found it hard not to associate his exuberance with the energy of the revolutionary era. Valerii Briusov, a doyenne of the Symbolists, observed in the journal *Print and Revolution* that whether Pasternak knew it or not, the poems were 'saturated with the spirit of contemporary life, perhaps unknown to the author'.

But in the 1920s Pasternak shied away from treating the 1917 Revolution for complex reasons that combined his misgivings about the state of life in Soviet Russia with developments in his own philosophy of history. In the completed fragments of a verse-novel *Spektorsky*, he sketched the development of a young Russian intellectual who comes of age during the Revolution. The result was a probing psychological portrait of an individual member of the intelligentsia and his views on historical action. Disenchantment of various kinds caused him to abandon this project. Close study of Pasternak's dense lines have shown how even in poems like the narrative *The Lofty Malady* (*Vysokaia bolezn'*) ambivalence marks his position in the 1920s. In scale the Revolution strikes him as a malady of the entire earth and another in a succession of upheavals from Troy and Herculaneum to the tragedy of the tsar and his family. Yet the malady is also the poet's feverish need to sing a not necessarily easy tune.

The continuation of NEP allowed poets to address the theme of social renewal through diverse methods. But by the end of the 1920s, the dissolution of NEP and industrialization were favourable to poets of a proletarian cast. In 1925 Taylorism and 'scientific management' were endorsed by the Soviet leadership, challenging more traditional collectivist labour organization, and by 1927 the attitude of the regime to the 'left front' of Soviet art hardened against the pluralism that had been defended by Lunacharsky, the first Soviet Commissar of Enlightenment from 1917 to 1929. Increasingly towards the end of the NEP period, as internal debate over economic policy sharpened, many poems regularly rehearsed the promise of liberation, equality and fairness that would be realized thanks to the will and effort of the people and its leaders; and these poems fine-tuned their message to be consistent with changes in economic policy. Pledges about a socialism of economic might and sufficiency were still largely aspirations at the end of NEP, and the rhetoric of a new socialist reality increased with the advent of the first Five-Year Plan:[11] the lyrics underscore the themes of solidarity, collective responsibility, determination, and optimism that reverberate in the poetry written in the late 1920s in anticipation of, and eventual support for, it. In this company Pasternak's 'To the October Revolution Anniversary' ('K Oktiabr'skoi godovshchine', 1927) is short on praise of the Revolution's achievements and prospects, offering instead a succession of scenes from Petrograd in 1917, which his use of metonymy and metaphor shape into Gogolian glimpses of wintry disorder cast in black and grey rather than in triumphant red.[12] The understatement hints at the conflict and ambivalence Pasternak faced in balancing strategies of survival and ideological accommodation with his own artistic beliefs in 1929 as RAPP imposed control over writers.

The poetry of dystopia and the absurd

The ideological tenor, formal conservatism, and monochromatic picture of much proletarian poetry forms a background against which the works of the OBERIU poets stand in sharp relief. Despite the striking individuality of the group's members, their belief that poetry is a type of linguistic and formal realm structured according to its own laws and processes of experimentation affiliates them with the spirit and goals of Futurism. The OBERIU poets (known collectively as the 'Oberiuty') aspired to reveal the true reality behind surface appearances by applying an analytical approach. While Konstantin Vaginov (1899–1934) and Nikolai Zabolotsky (1903–1958) regarded their outlook as 'realistic' because the perceptions were vivid, their highly visual world of tangible objects has been broken down into different parts and re-assembled in highly unfamiliar and often grotesque pictures. Their manifesto stated their conviction that only leftist revolutionary art could take them 'onto the highway to the new proletarian artistic culture', but the results strongly diverged from the growing preference for realism of a tendentious kind. Their work elicited immediate criticism and provoked lasting hostility that eventually led to their arrest. Zabolotsky's poetry stands in complex relation to developments in Soviet science, agriculture, and ideology in the 1920s. Implicit in his poetry is a commitment to the Revolution and the egalitarian promise of the new state. But his utopian vision grew out of a philosophical rather than a political outlook. Consequently, few if any of his poems treat social themes in an accessible way. Instead he focuses either on the lurid details of the present or on a natural world imbued with a mystical sense in which the animate and inanimate share consciousness, and transformation takes an evolutionary rather than an industrial or political course. The new consciousness in which his thinking animals and trees participate is not the revolutionary consciousness that literature was meant to be instilling in the peasantry and proletariat. Zabolotsky is at his most realistic and visceral in the urban scenes of his first collection *Scrolls* (*Stolbtsy*, 1929). Zabolotsky captured the excesses of the NEP period as a phantasmagoria without any disapproval or social comment, and he employed techniques of fragmentation and synecdoche to conjure up the febrile dynamism of city-life. In 'Evening Bar', Nevsky Prospekt looks 'shiny and languid/Having changed its colours during the night' and 'is different from a fairy tale only by a thread'.[13] In 'A New Life' ('Novyi byt'), biological change quickens to suit the speed of the times. The result is that appetites rather than as collectivist values increase: 'The factory sang forth: "Hurrah! Hurrah!"/And New Life, bestowing its grace,/Holds a sturgeon in a plate.'[14] The new reality of the NEP period is most vibrant and lurid in poems like 'At the Market'

('Na rynke'), which gives us a much more Dostoevskyan cross-section of the population than proletarian poetry where tubby women, cripples, and maimed soldiers seem to resemble the pickles and herrings and other food-stuffs on sale. 'The Wedding' ('Svad´ba') and 'The Foxtrot' ('Fokstrot') combine an Onegin-like elegance of narration with images of gluttony, peopling vignettes with 'a large flock of meaty dames', 'rich sweets', 'distended bellies', and 'thick slabs of fatty meat'.

To Zabolotsky, a migrant from the provinces to the city, this was an amoral, 'dream of a fortunate land' into which he inserted images of displacement, poverty, and entertainment. Despite the prosperity that spelled recovery from the Civil War, his Russia was not a socialist paradise. When Zabolotsky wrote the narrative poem *The Triumph of Agriculture* (*Torzhestvo zemledeliia*, 1933), a cycle of lyrics in six parts, dekulakization and collectivization had already begun. This work best illustrates why Zabolotsky's attitude to the political environment is ambiguous and, possibly, irreducible. The cycle opens with a village-assembly in which elders consider the material and corruptible nature of the soul; the conquest of nature and the vision of re-birth is a philosophical issue rather than a product of agricultural policy. This abstract vision emanates from Zabolotsky's scientific and philosophical interests, and bears no resemblance to the Neo-peasant socialist tradition of a poet like Kliuev. Yet the third poem, 'Kulak, Master of Farm Labourers', is more topical and treats the plight of the wealthy peasant who resists the new policy and would destroy the grain harvest rather than submit. While the profile contains some hints of satire, it evokes with pathos the solitude of an isolated and threatened figure. Section 2 ('The suffering of animals') again raises the vision of an ecological utopia in which animals and plants develop the consciousness of humans. Section 4 ('Battle with ancestors') depicts a dialogue between a soldier and the ghostly manifestation of dead ancestors who challenge the soldier as a child of reason to contemplate the fecundity of nature as an endless principle of birth and re-birth in which the dead also participate. The theme of modernization spills over into Sections 5 and 6, where the village structures are convulsed by panic and the birth of a new world does violence to nature and psychological damage to animals perhaps even more than humans. It has been interpreted convincingly as a bitter satire of the ruins of collectivization, but other arguments, perhaps less persuasively, have been made to show that Zabolotsky sees these changes as the precursor of utopian organic and metaphysical transformations in the organic structure of men, animals, and nature.

Daniil Kharms (1905–1942) is best known of the OBERIU group as a master of the comic absurd in prose, the heir to Gogol and the equal of Zoshchenko in his plotting of nonsense situations. Much of his poetry is written in the idiom of *zaum'* in which language, released from its referentiality, follows its own logic through etymological, imagistic, or phonological connections. But from the 1930s, when government policy on literature hardened, the source of the absurd in Kharms shifted from an existential, philosophical basis to a focus on the ethics of actions in the Soviet Union. In the poem 'Khniu' (1931), the invented name of a female figure who appears in several works, the poet remarks that 'we find it so pleasing to know the past/pleasant to believe in the confirmed/to re-read a thousand times books receptive to the rules of logic'. But the comfort of such a reality becomes scarcer in his poems where philistine, asocial, and even violently anti-social encounters occur. We can sample the flavour of his black humour in a poem like 'A dream of two swarthy ladies' ('Son dvukh chernomazykh dam', 1936):

> Two ladies sleep, well, that's not the case,
> they don't sleep, well, that's not the case,
> of course they do sleep and have a dream,
> It's as though Ivan walks through the door
> and behind Ivan comes the house manager,
> holding in his hands a volume of Tolstoy
> 'War and Peace', Part Two...
> But that's not the case, not at all,
> Tolstoy walked in and took off his coat
> removed his galoshes and his shoes
> and shouted: 'Vanya, help!'
> Then Ivan grabbed an axe
> And bashed Tolstoy on the noggin.
> Tolstoy fell. What a shame!
> There goes Russian literature down the bedpan.[15]

Nothing is what it seems as the boundaries between reality and dreaming crumble. The house manager, his office given in its bureaucratic Soviet designation of 'upravdom', would have been of modest social origins. His taste for Tolstoy reflects the new-found popularity of the classics among all grades of society, since the government, led on this by Stalin, believed that the best means of elevating the taste of the masses was by educating them in the classics of Russian literature. But murderous violence eliminates Tolstoy who demonstrates great politeness by removing his shoes. Even Tolstoy is not safe in a proletarian state where the polish of an everyman like Ivan is only skin deep and class hatred can swell up murderously. Far from conveying a spirit of collective harmony in which the New Soviet person has achieved his full human potential and contributes to social life, these poems depict subjectivity as mechanical and virtually inhuman, reduced to violent reflexes.

Similarly, Nikolai Oleinikov (1898–1937) inverts (and subverts) the priority given officially to the heroic, the large, and the progressive as features of Soviet literature. Poems like 'Praise to the Inventors' ('Khvala izobretateliam', 1932) and 'The Fly' ('Mukha', 1934) celebrate a love of small things that jars by contrast with the mass-produced propagandistic verse.[16] His teapots, sugar-tongs, and cigarette-holders are not the expected emblems of the industrial programme heralded by the Great Leap Forward and first Five-Year Plan. Oleinikov finds a place for crushed humanity in the sub-human world of insects, channelling his representation of reality through the viewpoint of the downtrodden and mortally wounded insect. 'The Death of a Hero' ('Smert´ geroia', 1933) buries a dismembered beetle, a soulless carapace in which 'the tendon of consciousness doesn't stir', a forgotten, unknown hero who is lamented only by the spider. In Oleinikov's world individuals seek to hide by changing their identity ('Changing surnames' ['Peremena familii'], 1934), and insects are more capable of human feeling than people who experience total alienation from their surroundings. Desperation reaches a crescendo in his famous poem 'The Cockroach' ('Tarakan', 1934), recounted in song-like trochaic stanzas, which chronicles the brutal execution of the cockroach by vivisectors. Desperate to survive despite his isolation and impending death, the insect feeds off his own blood while the lyric speaker ironically comments that science has established that the soul does not exist and is no more than a physical function. The clinical detachment of this voice-over contrasts with the brutality of the execution and the anguish of the baby cockroaches who cry out for their father. It is a grotesque parable of the debased value of individual life in a menacing and brutal context.

Poets across a range of artistic schools saw the Revolution as a social movement bringing redemption as well as retribution for the lower classes. For Blok, it was the inevitable result of the old regime's inability to reform. For others, utopias of different kinds (industrial, peasant, and cosmic) vindicated the Revolution. Still others, like Zabolotsky, based their view of the Revolution as the final stage of life on scientific and philosophical theories rather than Marxist doctrine, but their hopes were betrayed as absurdity triumphed over reason. Poets like Blok and Mayakovsky produced in response to their age memorable verse that has entered the canon of Russian literature. Even Mandelshtam, who from the start was ambivalent about the potential good of a regime change that would cause so much destruction, sought to capture the scale and energy of this historic attempt to create a 'heaven' on earth. By the late 1920s, however, he concluded that the

Bolsheviks had betrayed socialist ideals and were against the people. His 1930s poems intermittently reflect the collective hardships of urban poverty and brutal dekulakization. Dissonant individual voices like Mandelshtam's had no place in Stalinist culture and were thus eliminated. Surviving as the true spokesmen for the revolution and its legacy were the hundreds of minor or anonymous poets, now anthologized, who collectively expressed the change that swept the country and permanently altered its institutions of literature.

NOTES

1 Blok, Alexander, 'Intelligentsiia i revoliutsiia' in his *Sobranie sochinenii* (Moscow: Khudozhestvennaia literatura, 1962), vol. 6, p. 11.
2 See Steinberg, Mark D., *Proletarian Imagination: Self, Modernity, and the Sacred in Russia, 1910–1925* (Ithaca, NY: Cornell University Press, 2002), p. 57.
3 Quoted in Men'shutin, A. and Siniavskii, A., *Poeziia pervykh let revoliutsii. 1917–1920* (Moscow: Nauka), 1964, p. 51.
4 *Oktiabr' v sovetskoi poezii* (Leningrad: Sovetskii pisatel', 1987), p. 93 (no. 11).
5 McVay, Gordon, *Esenin: A Life* (London: Hodder & Stoughton, 1976), p. 86.
6 Azadovskii, K., *Nikolai Kliuev. Put' poeta* (Leningrad: Sovetskii pisatel', 1990), p. 206.
7 Khlebnikov, Velimir, *Tvoreniia*, ed. M. Ia. Poliakova (Moscow: Sovetskii pisatel', 1987), p. 290.
8 Terras, Victor, *Vladimir Mayakovsky* (Boston, MA: Twayne Publishers, 1983), chapter 3.
9 Maiakovskii, Vladimir, *Polnoe sobranie sochinenii* (Moscow: Khudozhestvennaia literatura, 1956), vol. 2, p. 86.
10 Maiakovskii, *Polnoe sobranie sochinenii*, vol. 2, p. 125.
11 Brooks, Jeffrey, *Thank You, Comrade Stalin! Soviet Public Culture from Revolution to Cold War* (Princeton, NJ: Princeton University Press, 2000), pp. 54–59.
12 *Oktiabr' v sovetskoi poezii*, p. 333 (no. 93).
13 Zabolotsky, Nikolai, *Stolbtsy* (St Petersburg: Izdatel'stvo 'Severo-Zapad', 1993), p. 41.
14 *Ibid.*, p. 48.
15 *Poety gruppy 'Oberiu'* (St Petersburg: Sovetskii pisatel', 1994), p. 341 (no. 118).
16 For Oleinikov's poems, see *Poety gruppy 'Oberiu'*, pp. 390–428.

FURTHER READING

Brown, Edward, *Mayakovsky: A Poet in the Revolution* (New York: Columbia University Press, 1973).
Cornwell, Neil, ed., *Daniil Kharms and the Poetics of the Absurd* (London: Macmillan, 1991).
Fleishman, Lazar, *Boris Pasternak: The Poet and his Politics* (Cambridge, MA: Harvard University Press, 1990).
Hackel, Sergei, *The Poet and the Revolution: Alexander Blok's The Twelve* (Oxford: Oxford University Press, 1975).

Johansson, Kurt, *Aleksej Gastev: Proletarian Bard of the Machine Age* (Stockholm: Almqvist & Wiksell, 1993).

Mally, Lynn, *Culture of the Future: The Proletkult Movement in Revolutionary Russia* (Berkeley, CA: University of California Press, 1990).

Markov, Vladimir, *Russian Futurism: A History* (London: MacGibbon & Kee, 1969).

Men´shutin, A. and Siniavskii, Andrei, *Poeziia pervykh let revoliutsii. 1917–1920* (Moscow: Nauka, 1964).

Mikhailov, Alexander, *Puti razvitiia novokrest´ianskoi poezii* (Leningrad: Nauka, 1990).

Pyman, Avril, *The Life of Alexander Blok*, 2 vols. (Oxford: Oxford University Press, 1979–1980).

Steinberg, Mark, *Proletarian Imagination: Self, Modernity, and the Sacred in Russia, 1910–1925* (Ithaca, NY: Cornell University Press, 2002).

4

BORIS WOLFSON

Prose of the Revolution

Revolution, writer, episode

The Revolution, taken episodically, appears quite insignificant. Where is the
Revolution, then? Here lies the difficulty. Only he will overcome it who fully
understands and feels the inner meaning of this episodic character and who will
reveal the historic axis of crystallization that lies behind it. 'Why do we need
solid houses?' the sect of Old Believers used to say. 'We are awaiting the coming
of Christ.' Nor does this Revolution build solid houses; instead it concerns itself
with resettlement [*pereselenie*], increases of residential density [*uplotnenie*],
and construction of barracks. All of its institutions give the impression of
being temporary, barrack-like. But not because it awaits the coming of Christ,
that is, contrasts its final aim with the present process of building life, but
because, on the contrary, it strives in endless gropings and experiments to find
the best ways of building a house that is solid.[1]

In a few charged sentences Trotsky offers his readers a remarkable reformu-
lation of the entire Bolshevik project. An act of cosmic creation, it does not
(we are told) derive its legitimacy from an infinitely deferred redemption –
the arrival of a messianic age. Instead, its meaning must come from a particular kind of ongoing revelation. What the Revolution needs is someone
who will explain it to itself by figuring out how the various pieces of the
existential and ideological puzzle ought to fit together. And that someone
must be a writer. First published in 1923, the treatise in which Trotsky
makes this claim, *Literature and Revolution* (*Literatura i revoliutsiia*), is
itself decidedly episodic – a collection of stylistically heterogeneous essays
and reviews, written before and after 1917, that seek in part to define the
place of art in the ideal society of the future. The book is by turn painfully
candid and unabashedly utopian. At the end of the programmatic essay
'Revolutionary and Socialist Art' Trotsky famously describes the ultimate
aim of all human activity, including art, as the development of a 'higher
social biological type, or, if you wish, a superman' (207). At the same time,

throughout the book he is preoccupied with the proposition that the Revolution may well fall radically short of the expectations that surround it. A crucial part of his solution to this problem lies in identifying 'the development of a new art' as the ultimate test of vitality for the new economic, political, and social arrangements (29). To rescue the Revolution from the spectre of irrelevance, Trotsky advocates a government policy in the arts that sanctions maximum freedom of experimentation for writers willing to work on behalf of the revolution to bring about the ever-elusive revelation of the 'historical axis of crystallization'. This final point is crucial: to Trotsky, only those writers who see themselves, at a minimum, as 'revolution's literary fellow-travellers' (*literaturnye poputchiki revoliutsii*, Trotsky's original coinage) hold genuine promise. The intensity of his attacks on, and dismissal of, 'extra-revolutionary' writers serves to remind his readers of Trotsky's primary occupation – in 1923, he is still People's Commissar of War. Yet in turning to the fellow-travellers as he explores a major political and existential anxiety – what if the Revolution is in the end less than the sum of its parts? – he invests imaginative literature with a sweeping ideological function.

Extremely influential as a work of criticism and an ideological statement when it first appeared, *Literature and Revolution* articulated more clearly than most such writings the peculiar relationship between the ideological expectations of new regime and the institution of the Soviet literary fellow-traveller. In this arrangement, the writers were offered minimal, often vague and sometimes contradictory 'guidelines' for their work, and were then expected to develop these ideas, anticipating and fleshing out the finer points of ideological and aesthetic principles. When they erred, they were to be corrected and possibly offered more general guidelines, which could either elaborate upon the previous set of remarks or – just as likely – contradict them.[2] In addition to theorizing this dynamic, Trotsky illustrates its workings in practice. The passage with which I began, about the Revolution's 'episodic character', comes from a section devoted to the work of Boris Pilniak (1894–1938). Pilniak's anti-novel *The Naked Year* (*Golyi god*, 1921–1922), which Trotsky analyses in some detail, was one of the earliest and most prominent large-scale attempts to create a paradigm of 'the new prose' about the Revolution. A self-consciously experimental, openly modernist work, *The Naked Year* receives ample and fairly specific praise from Trotsky. The objections-cum-recommendations for improvement Trotsky offers are, by contrast, monumental yet evasive – weighed down by ideological and existential implications that reveal more about his own predicament as an advocate of a permanent, and decidedly un-fragmented, revolution.

Trotsky's career as a theoretician of party policy regarding the arts was short-lived, and new developments on the Russian literary scene quickly made some of the book's claims seem dated. For instance, Trotsky's one-line dismissal of Mikhail Zoshchenko's early short stories as jejune and inferior to the efforts of the other 'Serapion Brothers' looked at best premature by the time *Literature and Revolution* was reprinted in 1924: in the intervening months Zoshchenko had become one of the most important, well-read, and widely praised figures on the Soviet literary scene. Trotsky writes nothing about Isaac Babel or Andrei Platonov, about Valentin Kataev, Mikhail Bulgakov, or Iurii Olesha – because in 1922–1923, when Trotsky's essays were being composed, these were still at best marginal figures, with few well-known publications to their name. Yet the tension to which Trotsky points in his discussion of Pilniak's experiments – the ideological and aesthetic implications of the Revolution's 'episodic character' – proves one of the book's most abiding insights, and continues to illuminate the workings of the post-Revolutionary literary experiment as it unfolds in the early 1920s.

This is in part a matter of technique and of genealogy: Soviet writers, especially fellow-travellers, found themselves contending with the legacy of Modernism, which had established fragmentation – of narrative, of consciousness, of identity – as a privileged mode of structuring a fictional world. At the same time, the prominence of the Revolution and its aftermath as primary themes and topics of reflection invited new approaches to investigating fragmentation, discontinuity, and impermanence as literary problems. First, debates about the place of revolutionary change in history put questions of causality and agency centre stage. Second, the chief method of Revolution – destruction of the enemy by all necessary means – endowed revolutionary violence with a set of symbolic meanings that seemed to bear directly on the question of literary process. 'Revolutionary literature', Trotsky reminds his readers, 'cannot but be imbued with a spirit of social hatred, which is a creative historic factor in an epoch of proletarian dictatorship' (188). Finally, the tropes that dominate Trotsky's discussion of the Revolution's 'temporary' character point to another set of questions implicated in taking on the Revolution. To recast the (post-)Revolutionary condition in the well-worn bureaucratic argot of the housing shortage – to figure the Revolution, as he does, as redistribution of tenants (recall the *pereselenie* and *uplotnenie* in the quotation above) – is to beg a question: in what precise way do the objects, words, actions, and other realia relegated to the catch-all category of the 'everyday' shape, and how are they redefined by, the Revolutionary experience?

For Trotsky, the Revolution's 'character' – episodic, transitory, brutal – is a source of apprehension and inspiration precisely because it renders literature uniquely equipped to partake in the symbolic and physical re-making of the world. For the generation of Soviet writers who identified themselves as literary fellow-travellers in the first post-Revolutionary decade the vision articulated by Trotsky offers a chance to re-define their relationship to the Modernist tradition and negotiate the ideological implications of the writer's status in the post-Revolutionary society. In examining the range of ways in which four of these writers – Pilniak, Babel (1894–1940), Zoshchenko (1894–1958), and Olesha (1899–1960) – used the fragment as a figure, device, and mode of literary experimentation, let us consider how their major 1920s works brought the key preoccupations of the time to bear on one another: how visions of avant-garde innovation and attempts to conceptualize the implications of revolutionary violence came to define the literary re-invention of post-revolutionary everyday living.

Narrative, cycle, fragment

Pilniak's experiments in narrative form, which Trotsky read as symptomatic of an ideological and aesthetic predicament, proved especially important in fleshing out the terms of a broader debate about the status and coherence of an autonomous – and 'complete' – prosaic work of art: short story, novel, cycle, collection, book. Pilniak referred to *The Naked Year* as a novel – a designation that many readers and critics questioned.[3] Babel described the stories in his cycle *Red Cavalry* (*Konarmiia*, 1923–1925) as 'chapters', and insisted on following specific sequencing in all separate editions of the cycle.[4] Zoshchenko re-combined the same individual stories and mini-cycles in a multitude of sequences in numerous collections. Olesha's two-part novella (*povest'*) *Envy* (*Zavist'*, 1927) undermined fundamental principles of temporal and thematic sequencing without breaking the illusion of adhering to a conventional form. At stake in exploring these different modes of fragmentation, ultimately, are the authors' differing conceptions of the relationship between aesthetic experimentation and history.

Pilniak's is perhaps the most self-consciously modernist enterprise among the four authors. In an influential 1925 essay on Pilniak's achievement, Viktor Shklovsky attributed to Andrei Bely a quip that Pilniak's prose was like a painting, the audience of which could not figure out from what distance it ought to be viewed.[5] This response from Bely was especially significant, since many contemporary readers of *The Naked Year* remarked on the heavy indebtedness of Pilniak's style to Bely's works. The novel's key themes also re-visited some of the key concerns of Russian modernism: the contested status of Russian national identity (east vs. west), biological and moral degeneration, the apocalypse, and spiritual re-birth. Bely's reaction seemed to point to a crisis experienced by Russian modernist aesthetics in confronting the Revolutionary experience. For Shklovsky, however, Bely's metaphor held special resonance. Perhaps more than any other figure associated with the Russian Formalist school, Shklovsky was concerned with the workings of a particular literary device he called 'estrangement' (*ostranenie*). To defamiliarize elements of experience that have become routine, and so create art, is precisely to alter the conventional distance from which one perceives the everyday 'reality'.

To Shklovsky, then, Bely's metaphor suggests that the principal challenge of Pilniak's work lies in being constructed so as to thwart the attempts to construct a single overarching reading. It is a case of defamiliarization run so rampant that no single focus point can be found from which a 'familiar' picture of an experience can be reconstructed. *The Naked Year* consists of a series of brief episodes, many of which relate stories about happenings in a fictional provincial town of Ordynin-gorod, and describe events in the lives of its denizens and visitors: the aristocrats, the Bolsheviks (famously metonymized as 'the leather jackets'), the sectarians, etc. Though teeming with sentence fragments and sometimes-incomprehensible utterances, the stories are populated with numerous readily recognizable objects, actions, and even one-dimensional character types described with an eye towards verisimilitude most often identified with the nineteenth-century realistic tradition. And the stories' plots are on the whole recognizable: impoverishment of the landed aristocracy, generational conflict of fathers and sons, love, and betrayal.

Yet the novel as a whole is radically 'unfamiliar'. Fashioned from what originally was a collection of individual short stories, most of them previously published, the text makes no ostensible attempt to connect them by means of any conventional narrative links. Characters disappear at the end of a chapter or a paragraph, never to appear again. Different characters share the same name, so that it is literally unclear who is speaking or being discussed (a confusion highlighted, rather than alleviated, by the sometimes-present narrator). In the book's final chapters, a series of what Pilniak calls 'triptychs' only serves to undermine the very principle of structural parallelism, since the 'triptychs' propose no coherent conceptual scheme for interpreting the events portrayed in the beginning of the novel.

While the book's title promises a clear temporal frame (a year), and the opening lines appear to announce a particular setting (Ordynin-gorod), both time and space are dramatically 'defamiliarized'. The Revolution rips the year 1919 out of the natural temporal sequence: it is perceived, by the novel's characters, as already belonging to an indeterminate historical past that is not connected to the present in any meaningful way, and yet no coherent notion of what the future holds can be divined from the year's events. In a striking move, this time segment – the 'naked' year – also becomes the novel's primary spatial setting; the 'leather jackets' and the Ordynin family are above all residents of that year rather than any specific Russian locality; in their chronotope, time has swallowed space. Events take place in the town square and on the outskirts, in the fields, and on the altar of a monastery; the weather changes, but the seasons are irrelevant.

The final chapter of the novel comprises three words, each set off on a separate line: 'Russia. Snowstorm. Revolution.' Yet the crucial final word is not a conceptual or aesthetic union/synthesis of the cultural (Russia) and natural (snowstorm) signifiers but, instead, a filter that blurs the distinctions between the first two parts of this mini-triptych: a camera out of focus that suspends the moment of recognition infinitely, with no promise of a clear picture.

Pilniak's radical defamiliarization of the novel is a transparent extension of the modernist experiment; but rather than showcasing for his contemporaries – Trotsky, Shklovsky, and Bely among them – the wealth of resources the modernist paradigm could offer for conceptualizing the revolutionary cataclysm, it alerted them to the need to develop an aesthetic mode more adept at restraining its own centrifugal impulses. The task Trotsky assigns to the writers of the future is precisely the responsibility Pilniak works to avoid by fragmenting the texture of his fictional world. The cataclysm he offers for his readers' contemplation can transfigure history by obliterating now-obsolete notions of causality, but this transfiguration cannot yield its meaning to a page.

The principal conceit of Babel's project mirrors Pilniak's. *The Naked Year* is a collection of stylistically and thematically heterogeneous fragments, some of them published earlier, which continues to question its own generic status and ultimately subverts the designation of the novel assigned to it by the author. *Red Cavalry* never lays claim to the status of a novel; it consists entirely of stories published previously, piecemeal, over the course of two years, in Moscow and Odessa, in mass-circulation daily newspapers and prestigious literary magazines; yet, put between the covers of a separate edition and presented as a cycle, these stories invite precisely the kinds of questions about the links and tensions among them that are typical of a larger-scale prose work.

Beyond insisting that the sequence he established be observed in all editions, Babel himself offered no authoritative statement on the principles governing the construction of the cycle. He did add one story at the very end of the cycle in 1931, five years after the first book edition appeared, and there are some indications that he planned to add another one; at the same time, a few stories linked to the *Red Cavalry* cycle by common themes and characters were never included in the cycle. The meaning of the cycle's structure is a topic of an ongoing scholarly conversation.[6] All attempts to make sense of the cycle as a whole, however, are compelled not merely to draw conclusions from the many points of contact among particular stories – chronology, setting, characters, themes – but to account for the peculiar way in which Babel violates his readers' expectations of narrative coherence by breaking up thematic and chronological sequences.

All stories – thirty-five including the 1931 addition, 'Argamak' – take place during the brief, bloody, and ultimately disastrous Polish campaign of 1920, in which Babel participated as a correspondent for an army newspaper. The campaign was portrayed by the Soviet side as an extension of the Civil War, and the Cossacks of the First Cavalry with whom Babel travels were accordingly meant to serve as agents of a world-historical force – the Revolution – whose mission was to liberate and enlighten the residents of the many small towns of the former Pale of Settlement the Red Army encounters en route to Warsaw. An important ideological problem with this meta-narrative comes into view when the Cavalry, retreating, re-visits the locations it had liberated a few months earlier to discover that the revelation it was supposed to have brought with it has not produced the requisite transformation. One of the effects of the cycle's structure is to obscure precisely that teleological failure: the stories do not follow a strict chronological order, with strategically placed references to the months in which certain events take place serving to emphasize that the action moves back and forth in time. In its early editions, the collection followed the larger outlines of the campaign: the first story, 'Crossing the [River] Zbrucz' ('Perekhod cherez Zbruch') described, with many factual imprecisions,[7] the advance of the Cavalry onto Polish territory; the final story, 'Rabbi's Son' ('Syn rabbi'), was narrated from a train that was headed back east, and the allegorical charge of the death that takes place in the story's final line was transparent. With the addition of 'Argamak', the only story in the cycle that unfolds over the course of the entire campaign, the finale offered a conciliatory coda – an uneasy peace is established once again between the narrator and the Cossacks whose respect he is trying to win over the course of the book – and the impact of anti-climactic 'real' chronology was further diluted.

Without an overarching meta-narrative, the reader is left with a series of recurring themes, devices, characters, and existential problems that render the happenings in and out of battle as essentially circular; the universe

Babel describes becomes even more self-contained, its existential boundaries defined more sharply with each new rape, each new death (human or equestrian). The recurrence of themes and devices can be (and has been) read as a marker of pervasive and inescapable circularity, or an elaborate, and equally hermetic, structure of thematic triads; in either case, each rotation of the circle and each new layer in the structure exhibits the same fault lines. A striking anti-sequence is formed when 'Gedali' and 'The Rabbi' – stories that take place on the same night and both describe the narrator's encounter with the world of Hasidic Jews – are split by the insertion of 'My First Goose' ('Moi pervyi gus´'), one of the handful of stories in which the narrator attempts to secure the approval of the Cossacks. The key device in this puzzling arrangement is inversion and fragmentation.

It is easiest to see the contrasts drawn by this sequence and others like it in binary terms: the Cossacks and the Jews, the Revolution and the tsarist past, the effete and the masculine, the poetic and the grotesque. The narrator's attraction to the glamourous figure of the Cossack is accompanied by his pity for and disgust with the world the Cossacks are destroying. His celebration of the power of the ideological word, as he reads one of Lenin's public speeches to the Cossacks in 'My First Goose' or rhapsodizes (with some degree of exaggeration) about the By-Laws of the Communist Party in 'Evening' ('Vecher') are counterbalanced by a mini-cycle of *skaz* stories – 'The Letter', 'Salt', 'Treason' ('Pis´mo', 'Sol´', 'Izmena'), 'Konkin', and others – in which the extreme ideologization of the speakers' language is portrayed as a symbolic equivalent of violence that neither sacralizes nor redeems.[8]

Yet throughout Babel's chief device is to speak 'of stars above and of gonorrhea' in *the same* tone of voice.[9] Scenes of violence in *Red Cavalry* are in a few cases graphic and their effects are occasionally refracted through the prism of the narrator's perspective – by turn mesmerized and repulsed – but the actual portrayal of violence as a whole is remarkably detached, with the requisite remove sometimes achieved with the help of *skaz*. In 'Salt', a soldier first protects a woman from rape by his fellow Cossacks because he thinks she is nursing a child; then, on discovering that the 'child' is a bag of smuggled salt, uses his 'loyal rifle' to 'wipe that blot off the face of the working land and the republic'.[10] The author's irony at the expense of virtually every character, above all the narrator and some of his reactions to violence, is palpable but diffused; his eroticization of the many perpetrators of violence and, by extension, of the acts in which they engage, shrewdly discomfiting: admirable masculinity is presented as exaggerated, with mythologized Cossacks invariably performing their displays of prowess for an eager audience.[11] Even as it builds up a series of mythical oppositions, the text works to undermine the very possibility of a genuinely binary opposition, and structural disruptions are key in achieving this effect.

Every story in the cycle is driven by a series of actions or events – except for one: the shortest story, 'The Cemetery at Kozin' ('Kladbishche v Kozine'). Positioned almost in the middle of the sequence, it substitutes quiet description for narration – a landscape, an elegy, a few declarative sentences with no direct causal linkages. Fragmentation itself is in this story enacted in the deliberately paced account of gravestones and sepulchres, rather than through explicit violence. The author's implicit challenge to the reader is not only to piece the sentences together but to account for this interruption in the sequence of what otherwise are well-emplotted stories. This suspension of hostilities raises the meta-literary stakes by offering itself to the readers as a key allegory of writing the Red Cavalry/Civil War/Revolutionary experience. A number of connections to major thematic concerns of the other stories can be drawn here: the collapse of the *shtetl* civilization; memory, death, and writing; liminal spaces and states. Yet the story's meaning does not ultimately reside in this accumulation of linkages; it comes from the process of accounting for a fragment in which nothing happens, and the conventional ideological oppositions are for a second suspended – not overcome, not reformulated: deferred, interrupted, fragmented.

In *Envy*, Yuri Olesha sublimates the Civil War, and with it war itself, by projecting ideological struggle not onto the battlefields of an empire's outskirts but onto the couches and soccer fields of a post-war, post-Revolutionary society firmly committed to seeing itself in terms of one enormous binary opposition: the new world and the old. The timing of the novella's publication – in 1927, amid preparations to celebrate the tenth anniversary of the Bolshevik rule – cast *Envy*, in the minds of many of its original readers, above all as an attempt to take stock of the Revolution's accomplishments and failures. Yet instead of trying to reflect the collision of two worldviews Olesha refracts it, and he does so by placing the process of refraction itself at the centre of the reader's experience of the text.

The critical response to *Envy* was remarkable not only for its intensity (Olesha was instantly propelled to literary-celebrity status) but for the interpretive awkwardness that accompanied it. Several prominent publications found themselves retracting their original reviews of the book. Olesha's literary pedigree – he was well known for feuilletons in verse published in the newspaper of the railway workers' union, *Gudok* (*The Whistle*), under the pen name Zubilo ('Chisel') – helped shape readerly expectations of ideological transparency and dependability. *Envy*, however, proved to require re-reading, and that process yielded decidedly contradictory results. The question, for reviewers who first embraced the book and then repudiated its vision, was that of perspective: from what viewpoint does the author's 'authentic' ideological and aesthetic stance become visible? To a greater degree than Pilniak, Babel, or Zoshchenko, all of whom provoked similar reactions, Olesha invited and even compelled these questions – first, by using the idiom of a recognizably novelistic (and ostensibly more traditional) narrative and, second, by figuring interpretation as viewership, and so emphasizing the centrality of the search for a stable point of view.

Using as its starting point the relationship between a well-educated but unemployed young man, Nikolai Kavalerov, and the stranger who offers him shelter, Soviet food-industry functionary Andrei Babichev, *Envy* inquires into the workings of the world that surrounds the two characters. The novel identifies Andrei Babichev, his niece Valia, and his adopted son Volodia Makarov as models of 'new Soviet people', and proceeds to examine their physiological and ideological makeup from distinctly different, often contradictory, perspectives. Frequent references to lamps, mirrors, binoculars, glasses, reflections, shadows, and squinting posit the importance of vision in understanding the 'new people' and their world. Kavalerov's authority as a viewer, narrator, and interpreter is undercut from the very beginning of the novel because his perspective is so patently skewed: he observes his benefactor and those who visit him by looking up from the couch on which he has been allowed to sleep – a vantage point that is, furthermore, available to him only because the person who usually occupies the couch, the 'new man' Volodia Makarov himself, is away, helping build the new world. How well can such a character see; how much can he understand; could he ever amount to more than a shadow of 'the new man'? And yet Kavalerov's mode of seeing the world – the vividness and inventiveness of his perception, his insistence on treating virtually every object as a source of a metaphor – is a marker of a different kind of authenticity. He does not create the same things, or in the same way, as Andrei Babichev and Volodya – but Kavalerov is still a genuine creator; how could the Revolution, with its grand programme for transforming all aspects of human existence, not leave room for him in the world of the future? Vision, in *Envy*, becomes the principal criterion of intellectual and artistic viability; and the privileged mode of vision is, in another reverberation of the Formalist doctrine of art as estrangement, 'through the wrong end of the binoculars': the novella's first part culminates in Kavalerov's long-awaited meeting with an eccentric, quasi-messianic inventor and artist, Andrei Babichev's brother Ivan, who appears to Kavalerov first as a distorted reflection in a convex street mirror.

The main terms of the ideological oppositions drawn in the novel – the contrast between the new and the old, progress and decadence, robust and impotent physicality – are first translated into vivid visual emblems, and then rendered problematic by means of those very images. The famous description of Andrei's body from Kavalerov's perspective waxes lyrical about Babichev's vigorous masculinity even as it points to his surprising, uncomfortable femininity (echoed in the 'effeminate' root of his last name, *baba*). The ideological impact of a scar on Babichev's chest – a visceral reminder of his status as a genuine Civil War hero who has paid his ideological dues with his sacrifice – is attenuated not only by an 'aristocratic' birthmark on his back but, above all, by his large 'breasts'. The epic war for the future he wages in the novel is, likewise, undermined – rendered alarmingly commonplace – with the help of a single powerful image. Babichev and his associates view his grand project, the construction of an enormous experimental dining hall for the workers, as a battle in a new war, the 'war on kitchens': a struggle to liberate humanity from the prison of everyday household chores. Their entire effort, however, is emblematized by a prototype of the delicious and inexpensive foodstuff the new kitchen-factory is meant to produce: a new kind of veal bologna sausage. The violence that helps give birth to the new world, and is marked visibly on Babichev's body by a scar, is expended on justifying the Revolution's preoccupation with something as mundane as a piece of sausage.[12] Revolting in its utter banality, the bologna is also revolutionary in serving as a perverse mark of Andrei's potency. For all the gleeful carnivalization – ironizing about grown men slicing wieners, or comparisons between stuffing a casing and the mechanically rationalistic nature of the future as Babichev imagines it – and for all of Andrei's lack of education, the sausage and his task are presented as powerful tools in a war that Kavalerov is losing.

Kavalerov, too, is waging a war with the everyday, but his fight (and Ivan Babichev's) can be best understood in terms of another key implication of the Formalists' theoretical vocabulary: resistance to the routine. Olesha's readers remark that his prose aims not at mimetic verisimilitude, not at emulation of the idiosyncratic rhythms of street speech, but at revealing a surprising implication of an image.[13] Obsessed with the everyday, *Envy* seeks to capture the effects of the everyday by avoiding the very semblance of the mundane. The trick here is to represent the object of excoriation – the degradation of the imaginary and the encroachment of the material – by both showing the alternative and, simultaneously, by *talking about* showing the alternative. From the very beginning, Olesha builds a meta-level into the discussion by having the narrator (Kavalerov) use vivid metaphors of vision in this commentary on the outside world's perception of his existence. Olesha's reworking of a Dostoevskian 'notes-from-underground' narrative thematizes Kavalerov's everyday struggle to establish himself in the world against the resistance of objects (animated by his imagination) and people (whose benevolence is portrayed, by turn, with near-hysterical self-flagellation).

This presence of a meta-commentary may anticipate but cannot fully prepare the reader for the chasm that separates Part One and Two of the novella. The stance assigned to Kavalerov is ideologically controversial but coherent, and the perspective on the world articulated in the novel is consistent – until the final scene of Part One, in which Kavalerov meets Ivan. In the novella's Part Two, the narrative voice switches suddenly to a third-person omniscient narrator. This narrator has access to knowledge about Ivan's past that makes many sections of Part Two seem as if they reflect Ivan's perspective, but no direct equivalence is established. More than that: as the narrative develops, sequences that bridge the characters' dreams and their experiences while awake proliferate. Locales and images grow more vivid, but their relationship to the characters becomes more and more tenuous. The narrative of Part One is also episodic, and is certainly not chronologically linear, but all events and impressions described there issue from the same fictional consciousness. In Part Two the connection between time and space is disrupted over and over. The structure of the fragments changes as well: the third-person narrator uses fewer of the kinds of metaphors (especially tropes of vision) that were so characteristic of the Kavalerov narration in Part One. The relationship between each chapter and the novel as a whole becomes more and more difficult to establish clearly, and the narrative is ultimately broken up into progressively smaller units of meaning. This ostensible distancing of the narrative from the figure of Kavalerov allowed those who saw Kavalerov as an unambiguously negative character to suggest that Olesha, too, offers a critical portrait of a dying world. Structurally, this fragmentation translates a particular ideological and rhetorical problem into a meta-literary predilection.

And it is here, in the novella's Part Two, as the narrative becomes more fragmented and a coherent story gives way to a series of daydreams (or nightmares), that the implications of the war(s) described in the book's first part are fleshed out. Immediately after he describes the scar on Andrei's chest in Part One, Kavalerov changes the topic suddenly and reports that Andrei once asked him, 'Who is Jocasta?' Kavalerov's narrative notes Babichev's general ignorance with glee but does not report the outcome of the conversation. Olesha's text teems with allusions, but the meaning of this one is suspended until, at the end of Part Two, as the narrative is disintegrating, Ivan Babichev throws his arms around his daughter's legs in despair and says: 'Valia, put out my eyes. I want to be blind.' The central role assigned in the text to the rhetoric of vision brings the mythical implications of this gesture to the fore and illuminates the significance of the Jocasta reference:

when, as Sophocles tells us, King Oedipus discovered that his wife Jocasta was actually his birth mother, he blinded himself in quest of ultimate self-knowledge. Violence and sexuality are intermixed and sublimated elsewhere in the novella. But here the claim is that the generational divide is re-enacting and re-enabling a tragedy of classical proportions; that the only relationship between the two worlds that is ultimately possible is a relationship that both violates and eroticizes links of family; that the foundational moment of the new world lies not only in the abolition of 'feelings' or familial links (as both Kavalerov and Ivan claim on a number of occasions) but in the conceptualization of war as a family relationship, and *that* principle can only be rendered via splitting (radically, if need be) the narrative voice. The war bred of the Revolution – the war of the worlds – is in the end not the war of the past and the future, of the mundane and the artistic, but a kind of eternal linkage of the forbidden and the desired; it is necessarily unending and unresolved because it is unavoidable and irresolvable. The meaning of this war, Olesha suggests, can only be captured by a narrative structure that both masks and flaunts its fragmentariness; a fictional world that demarcates the everyday through – and *as* – violence; and a story that posits a conventionally recognizable fictional consciousness as the source of narrative authority only to undermine the very possibility of such a coherent fictional subject.

Language, persona, author

That Olesha's sleight of hand in *Envy* – a peremptory change of narrative voice that fragments the text without breaking the illusion of recognizably novelistic form – was so disorienting to the book's earliest readers is an index not only of the novella's success in complicating the very ideological oppositions it ostensibly asserted, but of the intimate, uneasy relationship between the fellow-travellers' experiments in fragmentation and the problem of post-Revolutionary authorship. By asking, indirectly but forcefully, *who* is speaking in *Envy*, to *whom*, and what conventions govern that conversation, Olesha pointed to a key implication of the 'ongoing revelation' that Soviet writers of the 1920s were being urged to bring about through their work. Above all, works that used fracturing as a key device had to produce meaning by conjuring a compelling authorial persona for whom these 'episodes' of the post-Revolutionary experience, saturated as it was with violence and obsessed with the transformation of the everyday, could be integrated in a cohesive worldview. To solve the problem of literature's relationship to the Revolution in their fiction, they had to devise a new mode of seeing the world, and so create themselves as Soviet authors. In the late 1920s and early 1930s Olesha attempted to find such a solution in an intensely personal, experimental, fragmentary diary, but found himself at an ideological and narrative dead end. By contrast, the model of authorial self-presentation (or self-concealment) contained in the narrative structure of *Envy* proved resonant with Olesha's peers and critics because it was of a piece with a broader fellow-traveller project underway at the time: a series of attempts to shape coherent but supple writerly identities through strategic fragmentation.

One of the earliest and most prominent such attempts was Mikhail Zoshchenko's. A year after the publication of *Envy* the prestigious publishing house Academia launched a new series of critical studies entitled 'Masters of Contemporary Prose'. The series' inaugural issue focused on Zoshchenko – an important validation of his status as a writer whose artistic undertaking had succeeded in the new Soviet world. This canonization took place just seven years after Zoshchenko published his first collection of stories, which included 'The Tales of Nazar Ilich Mister *Sinebriukhov*'. Unlike his exact contemporaries Babel and Pilniak (all three were born in 1894), Zoshchenko had published nothing at all before the 1920s, and even though he belonged to the 'Serapion Brothers' – an influential, well-connected group of self-consciously experimental fellow-travellers – he quickly established a reputation of a distinctive and mature figure, an exotic literary 'find' from the provinces the likes of which had not been seen since Gogol. While it soon became commonplace for Zoshchenko's readers to question whether the plots and themes of his stories – vicious fights among tenants of communal apartments, petty theft of clothing and jewellery items, embarrassing mishaps at bathhouses and theatres, humiliating misunderstandings resulting from insufficient knowledge of social etiquette – were sufficiently 'serious' to qualify as high literature, many critics agreed that the exploits of his characters mattered primarily because of the way they spoke. The 'raw material' for Zoshchenko's stories was fundamentally similar to that used by Olesha for his feuilletons at *Gudok* – accounts of daily life under the new order; what propelled Zoshchenko to the rank of master in many critics' view was his confident and sophisticated use of *skaz* in using that material.

The critical consensus regarding Zoshchenko's status as a major post-Revolutionary writer is remarkable especially because in Zoshchenko's early stories (unlike the work of Pilniak, Babel, or Olesha) direct conversations *about* the Revolution are almost entirely absent. Life after 1917 is presented as a recently created but utterly permanent arrangement in which people *always* behave the same way, make the same mistakes, complain about the same issues. When an explicit historical perspective is offered, as in the Sinebriukhov cycle, which begins during the First World War, more attention is devoted to the February Revolution than to the arrival of the Bolsheviks. And when a story directly invokes the events of the October Revolution, as in 1923's 'Victim of the Revolution' ('Zhertva revoliutsii'), the event itself passes unnoticed by the protagonist: having polished the floors for a local nobleman on a Monday, and having been accused, on that Tuesday, of stealing a wristwatch from his employer's wife, he remembers, on the following Sunday, what he had done with the watch; but when he rushes back to share the news, he discovers the nobleman's family being taken away as a result of the revolution that had happened the day before, on Saturday, and which he missed entirely. Key historical events – the Revolution, the Civil War – may not be that significant in themselves, but their consequences are here to stay, and they do matter: the truck that drives away with the nobleman's family injures the protagonist's foot – the injury that allows him to claim the status of the Revolution's victim. A sly travesty of the famous metaphor of Juggernaut's chariot as the inexorable force of world-historical progress, the image of the Revolution as a truck that runs over a hapless floor-shiner shifts the rhetorical and ideological emphasis from the overtly historical, political, 'Great' time of the national narrative onto the minute experiences of the stories' protagonists.

The meaning of the Revolutionary experiment is linked intimately to the accounts of these shards left in the wake of revolutionary implosion of time and space. The minuteness of these experiences is emphasized repeatedly: incidents described in the stories, no matter how grotesque, are framed as emblems of particular problematic social phenomena rather than as individual extraordinary occurrences. Likewise, the narrators of these (funny) stories about an all-too-imperfect way of life, for all their colourful language, are framed in a way that lays claim to social and psychological authenticity by virtue of being un-remarkable.[14] Zoshchenko's entire fictional world is premised on convincing readers that its inhabitants, as well as the social structures they create and sustain, are not extraordinary, and are not, at their core, ideologically charged. To achieve this effect, however, Zoshchenko manipulates conventions of the literary language in strategically destabilizing ways. The precise modality of *skaz* he uses varies, but Zoshchenko's principal achievement – the foregrounding of verbal performance – is arrived at, over and over, by breaking with the conventions of syntax and layout. Exclamations and tautological 'parasite words' begin Zoshchenko's sentences. New lines and new paragraphs begin with afterthoughts and conjunctions. A single incongruous word or action is placed at the grammatical and semantic centre of the sentence. The narrative often explicitly subjugates the workings of the plot to the whims of the characters' gab: at one point Sinebriukhov informs his readers that the character he had mentioned earlier was actually not around for those events, and belongs in a different story.[15] In addition to stand-alone short stories, Zoshchenko published novellas and story cycles, but what he fragmented above all – and then reassembled in such a way that a memorable and ostensibly authentic illusion of an autonomous consciousness comes into view – were conventions of syntax, usage, and layout. Each subtle fracture – mangled phrases, mispronunciations, and misused clichés, among others – propels the text forward precisely by registering as a destabilizing disturbance that manages to alter the rules of the game, but does not seek to suspend them altogether.

However fine, the cracks are palpable: the meanings generated by Zoshchenko's 'distrustful narratives about a fickle universe'[16] begin to unravel almost as soon as they start to come into focus. What holds the stories together? The texts' unreliable narrators do play a role in creating and slackening dramatic tension but, no matter how ostensibly insignificant the events being described, no matter how unsophisticated the thinking processes of the characters taking part in them (including the narrators), virtually every action points to, and is generated by, a potent undercurrent of violence, physical and symbolic. Violence, in these early stories, is showcased as a routine attribute of everyday life that simultaneously serves as an engine of especially eccentric plot developments. The *Sinebriukhov* stories move from one instance of misery and pain to another. Nazar Ilich is repeatedly beaten up, is arrested and mistreated in jail; he rips his hands into shreds while crawling through barbed wire and constantly witnesses violence being done upon those around him. Most of these violent acts are presented as utterly arbitrary – this is a key premise of Zoshchenko's numerous subsequent stories about domestic quarrels, humiliating public exposures of character flaws, and sub-standard manners. No matter how unjustified, or unjustifiable, the aggression, Zoshchenko's narrators domesticate and, in many cases, belittle the violent gestures on which they report. The most outrageous conflicts and heated emotional exchanges are rendered with a detachment that reads as ironic but is figured as narratorial naiveté. Several generations of critics of various ideological persuasions agreed that Zoshchenko's narrators are, as a rule, 'uncultured'. What earns them this distinction, however, is not merely their ignorance of the social graces, but their lack of agency, their complete dependence on misshapen linguistic structures. Produced and circumscribed by the fractured cadences of Zoshchenko's *skaz*, these characters defamiliarize the banal predicaments from which they are unable to extricate themselves precisely by succumbing to the violence that makes their deformed language so powerful.

The authorial position that emerges from these careful fragmentations of grammatical conventions is likewise bound above all to the power of linguistic experimentation. Zoshchenko creates a vivid authorial persona even, or especially, in those stories in which he does not rely on a meta-literary figure of the commenting and deliberating author (a device central to some of his works in the later 1920s and early 1930s, such as *The Sky-Blue Book*). Yet it remains fundamentally unclear what defines this author's relationship to any historical reality, from the facts of his own biography to the ideological anxieties of the NEP era: his readers know how he speaks but cannot agree about the meaning of what they hear. Just as Zoshchenko's jokes are born of acts of violence, his status as a master of Soviet prose is predicated on the savvy ruthlessness with which he fragments and re-shapes literary language. By re-arranging words he attempts to write himself into the post-Revolutionary literary reality yet suspend the very question of authorial stance – and, for a brief but crucial period in the 1920s, seems to succeed.

The ideological stakes of this suspension come further into view when we consider another critically successful model for fragmenting language itself – Babel's masterful use of *skaz* in *Red Cavalry*. (Volume Two of the Academia 'Masters' series, published a few months after the Zoshchenko collection, was devoted to Babel.) With the exception of 'The Cemetery at Kozin' (a special case, as we saw earlier), the stories of the cycle are narrated either by a fictional correspondent of an army newspaper, Kirill Liutov, or by the perpetrators/victims of the war on which Liutov is supposed to report. The latter set of voices is usually mediated by the generic conventions of a letter – written by Liutov on behalf of a soldier ('The Letter') or by a soldier directly to a newspaper editor ('Salt'). Babel's use of *skaz* is more controlled, more clearly framed (readers of *Red Cavalry* distinguished Liutov's voice from that of the *skaz* narrators); but his technique focuses on a similarly painstak-ing, non-spectacular but (verbal-) performance-oriented restructuring/ fragmenting and merging of incongruous or outlandish lexical and syntactic units into structures that, paradoxically, lay claim to verisimilitude and triv-iality. Crucially, Babel's narratives, unlike Zoshchenko's, do not shirk from incorporating elements of explicitly ideological speech. Babel's narrators, including Liutov, do talk directly about the Revolution and its meaning; they talk about it obsessively and sometimes to one another. Because in this process they operate with a shared vocabulary of ideas and names (Trotsky's included), the contrast between Liutov's anguished relationship to the Soviet cause and the Cossacks' attitude seems especially stark. For him, a mixture of horror and pity can give way to moments of cynical detachment but manages to co-exist with a vigorous will-to-believe. For them – 'soldiers of the Revo-lution' – writing letters and waging war are both matters of prosaic justice: putting their experiences into words is another way of building a new order, no matter how bloody these experiences or jarring their rhetoric. Like other contrasts drawn in *Red Cavalry*, this one does not translate into a direct and reductive opposition. Liutov's eagerness to see himself as both a Cossack and a Jew, his repeated attempts to testify with a compassion untainted by weakness – all are embodied in striking metaphors that burst open the earlier literary conventions. Babel's cycle, however, establishes a series of unnerving parallels between a creative, deliberate, and measured manipulation of imaginative language in Liutov's narrative and the brutal, ostensibly unselfconscious mangling of lives and idioms in the *skaz* stories. By having a Jewish fellow-traveller masking himself as a Russian Bolshevik record, cite, or archive the Cossacks' letters, Babel re-imagines and re-enacts not only his own experience in the First Cavalry but the experience of a generation of writers that came to define the prose of the Revolution. Whether or not they deliberately cultivate ambiguity as a literary and ideological value, the literary fellow-travellers of the 1920s dissect the post-Revolutionary experience by injecting different modes of fragmentation into their testaments to the era's experiments. As they reflect upon the metaphoric and mundane implications of literary violence, they search for the meaning that emerges from the fragments they so carefully crafted – but in the end, in a utopian move worthy of Trotsky's vision, strive to be revealed in the text together with the Revolution, not to be liberated by it.

NOTES

1 Trotsky, Leon, *Literature and Revolution*, ed. William Keach, trans. Rose Strunsky (Chicago, IL: Haymarket Books, 2005), pp. 76–77, with emendations; subsequent citations parenthetically.
2 Chudakova, Marietta, 'Sud′ba "samootcheta-ispovedi" v literature sovetskogo vremeni (1920-e–konets 1930-kh)' in *Literatura sovetskogo proshlogo* (Moscow: Iazyki russkoi kul′tury, 2001), pp. 393–420, p. 394.
3 Jensen, Peter Alberg, *Nature as Code: The Achievement of Boris Pilnjak, 1915–1924* (Copenhagen: Rosenkilde & Bagger, 1979), pp. 175–180.
4 Rougle, Charles, 'Isaac Babel and His Odyssey of War and Revolution', in *Red Cavalry: A Critical Companion* (Evanston, IL: Northwestern University Press, 1996), pp. 1–65, p. 28.
5 Shklovskii, Viktor, 'O Pil′niake', *LEF*, no. 3 (1925), p. 128.
6 Dobrenko, Evgeny, 'Logika tsikla' in *'Konarmiia' Isaaka Babelia*, ed. Galina Belaia, Evgeny Dobrenko, and Ivan Esaulov (Moscow: Rossiiskii gosudarstvennyi gumanitarnyi universitet, 1993), pp. 33–101; Rougle, 'Odyssey of War'; Bojanowska, Edyta M., 'E Pluribus Unum: Isaac Babel's *Red Cavalry* as a Story Cycle', *Russian Review* 59, no. 3 (2000).
7 Rougle, 'Odyssey of War', pp. 18–19.
8 Carden, Patricia, *The Art of Isaac Babel* (Ithaca, NY: Cornell University Press, 1972); Falen, James E., *Isaac Babel, Russian Master of the Short Story* (Knoxville,

TN: University of Tennessee Press, 1974); Sicher, Efraim, *Style and Structure in the Prose of Isaak Babel'* (Columbus, OH: Slavica Publishers, 1986).

9 Shklovskii, Viktor, 'I. Babel'. Kriticheskii romans', *LEF*, no. 2 (6) (1924), p. 153.
10 As rendered by Peter Constantine in the Norton *Complete Works of Isaac Babel* (New York: W.W. Norton, 2001), p. 276.
11 Borenstein, Eliot, *Men without Women: Masculinity and Revolution in Russian Fiction, 1917–1929* (Durham, NC: Duke University Press, 2000), pp. 73–124.
12 LeBlanc, Ronald D., 'Gluttony and Power in Iurii Olesha's *Envy*', *The Russian Review*, 60, no. 2 (2001), pp. 220–237.
13 Chudakova, Marietta, 'Masterstvo Iuriia Oleshi,' in *Literatura sovetskogo proshlogo* (Moscow: Iazyki russkoi kul'tury, 2001), pp. 13–72, p. 26.
14 Popkin, Cathy, *The Pragmatics of Insignificance: Chekhov, Zoshchenko, Gogol* (Stanford, CA: Stanford University Press, 1993), pp. 53–124.
15 Chudakova, Marietta, 'Poetika Mikhaila Zoshchenko' in *Literatura sovetskogo proshlogo* (Moscow: Iazyki russkoi kul'tury, 2001), pp. 79–204, pp. 99–117.
16 Zholkovskii, Alexander, *Mikhail Zoshchenko: poetika nedoveriia* (Moscow: Iazyki russkoi kul'tury, 1999).

FURTHER READING

Borenstein, Eliot, *Men without Women: Masculinity and Revolution in Russian Fiction, 1917–1929* (Durham, NC: Duke University Press, 2000).
Carleton, Gregory, *The Politics of Reception: Critical Constructions of Mikhail Zoshchenko* (Evanston, IL: Northwestern University Press, 1998).
Freidin, Gregory, 'Revolution as an Esthetic Phenomenon: Nietzschean Motifs in the Reception of Isaac Babel' in *Nietzsche and Soviet Culture: Ally and Adversary*, ed. Bernice Glazer Rosenthal (Cambridge: Cambridge University Press, 1994), 149–173.
Maguire, Robert A., *Red Virgin Soil: Soviet Literature in the* 1920s, rev. edn. (Evanston, IL: Northwestern University Press, 2000).
Naiman, Eric, *Sex in Public: The Incarnation of Early Soviet Ideology* (Princeton, NJ: Princeton University Press, 1997).
Rougle, Charles, ed., *Red Cavalry: A Critical Companion* (Evanston, IL: Northwestern University Press, 1996).
Salys, Rimgaila, ed., *Olesha's Envy: A Critical Companion* (Evanston, IL: Northwestern University Press, 1999).

5

PHILIP ROSS BULLOCK

Utopia and the Novel after the Revolution

In the penultimate paragraph of *The Rout* (*Razgrom*, 1927), Alexander Fadeev abandons the action that has constituted the narrative thus far, turning instead to an unexpectedly lyrical evocation of the pastoral life that awaits the heroes upon their return from the Civil War in the Far East:

> The trees came to an end quite unexpectedly, and they saw before them a vast expanse of light blue sky and red-brown, harvested fields that were flooded with sunlight and stretched away as far as the eye could see. Near a clump of willows by the deep, blue water of a small river lay a wide threshing-ground, resplendent with its peaked haystacks and golden sheaves of corn. Here a completely different life was in progress, a life that was sonorous, busy, and gay. The threshing-machine whirred with a dry, clear sound, sheaves of wheat flew through the air, and excited voices and bursts of girlish laughter could be heard amid the swirling clouds of chaff glittering in the light. Beyond the river, their lower slopes standing deep in curly-yellow woodland, dark blue mountains towered into the sky, and over their jagged peaks translucent, pinkish-white clouds, risen like foam from the salt sea far beyond, came pouring down into the valley, bubbling and frothing like milk fresh from the cow.[1]

This transformation of both tone and content might be seen as a premonition of the aesthetics of Socialist Realism, of Fadeev's commitment to ideology rather than art. After the Civil War, Soviet fiction would move away from the elemental chaos and élan of warfare and revolution as depicted in Isaac Babel's *Red Cavalry* (*Konarmiia*, 1926) or Boris Pilniak's *The Naked Year* (*Golyi god*, 1921). Writers turned instead to the search for new ways of constructing society and human relations; works such as Fedor Gladkov's *Cement* (*Tsement*, 1925) and Iurii Olesha's *Envy* (*Zavist'*, 1927) treated the passing of the old order and the establishment of the new, however different their authors' attitudes to this process.

At the same time, the conclusion to *The Rout* suggests another direction available to writers. As the partisans leave the forest, they see a vision of a promised land, at once an echo of a lost past and an anticipation of a radiant future – a vision of utopia. In keeping with the word's etymology, this is both a 'good place' (εὐ-τόπος) and 'no-place' (οὐ-τόπος): it is a good place because it is vital, productive, and bountiful; yet it is also 'no-place' because Fadeev's description deliberately eschews verisimilitude in favour of myth and archetype. The utopian instinct was particularly strong in the first two decades of Soviet rule, whether in the immediate aftermath of revolution, as a counterpoint to the perceived compromise with bourgeois capitalism during the years of the New Economic Policy (1921–1928), or as a result of Stalin's subsequent transformation of industry, agriculture, and society itself. And this instinct was variously embodied, reflected, and parodied in a number of the novels written at the time. In Evgenii Zamiatin's *We* (*My*, 1920–1921), utopia is located in the distant future. The novel's setting – One State – is a technologically advanced and rationally ordered society, isolated from the surrounding world by defensive walls. The narrator of *We* is D-503, an engineer and seemingly loyal subject, who has designed a spacecraft intended to spread the ideology of One State to other worlds. However, he falls in love with the sexually alluring and ideologically rebellious I-330, who uses him to gain access to the spacecraft on behalf of a group of revolutionaries intent on destroying One State and all that it represents. Although by the end of the novel I-330 has been captured and executed, the outcome of the rebellion remains unclear; D-503, however, has consented to a state-sponsored operation in which his imagination is excised.

We is the most famous treatment of the utopian theme in Soviet literature and, in its indebtedness to tropes borrowed from science fiction, is the most classical in its evocation of a society on its way to perfection. Andrei Platonov, by contrast, concentrated on the realities of contemporary society. His novel *Chevengur* (*Chevengur*, 1926–1929) is a long and amorphous work that falls into two halves. The first can be seen as a *Bildungsroman* (novel of education) depicting the growth of the hero, Alexander Dvanov, as both a human being and a revolutionary, from the rural poverty of the late Imperial era, through the violence and excitement of the Revolution and Civil War, to the establishment of Soviet power. The second half of the novel portrays the attempts of a group of eccentric revolutionaries to establish something called communism in the town that gives the novel its name; their experiment ends in failure when it is destroyed by a cavalry detachment. *The Foundation Pit* (*Kotlovan*, 1929–1931) also falls into two halves; the first portrays the attempts of a group of labourers to dig the foundations of a vast dwelling to house the proletariat; the second depicts the expulsion of kulaks (rich peasants) from the local collective farm. The unfinished *Happy Moscow* (*Schastlivaia Moskva*, 1932–1936) abandons the provincial settings of Platonov's first two novels in favour of the Soviet capital in the mid-1930s, when a new technical, artistic, and intellectual elite was enjoying the transformation of the city into a modern – even utopian – metropolis.

If Zamiatin and Platonov are obvious figures in any consideration of Soviet utopianism, then Bulgakov is an altogether more unexpected candidate for inclusion. Yet for all his ironic attitude both to Soviet reality in particular and to utopian idealism in general, his works evince considerable structural and thematic similarities to more obviously utopian works already mentioned. In *White Guard* (*Belaia gvardiia*, 1922–1928), Bulgakov depicts the battle for an unnamed city (in fact, Kiev) during the winter of 1918–1919, and with it the transition from the bourgeois, European culture of its Imperial past, initially to the brief rule of Ukrainian nationalists, but ultimately to the advent of the Bolsheviks. Yet rather than illustrate the triumph of the victors, Bulgakov concentrates on the personal lives of the Turbin family and their sympathy with the White cause. Whereas in *White Guard* Bulgakov merely adumbrates Soviet rule, it becomes the explicit target of his satire in *The Master and Margarita* (*Master i Margarita*, 1928–1940). Here, the weaknesses of *homo sovieticus* are exposed by the arrival of the Devil in modern-day Moscow. The utopian aspirations of Soviet society are certainly debunked with the author's usual withering irony, but Bulgakov also erects his own literary utopia. This takes the form of an idealistic counterplot; the story of the novel's eponymous hero and heroine. The resurrection of the Master's missing novel constitutes Bulgakov's own attempt to conceptualize the ultimate victory of his own literary posterity.

Because of the heretical philosophical content and unorthodox literary form of these works, most of them went unpublished at the time (at least in the Soviet Union). Only Bulgakov's *White Guard* was at all known to contemporary readers (its first thirteen chapters appeared in the journal *Rossiia* in 1925; the novel was published in its entirety in France in 1927–1929, and in the Soviet Union only in 1966). *The Master and Margarita* was published in 1966–1967 in a somewhat censored version (a complete text appeared in Germany in 1969 and in the Soviet Union in 1973). Although Zamiatin's *We* was known by reputation to writers and critics in the 1920s, it was not published in the Soviet Union until 1988, long after its first appearance in the West (in English translation in 1924 and in Russian in 1927). Similarly, Platonov's three long prose works were unknown anywhere until the late 1960s, despite Platonov's attempts to have them published during his lifetime. *The Foundation Pit* was eventually published in London in 1969, followed by *Chevengur* in Paris in 1972; only with the advent of *glasnost'* could they be published in Russia itself (in 1987 and 1988, respectively). *Happy Moscow* was rediscovered as late as 1991, at the very time the Soviet Union was coming to the end of its existence.

The non-publication of the majority of these works at the time of their composition means that they were unable to participate in an ongoing intertextual dialogue with each other. Nevertheless, they evince considerable similarities. Partly, this is because they are shaped by and respond to similar contemporary literary and ideological developments. They all look back on an existing canon of works dealing with utopian questions (particularly important here is the legacy of Dostoevsky), although certain typological similarities may also be the result of generic traits common to all texts of this nature (whether utopias, dystopias, anti-utopias, or meta-utopias). A final similarity between these three figures is that each was engaged in another unrelated field before turning to literature professionally: Zamiatin worked as a naval engineer, Bulgakov as a doctor, and Platonov as a land reclamation specialist. The comparison is a significant one, with each writer responding to the balance (and, indeed, tension) between scientific observation and artistic imagination in different ways.

For all their similarities, however, there are important differences between the three novelists and their attitude to questions of utopianism. Zamiatin's *We*, for instance, is a first-person narrative, in which the hero records in the form of a diary the events of his life as they actually happen. Bulgakov favours a more traditional form of omniscience, in which a narrator reports, and occasionally comments on, the thoughts and actions of the protagonists. Platonov, by contrast, eschews narration by either specific characters or a tangible narrator. Instead, he pursues a fluid and shifting form of consciousness, in which 'there is hardly a statement, idea or emotion that can confidently be attributed to a single narrative authority'.[2] These varying forms of narration delineate the three authors' contrasting responses to Soviet utopianism, while shaping how the reader might interpret such responses. Zamiatin's use of the first-person diary allows him to present the justification for utopia in its own terms, while simultaneously implying the very opposite and encouraging the reader to distinguish between the two. Bulgakov, by contrast, repudiates the rationalism and materialism of Soviet utopianism as something beneath his contempt, in the expectation that his reader will share and revel in this iconoclastic attitude. It is Platonov, however, who takes us most fully into the heart of utopian thinking, exploring both its allure and its absurdities, and carrying out a thought experiment so uncompromising that it morally implicates the reader in the values of the fictional world itself.

Topology and geography

Because the utopian genre harks back to religious traditions of apocalypse and eschatology, it frequently conceives of itself in spatial terms. Much of its imagery derives from descriptions of the Heavenly City in Revelation, the final book of the Christian New Testament:

> And there came unto me one of the seven angels . . . and shewed me that great city, the holy Jerusalem, descending out of heaven from God, having the glory of God: and her light was like unto a stone most precious, even like a jasper stone, clear as crystal; And had a wall great and high, and had twelve gates, and at the gates twelve angels, and names written thereon, which are the names of the twelve tribes of the children of Israel: On the east three gates; on the north three gates; on the south three gates; and on the west three gates . . . And the twelve gates were twelve pearls: every several gate was of one pearl: and the street of the city was pure gold, as it were transparent glass.
>
> (Revelation, 21: 9–21)

This vision of the New Jerusalem is most thoroughly reproduced in Zamiatin's *We*. Here, the emphasis on the numerical perfection and material luminosity of the New Jerusalem translates into the importance of mathematics in One State, as well as the recurrent use of glass in its construction. Moreover, by means of a series of descriptive entries in his diary, D-503 guides us through the institutions and customs of One State like the angel in Revelation. However, the impact of Zamiatin's representation of the utopian city rests equally on its place within the Russian literary tradition; One State can be seen as an evocation of St Petersburg, a city described by Dostoevsky in *Notes from Underground* (*Zapiski iz podpol'ia*, 1864) as 'the most abstract, most premeditated city in the whole wide world'. Platonov's responses to the model of the New Jerusalem similarly fuse references to his native culture with the inherited biblical archetype. In *Chevengur*, he relocates the utopian community to the isolated depths of the steppe, deftly suggesting the process whereby Marx's vision of proletarian revolution in urban, capitalist Europe was ultimately realized in the vast agrarian spaces of Russia (and subsequently, the Soviet Union). Similarly, the construction of the vast 'all-proletarian home' in *The Foundation Pit* is a dystopian vision of the city as a single communal dwelling. The frequent instances of violence in the novel only serve to reinforce the apocalyptic subtext, with the implementation of class warfare (specifically in the liquidation of the kulaks) matching the judgement of the justified and the damned in Revelation.

Platonov's interest in provincial and rural Russia is juxtaposed with his unsympathetic attitude towards Moscow, which he portrays as a kind of

Babylon, the biblical antipode to the New Jerusalem. Towards the end of
Chevengur, for instance, the narrative shifts from the communist experiment
in the steppe to the Soviet capital in the years of the NEP. It is a centre of
bureaucratic interference that will eventually destroy the spontaneous idealism of the town of Chevengur; it is also a city of degeneracy and fornication
(in one of the novel's most astonishing scenes, a character has sex with a
woman on his mother's grave). The muscovite digression in *Chevengur* was
to serve as a kernel for the whole of Platonov's later novel, *Happy Moscow*,
in which the lives of the Stalinist technical and cultural elite of the 1930s
are depicted in unremittingly sardonic detail. The notion of Moscow as a
modern-day Babylon is also taken up in Bulgakov's *The Master and Margarita*; the arrival of the Devil in Moscow reveals that, despite their claims to
a superior rationalism, its citizens are as credulous, sinful, and deserving of
punishment as their Babylonian counterparts. Moreover, Bulgakov's representation of Moscow translates many of those demonic elements previously
associated in Russian literature with St Petersburg to the new Soviet capital,
and simultaneously parodies a traditional nationalist view of Moscow as the
'Third Rome' (namely, the idea advanced by the monk Filofei of Pskov in
1510 of Moscow as a safeguard of Christian orthodoxy and imperial destiny
after the fall of Rome and Constantinople).

If Zamiatin's *We* is indebted to the myth of St Petersburg in Russian
literature, and both Platonov and Bulgakov turn their gaze on Moscow,
then Bulgakov also incorporates Kiev into this genealogy. In fact, in *White
Guard*, Kiev is never referred to by name; instead, it appears as 'the City'.
The depiction of revolution and civil war, an epigraph (the second of two)
from Revelation itself – 'and the dead were judged out of those things
which were written in the books according to their works' (Revelation,
20: 12) – and frequent references to the advent of the Anti-Christ, further heighten the novel's apocalyptic tone and illustrate its relevance for an
understanding of the utopian tradition to which it is obliquely related. Kiev
is often portrayed in loving and nostalgic detail by the rapturous narrator,
but its glory is entirely historical: the city has now been transformed into
Babylon – 'hectically sybaritic, with all-night cafes, cabarets, card clubs,
blasphemous poetry, shops pandering to fat purses and salacious habits'
– by the arrival of a flood of 'moneyed refugees' from Russia itself.[3] Bulgakov's depiction of Kiev also reveals a further feature of utopian fictions,
namely their interest not only in the utopian city itself, but in its borders and
encircling territory. Kiev may be 'the mother of all Russian cities', and the
novel's characters may look to Russian culture for solace and satisfaction,
yet the city is surrounded by (and, indeed, defined in relation to) the vast
and unknown Ukrainian lands. Platonov's works, too, are frequently set in

border zones; a favourite location is the edge of an unspecified provincial town, neither urban centre nor rural periphery, but some ill-defined combination of the two. Even *Happy Moscow* contains a number of pointed references to the city's outskirts and to the very different way of life that exists beyond the confines of the privileged utopian space.

But of all the novels considered here, it is Zamiatin's *We* that most comprehensively explores the dynamic relationship between the utopian city and the world beyond. One State is sealed off from the imperfect, unreconstructed world outside by a glass wall that serves to defend utopia from infection, destruction, and alternative ways of being (as represented by the community that lives outside and the rebellion of the Mephi). As D-503 argues, 'walls are the basis of everything human'.[4] However, the presence of a wall is no guarantee of utopia's impregnability, as Eric Naiman suggests:

> A constant feature in the construction of a would-be perfect world is the isolation of the ideal society; millenarian communities strive to wall themselves off from the rest of the world, and authors of utopian projects frequently seek to bracket their descriptions with protective narratives and framing devices that serve as a moat's narratological equivalent. In the fact of description, however, lies the seed of the utopia's disintegration.[5]

By specifying what utopia is (or at least should be), utopian fictions inevitably call into being what is not (or, indeed, should not be), thereby questioning their own validity. The depiction of borders is thus a topographical means for exploring this anxiety (or, in the case of parodic works, exposing and exploiting it).

The importance of the image of the city as a marker of utopian aspirations also means that other spatial motifs take on special significance. Compare, for instance, the representation of domestic space in *We* and in *White Guard*. In *We*, the use of glass as a building material results in the elimination of privacy (other than when One State's citizens have sex behind blinds) and the dissolution of individual space within the greater whole (likewise, the labourers in *The Foundation Pit* sleep in a communal dormitory and the residents of Chevengur abolish private property in a bid to create shared ownership of their precious community). In *White Guard*, by contrast, the Turbins' apartment constitutes a private refuge from revolution, war, and politics, and domesticity is a precondition of humanity rather than an impediment to social equality. At the opposite end of the scale, such images of intimacy (whether negative or positive) are juxtaposed with evocations of infinity and the universe, whose relationship to the utopian city is equally problematic. In *We*, the universe is a place to be colonized and civilized, subjugated to the absolutist principles of One State. In *Chevengur*, though, the insistent descriptions of the horizon and the seemingly boundless sky above the earth illustrate the very fragility of the utopian experiment, and hint at unknown territories from which danger and destruction will eventually come. And both Platonov and Bulgakov wrote remarkable scenes in which the stars and infinity are contemplated, but to strikingly different effect. In *The Foundation Pit*, a character stares at the Milky Way and wonders: 'When would a resolution be passed there to curtail the eternity of time and redeem the weariness of life?'[6] Here, the universe reminds man of his continual subjugation to the laws of time and space, and of his apparent meaninglessness in the universal plan. In the conclusion to *White Guard*, however, the narrator draws comfort from the way in which human affairs are contextualized and perhaps even redeemed by the infinite wisdom of the stars:

> All this will pass. The sufferings, agonies, blood, hunger, and wholesale death. The sword will go away, but these stars will remain when even the shadows of our bodies and our affairs are long gone from this earth. There is not a man who does not know this. So why are we reluctant to turn our gaze to them? Why?[7]

Whether they offer the promise of redemption or raise the possibility of our essential irrelevance, the stars expose the limitations of the utopian space by evoking a realm that exists well beyond its topographical and ideological reach.

Temporality and chronology

The infinite universe evoked by Platonov and Bulgakov is in part a spatial image, but it also has ramifications for the construction of temporality within utopian fictions. Apocalypse, after all, involves not only the establishment of 'a new heaven and a new earth' (Revelation, 21: 1), but the abolition of time itself: 'and there shall be no more death, neither sorrow, nor crying, neither shall there be any more pain: for the former things are passed away' (Revelation, 21: 4). As Hallie White argues, 'the desire to transform or even abolish time is a frequent characteristic of utopian thinking'; accordingly, utopia might also be termed 'uchronia'.[8] Appropriately enough, then, Alexander Dvanov – the main hero of *Chevengur* – invents a symbol that fuses both the temporal and the physical aspects of revolutionary idealism: 'The eight on its side signifies eternity of time and the upright arrow with two heads means infinity of space.'[9]

In the context of the Russian Revolution and the establishment of Soviet power, the temporal aspects of utopia were invested with particular urgency.

The teleological development of world history under socialism and the scientific inevitability of the dictatorship of the proletariat functioned as secularized versions of the apocalyptic narrative. The representation of utopia as the end of time is common to both Zamiatin and Platonov. For instance, the thirty-seventh entry in *We* (in which the world outside the wall breaks into One State) has as one of its subtitles the word '*svetopredstavlenie*' – 'doomsday'. *Chevengur* is similarly replete with eschatological imagery: for the Bolsheviks of the utopian town, communism is frequently perceived as the end of history and indeed time itself; similarly, the annihilation of the bourgeoisie in *Chevengur* is described as 'the second coming', a reference to the apocalyptic notion that the return of Christ would herald the end of the world (although the commune's claim to have brought about the end of time and initiated the communist paradise is subsequently undermined when it is destroyed by a cavalry detachment, a parodic reference to the four horsemen of the Apocalypse).

Cataclysmic violence and the ensuing end of time may bring about the advent of paradise, yet this presents the author with a peculiar problem of narration. As Zamiatin noted in his 1922 essay on H. G. Wells, 'a utopia is always static; it is always descriptive, and has no, or almost no, plot dynamics'.[10] Change, conflict, development, and even psychology – all of which are made possible by the workings and awareness of time – are no longer possible in the truly utopian narrative, which can do nothing but depict the static perfection of paradise itself. Zamiatin's awareness of the ultimate stasis of utopia also informs his famous argument about the opposition between entropy and energy; the utopian fiction achieves a state of entropy by claiming for itself the status of a final and perfect realization of revolution. In the penultimate entry of *We*, D-503 encounters an enthusiastic proponent of the finality of One State:

> There is no infinity. If the world were infinite, then the average density of matter in it would equal zero. But since it is not zero – this we know – it follows that the universe is finite. It is spherical in shape and the square of its radius, y^2, is equal to the average density, times the . . . I've just got to calculate the numerical coefficient, and then . . . You see, everything is done, everything is simple, everything is calculable. And then we'll win philosophically, don't you see?[11]

By contrast, I-330, D-503's lover and a member of the rebellion, refuses to accept this view of the world as inert, closed, and finite, asking instead 'how can there be a final revolution?' and arguing that '[t]here is no final one. The number of revolutions is infinite.'[12] This argument is used to defend a world in which boundless energy, and not entropy, is the defining feature (along with related notions of spontaneity, unpredictability, and heresy). For Zamiatin, it is the figure of the Scythian horseman who best represents such elemental energy: 'A solitary, savage horseman – a Scythian – gallops across the green steppe, hair streaming in the wind. Where is he galloping? Nowhere. What for? For no reason.'[13] Platonov, by contrast, celebrates a kind of foolish and aimless wandering as the best defence against utopian stasis. In *Chevengur*, for instance, the figure of Stepan Kopenkin rides the steppe on his horse, Proletarian Strength, in a parody of Cervantes' *Don Quixote*. Kopenkin's wanderings (as well as those of other similar characters in *Chevengur* and elsewhere in Platonov's other works) stand in direct contrast to the teleological view of history and motion suggested by the image of the train that Platonov employs early on in the novel. This image – which derives from the Marxist metaphor of revolution as the locomotive of history – is parodied by Platonov; instead of reaching its desired goal in the radiant future, the engine comes off the rails as it crashes into an oncoming train.

Utopia's tendency to conceive of itself as the final point in the historical process also explains why the representation of women is such a crucial feature of many utopian texts (and not only because their violent, apocalyptic tone often presupposes a stereotypically martial view of masculinity). If utopia presupposes the abolition of time, it may also imply the curbing of fertility and reproduction; the birth of a new generation suggests that the present moment cannot claim to be the last. Moreover, the connection between fertility, reproduction, and femininity also sets up a view of history as cyclical and seasonal, rather than teleological and utopian. In *We*, for instance, motherhood is strictly controlled and eroticism explicitly regulated by the state; O-90's rebellion consists of having a baby by her own volition and eventually escaping beyond the wall to a world where reproduction is part of the natural order. Platonov takes the idea of utopia's inherent masculinity to a characteristically absurd level; women are few in his works, and function either as an impediment to the establishment of a utopian community, or as the embodiment of an otherwise abstract idealism. In *The Foundation Pit*, for instance, the men strive to build communism as a dwelling for the young girl, Nastia, whom they take as their mascot; in *Chevengur*, by contrast, women are so comprehensively excluded, and relations between men so intensely valued, that Boris Paramonov has dubbed the novel 'a Gnostic utopia founded on homosexual psychopathology'.[14]

The presence of women in utopia is also linked to the question of mortality; awareness of our own birth leads us to the realization of the possibility of our own death, and hence of the world's essential mutability and inherent imperfection. In *We*, for instance, the narrator muses on the extent to which we comprehend the possibility of our own mortality: 'Do you believe that you will die?' We may know that we will die' (the narrator expounds the syllogism 'man is mortal, I am a man, ergo . . . '), but do we understand what this really means ('not with your mind but with your *body*')? On his trips to the Ancient House, he has seen the elderly guardian, whose age and decrepitude indicate that she belongs to another, earlier, age. The narrator, however, does not consider himself in thrall to time:

> I know that this little black hand on my watch is going to creep down to here, midnight, and that it will then climb slowly back upward, to cross at a certain moment some final point, at which time an incredible tomorrow will commence. This I know, but I somehow do not *believe* it[.][15]

He witnesses time in action, but seems little aware of its implications. Death (like birth) ought not to be possible in utopia (other than the kind of judicial execution by which One State dominates its citizens). Aptly enough, then, Platonov's doubts about the direction of Soviet society during the first Five-Year Plan (as suggested in *The Foundation Pit*) are expressed through the death of the child for whom the ideal world is being constructed.

It is, however, in *Chevengur* that Platonov most fully and strangely explores the association between death, birth, and femininity, and suggests that in utopia time is not so much abolished as reversed. Jacques Catteau suggests that the novel is filled with images that suggest 'the descent towards childhood and the reunion with the amniotic fluid'.[16] The most striking scene of this nature involves the death of a man whose final moments are perceived as a return to the womb:

> Then the foreman remembered where he had last seen this quiet burning blackness. It was simply the closeness within his mother, and now once again he was pushing between her parted bones. But he could not crawl free, because of his aged and too large size . . .
>
> 'Push me farther down the tube', he whispered with childish and swollen lips, clearly aware that he would be born again in nine months' time.[17]

Here, time turns in upon itself; the utopian instinct is revealed to be little more than a longing to undo the burden of adult knowledge and return to a prelapsarian state of innocence and contentment. Platonov was not alone in this view: throughout *We*, Zamiatin portrays D-503's fear of true knowledge (as represented by his terror on learning of the existence of irrational numbers and, in particular, the conundrum of $\sqrt{-1}$) and his ultimate desire to conform as indicative of his philosophical puerility. Similarly, the frequent references to the story of Adam and Eve posit a tension between a state of idealism associated with lost innocence and an adult world of choice and responsibility.

If the discussion of time in utopia so far has dealt little with Bulgakov, it is because his construction of temporality is quite different from the models of stasis and regression explored by Zamiatin and Platonov. In *The Master and Margarita*, the supposedly utopian present of Soviet Moscow in the late 1920s and 1930s is a locus of banality: hubristic in its claims to have achieved the ultimate in scientific rationalism; and unexceptional in the petty humanity of its citizens' misdemeanours. If it is an unconvincing New Jerusalem, neither is it a compelling Babylon: as Woland and his retinue depart, it is subject to only the most bathetic of apocalypses. Bulgakov belittles the Soviet present in order to illustrate the extent to which it is irrelevant in the context of other, more significant events, which occur, moreover, beyond the constraints of time and space to which only the elect have access. In *The Master and Margarita*, this realm is presided over by Ieshua and Woland; and it is to this realm that the Master and Margarita are eventually spirited. In *White Guard*, by contrast, it is the stars of Venus and Mars that preside over a universe far removed from human history. The intersection of the historically determined present with events that have either already happened, are yet to happen, or happen beyond ordinary time, illustrates how Bulgakov replaces the unfolding of history on a contingent scale with a far grander, almost theological conception of how the supernatural interacts with human existence.

An understanding of the relationship between these intersecting planes (in both *The Master and Margarita* and *White Guard*) has profound implications for how Bulgakov treats the question of judgement that is so central to utopian fictions. As Gary Saul Morson argues, utopias view the world in black and white, dividing ideas and people into diametrically opposed camps:

> In both utopias and apocalypses, the explicit division of the audience functions as a provocation to choose one side or the other. The logic of both traditions is that of the excluded middle: there can be no innocent bystanders at the apocalypse, no disinterested contemplators of the revolution.[18]

Thus, the rebels in *We* are tortured and executed and the citizens of One State transformed into docile servants by means of the removal of their imagination. Platonov likewise illustrates the brutal logic of class warfare by depicting the destruction of the bourgeoisie in *Chevengur* and the liquidation of the kulaks in *The Foundation Pit*. In both cases, the victors arrogate to themselves the task of judgement that is normally associated in the apocalyptic tradition with the end of time. Bulgakov, by contrast, illustrates the suspension of judgement, preferring the exercise of compassion to that of retribution (most notably in the actions and attitudes of Ieshua and Margarita). His interest in what Morson calls 'the excluded middle' – neither the righteous nor the damned, but the flawed reality of humanity (not for nothing is the Master a coward who doubts the value and permanence of his own novel) – stems from his conception of a realm beyond the grasp of human politics, history, or ideology. This is the implication of the dream that Aleksei Turbin experiences in *White Guard* (Part 1, Chapter 5), in which God explains to a White officer why the atheistic Bolsheviks also enjoy their place in heaven. Here, the black-and-white, all-or-nothing logic of utopianism is replaced by an infinite variety of greys that makes sense only in the context of an infinity and an eternity beyond the grasp of human comprehension.

Narrativity and textuality

The Master correctly intuits the events he describes in his novel because he seems to have special insight into a world that is beyond the rational, materialist philosophy on which Soviet Russia is built; his manuscript is returned to him because of the intervention of Woland, an emissary from this other world. In both cases, Bulgakov conceives of the irrational and the transcendent as a justification for and defence of the writer's vocation, confident that posterity and immortality will judge him more fairly than his own age. For all that they seek to present (or parody) a supposedly ideal environment, utopian narratives – and narratives about utopia – also frequently comment on their own status as fictions. *The Master and Margarita* contains a novel-within-a-novel, whose events, themes, and characters are subtly parallelled in the novel as a whole. Moreover, the narrator (especially at the opening of Part 2) directly addresses readers both real and imaginary, inviting them to participate in the literary process and to identify with the Master, Margarita, and the novel's other sympathetic characters. In part, this meta-textual strain in Soviet fiction of the time was a response to increasing censorship and calls for literature to serve an explicitly social and ideological purpose. As David Shepherd argues: 'There would . . . seem to be no reason to argue with the view that the upsurge in meta-fictional writing in the late 1920s and early 1930s was part of a straightforward defence of autonomous literary–aesthetic value'.[19] In the early 1920s, Zamiatin had already used *We* as a vehicle for caricaturing the mechanistic aesthetics of early-Soviet proletarian poets; and in *The Master and Margarita*, Bulgakov depicted both the Russian Association of Proletarian Writers (who had waged a hostile campaign against him the late 1920s) and the subsequent bureaucratization of literature in the form of the Union of Soviet Writers. At the same time, utopian (and anti-utopian) fictions may also have an inherent inclination to meta-fictionality, not least because influential precursors in the Russian tradition – such as Chernyshevsky's *What is to be done?* (*Chto delat´?*, 1863) or Dostoevsky's *Notes from Underground* – had established self-awareness as a key element of the genre.

Where Bulgakov juxtaposes a series of contrasting narratives – *The Master and Margarita* consists of a satire on Soviet life in contemporary Moscow, an archaic rewriting of the Passion, the love story of the eponymous hero and heroine, as well as the philosophical interaction between Woland and Ieshua; *White Guard* fuses a Chekhovian family drama with a meditation on the nature of history and epic in a way that explicitly echoes the meta-literary devices of Tolstoy's *War and Peace* (*Voina i mir*, 1865–1869) – Zamiatin takes instead a discrete and specific genre, that of the diary. Moreover, the diary serves not just as a vehicle for recording events and emotions, but also for meditating on the act of writing itself. What begins as a mere transcription of life – as D-503 writes at the outset, 'I am merely copying here, word for word, what was printed today in the *State Gazette*', and 'I shall attempt nothing more than to note down what I see, what I think – or, to be more exact, what we think' – soon defies the generic limitations the narrator has set himself. As events unfold, and dry, factual entries are increasingly set alongside more feverish and incoherent ones, D-503 laments about his diary that 'instead of the elegant and strict mathematical poem in honour of One State, it's turning out to be some kind of fantastic adventure novel'.[20] It is as if the act of writing itself – especially the kind of ornamental, Modernist prose in which Zamiatin excelled – necessarily undoes the conventional premises of scientific rationalism, replacing them with something altogether more ambiguous and unpredictable. This sense that language is caught between two radically opposed modalities – referential certainty vs. imaginative ambiguity – means that utopian fictions will tend to display awareness of their nature and hint at doubts about their own efficacy. As Naiman suggests:

> There is no such thing as 'safe speech.' The utopian enterprise is doomed by the necessity of being expressed and limited through the nonutopian, historically determined communicative instrument of language. The perfect utopia – a utopia immune to linguistically transmitted diseases – would be like the perfect crime: we would be ignorant of its existence.[21]

It is, therefore, apposite that in *We*, the diary should finish when D-503 submits to the removal of his imagination, and with it, his ability to use (or perhaps even be used by) the power of language itself. The battle between One State and the rebel forces may continue, and O-90 has escaped beyond the wall where she will bear the narrator's child: but for D-503 at least, utopia has been re-established by the subjugation of language to silence.

The resistance of utopia to both narrative and language is a key feature of Platonov's writing. As A. A. Kharitonov has suggested, *The Foundation Pit* can be interpreted as a Soviet version of Dante's *Commedia*: the digging of the foundations for the vast proletarian dwelling corresponds to Dante's subterranean exploration of hell; the ascent through purgatory becomes the liquidation of the kulaks on the collective farm as society is cleansed of its hostile elements. However, if Platonov can find contemporary equivalents for *Inferno* and *Purgatorio*, *Paradiso* resists such analogies. *The Foundation Pit* contains no vision of paradise, concluding instead with the death of the young girl, Nastia, in a tragic inversion of the image of Beatrice.[22] After completing *The Foundation Pit*, Platonov offered this commentary on his intentions as an author:

> Will our soviet socialist republic perish like Nastia or will she grow up into a whole human being, into a new historical society? This alarming feeling is what constituted the theme of the work, when the author was writing it. The author may have been mistaken to portray in the form of the little girl's death the end of the socialist generation, but this mistake occurred only as a result of excessive alarm on behalf of something beloved, whose loss is tantamount to the destruction not only of all the past but also of the future.[23]

Platonov's unwillingness – or, indeed, inability – to provide *The Foundation Pit* with the kind of ending that would transfigure its initial depiction of doubt and suffering stem in part, of course, from his complicated attitude to the culture of the first Five-Year Plan. Yet equally, paradise resists incarnation in language because no language is fit to depict perfection and no prose narrative can adequately describe its concomitant stasis (as Zamiatin knew well full). As Joseph Brodsky suggests, 'the idea of paradise is the logical end of human thought in the sense that it, that thought, goes no further; for beyond paradise there is nothing else, nothing else happens'. Thus, the power of Platonov's writing consists of his relentless search for a language that might possibly approach 'the logical end of human thought', thereby revealing 'a self-destructive, eschatological element within the language itself'. If utopian language strives towards the expression of the absolute and the ineffable, it is also burdened with the contingency of its own context. As Brodsky observed, Platonov 'appears to have deliberately and completely subordinated himself to the vocabulary of his utopia – with all its cumbersome neologisms, abbreviations, acronyms, bureaucratese, sloganeering, militarized imperative, and the like'.[24] It is with this historically determined, impoverished form of language that Platonov's characters struggle to communicate, aware that language offers only an inadequate representation of the world, yet also conscious that it is their – and our – only tool for understanding themselves and their surroundings.

Conclusion

Mikhail Bakhtin suggested that of all literary genres, the novel was the most flexible, capacious, and dynamic because of its commitment to and interaction with the contemporary moment: 'The novel comes into contact with the spontaneity of the inconclusive present; this is what keeps the genre from congealing. The novelist is drawn toward everything that is not yet completed.'[25] Elsewhere, Bakhtin defined the novel as 'a phenomenon multiform in style and variform in speech and voice'.[26] This emphasis on a polyphony of contrasting voices and ideologies, as well as the implied invitation to the reader to engage in the task of weighing the truth claims of various competing points of view, mean that the novel is perhaps a poor vehicle for the single-minded preaching of utopian philosophy. Indeed, as Morson suggests, the very presuppositions of the novel as a genre may be 'antithetical to those of utopia'.[27] Just as the novel resists the utopian instinct (whether satirically or earnestly), so too does it refuse to offer a coherent philosophy of its own (which is not to say that it does not deal with philosophical themes more generally), since to do so would be merely to replicate in inverse form the black-and-white premises of utopianism, and therefore fall victim to an identical didacticism. Thus, in *The Master and Margarita*, Ieshua's belief that 'there are no evil people in the world' and his prediction of a 'kingdom of truth and justice, where generally there will be no need for any authority' constitute an anarchic gospel that promises to undo rules and institutions of *any* variety.[28] Similarly, Platonov's disenchantment with revolutionary utopianism did not subsequently provoke in him a reaction against and rejection of that ideology; instead, the troubled embrace of domesticity in his later works represents an exit from the utopian chronotope into an altogether more uncertain world. And critics who have sensed that Zamiatin was 'prone to romanticise the instinctual life as one which is free from the constraints of convention'[29] arguably ignore his warning about the ossification of *all* thought; rather, as Morson argues, '[t]he rebels of *We* seek to re-establish the possibility of possibility'.[30] It is this sense of eternal and unpredictable potentiality that the novel most effectively juxtaposes against utopianism. By dwelling on 'the spontaneity of the inconclusive present', the novel simultaneously evokes the inevitability of the future, and thus brings into question the possibility – and even desirability – of perfection itself.

NOTES

1 Fadeev, Alexander, 'The Rout' in Luker, Nicholas, ed., *From Furmanov to Sholokhov: An Anthology of the Classics of Socialist Realism* (Ann Arbor, MI: Ardis, 1988), pp. 313–379 (pp. 377–378).

2 Hodel, Robert, *Erlebte Rede bei Andrej Platonov: Von 'V zvezdnoj pustyne' bis 'Čevengur'* (Frankfurt am Main: Peter Lang, 2001), p. 1.

3 Milne, Lesley, *Mikhail Bulgakov: A Critical Biography* (Cambridge: Cambridge University Press, 1990), p. 81.

4 Zamiatin, Evgenii, *We*, trans. Clarence Brown (London: Penguin, Harmondsworth, 1993), p. 40.

5 Naiman, Eric, *Sex in Public: The Incarnation of Early Soviet Doctrine* (Princeton, NJ: Princeton University Press, 1997), p. 13.

6 Platonov, Andrei, *The Foundation Pit*, trans. Robert Chandler, Elizabeth Chandler, and Olga Meerson (New York: New York Review Books, 2009), p. 85.

7 Bulgakov, Mikhail, *White Guard*, trans. Marian Schwartz (New Haven, CT and London: Yale University Press, 2008), p. 310.

8 White, Hallie A., 'Time Out of Line: Sequence and Plot in Platonov's *Chevengur*', *Slavonic and East European Journal*, 42, no. 1 (1998), pp. 102–117 (p. 103).

9 Platonov, Andrei, *Chevengur*, trans. Anthony Olcott (Ann Arbor, MI: Ardis, 1978), p. 108.

10 Zamiatin, Evgenii, 'H. G. Wells' in *A Soviet Heretic: Essays by Yevgeny Zamyatin*, ed. and trans. Mirra Ginsburg (Chicago, IL and London: University of Chicago Press, 1970), pp. 259–290 (p. 286).

11 Zamiatin, *We*, pp. 222–223.

12 *Ibid.*, p. 167.

13 Zamiatin, Evgenii, 'Scythians?' in Ginsburg, ed. and trans., *A Soviet Heretic*, pp. 21–33 (p. 21).

14 Paramonov, Boris, 'Chevengur i okrestnosti', *Kontinent*, 54 (1987), pp. 333–372 (p. 334).

15 Zamiatin, *We*, p. 180.

16 Catteau, Jacques, 'De la métaphorique des utopies dans la littérature russe et de son traitement chez Andrej Platonov', *Revue des études slaves*, 56 (1984), pp. 39–50 (p. 47).

17 Platonov, *Chevengur*, p. 40. The final sentence has been omitted from this translation.

18 Morson, Gary Saul, *The Boundaries of Genre: Dostoevsky's 'Diary of a Writer' and the Traditions of Literary Utopia* (Austin, TX: University of Texas Press, 1981), p. 101.

19 Shepherd, David, *Beyond Metafiction: Self-Consciousness in Soviet Literature* (Oxford: Clarendon Press, 1992), p. 26.

20 Zamiatin, *We*, pp. 3–4, p. 99.

21 Naiman, *Sex in Public*, p. 13.

22 Kharitonov, A. A.,'Arkhitektonika povesti A. Platonova "Kotlovan"' in *Tvorchestvo Andreia Platonova* (St Petersburg: Nauka, 1995), pp. 70–90.

23 Platonov, *The Foundation Pit*, p. 150.
24 Brodsky, Joseph, 'Catastrophes in the Air' in *Less than One: Selected Essays* (London: Penguin, 1987), pp. 268–303 (pp. 286, 287, and 288).
25 Bakhtin, Mikhail, 'Epic and Novel: Toward a Methodology for the Study of the Novel' in *The Dialogic Imagination*, ed. Michael Holquist, trans. Caryl Emerson and Michael Holquist (Austin, TX: University of Texas Press, 1981), pp. 3–40, p. 27.
26 Bakhtin, Mikhail, 'Discourse in the Novel', *ibid.*, pp. 259–422, p. 26.
27 Morson, *The Boundaries of Genre*, p. 117.
28 Bulgakov, Mikhail, *The Master and Margarita*, trans. Richard Pevear and Larissa Volokhonsky (London: Penguin, 1997), pp. 27 and 30.
29 Barratt, Andrew, 'Introduction' in E. Zamiatin, *My/We* (Bristol: Bristol Classical Press, 1994), pp. v–xx, p. xix.
30 Morson, *The Boundaries of Genre*, p. 132.

FURTHER READING

Barratt, Andrew, *Between Two Worlds: A Critical Introduction to* 'The Master and Margarita' (Oxford: Clarendon Press, 1987).
Bethea, David, *The Shape of Apocalypse in Modern Russian Fiction* (Princeton, NJ: Princeton University Press, 1989).
Brodsky, Joseph, 'Catastrophes in the Air' in *Less than One: Selected Essays* (London: Penguin, 1987), pp. 268–303.
Bullock, Philip Ross, *The Feminine in the Prose of Andrey Platonov* (London: Legenda, 2005).
Curtis, Julie, *Bulgakov's Last Decade: The Writer as Hero* (Cambridge: Cambridge University Press, 1987).
Edwards, T., *Three Russian Writers and the Irrational: Zamyatin, Pil'nyak, and Bulgakov* (Cambridge: Cambridge University Press, 1982).
Milne, Lesley, *Mikhail Bulgakov: A Critical Biography* (Cambridge: Cambridge University Press, 1990).
Mørch, Audun, *The Novelistic Approach to the Utopian Question: Platonov's Čevengur in the Light of Dostoevskij's Anti-Utopian Legacy* (Oslo: Scandinavian University Press, 1998).
Morson, Gary Saul, *The Boundaries of Genre: Dostoevsky's Diary of a Writer and the Traditions of Literary Utopia* (Austin, TX: University of Texas Press, 1981).
Naiman, Eric, *Sex in Public: The Incarnation of Early Soviet Doctrine* (Princeton, NJ: Princeton University Press, 1997).
Russell, Robert, *Zamiatin's 'We'* (London: Bristol Classical Press, 2000).
Seifrid, Thomas, *Andrei Platonov: Uncertainties of Spirit* (Cambridge: Cambridge University Press, 1991).
    Companion to Andrei Platonov's 'The Foundation Pit' (Boston, MA: Academic Studies Press, 2009).
Stites, Richard, *Revolutionary Dreams: Utopian Vision and Experimental Life in the Russian Revolution* (New York: Oxford University Press, 1989).
Weeks, Laura, ed., *The Master and Margarita: A Critical Companion* (Evanston, IL: Northwestern University Press, 1996).

6

EVGENY DOBRENKO*

Socialist Realism

Origins: Socialist Realism and Soviet literature

The Revolution signified the end not only of an entire epoch in Russian history, but also of the nation that had developed in Russia over the course of two centuries. Stalinism became the epoch of the birth and rise of a new, Soviet nation. The political culture of Russia – with its absolutism and lack of freedom – presupposed a wholly distinctive status for literature. Since, under these conditions, literature became virtually the only platform for political thought and the sole refuge of spiritual freedom, Russian culture was literature-centric. And yet – despite the naturally differing political, ideological, and aesthetic viewpoints of its authors – before the Revolution Russian literature developed as a unified national literature. The end of the historical epoch and of the nation, accompanied by the destruction of the political and cultural elites, also meant the end of the previous literary paradigm.

The Revolution sharply disrupted the organic development of literature by creating entirely new conditions under which it had to function. The new government imposed agitational and propagandistic functions that were not characteristic of the earlier literature, and the concept of the 'social mandate' took shape. Private publishing houses and literary journals closed or were immediately monopolized by the state. The party began to actively interfere in literary matters, a process that culminates in the state assuming complete control over literature.

But it is not just the conditions under which literature operates that change. The very composition of literature changes: with the bitterness of civil war and the exodus of the former cultural elites, national literature starts to come apart. By the early 1920s, the very term 'Russian litera-ture' already begins to fall out of usage. Instead, other definitions emerge for the literature developing in the country, such as 'proletarian' literature (the type openly supported by the new regime), 'peasant', 'bourgeois', and 'petit-bourgeois' literature. The latter was also called 'fellow-traveller' (*pop-utchik*) literature, a definition introduced by Trotsky. The 'fellow-travellers' were writers of different generations who were too tied to the past (ideologically, aesthetically, spiritually) and who were thus going 'in the same direction' as the Revolution, but only for a time. Since it was impossible to believe in the political trustworthiness of the fellow-travellers, they could be afforded only limited trust.

As can be seen, a 'class principle' lay at the root of the rupture: even more specifically, the social origin of the writers. The ideologues of the numerous post-Revolutionary literary groups exaggerated the antagonisms and conflicts. However, certain other forces were also at work within the literary world. There were those who understood the danger of the schism, since it was leading to the disintegration of the already thin and fragile layer of culture in Russia, weakening the new power holders, and pushing sympathizers away from the new regime. And so a new term arises: 'Soviet literature', which initially indicated a certain degree of national unity after the bloody Civil War, and was a sort of admission that authors with differing viewpoints could be allowed to co-exist.

The term 'Soviet literature' was coined by Alexander Voronsky, the most authoritative literary critic of the time and the editor of the first Soviet 'thick journal', *Red Virgin Soil*, who also enjoyed the support of Lenin and Trotsky. In his article 'From Contemporary Literary Moods', published in the main party newspaper *Pravda* on 28 June 1922, he wrote: 'It is not proletarian literature nor is it communist . . . On the whole, this literature is Soviet.' According to Voronsky, this new literature, although variegated in its composition, was nonetheless loyal to the political system (we should remember that in 1922, in connection with the end of the Civil War and the introduction of the NEP, romantic hopes were very strong: for a 'democratic evolution' of the Bolsheviks, for example, or for liberalization of the regime, or for the ideas of the Changing Signposts movement [*smenovekhovstvo*], which predicted the regime's inevitable ideological degeneration and a return to the Imperial order and the traditions of the strong state). However, 'Soviet literature' very quickly acquires an entirely different meaning from the pluralistic slogan of NEP.

The year 1929 is a singular date in Soviet history. In Stalin's Russia it was called 'the year of the Great Break', and in the West, the beginning of the Stalinist revolution. This is the year in which Stalin usurps power once and for all, becoming the 'leader' (*vozhd'*) and ridding himself of all opposition, and in which he begins the collectivization of the countryside. In this year, the attack on the ideological front also begins. In a 1929 letter to the playwright Bill-Belotserkovsky, Stalin transforms the term 'Soviet' from a synonym for heterogeneity into a synonym for polarization: 'It would be truer in the case of literature to use *class* terms, or even the terms "Soviet", "anti-Soviet", "revolutionary", "anti-revolutionary", etc.' Stalin points out that 'literature, at its present stage of development, has all trends, and of every possible kind, even down to the anti-Soviet and the outright counter-revolutionary sorts'. As an example of 'unproletarian trash' he cites the works of Mikhail Bulgakov. Stalin's approach to the concept of 'Soviet' literature immediately becomes the foundation for all literary policy.

A marked stratification of literature occurs. Stalin grants a virtually monopolistic power in literature to the Russian Association of Proletarian Writers (RAPP), which he supports in its most radical endeavours. Within the course of a few years RAPP completely bureaucratizes literary life. It announces the end of 'civil peace in literature' and unveils a new slogan: 'Not a fellow-traveller, but either an ally or an enemy.' Evgenii Zamiatin, Mikhail Bulgakov, and Boris Pilniak are targeted. At this moment RAPP announces the populist 'call of shock workers into literature': workers from the machines and peasants from the ploughs must replace professional writers. (And, by 1932, RAPP had 15,000 members!) The tension and bitterness in the literary battle reach their apogee. And then, like a bolt from the blue, in April 1932 Stalin disbands RAPP, establishes a single Union of Soviet Writers, and declares a single 'artistic method' for literature and culture, obligatory for all writers: Socialist Realism.

The 1932 decree was a turning point in the history of Soviet literature and art (inasmuch as it disbanded not only literary groups but also 'creative associations' in all art forms and assumed the establishment of single 'creative unions' in each of them). It abolished the system of literary polycentrism, in which writers had been able to unify in various groups on the basis of their shared ideological and aesthetic views. Now everyone had to have identical political views and adhere to a single aesthetic principle: Socialist Realism. From then on, all writers would be declared 'Soviet'. The reward for this would be an abrupt increase of their social status. The Union of Soviet Writers is transformed into a unique ministry of literature, and the writers, in essence, into privileged state bureaucrats on the same footing as the political elite, with luxury apartments, dachas, cars, honoraria, and special distributions of scarce goods – and at that time everything was scarce, from clothing and soap to bread and butter. In the course of two decades, the new Russian literature, having been almost completely re-born, travelled the path from absolute revolutionary nihilism to just as absolute Imperial servility.

Literature became controllable. The functions of the writer also changed. Now only high-level 'instrumentalism', 'craft', and 'execution' are demanded of the artist. This led to a radical change in the literary situation: in the public sphere only the new Soviet literature – that is, the literature of Socialist Realism – remains. Émigré literature is now completely cut off from the 'Soviet literature', and those writers who had remained in the country but, for whatever reasons, had not joined the new system, were now either repressed or forced to write 'for the desk drawer', without any hope for publication. In the years of the Great Terror, Isaac Babel, Boris Pilniak, Osip Mandelshtam, Nikolai Kliuev, Artem Veselyi, and many others were repressed – a total of almost 2,000 writers (among them, more than 250 of the roughly 600 delegates to the First Congress of the Union of Soviet Writers (1934)). Mikhail Bulgakov, Andrei Platonov, Anna Akhmatova, and Mikhail Zoshchenko all wrote without hope of being published. And even after Stalin's death, a number of writers either published abroad, such as Vasilii Grossman and Boris Pasternak, or were exiled from the country, such as Alexander Solzhenitsyn and Joseph Brodsky.

But it is not only literature itself that changed, but also its audience. The cultured reader of earlier times was either eliminated during the years of civil war or else fled the country. But the new mass reader was organically unprepared to comprehend complex culture. He was yesterday's illiterate peasant, fleeing to the city from the horrors of collectivization, with its famine and devastation. On the whole, these new masses of readers, although they had (just recently) learned to read, did not perceive urban culture as their own. This was the source of the strong demand for cultural simplification. The new readers did not need complicated literature so much as spiritual support and the comfort of melodrama. They could not comprehend Modernist experiments, since they were infected by 'naive realism' and demanded verisimilitude from literature. A total infantilization of culture took place, a peculiar return to a primitive spiritual childhood with suitable stylistic and plot paradigms: noble heroes, infernal villains, the ideals of collectivism, and so on.

The Socialist Realist canon: the doctrine

Socialist Realism was, above all, a political–aesthetic doctrine based upon certain 'principles of the artistic method', such as 'ideological commitment' (*ideinost´*), 'party-mindedness' (*partiinost´*), 'popular spirit' (*narodnost´*), 'historicism', and 'typicality'.

Ideological commitment denied the possibility of 'art for art's sake'. This kind of art was 'unideological', and the lack of this *commitment* had been the hallmark of bourgeois art – which had served the interests of the ruling classes and distracted workers from the battle for their rights. Naturally, there was no place for such art under socialism. Soviet literature had to be not only openly politically tendentious, but also – since *'communist ideological commitment'* lay at its foundations – the 'most ideologically committed in the world'. According to this principle, art cannot be party-neutral since it always reflects some kind of political ideas.

Party-mindedness is the basis for any art: because art is social, it is necessarily *class-oriented* and thus it participates in class struggle on the side of one party or another. *'Communist party-mindedness'* lies at the foundation of Soviet art. In other words, art must openly follow party leadership, be directed by the party, and serve the party's political goals. And since the Communist party expresses the 'interests of the progressive class', adherence to it means adherence to the only true 'historical legitimacy'. At the same time, the interpretation of this 'legitimacy' is exclusively controlled by the main party priest – the party leader.

Popular spirit was just where Soviet art found its supreme legitimacy. Lenin's maxim, 'Art belongs to the people', was written on the banner of Soviet art. This formulation is exceptionally broad, and thus the very concept of popular spirit is multi-faceted. First of all, as Hans Günther observes, the idea is connected with perceptions of organicity and wholeness and is opposed to the mechanical and the abstract. Second, it contains an objective or atemporal ideal that contrasts with the contemporary era of modernist style. Third, it signifies simplicity and comprehensibility, which are antithetical to elitist obfuscation and modernism. Fourth, the battle against the morbid and the decadent is waged in the name of a healthy popular spirit. Fifth, a popular folkloric style is contrasted to professional art as the ideal model. Finally, within the concept of popular spirit, 'one's own' culture is disassociated from any elements that are 'against' the people (*antinarodnye*) or 'foreign' to them.[1]

Historicism presumed that literature should reflect 'life in its revolutionary development'. In other words, the past, present, and future all had to be depicted in accordance with the 'laws of historical development' revealed by Marxism. The difficult past had been preparation for socialist revolution. The present day had to display 'signs of the future'. But the future itself was not subject to representation, since all of time converged in the present, in which the 'visible features of communism' were revealed at every turn. According to Soviet literature, communism had practically arrived.

Typicality meant that 'life must be depicted in the forms of life itself' (this is why Socialist Realism did not tolerate any form of non-realism, fantasy, or play). But this was a particular kind of verisimilitude. Everything that the authorities deemed 'atypical' (economic hardship, difficult living conditions, not to mention political repression) – that did not produce a sense of 'revolutionary development' or promote social mobilization – was not subject to representation, and so was virtually excluded from the public sphere.

In addition to these doctrinal ideological characteristics, Soviet literature was also characterized by a number of aesthetic peculiarities, including superrealism, monumentalism, classicism, and heroic spirit.

Superrealism is a special quality of 'realism' to which Soviet literature aspired. Stylistically, it is reminiscent of classical realism. However, as Hans Günther notes, 'superrealism does not aim for an analytic picture of reality, it only uses realistic drapery for its goals. It does not need realism of a descriptive, "naturalistic" bent, but rather a realism of a "higher", ideal type. Essentially, we are dealing not with realism but with mythology disguised in realistic clothing.'[2] The appeal to an ideal, synthetic principle is evident in the very evolution of the concept of 'Socialist Realism'. Throughout the 1920s, debates raged in Soviet art about what form the art of the future would take, with preference given to notions such as 'heroic', 'monumental', 'social', 'tendentious', or 'romantic' realism.

The *monumentalism* to which all 'ascendant' cultures asserting their novelty, youth, and strength appeal, characterized many of the cultures of the twentieth century. It reveals itself not only in the idea of the synthesis of art forms (*Gesamtkunstwerk*), but also in the triumph of the so-called Soviet Grand Style, which is associated primarily with the big genre forms.[3] In painting, this is the ceremonial portrait and the battle genre; in music, the opera, oratory, cantata, and symphony; in urban planning, ensemble and pompous architectural projects; in prose, the 'epic novel'; and in poetry, the narrative poem. The combination of the big generic forms with a heroic spirit rendered them the embodiment of synthetism and 'epic thought' and thus especially close to the Socialist Realist aesthetic.

Classicism, intrinsic to Socialist Realism and characteristic of the aesthetics of all dictatorships in general, should not be understood literally, of course. It enters the Socialist Realist aesthetic, as did realism and romanticism, only in some aspects. Soviet art arises from revolutionary art, which had initially fed upon romantic mythology. But, with the realization of the utopian nature of the revolutionary ideals and the necessity of glorification for the established order, romantic mythology begins to acquire the stylistic forms of a classicist aesthetic. This is evident not only in the monumental style, but also in the gravitation toward a classicist type of portraying the conflict between duty and emotion – whether the rejection of love in the name of revolution or the rejection of family and comfort in the name of a worker's duties. At the same time, the appeal to the classics as the ideal of harmony, order, and wholeness became a reaction against modernism, which was incomprehensible to the mass consumer demanding 'beauty' from art. The battle against formalism and naturalism in Soviet art was an acute form of Stalinist anti-modernism and the basis for asserting the 'eternal ideals' of the classics.

A *heroic spirit* is inherent to all art, from romanticism to classicism. But, not coincidentally, Günther calls the heroic principle the 'final component of the totalitarian synthesis of art, penetrating all of its structures' and argues that 'the totalitarian myth manifests itself in the heroic like nowhere else. Heroism is a dynamic principle that is closely connected with activism and the extreme polarization of cultural values. The hero emerges as the builder of a new life, overcoming all obstacles and defeating all enemies. It is not a coincidence that totalitarian cultures have found a designation that suits them: heroic realism.'[4]

The Socialist Realist canon: a history

Socialist Realism, despite its connection to the Soviet historical situation and its apparent cultural organicity, did not contain anything 'natural'. Starting with the term itself, which Stalin invented, and ending with its selection of formative models and the pre-history created for it, it was a wholly constructed project.

Socialist Realism was proclaimed to have emerged from the very history of Russian literature – as if, before the appearance of Marxism, it had been wandering in the wilderness in search of a 'positive ideal of reality'. The attempt to locate its origins in Maxim Gorky's *Mother* (*Mat'*, 1906) reveals how artificial this construct was from the very beginning. At the time of the novel's creation, Gorky was enthralled by ideas of 'God building', and these religious overtones (motifs of sacrifice, spiritual transformation, and universal redemption) are very strong in the novel. And they did not disappear immediately after the Revolution.

Alexander Serafimovich's novel *The Iron Flood* (*Zheleznyi potok*, 1924), for example, describes how the Red commander Kozhukh leads a detachment of revolutionary partisans out of encirclement. At the same time, the novel also reproduces an Old Testament story: Kozhukh himself is like Moses, and the escape of the Taman division from the encirclement is strikingly reminiscent of the story of the exodus of the Jews from Egypt to the Promised Land; the text of the novel contains direct indicators of this parallel. Early proletarian poetry – with its cosmism, romanticism, and the desire to convey in the new art the grandeur and boundless power of the proletarian revolution that had triumphed in Russia and, as the proletarian poets thought, had been kindled in the whole world – bore even less resemblance to 'the truth of life'. This supposition engendered images of cosmic revolution: 'For our planet we will find a dazzling new path' (Vladimir Kirillov); 'We will construct rows of stars, hitch the moon to our reins' (Kirillov); 'Along Martian canals we will erect a palace of World Freedom' (Mikhail Gerasimov), and so on.

But then the 'era of reconstruction' begins. Characteristic of this era is a rejection of the utopian excesses of the early revolutionary period; a reliance on the realist tradition is found to be much more congenial. The beginning of 'peaceful construction' and of the NEP era thrusts an entirely different kind of poet into the foreground. One such figure is Alexander Bezymensky, who demands that the poets of *'The Smithy'* group 'stop turning planets over like lumps' and proclaims: 'Enough of heaven and prophetic wisdom!/Give us more living nails./Away with heaven! Throw away these things!/Give us the sky and living people.' But this demand is not really as much about 'living people' as it is about 'life in its revolutionary development': 'heaven and prophetic wisdom' is a direct euphemism for the 'Marxist orthodoxy' of the proletarian poets. Bezymensky would later express this idea even more clearly, in the narrative poem 'Guta' (1924): 'Grab with your eyes/this life that we ourselves build.' But, according to Bezymensky, this 'life being built' is valuable in and of itself, and not subject to scrutiny by ideas: 'They [young poets – E.D.] cause to stir/The living, genuine faces/Of living, very real people,/Not those of wobbly ideas.' The notion of 'wobbly ideas' shows the apex of the party-mindedness principle as the writer's mind masters it: 'wobbliness' is finally ascribed to ideas, while 'life' is proclaimed to be 'genuine' and 'very real'. Obviously, only realism is necessary for the representation of this kind of life.

In prose, the work of the RAPP writers, who had advocated psychologism, assumes centre stage. Alexander Fadeev's *The Rout* (*Razgrom*, 1927) provides a most characteristic example of this type of writing. A former leader of RAPP and later a leader in the Union of Soviet Writers, Fadeev comes out with the slogan 'Down with Schiller!' in 1929 and advocates the depiction of the 'living person' in literature. The heroes of *The Rout* became exemplars of this kind of 'living person'. The novel – about the Civil War in the Far East – contains long, Tolstoy-like interior monologues that describe the complicated psychological anxieties and moral dilemmas of the heroes: the Bolshevik commander Levinson; a partisan from the popular masses, Morozko; and the harried intellectual, Mechik.

The genre of the *Bildungsroman* (novel of education) proved to be most suitable for simultaneously realizing the heroic principle and injecting an element of psychologism. Writing the story of a hero's formation allowed the author to reveal the process of the growth of party consciousness in his character, a conflict that Katerina Clark defined as central to the 'master-plot'

of the Soviet novel. This type of story reproduced the fundamental collision of Bolshevism in Russia: the party's task was to 'instill' revolutionary
consciousness in the masses.[5] Under the influence of the Bolsheviks' efforts,
the 'masses' gained experience not only with class struggle, but also with
'socialist construction'. Dmitrii Furmanov's *Chapaev* (1923) is of this genre:
based on real events, it describes the legendary commander Chapaev's heroic
participation in the Civil War. Under the influence of a Bolshevik commissar, Chapaev rids himself of elements of spontaneity and partisanship and
is transformed into an ideal Red Army commander.

Nikolai Ostrovsky's novel *How the Steel Was Tempered* (*Kak zakalialas'
stal'*, 1932–1934) represents the apogee of this genre in Socialist Realism.
The metaphor of 'tempering of steel' was extremely popular in both Revolutionary and Stalinist culture. But this autobiographical novel, written
by an author who had become paralyzed, blind, and confined to his bed –
about how he had earlier survived the Civil War, organized a Communist
youth league, worked on a railroad-building crew, and toiled in waist-deep
icy water – became an event that transcended the boundaries of literature.
Pavel Korchagin, the hero of the novel, possessed a limitless faith in the
Bolshevik cause. And, even though paralysed and blind, he still manages
to 'find his place in the system' by writing a novel for young people. *How
the Steel Was Tempered* is a novel about a martyr for an idea. However,
unlike earlier martyrs, Korchagin does not make a show of his suffering, but
instead hides it: 'Everyone knew that if Korchagin was moaning it meant
he had lost consciousness.' The book was immensely popular, and Korchagin became the same kind of extra-literary object as the reader himself. He became a 'fact of life', which is significantly bigger than a fact of
literature.

The degree to which the Soviet *Bildungsroman* evolved during the Stalinist
period can be judged by a comparison of Ostrovsky's work with Fadeev's
novel *The Young Guard* (*Molodaia gvardiia*, 1945, revised version 1951).
The latter work chronicles the quasi-documentary history of an underground
youth organization that resists the German occupation, but in a romantically
heroic style. *The Young Guard* contrasts sharply not only to *The Rout*, which
was written in the style of psychological realism *à la* Tolstoy, but also to
Ostrovsky's novel, which was based on autobiography.

The most outstanding example, perhaps, of the contrast between Revolutionary and Stalinist aesthetic projects is the fate of one of the supergenres of
Soviet literature, the 'industrial novel'. Born in the mid-1920s as a rejection
of the traditional family novel and as a (wholly literal) rejection of the family
itself, the industrial novel after the war returned to the family novel and to
melodrama. The novel of everyday family life had been impossible during

the Revolutionary period, when the family was considered a 'stronghold of the old world'.

The proletarian writer Fedor Gladkov's *Cement* (*Tsement*, 1925) is justly considered the first exemplar of the industrial novel. The novel, which enjoyed dizzying success, described the heroic struggle of the communist Gleb Chumalov to resurrect a factory after the Civil War. It answered anew questions about the role of women in socialist society and about the 'new Soviet family'. The novel (especially in its first version) contained strong elements of ornamentalism and 'proletarian romanticism'. Its popularity was such that, at the beginning of the 1930s, even the leading fellow-traveller writers adopted the 'industrial novel' genre. Leonid Leonov writes the novel *Sot'* (1930), Marietta Shaginian releases *Hydrocentral* (*Gidrotsentral'* 1930–1931), Valentin Kataev his *Time, Forward!* (*Vremia, vpered!*, 1932), and in 1933 Ilia Ehrenburg publishes *The Second Day* (*Den' vtoroi*). These works still retain obvious features of symbolism, avant-garde aesthetics, and documentalism.

However, the industrial novel, with its asceticism and obsession with production, ceased to satisfy the aesthetics of high Stalinism. Vsevolod Kochetov's novel *The Zhurbins* (*Zhurbiny*, 1952), about a long line of working-class shipbuilders, is the best example of this. It is impossible to determine conclusively whether this is a novel about the family or about workers and shipbuilding. The transformation of the industrial novel, its return to the family novel and to melodrama, would have been impossible without a rejection of revolutionary asceticism. 'The move beyond the aesthetics of asceticism', wrote Boris Riurikov in the year that *The Zhurbins* was published, 'is one of the most significant features of Socialist Realism . . . We are against cheap melodramas, against petit bourgeois, sentimental family tales, but we believe that all aspects of the life of a Soviet person have a right to be reflected in art. The spiritual wealth, the moral beauty of the Soviet man are revealed in his relationships with his comrades, with his beloved woman, with his children.'[6]

This new aesthetic of the consolidated utopia revealed itself most clearly in the 'collective farm novel' that flourished after the war. Sholokhov's *Virgin Soil Upturned* (*Podniataia tselina*, 1932) had described the process of collectivization and the conflicts of that era; but the post-war collective farm novels by Galina Nikolaeva, Elizar Maltsev, and Semen Babaevsky (which all received the Stalin Prize) exemplified what was called 'conflictless literature'. Babaevsky's *The Cavalier of the Golden Star* (*Kavaler zolotoi zvezdy*, 1947–1948), for example, tells of a hero returned from the war who achieves incredible successes: he rebuilds the collective farm, constructs an electrical station, makes an astounding career for himself, and marries a beauty who gives him twin sons. This fantastic character – idealized, selfless, and capable of overcoming all obstacles – typified the hero of post-war Soviet literature, which produced novel-fairytales that contained not only happy endings but also a whole series of happily resolved 'clashes'.

The 'new past' also corresponded to this happy present, into which the coming future had already seemingly capsized. If pre-Revolutionary literature had depicted the people's difficult past – when they suffered under the tsar and fought against him – and a whole series of historical novels had portrayed history as an endless concatenation of popular rebellions against oppression, now Russian literature was filled with national pride. A country rebuilt by the Bolsheviks and, what is more, one that had emerged victorious in war, needed a new, heroic, epic past, the kind in which the people and the state co-existed in harmony. Aleksei Tolstoi's *Peter the First* (*Petr I*, 1945) has been called the highest achievement in Soviet historical prose. This novel is a virtual apologia for the tsarist regime, affirming the tsar's progressiveness. It is difficult even to imagine such literature during the 1920s, when rigid, class-based, Marxist criteria had been in force. But this is just how 'party-mindedness' and 'historicism' functioned: Stalinism became an increasingly etatist system that used Marxist and socialist ideology and rhetoric to conceal its own nationalistic nature.

We have focused exclusively on the most famous examples of Socialist Realism, not only because they comprised the core of the Soviet literary canon, but also because they were actively promoted in Soviet schools. Many generations of Soviet citizens were raised on these very works. An entire network of institutions functioned like part of an enormous Socialist Realist machine: publishing policies, the library system, the schools. Indeed, Socialist Realism could exist only under specific institutional conditions: a repressive system of censorship; a government monopoly on ideology; and absolutely rigid Party control. The weakening of these institutions led to the breakdown of the Socialist Realist aesthetic itself. This is why the marginalization of Socialist Realism began with the death of Stalin and the beginning of Khrushchev's Thaw. The emergence of political dissidence in the 1960s–1970s, the development of a pluralistic (if still only underground) aesthetic, the return (though still not nearly complete) of those names and artistic movements forbidden during the Stalinist period – all led to the erosion of the canon. Its complete collapse became only a matter of time.

In these years, the themes of historical memory and social responsibility emerge in Iurii Trifonov's 'urban prose', which re-examines established viewpoints on the consequences of the revolution and of Stalinism. In the 'new war prose' by Vasil Bykov, Iurii Bondarev, Grigorii Baklanov, and

Vladimir Bogomolov, an understanding of one of the most important experiences in the formation of Soviet identity – that of the Second World War – develops through a description of the real conflicts and tragedies of war, far from the triumphal stock phrases of Socialist Realism. The 'village prose' of Fedor Abramov, Vasilii Belov, Valentin Rasputin, and Vasilii Shukshin introduces the theme of the destruction of the native way of life by Stalinist collectivization. It focuses on the collapse of the ethical and moral foundation of this way of life, on the themes of death and conscience, and on the ruin of the Russian village. These same themes of historical memory and responsibility for the past resounded not only in the works of Russian writers, but also in those of writers representing other national literatures of the former Soviet Union: the Kirghiz Chingiz Aitmatov, the Estonian Paul Kuusberg, the Lithuanian Ionas Avizhius, the Georgian Otar Chiladze, and many others. As we have seen, all of these themes had been absolutely taboo in the Socialist Realist canon which, as time went on, was increasingly viewed as merely an unavoidable backdrop for 'real literature'. This new literature now developed according to its own logic, retreating ever further into the realm of aesthetic experiments that had captivated writers of different generations, from Valentin Kataev to Andrei Bitov and Venedikt Erofeev. Conceptualist prose writers and poets, the representatives of Sots Art, such as Vladimir Sorokin, Evgenii Popov, Dmitrii Prigov, and Lev Rubinshtein, all devoted themselves to the deideologization of Soviet society and the ironic reworking of Soviet aesthetic and ideological clichés.[7] During the *perestroika* era, the canon completely disintegrated. The collapse of the Soviet Union signified the collapse of Socialist Realism as well, as an aesthetic doctrine inextricably linked to the Soviet regime.

Andrei Siniavsky, one of the first who managed to tell the truth about Socialist Realism (and ended up in a prison camp for doing so), called it 'half-*classicist* half-art, which is none too *socialist* and is not *realism* at all'.[8] We have seen what there was of classicism in this pseudo-classicism, and how little there was of art in this half-art. Now let us try to understand what was 'socialist' about it, and what it contained in the way of realism.

Functions: Socialist Realism and Soviet reality

Early Proletarian poetry was wholly romantic. However, by the late 1920s, when it became clear that the world-wide communist dream had collapsed, the building of 'socialism in one country' necessitated an entirely different aesthetic project: the illusion of reality, instead of an illusory utopia. And so Socialist Realism appeared – the realism of the dream. Or, even more concretely, utopian naturalism. This is why Socialist Realism aspires not so much to romanticism or to realism but rather to melodrama, this 'naturalism of the dream life', as Eric Bentley so accurately characterized it.[9]

The official definition of Socialist Realism, given at the First Congress of the Union of Soviet Writers by Stalin's right-hand man in matters of ideology, Andrei Zhdanov, stated that it was the 'truthful representation of life in its revolutionary development'. The contradiction inherent in this definition is by no means accidental. Many other definitions of Socialist Realism exist. One of them belongs to Aleksei Tolstoi: 'Marxism, mastered in an artistic way.' However, despite Marxism's effectiveness as a critique of reality, its positive aspects are equally utopian. In this sense, the very phrase 'Socialist Realism' is an oxymoron. Socialism is a goal, an aspiration, a hope. Romanticism would much more answer the needs of socialism, in a way that realism simply could not. Life can be depicted either 'truthfully' (then this would be realism) or 'in its revolutionary development' (i.e. not entirely truthfully, romantically). But reconciling these two things is not a simple task.

This was well understood by the people who created Socialist Realism. For example, the man officially proclaimed to be its founder, Maxim Gorky, emphasized in a speech delivered to young writers on the eve of the First Congress of the Union of Soviet Writers that 'Socialist Realism . . . can be created only from the facts of socialist experience',[10] only 'as a reflection of the facts of socialist creation as provided by working practice' (27, 218). But this experience and these 'facts' were not yet recognized as the product of Socialist Realism. Gorky demonstrated this train of thought, without fully realizing it, in the same speech. He complained that certain literary figures, 'apathetic know-it-alls', were submitting to the 'power of facts' and calling the goals of construction 'fantastic' and 'unattainable', whereas 'a striving toward a "fantastic" goal is a stimulus to amazing feats, heroic work, and bold intentions. This is not the place to enumerate the latter, but it would behoove writers to recognize them precisely as *intentions that become facts before they become reality*' (27, 220–221).

'Our reality is our teacher' (25, 455), Gorky affirmed, despite the fact that 'reality does not make itself visible. But then we are obliged to know more than just two realities – the past, and the present, the one in which we live and take part to some extent. We must also know a third reality – the reality of the future . . . We must somehow include this reality in our everyday lives, we must depict it. Without it we will not understand what the method of socialist realism is' (27, 419).

This 'third reality', however, was not some purely abstract 'dream'. Gorky yearned for a materialized dream. At the same time, this 'reality' is superempirical: even though it consists of certain 'facts', these facts also do 'not make themselves visible'. As Gorky would say elsewhere, 'a fact is not yet the entire truth; it is only the raw material out of which the real truth of art must be smelted and extracted. We must not fry the chicken together with its feathers . . . We must learn to pluck away the insignificant feathers of the fact, we must know how to extract meaning from a fact' (26, 296).

Since it comprised an essential part of the overall political–aesthetic project of Stalinism, Socialist Realism was included in the general system of social functioning. The ideology that not only dominated over the economy but also gave it meaning took shape within Socialist Realism. In this sense, Soviet literature, the quintessence of which was Socialist Realism, was a completely new and unique phenomenon. Its main function amounted not to propaganda, but to the *production of reality through its aestheticization*.

If we try, speculatively, to remove Socialist Realism – novels about enthusiasm for production, poems about joyous labour, films about happy life, songs and paintings about the wealth of the Soviet land, and so on – from the picture of 'socialism', then we are left with nothing that could genuinely be called socialism. Grey workdays, routine daily labour, and an unsettled and oppressive daily life are all that are left. In other words, since a reality like this could be attributed to any other economic system, nothing of socialism would remain in this hypothetical residue. Therefore, it can be concluded that Socialist Realism produced the symbolic values of socialism instead of its reality.

Naturally, art always produces substitutes; it is always a factory of dreams as well (one of its most important social functions). However, these substitutions are always either future-oriented or focused on the past. The particularity of Soviet culture stems from the fact that the here-and-now reality is also subject to substitution. We are dealing here with a specific kind of modality: this is not the future replacing the present, but an attempt to imagine the future as the present. If Futurism spoke about tomorrow, then Socialist Realism lays claim not only to tomorrow (and not even so much to tomorrow!) but also, specifically, to *today*. Everything that Socialist Realism creates already exists and has already taken place. Thus, a radical aesthetic effort (much more radical than in Futurism) is required to make this transformation of the present convincing.

Socialist Realism constantly produces new symbolic capital, namely, *socialism*. Evidently, this was the USSR's only successful product. One can say that *Socialist Realism is the means of producing socialism, the machine for transforming Soviet reality into socialism*. That is why its main function is not propagandistic but rather aesthetic and transformative.

It is commonplace to speak of censorship that did not allow the truth to be written while, at the same time, a huge amount of 'artistic production', considered to be the production of lies, took place. One should keep in mind, however, that this enormous output of images, which occupies the entire Soviet sphere, begins to define not only the political unconscious but also the entire realm of the imaginary. After some years, all these images return as '*truth*' for new generations: people now see the world as *being like this*. Socialist Realism created not 'lies' but *images of socialism* that, through perception, return as *reality* – or, more specifically, as *socialism*.

Whatever Soviet reality was (and it was, above all, a system of personal power, to which collectivization, modernization and terror were all ultimately subordinated), an art was needed to make *this* reality into socialism. It is specifically in art – through Socialist Realism – that Soviet reality is translated and transformed into socialism. In other words, *Socialist Realism is the machine that distils Soviet reality into socialism.* For this reason, it should be considered not only as the production of certain symbols, but also as the production of visual and verbal substitutes for reality. *Socialist Realism describes a world to whose existence it alone bears witness.* And, for this very reason, the function of Socialist Realism in the political–aesthetic project of 'real socialism' consists of filling the space of 'socialism' with images of reality. While derealizing life, Soviet literature created a new, 'socialist' life.

This life had no relationship to the reality. In reality, as Mandelshtam wrote, 'We live, not sensing our own country beneath us,/Ten steps away they dissolve, our speeches.'[11] In the words of Sergei Klychkov, 'In this gloom, in this darkness/It is terrifying to look beyond the door/There time is stirring/Like a beast in its desolate lair.' Anna Akhmatova wrote about this period: 'It was a time when only the dead/smiled, happy in their peace./And Leningrad dangled like a useless appendage/at the side of its prisons./A time when, out of their minds with suffering,/the convicted walked in regiments,/ and the steam whistles sang/their short parting song./Stars of death stood over us/and innocent Russia squirmed/under the bloody boots,/under the wheels of Black Marias.'[12] But the Soviet country was living in an entirely different 'reality.'

Thus, Socialist Realism became the key instrument of political action and an extremely important part of the overall political–aesthetic project and of the entire social apparatus of Stalinism. The influence of this apparatus extended to all facets of life: from the factory to the novel, from the plant to the opera, from the collective farm to the artist's studio. As we have seen, the various Socialist Realist genres contained nothing that was truly socialist. They are unified not by their content (many of them were, in essence, deeply anti-revolutionary), but by an aesthetic. The unity of this aesthetic can be traced back to its underlying function: all of these works are united by their function – the production of socialism. The industrial novel, the poem about the collective farm, the patriotic play, or the historical–revolutionary film – these are all means for the production of the most important and the only end product of the Soviet regime: socialism.

Hence, we can conclude that, if all previous literary movements had produced literature, then in Socialist Realism literature was merely a byproduct of production. The quality of the Socialist Realist product is questionable from an aesthetic point of view because Socialist Realism was not so concerned with producing literature as it was with producing reality itself. This is why Socialist Realism was and remains the only material reality of socialism. Thus, when reading these books today, the reader has the unique (if not the only) opportunity to feel as if he were within Soviet socialism, this product of a radical political–aesthetic experiment that went by the name of Socialist Realism. It is no coincidence that this 'artistic method' aspired to uniqueness: the works it produced are at once inferior as literature and significantly larger than literature.

NOTES

* Translated from Russian by Jenny Kaminer.
1 Günther, Hans, 'Totalitarnoe gosudarstvo kak sintez iskusstv' in *Sotsrealisticheskii kanon* (St Petersburg: Akademicheskii proekt, 2000), p. 12.
2 *Ibid.*, p. 10.
3 See Günther, 'Totalitarnoe gosudarstvo kak sintez iskusstv'; Groys, Boris, *The Total Art of Stalinism: Avant-garde, Aesthetic Dictatorship, and Beyond* (Princeton, NJ: Princeton University Press, 1992).
4 Günther, 'Totalitarnoe gosudarstvo kak sintez iskusstv', p. 13.
5 See Clark, Katerina, *The Soviet Novel: History as Ritual* (Chicago, IL: University of Chicago Press, 1985).
6 Riurikov, Boris, *Literatura i zhizn'* (Moscow: Sovetskii pisatel', 1953), p. 146.
7 See Balina, Marina, Condee, Nancy, and Dobrenko, Evgeny, eds., *Endquote: Sots-Art Literature and Soviet Grand Style* (Evanston, IL: Northwestern University Press, 2000).
8 Quoted in Ellen E. Berry and Anesa Miller-Pogasar, eds., *Re-entering the Sign: Articulating New Russian Culture* (Ann Arbor, MI: University of Michigan Press, 1995), p. 41.
9 Quoted in Brooks, Peter, *The Melodramatic Imagination: Balzac, Henry James, Melodrama, and the Mode of Excess* (New Haven, CT: Yale University Press, 1995), p. 35.
10 Gorky, Maxim, *Sobranie sochinenii v 30 tomakh*, vol. 27 (Moscow: GIKhL, 1954), p. 12. All subsequent references are to this edition, and are indicated in the text by volume and page number in parentheses; emphases are mine.
11 Translation by Scott Horton.
12 Translation by Richard McKane.

FURTHER READING

Clark, Katerina, *The Soviet Novel: History as Ritual* (Chicago, IL: University of Chicago Press, 1985).

Dobrenko, Evgeny, *The Making of the State Reader: Social and Aesthetic Contexts of the Reception of Soviet Literature* (Stanford, CA: Stanford University Press, 1997).

The Making of the State Writer: Social and Aesthetic Origins of Soviet Literary Culture (Stanford, CA: Stanford University Press, 2001).

Political Economy of Socialist Realism (New Haven, CT: Yale University Press, 2007).

Dunham, Vera, *In Stalin's Time: Middleclass Values in Soviet Fiction* (Cambridge: Cambridge University Press, 1976).

Ermolaev, Herman, *Soviet Literary Theories, 1917–1934: The Genesis of Socialist Realism* (Berkeley, CA: University of California Press, 1963).

Golomshtok, Igor, *Totalitarian Art in the Soviet Union, the Third Reich, Fascist Italy and the People's Republic of China* (New York: HarperCollins, 1990).

Groys, Boris, *The Total Art of Stalinism: Avant-garde, Aesthetic Dictatorship, and Beyond* (Princeton, NJ: Princeton University Press, 1992).

Günther, Hans, *Die Verstaatlichung der Literatur: Entstehung und Funktionsweise des sozialistisch-realistischen Kanons in der sowjetischen Literatur der 30er Jahre* (Stuttgart: J.B. Metzler, 1984).

Der sozialistische Übermensch: M. Gor'kij und der Sowjetische Heldenmythos (Stuttgart: Metzler, 1993).

ed., *The Culture of the Stalin Period* (London: Macmillan, 1990).

Günther, Hans and Dobrenko, Evgeny, eds., *Sotsrealisticheskii Kanon* (St Petersburg: Akademicheskii proekt, 2000).

Gutkin, Irina, *The Cultural Origins of the Socialist Realist Aesthetic, 1890–1934* (Evanston, IL: Northwestern University Press, 1999).

Lahusen, Thomas, *How Life Writes the Book: Real Socialism and Socialist Realism in Stalin's Russia* (Ithaca, NY: Cornell University Press, 1997).

Lahusen, Thomas and Dobrenko, Evgeny, eds., *Socialist Realism without Shores* (Durham, NC: Duke University Press, 1997).

Papernyi, Vladimir, *Kul'tura Dva* (Moscow: Novoe Literaturnoe Obozrenie, 2006).

7

STEPHANIE SANDLER

Poetry after 1930

The lasting prestige of twentieth-century Russian poetry flows from those poets who endured the Stalin years with honour and integrity. Poets are thought to have performed hidden acts of heroism when they took the simple risk of composing verse. Some famous images of the 1930s come from these poems, including the woman who whispers with blue lips in 'Requiem' by Anna Akhmatova (1889–1966). She described the internal exile of Osip Mandelshtam (1891–1938) as a time when fear and the muse stood guard. His poems, and the memoirs of his widow, Nadezhda Mandelshtam, made him the emblematic poet of Russia's modern time of troubles.

Life for Russia's poets was more complex than these dramatic images suggest. The dangerous 1930s were also an era for cultural negotiation and the sheer work of imagining a readership. Both efforts continued as the Soviet Union evolved, and as it collapsed in the 1980s. The flourishing of post-Soviet poetry merits separate treatment, but most contemporary poets came of age in the late Soviet period, so it makes sense to see these decades as a strangely unified epoch, with several persistent features. Indeed the late Mikhail Gasparov argued that rhythmic innovations and the presence of semantic aureoles for metrical patterns are surprisingly constant across the many decades.[1]

How readers were imagined early in the Soviet period has been well studied by Evgeny Dobrenko. He traces the multiple points of entry that the state-controlled system offered those seeking everything from entertainment to reassurance at their status as Soviet citizens.[2] Poets who participated in tasks of identity formation for the new citizen produced poems in praise of Stalin and odes extolling the heroic Soviet people during the Second World War. These poets were in many cases as sincere as marginalized poets, and the quality was not always inferior. The forging of national identity in a time of war could also lead to extraordinary poems of individual non-conformity, as in Mandelshtam's 1937 'Lines on the Unknown Soldier' or the poems of daily life written by Boris Slutsky (1919–1986). Such poems did not immediately reach their readers, however, and long delays in reception often shaped writers' and readers' experiences.

The poet faces the state

Poets who had found ways to adapt to Soviet rule in the 1920s faced staggering new challenges as Stalinism consolidated its hold on all public institutions in the 1930s.[3] The emergence of the official doctrine of Socialist Realism clarified some expectations, but complicated others: creators of narrative poetry were urged to pursue plots of successful integration into the new socialist order, and the requirements for lyric poetry were hotly debated. Some, including Boris Pasternak (1890–1960), wrote about the individual's merging with the collective will in simpler words and forms so as to meet the needs of the newly literate public. Critics have traced the 'poet's internal change triggered by outside pressure' in such poems as 'The Waves' (1931), where Pasternak says to his city, Moscow, 'I will accept you like a harness'.[4] For the poet who was famously compared to both an Arabian horse and its rider, this may seem a gesture of abject submission. Yet Pasternak retained sufficient independence to later write *Doctor Zhivago* (1958), with its ethos of Christian self-sacrifice.

Mandelshtam chose a more defiant path than Pasternak's search for accommodation and public recognition. Mandelshtam declared, 'And I am not one to draw. I do not sing. I do not play with a black-voiced bow,' as if renouncing public performance. Yet he also said that he had walked 'deeply into a deafened era', and he called on the air to witness his creative acts.[5] As Nancy Pollak has persuasively shown, the Christian principles Pasternak would later embrace contrasted with Mandelshtam's increasing identification with the fate of the Jewish people (neither practised, but both poets had been born Jews).[6]

Although cast as a pariah by the authorities, Anna Akhmatova maintained an identity as the voice of her people. (As Vladimir Kornilov [b. 1928] was to write much later, 'Motherland and state/Are not the same thing').[7] She steadfastly recorded the suffering and silence of others, and her own losses as well, often in code. Few poems attained the iconic status of 'Requiem' (1936–1940), with its terse recreation of night-time arrests, the bereft madness of women left behind. The poem's changing metrical schemes and quick thematic movement contributed to its success in recreating the forcible silence of the Stalin Terror. Some have come to see Akhmatova in a less flattering light in recent years, even suggesting a peculiar mirroring of authoritarianism in her acts of self-creation.[8] But she retained considerable admiration among Russian intellectuals, as was reaffirmed when 'Requiem' was first publicly recited in Leningrad in 1987 by Mikhail Kozakov, and when her centenary was celebrated in 1989. Her example of truth-telling, psychological firmness, and verbal precision has shaped the ethos of later poets, Oleg Chukhontsev (b. 1938) among them; her stoicism and conservative form finds a worthy successor in Mikhail Aizenberg (b. 1948) who, like Akhmatova, is also a keen literary critic.

A harsher stance toward the state was taken up by a quite different woman poet, Anna Barkova (1901–1976). Enthusiastic about the Revolution, Barkova grew as profoundly disenchanted as better-known Modernist poets. She was arrested and served out several long terms in the labour camps, where the severity of her circumstances earned her comparison to the long-suffering Varlam Shalamov (1907–1982). Barkova had written of firebrand revolutionary heroines in the 1920s, and her later work was marked by a zeal for cold realism and stony resilience. As a lesbian, she fitted poorly into the Stalinist-era artificial family cosiness, and her lyric heroine became something of a Holy Fool. The publication of Barkova's later work was another significant cultural event during *perestroika*, and the legacy of her stoical resistance persists. It was echoed in the fierce protest against the Soviet invasion of Czechoslovakia (1968) by the Moscow poet Natalia Gorbanevskaia (b. 1936), and Barkova's poetic persona as misfit inspired the later Leningrad poet Elena Shvarts (1948–2010).

Shvarts was among the poets who created a lively poetic underground in the 1970s, and this activity constituted a new chapter in the relations of poet and state. These poets reacted against the public showmanship of Evgenii Evtushenko (b. 1933) and Andrei Voznesensky (b. 1933), who performed before stadiums full of youths in the 1960s. But the 1970s underground poets were each others' small audiences, and their works were circulated in the same *samizdat*-like atmosphere that defined the dissident movement; indeed, their gatherings were subject to surveillance and occasional restriction. Some of these poets were visual artists and creators of happenings; among the best performers and instigators in Moscow was Nina Iskrenko (1951–1995), who broke taboos against explicit mention of women's bodily functions and desires. Officials were most likely to clamp down on events that attracted a public following, like the bulldozing of an art market in the Moscow suburbs in 1974. Poets increasingly sought larger public hearings, as permissions were gained for new anthologies and gathering places. Glasnost´ opened new outlets for publication and public reading, embracing young poets in the provinces and the capitals, and a huge backlog of works that had long been suppressed.

In post-Soviet Russia, the problem of the poet and the state would seem irrelevant: censorship has seemingly disappeared. The rise of the internet, new small presses, commercial venues for poetry readings, and the removal of travel restrictions have enriched connections between poets and their readers. Some say that there are now more poets than readers, but the freedom is invaluable, and it has allowed poets who see remnants of tyrannical rule in the post-Soviet state to speak their mind openly. If integrity is a lasting mark of twentieth-century Russian poetry, then this political courage remains significant. The anguished protest at violence in the Caucasus found in the work of Sergei Stratanovsky (b. 1937) stands out. Some poets have largely devoted themselves to the public discourse of politics. Lev Rubinshtein (b. 1947) is a prime example; others, including Tatiana Shcherbina (b. 1954), are outspoken voices on their blogs and on other widely read web sites.

War and historical catastrophe

Mandelshtam's 'Lines on an Unknown Soldier' stands as the major statement against war's violence in twentieth-century Russian poetry. A poem that recollects the appalling violence and losses of the First World War, 'Lines' also eerily foresees a coming conflict, and places Mandelshtam's generation squarely between these two experiences of human horror. Long unpublished, this poem invokes both a stable cosmic order and a chaotic human experience of death; like Moses speaking to an angry God, ready to destroy the Israelites for their idolatry, 'Lines' asks how humanity can have come to such an era of wholesale destruction. The poem's music is its salvation: the anapaest rhythm and frequent dactylic rhymes make it mesmerizingly intense.

The public face of wartime patriotism dominated official poetry during and after the Second World War. Just as there were dozens of poets willing to glorify the state or its leader, so there were those who wrote patriotic exhortations. Lasting value can be seen in poems by Akhmatova, Slutsky, Boris Chichibabin (1923–1994), and many others.[9] Slutsky was the only major poet who saw front-line service and survived, but he maintains an unusually even and dispassionate tone, even in recording terrible suffering or ethically indefensible crimes. Along with Konstantin Simonov (1915–1979) and Alexander Tvardovsky (1910–1971), Slutsky, Mikhail Kulchitsky (1918–1942), and David Samoilov (1920–1990) were perhaps the best-known poets of the wartime generation. Samoilov's poem 'The Forties' (1961) merged the themes of wartime losses and Stalin's Terror. Slutsky often embedded multiple points of view into his poems, and he wrote for a desk drawer that was found brimming with remarkable work at his death. A powerful theme in this work is the grieving of widows who, as he put it, continued to fight every night long after the war had ended.[10] Other poems convey the lives of soldiers, most famously in Tvardovsky's *Vasily Terkin* (1941–1945), and, in a poem that looks ahead to postwar calm, 'The Sky', by Kornilov (1931).[11] Simonov's tremendously popular 'Wait for Me' (1941) was the romantic opposite of these accounts of war's dailiness: it exhorts the beloved to be faithful and steadfast, for her love can bring her soldier home alive.

The 900-day Blockade of Leningrad proved a powerful subject for poetry, including the poems by Olga Berggolts (1910–1975) broadcast on the radio to bolster the courage of Soviet citizens. Berggolts' poems echo the heroic rhetoric of official writings, although her experience of imprisonment (pregnant, she was savagely beaten, and her child died) in 1938 and the death of her husband from starvation underlay her work with deep personal tragedy and, particularly in poems published only later, considerable aesthetic and political complexity. The poems of Natalia Krandievskaia-Tolstaia (1888–1966), another Blockade survivor, also provide terrible, evocative vignettes of daily life during the siege, with images of corpses frozen in the streets and rats living brazenly in communal kitchens.

The topic of war and loss proved important for later poets as well, some of whom insisted on the freedom to write about aspects of the war that had been passed over in silence. Shvarts, for example, evoked cannibalism in her 'Portrait of the Blockade' (1999). Any representation of the war's survivors as callous or unethical would have been impermissible earlier. Other poems broke taboos in the 1960s, including the murders and persecution of Jews and members of other minority groups, famously in Evgenii Evtushenko's 'Babii Iar' (1961). It fell principally to prose writers to fill in the documentary record of this period of historical catastrophe, but poetry could indirectly conjure up the sense of unnamed fears and enforced silences, as in Mandelshtam's 1930s poems and the later work of Akhmatova, for example, her 'Northern Elegies'. Mandelshtam's 'Voronezh Notebooks', published only much later, record with a fractured lyric subjectivity the threatened sense of personhood that was widespread during the Terror. In one poem, he imagines a future Mandelshtam Street, only to correct himself – it is not a street, but a pit; in another, he locates himself in a spider-web of light, and in still another he lies in his grave, lips still moving.[12] These sharp images appear fleetingly in the complex late poems, which are as filled with literary quotations and echoes as the earlier work; their power comes from the poet's enduring ability to draw deeply on the cultural tradition in formally beautiful poems of doom.

Poets' freedom after the Stalin period to think about Russia's catastrophic history saw the emergence of poems that assess larger patterns of violence and suffering. Akhmatova's late work 'Poem Without a Hero' (1940–1962) created a personal model for such retrospective work, with its private, often coded recollections. Although written about pre-Revolutionary Russia, the poem is infused with the emotions of a poet who had guiltily survived Terror, war, and postwar recriminations. Viktor Krivulin (1944–2001), a later Leningrad poet, wrote powerfully of Soviet citizens' shared history of trauma, including such poems as 'The Wine of Archaisms' (1973) and 'At the Public Festival' (2001). Krivulin's poetry is better known for employing the material of myth and religion. Indeed, some of the most powerful writing against the grain of official, jubilant public history has come from poets who draw on religious thinking and experience – for example, Shvarts, or Iurii Kublanovsky (b. 1947). Shvarts' longer lyric poems often layer historical eras, as in 'Kindergarten Thirty Years On', where motifs of Petrine revolution, Avvakum's seventeenth-century revolt, the 1905 workers' uprising, and the Blockade all appear.

Historical material also informed the work of poets describing life during the Cold War and the era of Stagnation, as the Brezhnev years came to be known. The Moscow Conceptualists' transformation of the everyday language of Soviet slogans and popular discontent in effect became a historical record of these years. Such poems – not all by Moscow Conceptualists, to be sure – as Dmitrii Prigov's (1940–2007) 'Screaming Cantata (Who Killed Stalin)', Sergei Gandlevsky's (b. 1952) 'There's our street, let's say –', Sergei Stratanovsky's (b. 1944) 'A Leningrad Stairwell', and Rubinshtein's 'A Little Night Music' displayed what Jed Rasula, writing of American poetry, called a 'documentary propensity'.[13] At times, unofficial poets put historical themes to work parodying the official language that had been used to describe the past, as in Prigov's 'Kulikovo' and 'The Year 1937', and in 'When Lenin Was a Little Boy' by Timur Kibirov (b. 1955). These poems can be difficult to capture in translation, so dependent are they on Soviet jargon, but the contribution of these prolific poets (especially Prigov and Kibirov) has been massive and their performances very popular. Their importance can be measured by the enormous outpouring of grief at Prigov's death in 2007. The legacy of poetry as public performance endures, particularly in the era of YouTube and the internet more broadly.[14]

Poems of mind, spirit, body

The poetry of private experiences suffered from overscrutiny and public attack during the Soviet period and, for quite different reasons, during the years of *glasnost'* and post-Soviet reconstruction. Yet such lyrics thrived over these decades, suggesting both the remarkable resilience of the form and the deep psychological demand to which lyric responds. Few poets demonstrated a keener awareness of the pressures to write of inner experience than Pasternak. In a long poem of the 1920s, *The Lofty Malady*, he forthrightly weighed the expressive benefits of lyrical speech against the responsibilities of listening to 'the music of the revolution' (as Blok put it). His writing demonstrated as well the many pressures against taking up the lyre. The choice of longer poetic forms was eminently logical; in fact, poets through the twentieth century tried to measure up to some notion of larger form. The task was difficult – the poems rarely succeeded – and Pasternak's eventual solution was to append the lyric poems Iurii Zhivago 'writes' to the large narrative that tells his story.

Pasternak's approach was to represent interiority as it was formed by the pressures of historical experience – this is the theoretical model developed by Lidiia Ginzburg.[15] Other poets sought to represent the process of identity formation as if from within, and Pasternak wrote in this way particularly in his last volume, *When the Skies Clear* (1956). Such poems often allegorize the creative process, as in Leonid Martynov's (1905–1980) 'Sunflower' (1932) or Akhmatova's poems about shattered identity.[16] Émigré poets are treated separately in this volume, but one should not forget that such representations of selfhood were important to poets who left Russia, Marina Tsvetaeva (1892–1941) among them. She and Mandelshtam were key figures for Arsenii Tarkovsky (1907–1989), who especially inherited the Acmeist insistence on purity of language and a love for classical themes. Tarkovsky may now be better known as the father of the film-maker Andrei Tarkovsky; from the 1950s onward, he exemplified a preservation of poetic ideals and public restraint (although he signed the letter of protest against the 1965 trial of Siniavsky and Daniel, which was a major act of public dissent). His poems celebrate natural phenomena and life itself, as in the splendid lyric 'Life, Life' (he reads this poem, along with three others, in the film *The Mirror*). In the lyrics' receptivity to the subtleties of the natural world, and in the poems' allegory of poetic creation as a similar form of aesthetic absorption, they recall early Pasternak, whose legacy Tarkovsky also carried on.

Among poets in Tarkovsky's generation and those slightly younger, Semen Lipkin (1911–2003) and Inna Lisnianskaia (b. 1928) stand out for their roles in the *Metropol* affair (1979), an independently assembled almanac of writings that aroused a scandal and caused a number of its participants to resign from the Writers' Union. Lipkin and Lisnianskaia, who lived as husband and wife for decades, crafted highly individualistic lyric voices, and both became enduring figures in the intelligentsia. Lipkin's superb artistry and original formulations produced poems of forthright beauty, as in the lines that open 'In the Desert': 'Like wanderers in elevated meekness,/We move in the fourth dimension.'[17] Lisnianskaia's lyric poems, many of them compactly introspective, explore the dimensions of subjectivity and memory. She employs mirror imagery in some poems, and the theme of loss weaves throughout her work, as in her reprisal of Elizabeth Bishop's 'One Art', which begins 'I rejoice when I lose things' and ends 'I've lost my ringing voice, And nests of words, and their soaring order' (1983).[18] As with Akhmatova, for whom loss was a crucial theme, Lisnianskaia became a premier practitioner of the modern elegy. Her decades of productivity and growth remind one of such long-lived poets as the Americans Robert Creeley and Barbara Guest, or the visual poet Elizaveta Mnatsakanova (b. 1922). Unlike them, however, Lisnianskaia's is not an experimental or radical voice in terms of form. Using traditional meters and measured expression, she has simply burrowed deeper into the topics that have long sustained lyric poetry.

One of Lisnianskaia's great themes and metaphors is illness, which bears special mention among lyric topics. Sickness and disease elicit allegorical comparisons to the failing body of the state and, conversely, dig into individual experience of physical integrity and vulnerability. Pasternak set this topic on its course, largely in poems written earlier in his career, for example those collected under the title 'The Malady'. A study of Pasternak's poetry in the 1920s has shown persuasively that the topic of hysteria was closely tied to his metaphors of poetic creation.[19] Maladies of both psyche and body (hysteria being the illness that links the two) are experienced by the lyrical heroes of some of the greatest poems of these decades, including Mandelshtam's descriptions of suffocation ('Oh the horizon steals my breath', 1937), swollen glands ('Leningrad', 1930), or repudiated migraine ('No, it's not migraine', 1935).[20] Diseases of spirit and being that infected survivors and victims found expression in lyric poetry that referred obliquely to the body's sufferings, as in these poems by Mandelshtam, in Lisnianskaia's cycle 'In the Hospital for Face Wounds' (1984), and in Bella Akhmadulina's (b. 1937) poem 'Fever'.

A poet who explored the topic of mental distress early in his extraordinary career (largely discussed elsewhere in this volume) was Joseph Brodsky (1940–1996), in the long poem 'Gorbunov and Gorchakov' (1968), set in a mental hospital.[21] Brodsky himself had been declared to display the traits of a psychopath at his trial for parasitism in 1964. Later poets with far deeper experience of mental illness would include this theme in their work, among them the Leningrad poet Vasilii Filippov (b. 1955), who has lived in a mental hospital for many years. Mental illness as interruption in one's life also appears as a theme in the work of other poets, including Olga Sedakova (b. 1949). Compare the terse expressiveness of her lyric poem 'In the Psych Ward' (1979–1983), or the longer lyric 'The Malady' (1978), which opens with a headache so powerful that it is alive. Illness teaches what other experiences cannot, writes the poet. Its lessons include a capacity to see the maladies of the culture in which the poet resides.

The enduring natural world

Lyric poets have long sought refuge from social ills in the natural world. Again, modernist poets were important models, especially Pasternak, although many poets reach back as well to the Romantic pantheism of Fedor Tiutchev or the simple diction and clear emotions of Pushkin. An unusual and powerful figure is Nikolai Zabolotsky (1903–1958), initially a member of the Oberiuty, who then seemed destined to become a mainstream Soviet poet, particularly in his poems in praise of agriculture. Zabolotsky's penal servitude, as well as his profound connections to peasant mentality and a religious sensibility, changed his later work. The purity of expression in such poems as 'A Lake in the Forest' (1938) impressed later poets. Sedakova praised his integrity and honesty of expression, noting that the compassion with which the poet turned to nature was a cover for a sense of 'shared orphanhood and sadness', and of solitude in the world.[22]

Many poets chose still simpler language, perhaps carried to extreme in the primitivism of Kseniia Nekrasova (1912–58). Minimalism distinguishes the work of Gennadii Aigi (1934–2006), famous in the West before his poetry was much available in Russia. After his earliest poetic output in his native Chuvash and translations, Aigi began to compose poems in Russian as well. His poems preserve Chuvash folk beliefs and absorb the influences of French poetry, which he had translated, and show as well the impact of Oberiuty minimalism. The result is an unusual body of work characterized by an intense formal compression and linguistic barrenness. His subject matter is frequently the simplest of natural events – a snowfall, a moving stream of water – imbued with an intense affirmation of human value and spirit, as in these lines from a poem dedicated to Pasternak, 'Here' (1958):

> and life had disappeared into itself like a road into the forest
> and a word became a hieroglyph
> to me, the word 'here'
> and it signified both earth and sky
> and what was in shadow
> and what we see eye-to-eye
> and what we cannot share in verse[23]

As an aside one might note that Aigi's preference for unpunctuated and uncapitalized lines has found many successors in contemporary poetry, poets as different as Kirill Medvedev (b. 1975), Andrei Sen-Senkov (b. 1968), and Anna Glazova (b. 1973), not all of whom would cite Aigi as a model, to be sure.

Mikhail Eremin (b. 1937) writes with more suspicion of the recompense of the natural world. The rapid urbanization and indifferent destruction of natural environments that accompanied the Soviet Union's rush to industrialization rendered the pastoral mode increasingly implausible. Eremin creates extraordinary tension in his poems of nature, holding fast to a single format, the eight-line lyric. But his language and imagery know no bounds, with splendidly opaque juxtapositions and transitions on vivid display, as in this poem from 1957:

> Polyhedral kernels of wisdom,
> Primordial form of space.
> All-Russian holiness, hodgepodge
> And the herony tang of swampland
> To be searched out in autumnal writing,
> Where the slush has left its traces,
> Where leaves, like the skirts of an onion
> Conceal tears in their creases.[24]

Traces of Zabolotsky's earthy images touch this poem (his name, in fact, is echoed in the swampland of l. 4, 'boloto' in Russian), as do familiar references to the act of writing, compared to slushy traces on an autumn landscape.

The complexity of Eremin's metaphors finds an apt counterpart in the rich metonymies of Ivan Zhdanov (b. 1948). His poems may take their subjects from mythology or urban spaces. As in Zabolotsky's work, Zhdanov's shows his origins in a provincial farming region (Altai). Poems like 'Hills' and 'Portrait of My Father' are splendidly visual in a dream-like, emotionally logical way. The result is an all-encompassing fantasy of the sights and sounds of the natural and agricultural worlds.

Poems of love

The legacy of Akhmatova's love poetry was as intimidating as it was inspiring for subsequent poets, but Akhmatova proclaimed that the best love poem of the twentieth century had been written by Mariia Petrovykh (1908–1979): 'Make a time to meet me' (1953). In its intensity of imprecation, this poem uses the usual rhetorical situation of love poetry, separation from the beloved, to recreate the passion of presence. Some poets preferred the pleasures of intimacy to evocations of absence, as in the poems of the 1930s by the lesbian poet Sofiia Parnok (1885–1933). First published by Sofiia Poliakova in 1979, these poems evoke the experience of aging alongside frank longings. Parnok's was not an entirely isolated lesbian voice: she may have read Barkova's early poems, for example, 'Sappho' (1922), and she clearly knew Sappho's own work. The love lyrics of lesbian poetry vanquish the gender barrier that separates poet and beloved in standard heterosexual love poetry. Akhmatova's innovative contribution lay in the strength she gave to the voice of the speaking woman poet. Her contemporary Tsvetaeva, who left one remarkable cycle of lesbian lyrics, 'The Girlfriend' (1916), was similarly undaunted by the tradition that associated erotic power with male power, also seen in her 'Attempt at Jealousy' (1924).

Many male poets continued to write love poems in the twentieth century. Leonid Aronzon (1939–1970) was highly regarded for his love poetry, which has a light touch and a fine sense of whimsy. More self-consciously substantial are the dozens of poems Joseph Brodsky dedicated to 'M. B.' (Marina Basmanova), beginning in the 1960s; they stand apart for their elliptical evocations of the entire cultural tradition of love poetry. Many of Brodsky's poems engage in philosophical speculation on the nature of human intimacy, and they indulge psychological theories about love's failures. Brodsky's cycle 'Twenty Sonnets to Maria Stuart' (1974) had perhaps the greatest resonance among later poets, producing three poems that were read at a 2008 evening in his memory in Moscow: 'Poems to Maria S.' (1994) by Elena Fanailova (b. 1962); 'Twenty Sonnets to M.' (2001) by Mariia Stepanova (b. 1972); and 'Twenty Sonnets to Sasha Zapoeva' (1995) by Timur Kibirov. Stepanova's poem is dedicated to her mother (a clever reassignment of Brodsky's letter 'M' to 'mama'), and Kibirov's are to his newborn daughter, moving the love lyric into the setting of family romance, while maintaining the usual feminine addressee. Fanailova prosaically addresses 'Maria, wife of the poet B., Nobel laureate' and Mary Queen of Scots, also Brodsky's addressee. She is comfortable with earthy vulgarity, as was Brodsky himself (more than one Brodsky poem to 'M. B.' refers casually to an erection).

One could argue that these three post-Brodsky poems are quite the opposite of love poems: not words addressed to the beloved so much as riffs on the theme of love, penned self-consciously in an age where sentiment is largely suspect. Successful love poets were rare late in the twentieth century. Tatiana Bek (1949–2005) would surely be among the exceptions. Although Bek once said that her shoulders were shaped for basketball, not for

Akhmatova's famous shawl, her love poems were built on Akhmatova's foundation, often sneaking into the territory of conflict and betrayal. Other poets have sought sharper breaks with the models of the past, among them Vera Pavlova (b. 1963). Her brief, colloquial poems play against the expectations of feminine speech and mix lyrical longings with prosaic assertions. In a more maximalist vein, Mnatsakanova created a strong sequence of incantatory lyrics to the beloved in her *Das Hohelied*, her Song of Songs.[25] Mnatsakanova's imperatives resemble those of Petrovykh, but with greater sound complexity and musical elaboration. She has also produced a range of richly illustrated albums. Mnatsakanova writes on the back cover of one album, in English, 'This is a book of permanent love. This is a permanent book.'[26] The transposition of the adjective is typical of her poetics, as is the urgent assertion that love, like poetry, endures against all encroachments.

Faith, belief, religious fantasies

Such faith in the power of love finds its counterpart in religious faith which, for all the intense prohibition during the Soviet period, endured as a theme in poetry across the decades, in both work published much later, like that of Zinaida Mirkina (b. 1926), and in poems that eventually grew quite famous, like Pasternak's *Zhivago* sequence. But it was poets fated to obscurity who produced the most unusual poetry of religious experience, including Daniil Andreev (1906–1959), whose *Rose of the World* fantasized a cosmic spirituality that envelops the material world. Also important is Vera Merkureva (1876–1943), who followed the intense, aberrant spirituality of the Symbolist Viacheslav Ivanov in poems that show a remarkable range of formal experimentation. She wrote of the self-abnegation that history seemed to press upon Russia. Her image of the world was less Orthodox than pantheistic, closer to the poetry of Shelley, whom she had translated. Like Mirkina's, Merkureva's later poetry became known only in the 1980s.

Religious themes were abundant in the underground poetry of the 1960s and 1970s, most importantly in the work of such Leningrad poets as Krivulin and Stratanovsky. Shvarts became the best-known Leningrad poet, and she continued to write poems and prose for nearly four decades. Her novel-length poetic sequence on the *The Works and Days of Lavinia, Nun of the Order of the Circumcision of the Heart* (1987) imagines women's religious and demonic visions. Shvarts' lyrics can invoke the ecstatic nature of religious experience as an analogue for other forms of rapture. A poet of greater restraint (and an admirer of Shvarts' poetry) is Olga Sedakova, who has re-imagined saints' lives and Biblical stories, including that of the Prodigal Son.

Sedakova can represent the universe in the tiniest of images (in one poem, a lentil), or an entire cosmic order in a small natural scene:

> The wild dogrose
>   walks by like a grim-faced gardener, knowing no fear,
> with a crimson rose,
>   compassion's concealed wound, under his savage shirt.[27]

How a climbing, flowering plant might move with the grim insight of one who tends this garden of Eden is a typical mystery for Sedakova's poetry, where compassion and injury are portrayed equally. With erudition and ease, Sedakova builds her poems on the foundations of the Russian tradition, as in her reprisal of Lermontov's, Pasternak's, and Zabolotsky's ballad structure in 'The Ballad of Continuing', or in her re-working of the folk–religious song tradition in 'Old Songs' (1980–1981).

Soviet anti-Semitism, among its other legacies, discouraged poets from treating Jewish themes, but some poets did so anyway. Slutsky sometimes told tales of a community's suffering and near disappearance, and his poems abound in Biblical references. Ian Satunovsky (1913–82) and Genrikh Sapgir (1928–99) also explored the meanings of Soviet Jewish identity. Sapgir is rightly admired for his transpositions of the Psalms, which effectively bring Yiddish phrases into the Russian lines. Satunovsky and Sapgir were members of the Lianozovo poetry group in a Moscow suburb, and their extensive poetic legacies touch on many other themes. Sapgir was admired for his light touch, and both poets worked as children's writers. Others turned to the Holocaust and the larger identity of Jews as outcasts in their poems – for example, Slutsky and Lipkin. In the post-Soviet period, most notable is the Odessa psychologist and poet Boris Khersonsky (b. 1950), whose *Family Archive* (2006) weaves an indirect history of Jewish experience in the Pale of Settlement. In its characters and plots, the volume is more like an epic than like lyric poetry (and thus participates in a strong trend in contemporary poetry, that of a new epic mode, exemplified also by the work of Fedor Svarovsky [b. 1971]). The prayers that punctuate *Family Archive* are especially remarkable as Russian settings of familiar Hebrew chants. One can anticipate considerable future work on Jewish themes, particularly from the substantial contingent of Russian poets now living in Israel, including Alexander Barash (b. 1960), Elena Ignatova (b. 1947), Gali-Dana Zinger (b. 1962), and Mikhail Grobman (b. 1939). Also significant among emigrants to Israel, but now deceased, are Mikhail Gendelev (1950–2009) and Anna Gorenko (1972–1999). Jewish themes by no means dominate the work of any of these poets, and Grobman is better known as an avant-garde visual artist. Life in Israel in part has meant that these poets record the political and cultural difficulties of living in a state at war. On this topic, the work of Aleksandra Petrova (b. 1964) is also quite striking, including the poems in *Residence Permit* (2000), although she has moved to Rome, a city whose myths and realities permeate her poetry.

Sites, locations, communities of poets

The mention of poets living in Israel and Rome brings up an aspect of twentieth-century Russian poets' experience that deserves special mention, the diaspora that has increasingly defined the cultural scene since the 1970s. Among the significant poets who chose emigration from the Soviet Union, apart from Brodsky, were Dmitrii Bobyshev (b. 1936), Lev Losev (1937–2009), Aleksei Tsvetkov (b. 1947), and Vladimir Gandelsman (b. 1948), Kublanovsky, Gorbanevskaia, and Mnatsakanova. Their departures were orchestrated by the Soviet Union's last attempts to manage intellectual ferment during the Thaw and its aftermath. Significant public trials of dissidents were meant to send messages of control and limitation, as were such public acts of forced exile as the stripping of citizenship from Mstislav Rostropovich and Galina Vishnevskaia (1978). The poets who left in the 1970s and early 1980s were cut off from families they had left behind, but after the collapse of the Soviet Union, poets and a good many others remained abroad out of choice. They maintained strong ties and in many cases spent long periods of time in Russia. Others left as the Soviet Union collapsed, in several cases after years of internal dissidence: Sergei Magid (b. 1947), Katia Kapovich (b. 1960), and Nika Skandiaka (b. 1978). Aleksei Parshchikov (1954–2009) and later Mikhail Gronas (b. 1970), Anna Glazova (b. 1973), and Polina Barskova (b. 1976) sought education abroad and found new homes. Some poets have created patterns of travel defined by affinities for a place or a people, as in Shcherbina's regular trips to France. Their access to an audience in Russia is undiminished, in fact a Moscow publishing series, Diaspora, presents their work regularly, as do major journals on-line and in print. The vast internet site *Literaturnaia karta* maps the many locales in which Russian poets now live. Moscow and Petersburg remain important centres for literary gatherings, book celebrations, and ever-increasing prize announcements, but provincial Russian cities and many European and American cities have sizable Russian-speaking populations, and can gather respectable audiences for local poets, poetry festivals, and visiting poets. The poetry itself has drawn upon this presence of new venues and changing readerships as an occasional theme, particularly in the way words from various languages are casually dropped into the Russian lines as signs of cosmopolitan comfort. The bitter air of exile, so much a theme for the poets who fled post-Revolutionary Russia earlier in the twentieth century, seems a distant cultural memory.

Translations, comparisons, connections

The large number of poets who travelled abroad extensively or left Russia has meant that the entire poetic tradition has become more open to registering the effects of other languages and other national traditions. That last is nothing new: Mandelshtam's absorption of Dante and Tsvetaeva's devotion to French, German, and Czech cultures are well known. In the Soviet period, poets turned to translation work to survive the long years when their original poetry could not be published. Much of this work involved translations from the languages of the various Soviet Republics. Many poets felt as if they were performing alienated labour, but some translations became justly famous, like Pasternak's Shakespeare. Among the excellent poet-translators, Sedakova stands out for the range of her linguistic and cultural skills (she has translated St Francis, Rilke, Celan, Dickinson, Pound, Eliot, Mallarmé, and Claudel, among others). Sedakova has said that she translated poems she wishes she had written herself, casting the work of translation as a wish to expand one's own skills as a poet. Sedakova's openness to a wide range of linguistic influences may be greater because of her knowledge of many languages, and some others have considerable facility in moving between cultures. Arkadii Dragomoshchenko (b. 1946) and the American poet Lyn Hejinian developed a strong relationship as each other's mutual translators, and Dragomoshchenko and the Moscow poet Vladimir Aristov (b. 1950) have now brought John Ashbery and Michael Palmer into Russian as well. Alexander Skidan (b. 1965) has translated Susan Howe, among others. A poet whose work shows rich integration of foreign words into his poetry is Tsvetkov, who has included self-translated poems in recent books and written poems like 'kennedy kennedy king with sundry other' (2006) that mark his verbal encounter with American culture.[28] Tsvetkov has also translated some of his poems into English.

How foreign cultures are integrated into Russian poetic experience remains a rich and telling process. During the Stalin years and the Cold War, the cultural discourse of the Soviet Union was organized around forms of separation and difference. If a non-Russian cultural influence was countenanced, it was that of nations that the Russian and subsequently Soviet state had colonized, and Western European and American cultures were construed as ideologically backward. That discourse of suspicion weakened during the Second World War, but one has only to recall how those returning to the Soviet Union, even from foreign captivity, were treated to see how much the foreign remained suspect. The effect on the counter-culture, especially during and after the Thaw, was to make the foreign all the more fascinating, and that produced the kind of openness that led to poets learning Polish, as Brodsky and Gorbanevskaia did, so that they could read the many foreign poets available in Polish translation.

Poetry has brought down aesthetic borders as well, to good effect. The exalted position of the poet may have lost some of its glamour in the post-Soviet era, but seeing poetry as one among many aesthetic enterprises has been quite salutary. The boundary between poetry and music has perhaps always been a permeable membrane, with poems offering the words that become songs, and poetry accepting into its repertoire the rhythmic innovations of musical composition (Zhdanov's 'Jazz-Improvisation', or Brodsky's poem 'In Memory of Clifford Brown', for example). There are several poets whose rich knowledge of music affects their style of performance and much of their work, including Pavlova, Sedakova, and of course Prigov. Also professionally trained in music history and performance is Mnatsakanova. Her best-known poem, *Requiem in the Lazaretto of Innocent Sisters*, draws on musical polyphony as well as the unusual form of the passacaglia.[29] Mnatsakanova is unusual as a poet of sound because she is equally committed to visual poetry. Other major visual poets include Anna Alchuk (1955–2008), Ry Nikonova (b. 1942), and Sergei Sigei (b. 1947); the trend generally shows the long-lasting impact of the visual experiments of the Russian futurists as well as the influence of visual poetry that has long flourished in France and in the United States. The futurist legacy is also seen in the work of poet and theoretician Sergei Biriukov (b. 1950), whose Academy of Zaum and far-reaching prose essays recall the fantastic, compelling schemes of Velimir Khlebnikov.

A different integration of music with poetry appeared in the work of the guitar poets, who flourished beginning in the 1960s and included Alexander Galich (1918–1977), Bulat Okudzhava (1924–1997), and the most genuinely popular poet of all time in Russia, Vladimir Vysotsky (1938–1980). Cinema has also exerted a profound effect on poetry, providing it both with thematic motifs and with the example of montage as a structuring principle; the work of Petrova, Fanailova, and Mara Malanova (b. 1970) is exemplary here.

Conclusion

This chapter has unfolded thematically, offering an account of many different poems and poets across the decades. By seeing these many decades as a single era, it has implicitly challenged a historical narrative of progress from the (totalitarian) Soviet to the (market-economy and politically free) post-Soviet eras. Poetry abounds in material that demonstrates and often thematizes this more complex historical dynamism.

The evolution of poetic trends over these decades has its own history, which this chapter has not discussed. How poetic groupings have formed or been imagined is useful interpretive work by critics, and the conditions of writing and reading as they have changed across the decades are thus far little studied (though excellent work on specific topics, like Moscow Conceptualism and the Leningrad underground, exists). One could argue that the poetic practices of each generation have opened new possibilities for their successors, even when poets looked to distinguish themselves sharply from their predecessors. Much of the groundwork for the post-Soviet era was laid in the 1970s, when the unofficial cultures of the major cities emerged, and that process and the diaspora it spawned await further study. Across these historical changes, however, poetry has sustained itself and its readers by re-imagining themes of national identity and personal struggle, of love and belief, of scepticism and poetry itself. Given the strong voices among poets writing today, this bodes well for the future, even as audiences seem smaller and as the culture itself continues to be in a state of dramatic flux.

NOTES

1 Gasparov, M. L., 'Russkii stikh kak zerkalo postsovetskoi literatury', *Novoe literaturnoe obozrenie*, 32 (1998), pp. 77–83.

2 Dobrenko, Evgeny, *The Making of the State Reader: Social and Aesthetic Contexts of the Reception of Soviet Literature*, trans. Jesse Savage (Stanford, CA: Stanford University Press, 1997).

3 See Smith, G. S., 'Russian Poetry Since 1945' in *Routledge Companion to Russian Literature*, ed. Neil Cornwell (London: Routledge, 2001), pp. 197–208.

4 See Zholkovsky, Alexander, *Text Counter Text* (Stanford, CA: Stanford University Press, 1994), p. 216.

5 Mandelshtam, Osip, *Selected Poems*, trans. Clarence Brown and W. S. Merwin (New York: Atheneum, 1974), p. 93; Mandelshtam, *Polnoe sobranie stikhotvorenii* (St Petersburg: Akademicheskii proekt, 1995), pp. 269, 268, 272.

6 Pollak, Nancy, *Mandelstam the Reader* (Baltimore, MD: Johns Hopkins University Press, 1995). Pollak's work follows a long and distinguished tradition of subtextual readings of Mandelshtam's allusive poetry; see her bibliography for these works.

7 Kornilov, 'An Argument' in *Contemporary Russian Poetry: A Bilingual Anthology*, trans. Gerald S. Smith (Bloomington, IN: Indiana University Press, 1993), pp. 54–55.

8 Zholkovsky, Alexander, 'The Obverse of Stalinism: Akhmatova's Self-Serving Charisma of Selflessness', *Self and Story in Russian History*, ed. Laura Engelstein and Stephanie Sandler (Ithaca, NY: Cornell University Press, 2000), pp. 46–68.

9 A fine example of Chichibabin's poetry is 'The Battle', *Contemporary Russian Poetry: A Bilingual Anthology*, pp. 22–23. That volume includes excellent translations of other poets mentioned here, Slutsky and Gorbanevskaia among them.

10 Gerald Smith recounts Slutsky's life and work, with extensive translations, in *Things That Happened* (Moscow: Glas Publishers, 1999).

11 Kornilov, 'The Sky' in *Twentieth Century Russian Poetry: Silver and Steel: An Anthology*, sel. and introd. Evgenii Evtushenko, ed. Albert C. Todd and Max Hayward, with Daniel Weissbort (New York: Nan A. Talese Doubleday, 1993), pp. 785–787.

12 For the poems, see Mandelshtam, *Selected Poems*, pp. 76, 89, 77; *Polnoe sobranie stikhotvorenii*, pp. 264, 240, 241.

13 Rasula, Jed, *Syncopations: The Stress of Innovation in Contemporary American Poetry* (Tuscaloosa, AL: University of Alabama Press, 2004), p. 15.

14 Segments of Prigov's funeral were posted to YouTube within hours of the event, for example, www.youtube.com/watch?v=RpGybrzaisk&feature=related (accessed 3 February 2008).

15 Ginzburg, L. Ia., *O lirike* (Leningrad: Sovetskii pisatel', 1974).

16 For Martynov, see *Twentieth Century Russian Poetry*, pp. 489–493.

17 *Twentieth Century Russian Poetry*, p. 581.

18 *Russian Women Writers*, 2 vols., ed. Christine Tomei (New York: Garland Publishers, 1999), vol. 2, p. 1369.

19 Ciepiela, Catherine, *The Same Solitude: Boris Pasternak and Marina Tsvetaeva* (Ithaca, NY: Cornell University Press, 2006).

20 Mandelshtam, *Selected Poems*, pp. 87–88, 58, 81.

21 For Brodsky's translation, see Brodsky, Joseph, *Collected Poems in English* (New York: Farrar, Straus & Giroux, 2000), pp. 163–208.

22 Sedakova, Ol'ga, 'O Zabolotskom' in *Proza* (Moscow: NFQ to Print, 2001), p. 671.

23 Aigi, Gennadii, *Razgovor na rasstoianii* (St Petersburg: Limbus Press, 2001), p. 118.

24 *In the Grip of Strange Thoughts: Russian Poetry in a New Era*, ed. J. Kates (Brookline, MA: Zephyr Press, 1999), p. 191.

25 One of the albums for *Das Hohelied* is held in Houghton Library, Harvard University; others are in the Albertina Museum, Vienna.

26 Mnatsakanova, *Das Buch Sabeth* (Vienna: n. p., 1988).

27 Sedakova, Olga, *The Silk of Time*, ed. Valentina Polukhina (Keele: Ryburn Publishing, 1994), p. 27.

28 Translated by Philip Nikolayev in *Contemporary Russian Poetry: An Anthology*, ed. Evgeny Bunimovich and J. Kates (Champaign, IL: Dalkey Archive Press, 2008), pp. 27–29.

29 Janecek, Gerald, 'Paronomastic and Musical Techniques in Mnacakanova's *Rekviem*', *Slavic and East European Journal*, 31, no. 2 (1987), pp. 202–219.

FURTHER READING

Agenosov, V. and Ankudinov, K., *Sovremennye russkie poety* (Moscow: Megatron, 1997).

Dolinin, V. *et al.*, eds., *Samizdat Leningrada. 1950-e – 1980-e. Literaturnaia entsiklopediia* (Moscow: NLO, 2003).

Epstein, Mikhail, 'New Currents in Russian Poetry' in *After the Future: The Paradoxes of Postmodernism and Contemporary Russian Culture*, trans. Anesa Miller-Pogacar (Amherst, MA: University of Massachusetts Press, 1995), pp. 19–50.

Ivanov, B. I. and Roginskii, B.A., eds., *Istoriia leningradskoi nepodtsenzurnoi literatury 1950–1980-e gody* (St Petersburg: DEAN, 2000).

Janecek, Gerald, *Sight and Sound Entwined: Studies of the New Russian Poetry* (New York: Bergahn Books, 2000).

Postnikova, T. V., *'Esli ty nosish´ nachalo vremen v ushakh...' (Avangardnaia poeziia 80-kh – 90-kh gg)* (Moscow: Rossiiskaia gosudarstvennaia biblioteka, 1995).

Sandler, Stephanie, ed., *Rereading Russian Poetry* (New Haven, CT: Yale University Press, 1999).

Smith, G. S., 'Russian Poetry: The Lives or the Lines?', *Modern Language Review*, 95, no. 4 (2000), i–xiii.

'Russian Poetry Since 1945' in *Routledge Companion to Russian Literature*, ed. Neil Cornwell (London: Routledge, 2001), pp. 197–208.

Songs to Seven Strings: Russian Guitar Poetry and Soviet 'Mass song' (Bloomington, IN: Indiana University Press, 1984).

Wachtel, Michael, *Cambridge Introduction to Russian Poetry* (Cambridge: Cambridge University Press, 2004).

Recommended anthologies, journals, and websites

Arion: Zhurnal poezii, ed. Aleksei Alekhin (1994–), Moscow, four issues annually, www.arion.ru.

Bunimovich, Evgeny and J. Kates, eds., *Contemporary Russian Poetry: An Anthology* (Champaign, IL: Dalkey Archive Press, 2008).

Deviat´ izmerenii. Antologiia noveishei russkoi poezii (Moscow: Novoe literaturnoe obozrenie, 2004).

Evtushenko, Evgenii, ed., *Strofy veka* (Minsk: Polifakt, 1995).

High, John, *et al.*, eds., *Crossing Centuries: The New Generation in Russian Poetry* (Jersey City, NJ: Talisman, 2000).

Johnson, Kent and Ashby, Stephen M., eds., *Third Wave: The New Russian Poetry* (Ann Arbor, MI: University of Michigan Press, 1992).

Kates, J., ed., *In the Grip of Strange Thoughts: Russian Poetry in a New Era* (Brookline, MA: Zephyr Press, 1999).

Kuz´min, Dmitrii, ed., *Nestolichnaia literatura. Poeziia i proza regionov Rossii* (Moscow: Novoe literaturnoe obozrenie, 2001).

Osvobozhdennyi Uliss. Sovremennaia russkaia poeziia za predelami Rossii (Moscow: Novoe literaturnoe obozrenie, 2004).

Novaia literaturnaia karta Rossii, www.litkarta.ru/mediateka, Vitalii Pukhanov, curator (2007–).

Open Space, openspace.ru/literature, website.

Polukhina, Valentina and Weissborg, Daniel, eds., *An Anthology of Contemporary Russian Women Poets* (Iowa City, IA: University of Iowa Press, 2005).

Smith, Gerald S., ed. and trans. *Contemporary Russian Poetry: A Bilingual Anthology* (Bloomington, IN: Indiana University Press, 1993).
TextOnly, textonly.ru, ed. Il´ia Kukulin (1999–), on-line journal.
Vavilon, vavilon.ru (1998–).
Vozdukh: Zhurnal poezii, ed. Dmitrii Kuz´min (2006–), Moscow, four issues annually.

8

KATERINA CLARK

Russian Epic Novels of the Soviet Period

During the Soviet period the epic as a genre was at the forefront of attention for many writers producing long novels, especially if the subject involved military combat. In Soviet literature, two related but distinct versions of epic were most germane. The first was the classical tradition, particular features of which were appropriated for ideological purposes and for the cause of national aggrandizement. The second was the specific model of the epic novel to be found in Tolstoy's *War and Peace* (1865–1869), itself an official model for Soviet literature. A complication here is that Tolstoy's novel is indebted to the classical epic (as his own diary entries attest), yet its Second Epilogue takes issue with certain fundamental assumptions of the 'epic' view of history.

A similar ambiguity can be seen in the work of the four writers I will discuss here. Each of them produced epic novels which both challenge, and draw on, the kind of 'epic' exemplified by canonical Socialist Realism, and also both challenge and draw on the reworking of the epic tradition in *War and Peace*. I am treating in particular: Mikhail Sholokhov's *Quiet Flows the Don* (*Tikhii Don*, 1928–1940); Boris Pasternak's *Doctor Zhivago* (*Doktor Zhivago*, 1957); Alexander Solzhenitsyn's *Cancer Ward* (*Rakovyi korpus*, 1968), *The First Circle* (*V kruge pervom*, 1969), and *August 1914* (*Avgust chetyrnadtsatogo*, 1989);[1] and Vasilii Grossman's *For A Just Cause* (*Za pravoe delo*, 1952) and its sequel *Life and Fate* (*Zhizn´ i sud'ba*, 1960/1980). These novels have become famous in the West: three of the authors won the Nobel Prize for literature (Pasternak in 1958, Sholokhov in 1965, Solzhenitsyn in 1970), and though Grossman was not so honoured, his *Life and Fate*, published posthumously, has been hailed by renowned Western intellectuals. But all of these novels are epic: epic in terms of length, but also epic in terms of their canvas, their historical sweep encompassing such critical moments in twentieth-century Russian history as the First World War, the Revolution, the Civil War and, for the later novels, the Stalin years and the Second World War. They have, then, the encyclopaedism that Franco

Moretti identifies as central to epic[2]: they attempt to cover the entire Soviet period up to the point of writing, and sometimes the pre-Revolutionary years as well. All of them foreground military engagement or state violence, defining features of the twentieth century. In doing so they raise major issues that encompass history, philosophy, and national identity.

In the Soviet Union the response to most of these novels contrasts with their enthusiastic reception in the West. Virtually all the post-war novels by Pasternak, Solzhenitsyn, and Grossman were banned from publication in the Soviet Union; they initially came out in the West and appeared in the Soviet Union only at the end of *perestroika*. Hence they came to enjoy the status of dissident, and even 'treasonous' (*kramol'naia*) literature; in the most extreme case, the manuscript of Grossman's *Life and Fate* was confiscated by the KGB, and the Central Committee's ideological spokesman, Mikhail Suslov, told the author that it could not be published for another 250 years.[3] These authors were also subjected to hostile political campaigns in response to their novels (some writers called for Pasternak to be executed for *Doctor Zhivago*; Solzhenitsyn was forcibly exiled in 1974). Sholokhov's *Quiet Flows the Don*, however, was officially a jewel in Socialist Realism's crown, and his career matched this status. He joined the Communist Party in 1932, after much of the novel had appeared, and from then on was a Soviet establishment figure, elevated to such offices as Supreme Soviet delegate and Academy of Sciences member.

In the fates of these novels and their authors, then, we seem to have the familiar binaries with which Western criticism has operated for decades: novels lionized in the West/novels vilified in the Soviet Union; good, serious, anti-Soviet literature/hack standard Socialist Realism. This chapter seeks to show the inadequacy of these binaries, to demonstrate that there are many gradations to be found when considering these works and writers. Though the novels of Pasternak, Solzhenitsyn, and Grossman have been read as counterposing the tradition of Socialist Realism, they in fact come from it, to varying degrees, or are in dialogue with it; and, in that sense, they emerge from within its purview. At the same time, the status of *Quiet Flows the Don* as an exemplum of Socialist Realism is questionable, as will be demonstrated.

The contrast between these authors is not absolute even in terms of publishability and censorship. In reality Sholokhov, too, had a great deal of difficulty getting sections of *Quiet Flows the Don* published because they were politically problematic.[4] They would not have appeared at all except for the intervention of such powerful patrons as the writers Alexander Serafimovich and Maxim Gorky, and even Stalin.[5] And Sholokhov's texts were subjected to major cuts and progressive censorship with each edition. In

Solzhenitsyn's case, somewhat as in Sholokhov's, the intervention of a powerful patron (Khrushchev) was critical in getting those of his texts that were
published accepted, and Khrushchev's demise in 1964 proved fateful in terms
of further publication.

It is not just the novels that are hard to fit into the standard binaries,
but also the careers of their authors. The straightforward oppositions of
black and white, of conformist/'time-server' and valiant nay-sayer, which
inform so much of the Western literary history of the Soviet Union, need
to be modified by shadings of grey. Sholokhov's own actions are less that
of the predictable Soviet yes-man than one might suppose in a Party member and establishment darling. While he did play an unsavoury role in the
post-war campaigns to vilify writers (including Pasternak and Solzhenitsyn), during the 1930s he performed some highly commendable deeds: he
petitioned successfully to save fellow Cossacks from starvation in the 1933
famine and also intervened on behalf of local Communists who were purged
in 1937. Only the whim of Stalin saved Pasternak, a Jew by birth (though
Russian Orthodox), from arrest during the campaign against 'cosmopolitans' (a mostly anti-Semitic term for intellectuals) in the late Stalin years.[6]
Grossman's conscience, too, was not uncompromised: during the purges of
the 1930s he signed a letter condemning the 'Trotskyite–Bukharinites' and
in the late Stalin years another against those (fellow Jews) who had been
arrested for the 'Doctors' Plot'.[7]

This chapter will argue that the novels of all four writers emerge from
the discursive space of the Stalin era and can be seen as representative of
intellectual orientations within it. Even within the orthodox Soviet literary
world there were competing senses of what Socialist Realism should be and
lobbies for it to follow a variety of literary and intellectual traditions. The
discussion will focus on the way the novels of these four major Soviet-
period authors *both* exemplify, *and* are counterposed to, the epic nature of
Socialist Realism (in Sholokhov's case, only prospectively, since the term
was not coined until 1932, after much of his novel had already appeared).

Epic and Soviet novel

Andrei Siniavsky in his essay 'What Is Socialist Realism?' (1959)[8] notes the
'classical' nature of Socialist Realism, but does not elaborate precisely in
what sense. Arguably, though the paradigmatic Socialist Realist text was
a novel, it was in mode epic, like many works of the classical era. Epic is
a contested concept, and the borders between it and other genres are far
from clear. But there were distinct parallels between the Socialist Realist
novel and the classical epic, particularly during the High Stalinist phase

of the 1930s. Generically, however, Socialist Realism is closer to the *Bildungsroman* (novel of education). More specifically, it might be called a sort of ideological *Bildungsroman*, in that the hero's development is largely in the area of political consciousness and acquiring Party discipline, a trajectory that follows a 'masterplot' which enables it to represent allegorically the progress charted in Marxism–Leninism. But there are distinct elements of the epic in any novel – or at any rate of the epic as it has been defined in such diverse sources as Aristotle, Erich Auerbach, and Georg Lukács.

It might immediately be asked: how could those sagas of the factory floor and collective farm field, the standard fare of Socialist Realist novels, be seen as epics? They treat, and were even enjoined from on high to treat, the 'most matter-of-fact, everyday reality', as the Central Committee spokesman, Andrei Zhdanov, put it in his keynote address to the First Congress of the Union of Soviet Writers in 1934, a *locus classicus* for defining Socialist Realism.[9] Here the word 'saga' is used advisedly: in chronicling events in some provincial Soviet production site – the typical locus of the Socialist Realist novel – the 'approved' authors contrived to give their 'positive hero' epic proportions, and depicted him as operating in an epic-like world of struggle against natural disasters or natural-disaster-like obstacles (including bureaucratic roadblocks). 'Struggle' conferred on the actions of the novel's hero the aura of feats, thereby making it like an adventure romance. But in Socialist Realism, the narration blurs somewhat with the epic, thanks in part to its august nature and the elevated, 'bookish' style. Since at least as far back as Aristotle's classic formulation of the epic in the *Poetics*, the form has been felt to encompass 'the imitation of noble subjects presented in an elevated meter' and an 'heroic meter'[10] (or at least some elevated style).

Socialist Realist novels are also like the classic epic in terms of their social functions and the dynamic of the tradition's evolution. Central to the Roman epic tradition is, as Franco Moretti writes, its 'very solid link between epic and power'.[11] In the case of the Socialist Realist novel, this link with power was mandated to be more than just 'very solid', but actually ineluctable (this is in effect the meaning of its base principle of 'party-mindedness' [*partiinost'*]). Christopher Phillips identifies 'the epic impulse, the drive to thrust oneself into a tradition of canonical authors for the purpose of using that tradition's cultural capital to forward a career, a political viewpoint, an aesthetic credo, or an act of devotion'.[12] The Socialist Realist novelist, in producing a variant on the masterplot, was 'forwarding' all four.

This is not to suggest that there was any conscious attempt or directive in the Soviet 1930s to emulate the classical epic. Though in that decade 'world literature' was officially valued, its canon was generally limited to such authors as Shakespeare, Goethe, and Cervantes – texts from the classical era of Greece and Rome were conspicuously absent from the standard enumerations of 'world' authors. Nevertheless, arguably, conventional Socialist Realist novels have some affinities with the classical epic.

The first of these affinities has to do with characterization. Lukács remarks that 'the epic hero is, strictly speaking, never an individual... [The epic's] theme is not a personal destiny but the identity of a community',[13] while Auerbach notes that Homeric poems eschew any 'problematical psychological situation... [Their heroes'] emotions, though strong, are simple and find expression instantly.'[14] Socialist Realism takes this kind of characterization to an extreme. Here heroes are not of interest for their individual selves, but only in terms of their feats, themselves subordinated to the interests of political allegory. Socialist Realist novels privilege the public plot over private life; they foreground duty, the call of the *patrie*, or the like. In a classic Socialist Realist novel there is effectively no interiority distinct from the exterior, no discrepancy between inside and outside – not in positive characters, at any rate. In what might be seen as a variant on what happens in the epic, everything has to be 'readable' on a character's face, so much so that the facial depictions can be called 'verbal icons'. Characters are described in terms of surface detail by means of standard epithets encoded to indicate their moral/political qualities.[15]

This lack of discrepancy between the inner and outer selves, and the lack of individuation in a Socialist Realist novel can be related to another defining feature of the epic, one emphasized by Lukács – the elimination of contingency. Lukács condemns the use of gratuitous facts and particularity – 'the contingent' – and calls instead for the hegemony of some overarching narrative in composition, insisting that all detail have a discursive function.[16] Lukács wants the details of the setting and characters to be connected in a narrative of action taking place in what he calls an 'epic' world; like the traditional epic, it might be episodic, but its structure is teleological. In fact, his ultimate condemnation of bare 'description' is that it functions as a 'writer's surrogate for lost epic meaning'.[17]

In the late 1930s, there was a call for a return to 'the lyric' in Socialist Realism, to a more 'authentic' (*podlinnaia*) and 'true' (*pravdivaia*) literature. In part, advocates called for the 'lyric' as an attack on the bombast and hyperbole of typical Socialist Realist texts. But they also asked for representation of a character's psychology and inner life, and for greater emphasis on the private and personal, giving less weight to the public sphere, the factory bench, and all that. The call for more 'truth' might seem dissident, but actually this movement was in various ways closely implicated with the mentality and culture of the purge era. Lobbyists for 'the lyric' often used the rhetoric of the purges in making their case.

The novels discussed here can be seen as representative of this shift toward 'the lyric'. Those by Pasternak, Solzhenitsyn, and Grossman were of course considered 'treasonous' because of their historical critiques; but they were also problematical because of the various ways they undermined official expectations of what amounted to the epic mode of Socialist Realism. These writers wrote novels about epic events, but it could be said of all of them, including Sholokhov, that they did not provide wholly positive, uncomplicated heroes, and instead accentuated 'lyric' aspects – private life, the emotions – in their narratives.

Mikhail Sholokhov

Quiet Flows the Don, though recurrently cited as an exemplum of Socialist Realism, actually only marginally and very intermittently shows traces of that tradition. The novel has as its hero Grigorii Melekhov, a Cossack from the village of Tatarskoe in the Don region. A valiant fighter and even a clever strategist, hard living and exuberant, Grigorii could potentially be the hero of an adventure romance, in the tradition of writing about the 'daring' (*udalye*) Cossacks and their exploits. But though Grigorii is distinguished in battle and the reader's sympathies are meant to be with him, events conspire to deny him the conventional heroic role.

The novel focuses on Grigorii's family, on neighbouring families with whom they intermarry, and on their friends. This social network is devastated by the Civil War that pits 'brother against brother' and unleashes an orgy of violence such that by the end of the novel almost all the major characters have died – most enduring gruesome, violent deaths. Even Grigorii's survival is open to question. Thus the novel might be called an epic tragedy. Central to the narrative is Grigorii's illicit passion for Aksinia, the wife of a fellow villager. Over the course of events, which include Grigorii's own marriage to Natalia, he and Aksinia come together, their relationship now part of a saga punctuated by revenge, rape, suicide, abortion, typhoid, and the death of offspring. Sholokhov's novel was tremendously popular among readers[18] because of this steamy love plot.

Though the novel has its share of local vendettas, its scope is much wider. Moretti stipulates that in an epic, both broad historical sweep and 'encyclopaedic' detail have to be subordinated to a world system. *Quiet Flows the Don* meets this criterion in the sense that the conflicts are, ostensibly, between two rival belief systems, the monarchist or liberal democratic for the Whites, the Communist for the Reds. Grigorii must negotiate a path for himself not only between his all-consuming passion on the one hand and social mores and family ties on the other, but also between these competing political systems. A complicating factor is his allegiance to the Cossack cause and the lure of Cossack autonomy. He alternates between fighting for the Reds and fighting for the Whites, sometimes joining one side in a gut reaction against the excesses of the other or because he thinks it will serve the Cossack cause, but sometimes the chaotic circumstances of civil war simply propel him to one side or another. In other words, there is an element of contingency in his successive affiliations. Grigorii is beset by doubts, and troubled by the violence even as he is a perpetrator. At one point he wishes he could be like two of his acquaintances: one joined the Whites, and the other the Reds – but for both the choice seemed clear-cut. Thus this novel does not provide the black/white juxtaposition among characters and events, the steadfast political allegiance that Socialist Realism later prescribed. The Communist authority figures who, also in accordance with this formula, should have served as mentors for Grigorii in his political maturation, are insignificant.

This lack of a clear-cut political binary is not the only aspect that renders *Quiet Flows the Don* problematic as an exemplum of Socialist Realism. In fact, it could be regarded in crucial respects as the least Socialist Realist of these four authors' novels. Socialist Realism, as stipulated in Zhdanov's canonical address to the First Congress of the Union of Soviet Writers of 1934 and implemented by the censors, was extremely puritanical, both in content and in language. In this official formulation of Socialist Realism, all 'physiologism' (read sex and lower bodily functions) was proscribed, as were sub-standard speech, dialecticisms and, needless to say, scatology. But Sholokhov's pithy, earthy novel abounds in swear words, dialecticisms, detail about bodily functions and about grisly, violent deaths; much of this was progressively cut out in later redactions.[19] In the early 1930s there was a bitter and public argument between Sholokhov's two literary patrons, Gorky and Serafimovich, about the sort of language that was appropriate for Soviet literature. Gorky won the debate, thanks to intervention from on high (in *Pravda*), ensuring that Soviet literature was 'cleaned up', but, had it gone the other way, Socialist Realism might have been very different; Fedor Panferov's novel *Ingots* (*Bruski*), which was at the centre of the Gorky/Serafimovich exchange, also features sexually explicit scenes. Ironically, the 'treasonous' novels of the other three writers discussed here were much more puritanical and bookish in their language (even in dialogue) and much less graphic in treating the physical, and in those respects were 'more' Socialist Realist.

In comparing Sholokhov's novel with those by the other three writers, one should not forget that his was a pre-war novel: those of the other three were post-war, and hence came out of a different historical moment. Indeed, prior to the Second World War, two of them, Grossman and Pasternak, produced very different texts from their post-war efforts – Pasternak highly complicated Modernist poetry and prose (he made a turn to greater 'simplicity' around 1940, about the time he began work on *Doctor Zhivago*), and Grossman an industrial novel that became a Socialist Realist classic (*Stepan Kol'chugin*, 1937–1940).

Alexander Solzhenitsyn

Solzhenitsyn was entirely a post-war writer, yet his novels are in important respects closer to Socialist Realism than those of Pasternak and Grossman. His message is anti-Soviet, but much of his basic literary approach is in the Soviet mode. In his three fictional works about the gulag he essentially works within Socialist Realism, but deliberately inverts some of its hallmark conventions. In Socialist Realist novels the majority of the action takes place in a single, isolated space, generally a provincial production site or town, which functions as a microcosm, a model for depicting Soviet society as a whole. But there is a second space, Moscow, which represents a more advanced stage in the progress towards a Communist society, one so advanced that generally only the hero is sufficiently 'positive' to be accorded the privilege of going there. Solzhenitsyn's prison camp fiction, which is autobiographically based, reverses this spatial dichotomy, placing positive characters 'far away from Moscow'. In *The Cancer Ward*, set in 1955 when the Soviet government had begun to release political prisoners and review their sentences, one such political prisoner, Kostoglotov, finds himself thrown together with a cross-section of civilians in a Tashkent cancer ward. The principal negative hero, Rusanov, a New Class Party man and bureaucrat who was responsible for many arrests during the purges, looks to Moscow as a mecca, while Kostoglotov yearns to return to the *Gemeinschaft* world of the bleak Kazakh village Ush-Terek (where he had formerly been exiled), in the far-flung and primitive reaches of the Soviet empire. And in *The First Circle*, in which a group of highly educated political prisoners has been incarcerated in a research station and forced to work on sinister inventions for the secret police, the worst camps stand for the Dantean inner circle of hell; yet it is only the most virtuous – those who most resist the Stalinist order – who are dispatched there. In other words, corresponding to this inverted, binarized hierarchy of space we find a division of characters into black and white.

The typical Socialist Realist novel also has a limited time frame, generally just the duration of a single cycle of the seasons, but in the Solzhenitsyn novels the time frame is even more condensed, ranging from just one day to a couple of weeks. The shortest duration is in his novella 'One Day in the Life of Ivan Denisovich' (1962), but here a simple Soviet citizen's unremarkable day at a Soviet prison camp – a tiny slice of time in that delimited space, and hence the opposite of the long journey that is so much a hallmark of epic – acquires epic grandeur as Ivan Denisovich retains his dignity. Moreover, in this novella, as in the two gulag novels, Solzhenitsyn expands his limited spatial and temporal frame through the recollections of characters and the narrator, thereby incorporating virtually the entire expanse and past history of the Soviet Union.

Vasilii Grossman and Boris Pasternak

Pasternak and Grossman also incorporated a broad historical canvas into their post-war novels. However, they privilege not the epic register, as in Solzhenitsyn, but an alternative or complement to the epic world in which their characters operate – the personal, the trifling, everyday, and even domestic. When in *Life and Fate* the narrator comments that a central character, Zhenia, in her painting tries to combine the 'the mighty power of the military' with the 'trivial items [*melochnost'*] in the kitchen, to represent not just actions but the feelings they arouse in her', this has the air of a statement of the principles that guide Grossman in his literary compositions. This trend is more marked in *Doctor Zhivago*. The novel chronicles the life of its hero from early childhood through the tumultuous times of the First World War, the Revolution, and the Civil War. In the dire conditions of the Revolution's aftermath, Zhivago and his family seek refuge in Varykino, a remote family farm in the Urals, where Zhivago is commandeered to serve a Bolshevik unit as a doctor. He ultimately escapes to live in Varykino not with his wife and child but with his love, Lara. In this remote setting he exercises his true vocation as a writer. In this context the narrator asserts that with great writers literary production comes from their personal experiences, from what is fundamentally 'private and individual' (*chastnost'*) but which becomes through their writing common to all (*obshchee delo*).

The post-war novels of Pasternak and Grossman, then, have pronounced 'lyric' elements. This is especially true of *Doctor Zhivago* inasmuch as its cycle of poems, appended at the end but allegedly composed by Zhivago at particular moments in the course of the novel, are intended as a dominant and as such undermine the linear nature of the narrative, providing an alternative temporality.

Grossman's Stalingrad novels come closer to meeting the criteria for the epic. They treat the great turning point in the Second World War, the Battle of Stalingrad, encompassing its immense human and material losses and the ultimate Soviet victory. The narrative shifts back and forth in focus, showing mostly the Soviet soldiers and civilians pitted against the Germans, but also intermittently presenting the perspective of the German combatants, occasionally depicting actual historical figures (mainly military commanders, but also Hitler and his entourage). The principal characters recurrently iterate a confidence that the Soviet forces will defeat the Germans, and by the end they do; in this sense, the novel has a teleological plot trajectory, like an epic. Unlike Pasternak's coverage of the Civil War, which highlights a Russian officer being lynched by a mob of rank-and-file soldiers, Grossman presents a more uplifting picture of Russians at war, showing multiple examples of individual bravery and determined patriotism. And he maintains an elevated tone and style: his characters converse in bookish language, and the narrator frequently uses rhetorical flourishes typical of epic such as repetition of key details and motifs.

The central focus of both Stalingrad novels is on the three generations of the Shaposhnikov family, presided over by its widowed matriarch, Aleksandra Vladimirovna. Much of this is autobiographical, with incidents from Grossman's own life spread around the characters. Like Solzhenitsyn he stretches beyond the time frame. Using the extended family as his main focus, Grossman was able, largely through flashback memories, biographical sketches, or allusions in conversation, to cover a vast swath of Russian history in the twentieth century, stretching back before the First World War. In *Life and Fate* Grossman effectively takes it forward beyond the novel's present of the Second World War by providing a version of what the reader would recognize as the 'anti-cosmopolitanism' campaign and the Doctors' Plot fabrication of the late Stalin years. Moreover, through the occupations and careers of his characters' family members Grossman introduces a cross-section of Soviet life, both sociologically and geographically.

The emphasis Grossman gave to the personal and domestic in his Stalingrad novels was an important factor in their being subjected to official opprobrium. This was so even with the initial novel, *For a Just Cause*, which appeared in 1952 at the end of the Stalin period, and which many Western commentators dismiss (wrongly) as merely Stalinist. At first the novel was enthusiastically received and proposed for a Stalin Prize; but such anticipation was crushed when in February 1953 Mikhail Bubennov published in *Pravda* an attack in which, though it praised the novel's 'epic sweep' (*epichnost*) condemned it overall. Grossman was faulted for failing to depict the powerful Stalingrad defence, to show how it was a 'triumph of Stalin's genius as a military commander and the mighty victory of the heroic Soviet army' and the Party's guiding role.[20]

Grossman's two Stalingrad novels could be described as heroic epics of the Russian intelligentsia as it goes through war and societal upheavals in the Soviet era. To some extent this could also be said of *Doctor Zhivago*, though that novel is more of a *Künstlerroman* about an individual poet and his intellectual friends, if in an epic setting.

Intellectuals are the heroes of most of these post-war epics, and in them all three novelists evince a cult of literature. Both Solzhenitsyn's gulag novels and Grossman's Stalingrad fiction feature individuals from the lower classes who are drawn to become avid, even discriminating readers, and thereby positive characters. Through them the authors were able to critique Soviet literary trends (especially the most hack varieties of Socialist Realism). In Grossman they also contrast with the image of a degenerate German soldier: the narrator remarks that for this soldier, women are the only form of reading (as sex objects) he recognizes. Part Two of *Doctor Zhivago*, the section where Zhivago emerges as a writer, is framed by Zhivago's notebook entries during his initial times in Varykino that chronicle the literary texts he is reading. Even Solzhenitsyn's *Gulag Archipelago* is punctuated by literary references, which undermine its purport to present an overwhelming condemnation of the camp system based on eyewitness accounts.

Though both Pasternak and Grossman lionize the intelligentsia, each promotes a very different conception of it. They were both Jewish, but came from upper-middle-class, cosmopolitan, and assimilated backgrounds that included study abroad (Pasternak in Marburg; Grossman's parents were both educated in Switzerland, where he spent some time as a child). Grossman, largely through another central character, Krymov, a son-in-law of Aleksandra Vladimirovna and a former Comintern official now serving as a Commissar with the Soviet Army, evinces a preference for the cosmopolitan, international leftist intelligentsia – the Comintern in its more idealist guises. But Grossman also gives positive billing to the Jewish Bund, the Mensheviks, and the nineteenth-century radical intellectuals Herzen and Ogarev – all, implicitly, as distinct from the Bolshevik Party.

The fate of Jewish people is another major theme in Grossman's two Stalingrad novels. Both of them, but *Life and Fate* most particularly, include strong writing about the Holocaust. One section that has particularly captivated the attention of Western critics is a poignant attempt to recreate in fiction a 'letter' written by one of the characters which in effect tries to convey the last days of Grossman's own mother, who perished among the 20,000 executed in his home town of Berdichev, west of Kiev. The topic of the Holocaust marked Grossman's war and post-war career: he was the first to report on a Nazi extermination camp (Treblinka) and, in 1946, together with Ilia Ehrenburg, produced the *Black Book* (*Chernaia kniga*) on the Holocaust in the Soviet Union, one of his many projects that could not be published at the time. Pasternak, however, shows little sign in *Zhivago* of interest in a Jewish identity, being more concerned with Christian experience. The novel gives a sympathetic account of the liberal democratic intelligentsia, but has also been read as critical of Bolshevism and the Revolution: Pasternak comments, for example, that Zhivago's beloved uncle Nikolai, an unfrocked priest, has 'been through Tolstoyism and revolutionary [ideas]' but is 'constantly moving on farther'.

These novelists themselves all went 'farther' in their thinking over time, as Soviet society also did to a large extent. After Stalin's death in 1953 there was a reversal of fortune when writers began again to call for a restoration of 'the lyric' in literature, an early harbinger of 'Thaw'. The stilted, triumphalist fiction of the past decade was derided. This was the historical moment in which it was even thought that Pasternak might be able to publish *Doctor Zhivago* in the Soviet Union, especially after Khrushchev's 'Secret Speech' to the Twentieth Party Congress in February 1956, attacking Stalin's excesses. Some of the views to be found in *Doctor Zhivago* fit in with the new thinking of the Thaws, such as decrying the force exercised by men of power – '*vozhdi*', as Pasternak explicitly calls them, using the word normally used for the Bolshevik leadership. Unlike Soviet commentators at the time, however, he counterposes this 'Roman' trend to what he sees as the true spirit of Christianity, which favours individual self-determination and 'freedom'. At one point Lara calls for exercising 'one's own opinion', which was a catchcry of Soviet literature in 1956 following Khrushchev's 'Secret Speech'.

Grossman's *For a Just Cause*, too, was republished soon after Stalin's death and ran through several editions, the 1955 redaction considerably revised to slough off some of the concessions to Stalinism. In that year Grossman began *Life and Fate*, in which he pulled fewer punches in his account of the Stalin era. Then a third thaw of 1962 made it possible to publish accounts of the camps; a character who in the 1952 redaction of *For a Just Cause* is said to have died after a stint working in the far north is in this later book said to have been purged in 1937 and later perished in the camps. Solzhenitsyn wrote *The First Circle* at approximately the same time, between 1955 and 1964, and began *The Gulag Archipelago* in 1958.

As Pasternak died in 1960, *Doctor Zhivago* could not see the successive rewrites that Grossman and Solzhenitsyn were able to make to their post-war novels. The latter two writers underwent progressive revisions of their positions, reflected in their fiction, but their thinking evolved in contrary directions. Solzhenitsyn in *August 1914* evinces contempt for the radical tradition of the Russian intelligentsia in the figure of the negative character Lenartovich; the novel has also been accused of anti-Semitic overtones.

Grossman did not abandon his faith in socialist internationalism, but *Life and Fate* is inflected by new attitudes: 'freedom', for example, is the most fundamental value, and the great error of the Bolsheviks was in not recognizing this. In this novel, Grossman emerged as one of the earliest Soviet intellectuals to liken Stalin's Soviet Union to Nazi Germany as a totalitarian regime. In sections omitted in some published versions, Grossman draws several pointed parallels including between the worst purge year of 1937 and the Nazi Night of the Long Knives (1934) and even the Holocaust. In his analysis, the extraordinary violence of the totalitarian social systems paralysed their populations, who thus acquiesced in it, hiding their horror of the killings even from themselves. These remarks are, in effect, an attack on the fundamental tenets of Soviet history.

These post-war novels were problematic not only thematically but also in their very composition. For example, Mikhail Bubennov, in the aforementioned review of *For a Just Cause*, objects that: 'The plot lines are not thought through, everything is built on chance and coincidences [*sluchainosti*].'[21] There is a larger point here: how can a novel be 'epic' – or Socialist Realist – when so much of it is built on contingency? But in these novels the role of contingency goes beyond a compositional ploy of the novelist and becomes a central philosophical, and hence ideological, issue. The novels discussed here, particularly those by Pasternak and Grossman, engage in their texts questions having to do with time and history. On closer inspection, their literary antecedent is more Tolstoy than Socialist Realism or the classical epic.

In all these novels Tolstoy is a recurrent reference (he is less explicitly present in *Quiet Flows the Don*, though there are some characteristically Tolstoyian compositional features). Some of these novels' motifs and incidents hark back to *Anna Karenina*, but *the* shadow text is *War and Peace*, especially for the novels that deal with military combat. This was far from a dissident gesture by these authors: Tolstoy had been made into an acclaimed historical precedent for Socialist Realism, and *War and Peace* had been a favourite text of Lenin's. During the Second World War, official Soviet texts and speeches frequently referenced the battle of Borodino and the defence of Moscow against Napoleon in 1812 in discussing how to repel Hitler; Stalin, in thinking through his own strategy, identified with Mikhail Kutuzov, the historical military leader who figures in *War and Peace*.

As early as 1938, as the Soviet Union stood in the shadow of an anticipated war, creative people were enjoined to produce versions of *War and Peace* in their own writings. Alexander Fadeev, the emerging head of the Writers' Union, revealed at a special meeting of the Union in February 1938 that he had been asked to write a stage version of *War and Peace*; he commented, however, that it was not essential to choose military topics in order to inspire patriotism in the populace. Pushkin's novel in verse *Eugene Onegin* could also be used for that purpose.[22] In other words, the writers felt that patriotism did not require the epic, and could be conveyed in a lyric mode. Incidentally this Russian classic is a preoccupation of Zhivago as he limbers up to write while secluded at Varykino. He, like Fadeev, prefers it to *War and Peace* (which he also reads there).

War and Peace as an official model for writing about military engagement provides us with interesting parallels. Bubennov takes exception to the character Krymov in *For a Just Cause*, who wanders around, never joining in the combat but just 'observing'. However, Bubennov might have noticed the parallels with Pierre, the onlooker at Borodino. Similarly, Zhivago in Pasternak's novel for two years of the Civil War moves around with a unit of Reds, observing rather than engaging militarily, a situation motivated by the fact that he is a doctor. Far from the epic hero, in general Zhivago shows great passivity, right down to the way his marriage breaks up while he is absent. But, as Moretti tersely states: 'Without action, in short, no hero. Hence no epic.'[23]

Another plot feature that could be associated with Tolstoy is that all four novelists, as established already, to varying degrees used the compositional strategy of *War and Peace* for their 'epic' texts by hanging a huge slice of history on a single family and its filiations. But the links to *War and Peace* go beyond mere references and an overall compositional strategy. The four novelists all (though in Sholokhov's case not overtly or even perhaps consciously) address this novel in terms of its Second Epilogue, where Tolstoy ridicules the notion that individual heroes affect the course of history. In other words, though *War and Peace* provides an epic coverage of historical events, its author questions defining features of the epic mode.

All the post-war novels discussed here address Tolstoy's Second Epilogue fairly clearly. In Solzhenitsyn this is most overtly the case in *August 1914*, at the centre of which is Russia's disastrous failure at the Battle of Tannenberg. In this novel Solzhenitsyn takes issue with Tolstoy's fatalistic philosophy of history, with the notion that there is an inevitable course of events that cannot be altered and that it is not great men, great generals, or heads of state, who move history; he debunks Tolstoy's lionization of Kutuzov, the Russian commander at Borodino, as one who understood this. In analysing the causes of the failure at Tannenberg, a key moment in the progression leading to the break-up of the tsarist regime and the fateful accession to power by the Bolsheviks, Solzhenitsyn brings out such factors as corruption among the upper elites resulting in the promotion of clearly incompetent officers, and the lack of attention to military science and technology, factors that Tolstoy had sought to diminish. In contrast to the other writers discussed here, Solzhenitsyn also rails against Tolstoy's doctrine of non-violence, which he sees as having contributed to the disastrous lack of military commitment.

Pasternak and Grossman, while emphasizing the power of contingency, do not idealize contingency itself. Their novels tell epic tales of war, revolution, and suffering, but reach out beyond these tales to another, greater, possibility – a transnational intellectual space, the 'farther' of Zhivago's uncle Nikolai. Pasternak's novel views history as a suprahuman process. Zhivago triumphs over contingency with his writing. Creativity propels him to a different time–space, that of timeless high culture, which has roots going back to ancient Egypt. Thus the hero attains epic time not in world-historical military engagement but in a creative act. 'Farther' in the terms of this novel is Christianity and art, linked by their association with God: the genius of the poet-creator comes not from within, but from words, and he is the mere afflatus of the divine. Scenes where Zhivago creates occur not within an epic frame but always within the domestic. At Varykino, when the house and its inhabitants have been cleaned and scrubbed, Zhivago settles down to write, a version of the Orthodox tradition whereby the icon painter must purify himself before presuming to address a divine subject.

The theme of the redemptive power of art, its capacity to transcend, can be found also in *Life and Fate*. And, like Pasternak, whose poems in *Zhivago* are organized in clusters determined by particular seasons, recurrent time, Grossman is impressed by the power of cyclic, rather than linear, time. He developed this theme in a play about an eternal cyclicity, *If We Are to Believe the Pythagoreans* (*Esli verit´ pifagoreitsam*), which he published in the summer of 1946, while working on *For a Just Cause*, and further elaborated it in *Forever Flowing* (1955), as the title implies. At the same time, despite the fact that Grossman admits different temporalities in these novels, and despite his more outspoken criticism of the Soviet system, he more than the other writers appears (at least sometimes) to subscribe to a view of history's inevitable onward march. This trans-personal force, which Grossman, like Tolstoy, sometimes identifies with 'the people,' always, he claims in *Life and Fate*, unmasks forces that are false or illusory in favour of the true. In such statements there is a historico-political binary of false and true, the false being those 'forces' that conduced to 'totalitarianism', the purges, the prison camps, the persecution or outright genocide of Jews, while the true, implicitly, are forces of the *longue durée* that are not deterred by such dark interludes.

Thus at least three of these novelists are both influenced by, and directly challenge, Tolstoy's maverick questioning in the Second Epilogue of the view that heroes move history. They equally reject Socialist Realist historical determinism and Bolshevik triumphalism. Sholokhov's *Quiet Flows the Don*, much of which appeared before Socialist Realism existed even in name, entered the great debate about history implicitly, thus less obviously. But of all the four writers discussed here it could be said that they, effectively, resist the expectation (which is a legacy of Lukács) that detail in a novel be subordinated to an overall plot scheme, that the novel's trajectory be teleological and ineluctable. These 'epic novels' challenge some defining features of epic. While they critique official accounts of Soviet history, they also challenge Soviet historiography at a more fundamental level.

NOTES

1 *August 1914* is Part I of his series on the First World War, *The Red Circle* [*Krasnoe koleso*]). The later volumes in this series are largely post-Soviet and will not be discussed.
2 See: Moretti, Franco, *The Modern Epic: The World-System from Goethe to García Márquez*, trans. Quintin Hoare (London and New York: Verso, 1996).
3 Garrard, John and Garrard, Carol, *The Bones of Berdychev: The Life and Fate of Vasily Grossman* (New York: Free Press, 1996), p. 268.
4 Ermolaev, German, *Mikhail Sholokhov i ego tvorchestvo* (St Petersburg: Akademicheskii proekt, 2000), p. 56.
5 Ermolaev, *Mikhail Sholokhov i ego tvorchestvo*, pp. 23, 33, 40, 46, 51, 56.
6 Barnes, Christopher, *Boris Pasternak: A Literary Biography*, vol. II (1928–1960), (Cambridge: Cambridge University Press, 1998), p. 259.
7 'Trotskyite–Bukharinites' was an accusatory label pinned on Stalin's political opponents during the late 1930s purges, implying conspiracy and treason against the Soviet people and alleging collaboration with Lev Trotsky and Nikolai Bukharin. Trotsky was expelled from the Party and in exile from 1929 onwards (and assassinated on Stalin's order in 1940, in Mexico), and Bukharin, one of the most prominent members of the 'old Bolshevik guard', was ultimately executed as an 'enemy of the people' in 1938. The Doctors' Plot (1953) was one of Stalin's last fabricated trials, accusing a group of prominent medical doctors, predominantly Jewish, of a Zionist plot/conspiracy to eliminate the leadership of the Soviet Union, including Stalin himself, through malpractice and poisoning. See Garrard and Garrard, *The Bones of Berdychev*, p. 128.
8 Siniavsky's essay was published (1960) in English as *On Socialist Realism*, trans. George Dennis.
9 'Rech´ sekretaria TsK VKP(b) A. A. Zhdanova' in *Pervyi s´´ezd pisatelei: Stenograficheskii otchet* (Moscow: Ogiz, 1934), p. 5.
10 *Aristotle's Poetics*, trans. Leon Golden (Tallahassee, FL: University Presses of Florida, 1981), pp. 10, 44, respectively.
11 Moretti, *Modern Epic*, p. 49.

12 Phillips, Christopher, 'Lighting out for the Rough Ground: America's Epic Origins and the Richness of World Literature', *PMLA*, 122, no. 5 (October 2007), p. 1501.

13 Lukács, Georg, *The Theory of the Novel: A Historico-Philosophical Essay on the Forms of Great Epic Literature*, trans. Anna Bostock (Cambridge, MA: MIT Press, 1971), p. 66.

14 Auerbach, Erich, *Mimesis: The Representation of Reality in Western Literature*, trans. Willard R. Trask (Princeton, NJ: Princeton University Press, 2003), p.12.

15 Clark, Katerina, 'Socialist Realism *with* Shores: The Conventions for the Positive Hero' in Thomas Lahusen and Evgeny Dobrenko, eds., *Socialist Realism without Shores* (Durham, NC: Duke University Press, 1997), pp. 27–50.

16 Lukács, 'Rasskaz ili opisanie' (trans. from the German manuscript by N. Vol'kenau), *Literaturnyi kritik* (1936), no. 8, pp. 44, 65.

17 *Ibid.*, p. 55.

18 Ermolaev, *Mikhail Sholokhov i ego tvorchestvo*, p. 35.

19 *Ibid.*, pp. 82–85.

20 Bubennov, Mikhail, 'O romane V. Grossmana "Za pravoe delo"', *Pravda*, 13 February 1953.

21 *Ibid.*

22 RGALI, F 631, op. 15, e/kh 275.

23 Moretti, *Modern Epic*, p. 14.

FURTHER READING

Afiani, V. and Tomilina, N., eds., '*A za mnoiu shum pogoni . . .*'. *Boris Pasternak i vlast'*. Dokumenty, 1956–1972 (Moscow: ROSSPEN, 2001).

Barnes, Christopher, *Boris Pasternak: A Literary Biography*, vol. II (1928–1960) (Cambridge: Cambridge University Press, 1998).

Bocharov, Anatolii, *Vasilii Grossman. Zhizn', Tvorchestvo, Sud'ba* (Moscow: Sovetskii pisatel', 1990).

Clark, Katerina, *The Soviet Novel: History as Ritual*, 3rd. edn. (Bloomington, IN: Indiana University Press, 2001).

Dunlop, John, Haugh, Richard, and Klimoff, Alexis, eds., *Alexander Solzhenitsyn: Critical Essays and Documentary Materials* (New York: Collier Books, 1975).

Ermolaev, Herman, *Mikhail Sholokhov and His Art* (Princeton, NJ: Princeton University Press, 1982).

Garrard, John and Garrard, Carol, *The Bones of Berdychev: The Life and Fate of Vasilii Grossman* (New York: Free Press, 1996).

Livingstone, Angela, *Boris Pasternak*: Doctor Zhivago (Cambridge: Cambridge University Press, 1989).

Murphy, A. B., Butt, V.P., and Ermolaev, H., *Sholokhov's Tikhii Don: A Commentary in Two Volumes* (Birmingham: Slavonic Department, University of Birmingham, 1997).

Scammell, Michael, *Solzhenitsyn: A Biography* (New York: W.W. Norton, 1984).

Siniavsky, Andrei, *On Socialist Realism*, trans. George Dennis (New York: Pantheon Books, 1960).

9

MARINA BALINA

Prose after Stalin

The liberal changes that started in Soviet Russia after Stalin's death (5 March 1953) came to be called 'The Thaw', after the 1954 novel of this title by Ilia Ehrenburg, in which the writer advocated for the artist's right to self-expression, criticized the events of recent history, and expressed hope for change. During the ensuing decade, 'thaws' and 'freezes' alternated with each other; but throughout this period observers could see the seemingly unified, monolithic stratum of Soviet culture that had been shaped and consolidated in the preceding Stalinist period erode rapidly. A special role in these changes was allotted to literature, both documentary and *belletristic*, thereby affirming the classical postulate about the literature-centredness of Russian culture as a whole. Thaw literature had its own pioneers: the writer and critic Vladimir Pomerantsev is usually considered the main one of the 'first Thaw' because of the groundbreaking statements he made in his December 1954 article 'On Sincerity in Literature' ('Ob iskrennosti v literature') in the literary journal *Novyi mir*, in which he insisted on the sincerity of a writer's work as the measure of artistic achievement. His claim that the writer should follow his own creative impulses rather than official party doctrine drew both accolades and harsh criticism; but it broke the silence about the situation in literature and the arts, and vigorous discussions about the state of literature began.

For many of his contemporaries, the undoubted champion of Thaw reforms was the Communist Party's First Secretary Nikita Khrushchev, who in his 'Secret Speech' at the Twentieth Party Congress (on 25 February 1956) denounced Stalin's 'cult of personality' and held him responsible for the destruction of many innocent lives during the purges. The speech became a turning point in the re-evaluation of the Soviet past. The revolutionary past was still considered to be the glorious rebirth of Russia, and the greatness of the Communist cause remained indisputable: accordingly, a call arose for a return to 'Lenin's norms' for managing the Party's affairs. The removal of Stalin's body from its position next to Lenin's in the Red Square mausoleum in October 1961 was more than a symbolic gesture: a big chunk of recent Soviet history had to be re-evaluated and re-written. The return of the victims of Stalinist purges from the forced-labour gulag camps, which had already started in the late 1950s, contributed to these efforts by providing eyewitness accounts of life (and survival) in the gulag system – the Stalinist Terror's powerful machine of human destruction. A new body of fictional texts based on the facts of these experiences was also created. The most remarkable event in this respect was the November 1962 publication in *Novyi mir* of Alexander Solzhenitsyn's story *One Day in the Life of Ivan Denisovich* (*Odin den´ Ivana Denisovicha*), which for the first time introduced the topic in literature.

A peculiar feature of the Thaw renaissance that spilled over into the Brezhnev-era 'Stagnation' that followed it was the stratification of not only Soviet literature but also of its practitioners – Soviet writers. Simultaneous actors on the literary scene were the older generation of writers shaped by 1920s avant-garde culture ('writers of the Soviet period', in Marietta Chudakova's 2005 definition[1]) such as Ilia Ehrenburg and Valentin Kataev; politically correct Soviet writers (Anatolii Ivanov, Petr Proskurin, Georgii Markov) whose literary products promoted the official party line; and the generation of writers labelled as 'Sixtyists' (*shestidesiatniki*), known as the 'children of the Thaw', whose creative life was a constant balancing act between the demands of censorship and the attempt to remain true to their creative credo.

Though full of liberal potential during its brief 'lifetime' (and to some extent, benefiting Stagnation-era literature as well), the Thaw turned out to be a traumatic period, because it led to a re-examination of the basic postulates of the Soviet experience. Literature – and more than any other kind, *belles lettres* – became the battlefield on which the country's conservative and progressive forces engaged to scrutinize the Soviet past, for both their own reasons and for society, yet once again. The generation born in the 1920s did not experience the trauma of the Revolution directly, as their parents had; but like their parents, they found themselves (as Mandelshtam said) 'cast out of their own biographies' by the Thaw's re-examination of the historical values instilled in them from their earliest years in school. For this generation, the main measure of truth was their personal experience of the preceding war: for its writers, wartime brotherhood and the nation's unity when facing the enemy eclipsed the direct experience of Stalinist Soviet existence. And although the war theme became a significant part of Soviet mythology, it was just this generation of authors (Viktor Nekrasov, Grigorii Baklanov, Konstantin Vorobev, and Vasil Bykov) that steered wartime discourse back into the direction of 'sincerity in literature', when the story of the war was imagined not only as a test of the nation but also as a personal experience.

Separated by a mere decade from the authors who had lived through the war, the generation born in the 1930s experienced Stalin's Great Terror (1936–1938) (families devastated by arrested parents, life in orphanages), and it became a defining factor of their personal biographies. It was just this personal experience that the Sixtyist writers addressed. The Thaw's lasting contribution to literature was a liberation from the necessity to substitute national memory, which the Soviet political system had corrupted and usurped, for personal history. The re-examination of personal history became a trigger for re-examination of the history of the state: indeed, it was individual memory that had to return the status of *homo historicus*, the possessor of collective memory, to the person living during the Thaw, and to replace the sense of being 'cast out' of history with a feeling of belonging to it. Particularly significant in the context of this re-examination was Ehrenburg's memoir *People, Years, Life* (*Liudi, gody, zhizn'*, 1960–1965), in which the author correlates the significance of his own story with the events of cultural history. Kataev, another representative of the older generation of the writer's profession, also played a considerable role in freeing individual memory. He takes liberties in his treatment of apparently 'petrified' history, creating a fictional image of Lenin in *The Little Door in the Wall* (*Malen'kaia dver' v stene*, 1964), for instance, or with his no less frivolous treatment in *The Grass of Oblivion* (*Trava zabveniia*, 1967) of the memory of the poet canonized in Soviet literature, Vladimir Mayakovsky.

Thus, the story of the Soviet nation appeared as a multi-layered narrative written in palimpsest modality by official history as well as individual history. The 'Short Course' History of the Bolshevik Party, for instance, created by Stalin-as-writer and thenceforth established as the obligatory text for studying the history of the Revolution, was now overlaid with the text of Khrushchev's Secret Speech. This latter text, full of revelatory details about Stalin's 'cult of personality' and transgressions against 'Leninist norms' in politics, did more than anything else to shatter the notion of a monolithic Soviet history. The spaces that unexpectedly opened up in this new overlay had to be filled with new history. It was not historical documents, however, that began to function in this new history – the opening of Party archives did not come until later, as a phenomenon of the *perestroika* period – but literary texts: memoirs and fiction, the primary task of which was to unlock human memory.

Paul Ricoeur, in his studies of the relationship between memory and history, and memory and forgetfulness, suggests three types of memory: blocked memory, manipulated memory, and abusively controlled memory.[2]

The shaping of the collective memory of the pre-war generation – with the obligatory deletion of the names of 'enemies of the people' from history text-books, the removal of repressed authors' books from libraries, and collective condemnations of the guilty – is an obvious example of abusive control. But even the half-truths of official Thaw-period documents were more an attempt to manipulate collective memory than to liberate it. Nonetheless, it was Thaw literature that began the work of unlocking memory: not simply individual memory, but the memory of the whole generation born during the ascent of revolutionary zeal and suffering through the traumatic losses of Stalinism and war. This generation's collective experience was constructed from that of different social groups – dwellers from city and countryside, intelligentsia and workers, and children of Stalin's elite as well as those of repressed parents. Thus the liberation of their memories highlights differing temporal and spatial connections in the works of Thaw literature, which allows us to divide this prose, perhaps somewhat provisionally, into wartime narratives, 'village prose', and urban prose.

'The truth of the trenches': personalizing war memory

Cultural historian Boris Dubin explains that the tragic experience of the Second World War provided the most stable *collective* identification for the Soviet people.[3] War prose, which offered an alternative history of this war, took shape in the Thaw period; it started with a privatization of war history that put the official version of the war to the test against an individual's experience, making history into a mere backdrop of an individual story. This trend served as a formative element in the 1950s and 1960s war prose of Iurii Bondarev (b. 1924), Grigorii Baklanov (1923–2010), Konstantin Vorobev (1919–1975), Vasil Bykov (1924–2003), and Viktor Astafev (1924–2001). To some degree, these authors' works were an antithesis to the official Stalinist version of the war, with its focus on heroic deeds: they intentionally brought the war narrative down to the register of the ordinary, to everyday survival at the front.

The most commonly used designation for this new literature is 'lieutenants' prose,' which contrasts it with the widely published memoirs of higher-ranking Soviet military officialdom. By moving away from the glamourization of the Soviet heroism, the authors – actual participants of military operations, survivors of bloody battles – shared with readers *their own* reality of 'the truth of life in the trenches'. By focusing their narratives on the profound effects of the war experience on the human spirit, these writers provided common human dimensions to the tragedy, thus replacing the locality of *patrie* (Russia) with the universal image of human suffering.

Viktor Nekrasov (1911–1987) is viewed as a precursor of this significant shift in war narratives; he was the first to reveal the war's unglamorous reality in his novel *In the Trenches of Stalingrad* (*V okopakh Stalingrada*, 1946). This very aspect of the novel, which critics of the time considered its downfall, became a major narrative device of 'lieutenants' prose' and affected the choice of narrative form – giving preference to the novella (*povest'*) over the novel (*roman*).

The main protagonist of these novellas is a prosaic character, an *intelligent* – a high school graduate, or a student – the sort who would appear the least prepared for war. Critics have often complained that the autobiographical character of these narratives makes them highly subjective; it is important to realize, however, that the autobiographical experience was just the impulse that led these writers to create works of fiction. The plots of the novellas are often restricted in both their temporal and spatial dimensions to a single episode that focuses on only a few hours in the lives of the soldiers (Bykov, *The Cry of the Cranes/Zhuravlinyi krik*, 1960), or perhaps a few days, like the march towards a battlefield (Vorobev, *Killed at Moscow/Ubity pod Moskvoi*, 1963).

The same restrictive principle is applied to the scope of the military engagements depicted, making geographical accuracy an important feature of the stories. The function of this structural device is twofold: it provides factual support to fiction with a specific historical event and, with this specificity, simultaneously challenges the epic depiction of history that had been so popular during the previous decade. In *The Battalions Are Asking for Fire* (*Batal'ony prosiat ognia*, 1957) Bondarev constrains his narrative to the capture of one town on the right bank of the Dnieper. In *The Foothold* (*Piad' zemli*, 1959), Baklanov references a line from a popular pre-war (1939) song, 'The March of the Soviet Tankmen': 'We don't crave a foothold on any foreign land/But every single inch of ours we will defend.' Only when confronted with the concrete experience of a military battle does the main character, Lieutenant Motovilov (and the rest of his generation), understand the real portent of these words, realizing the true cost of defending an 'inch of ground' and discerning the fatal discrepancy between the emptiness of propaganda rhetoric and the bloody reality of this war.

The focus on individual experience in 'lieutenants' prose' has an interesting impact on the relationship between the history *of* the war and an individual's story *in* the war. The writers do not so much care about the chronology of the war: they introduce characters at moments when their experiences become a litmus test for their human dignity rather than their level of military success. The protagonists feel a personal responsibility for the course of the war: they measure victories not by the capture of towns and villages but by the human losses accompanying them. Thus the personal story dominates the depiction of history and becomes a sort of *Bildungsroman* (novel of education) by focusing on the moral dilemmas confronting the characters.

Protagonists in 'lieutenants' prose' are faced with the massiveness of human sacrifice in this war, and they react differently to the human losses they witness. In Vorobev's *Killed at Moscow*, company commander Riumin leads the young cadets of the Kremlin's military school to Moscow to participate in the defence of the capital, one of the most significant moments in Second World War history. Out of 240 cadets, only one survives this march. Riumin, an ideal officer who follows orders without questioning them, commits suicide. He cannot bear his feelings of guilt and personal responsibility for the senseless losses, nor can he justify his own wrong decisions by shifting the moral authority to his superiors. Bondarev's captain Boris Ermakov (*The Battalions Are Asking for Fire*) can never consider the liberation of Dnepropetrovsk a victory, since it was determined by the needless sacrifice of two battalions, and he is not afraid to confront Colonel Iverzev, the superior responsible for this operation. In Bondarev's *The Last Volleys* (*Poslednie zalpy*, 1959), the rigorous Captain Novikov is immune to any manifestation of kindness, hardened by his constant confrontations with human losses. Literary critics have likened the outlook of these characters to those of the 'lost generation' in the novels by the German writer Erich Maria Remarque, thus coining the derogatory term *remarquism*, which signifies a focus on disappointment and mistrust in life, and high naturalism in the portrayal of life at the front.[4] Frank depiction of dead or dismembered bodies was both novel and frightening, and Soviet society, which was undergoing major existential changes in the 1950s and early 1960s, had not yet developed a suitable vocabulary for discussing these brutal aspects of war.

The war novellas of the 1950s–1960s present their readers with an interesting depiction of time: their characters live in a fragile moment of the present, and seldom recall their pasts. Astafev called his novella *The Shepherd and His Wife* (*Pastukh i pastushka*, 1971) a 'contemporary pastoral', thus emphasizing his idealistic approach to the depiction of love during a time of war: he concentrates on the effects of war on the human soul, which in wartime is destroyed before the body is. While liberating a small village, soldiers discover the bodies of an old shepherd and his wife next to each other, their hands literally locked together. This picture of inseparability even in death becomes a leitmotif in the tragic love story of Lieutenant Boris Kostiaev and the nurse Liusia, a jaded woman who is 'rejuvenated' by the image that Kostiaev creates of her. But their love, though idealistic, is also artificial: dismissing the reality of the war, the pair could easily be following a beautiful 'script' of the pre-war ideal of happiness as they plan their post-war life together. Astafev foreshadows the bitter end of the story (Kostiaev dies from wounds) by incorporating his own commentary into the texture of the narrative: he follows every new version of the lovers' future meetings with a comment such as 'but it never happened'. Astafev refuses to create a new myth of the healing power of love: penetrating every realm of human existence, the war alters even the world of emotions. What is left to the characters (and, consequently, to readers) is the redeeming power of remembrance, which allows the fallen soldiers of the Second World War a continued 'existence' in memory. Thus Liusia's much-anticipated reunion with Boris turns out to be the discovery of his grave – the place of memory with which the story concludes. The individual story is raised to the level of history, thus making fiction more truthful than a lifeless document.

Concentration on story rather than history in the 1950s–1960s war narratives has the effect of shifting from depiction of ideological conflict (Soviet Russia vs. Nazi Germany) to investigation of the capabilities of the human character and to the juxtaposition of good and evil within it. Writers examine comrades-in-arms who, cast into extreme circumstances, present a multitude of different human qualities. The narrative tone changes substantially, and these authors (who were, after all, direct participants in the events described) pronounce their own judgement on the actions of the characters not by the more lenient standards of wartime brotherhood but according to higher obligations of universal moral duty; the reader is denied the right to judge right and wrong. In this literature, protagonists constantly re-examine the very essence of ethical consciousness and come to realize that moral behaviour is not an inherent trait of the Soviet citizen but rather a growth process that requires difficult individual choices.

This problem is central to other works by Bykov but it pervades the very essence of his novella *Sotnikov* (1970).[5] Bykov constructs his narrative by interweaving the stories of two partisan fighters, Sotnikov and Rybak, who are captured by the police while trying to get food for their unit in a nearby village. Bykov investigates the psychological motivations for betrayal: Rybak, driven by the desire to survive, enters into a bargaining game with his captors, convinced that he will finally prevail. Bykov also highlights the peril of moral compromise through Rybak, who, gradually yielding to the demands of the enemy, first betrays the people who had helped him to hide (Petr, the village headman; Demchikha, a mother of three children; and Basia, a Jewish girl) and finally becomes the enemy's henchman, executing his fellow partisan, Sotnikov. Rybak is a good soldier, and is 'street-smart' and skilled: but he is also a person without any moral grounding, and his conscience is controlled by his desire to survive, without regard for the consequences. Sotnikov's convictions arise from a moral code that makes him wary of the cost of any compromise. The execution scene is raised to the level of a parable when Rybak, pulling the log from underneath Sotnikov, whispers 'Forgive me, brother'. The Bible that appears, when Rybak's other victim (Petr) reads it, reinforces this existential undertone of the story, suggesting a modern Cain and Abel. Yet again, story prevails over history by making the problem of moral choice the measurement of the real dimensions of human tragedy. In this context, the war theme in Bykov's prose has obviously expanded the narrational frame: the theme is perceived as existential, hitting at the very foundations of human life.

During the 1970s Stagnation, the focus in war narratives changed from the depiction of an individual experience to a more panoramic depiction of the war. Individual memories were once again subordinated to history, but this time with a particular focus on the role of personality in shaping historical events. These issues dominated the prose of the former 'lieutenants' as well, making them embrace the bigger narrative form – the novel – while keeping the war central to their work. In Baklanov's *June 1941* (*Iiun´ 41-go*, 1964), the issue of Stalin's personal responsibility for the defeats and human losses was addressed for the first time; Bondarev's *The Hot Snow* (*Goriachii sneg*, 1969) already manifests some features of the epic novel. Shifting his focus from personal experience to 'favourite' battles of official Soviet history, Bondarev in his later works (*Shore/Bereg*, 1975; *Choice/Vybor*, 1980) abandoned the sincerity of his war novellas, becoming one of the celebrated 'court writers' – the literary functionaries of the Soviet Writers' Union during the Brezhnev era.

Distinctive in this shift towards the new war epic are the works of Konstantin Simonov (1915–1979), for whom the telling of the Second World War story became a lifelong commitment. His trilogy *The Living and The Dead* (*Zhivye i mertvye*, 1959–1971) is based on his personal experiences as a war correspondent as well as his extensive archival research, and presents an interesting 'balancing act' between the state-approved depiction of history and the sincerity of a personal story. The first part of the trilogy focuses on the experiences of a war correspondent, Ivan Sintsov, and describes the turmoil of the early days of 1941. The work demonstrates the incredible *fear* of the unknown that the Soviet army experienced and consistently chips away the myth of the invincibility of this army on many levels, from ordinary soldiers to generals. Simonov is one of the first writers to introduce a character (General Serpilin) that had been a victim of the Stalin purges but who was returned directly from the camp to the front. A military professional – a former instructor at the military academy – Serpilin had constantly warned his students and colleagues of the dangers of the forthcoming war, thus directly contradicting the official myth of Soviet readiness to defeat any enemy. By demonstrating the moral superiority of Serpilin over Colonel Baranov (his former colleague at the military academy, one of those who accused him of 'treason'), Simonov brings to the forefront of his narrative questions surrounding Stalin's leadership and his responsibility for the massive losses. In the following parts of the trilogy, however, the author replaces the depiction of human lives with the re-creation of historical battles; his focus on human experience becomes trapped in the epic proportions of the novel.

Ironically, the main achievement of 'lieutenants' prose' – making the memory of the war a private domain – was reflected in the title of a war memoir by the most public figure of the ensuing decade, the Communist Party's General Secretary Leonid Brezhnev. Entitled *Small Land* (*Malaia zemlia*, 1978), his recollections elevated the defence of a small bridgehead near Novorossiisk to the level of the most decisive Second World War battles. Glorification of war achievements became the favourite subject in the works of the Soviet 'court writers'. Known as 'secretaries' prose', this state-sanctioned literature ranged from multi-volume epic novels (Ivan Stadniuk's *The War/Voina*, 1967–1980; Alexander Chakovsky's *Siege/Blokada*, 1968–1974, *Victory/Pobeda*, 1978–1981) to entertaining detective novels (Vadim Kozhevnikov's *Shield and Sword/Shchit i mech'*, 1965, Iulian Semenov's *Seventeen Moments of Spring/Semnadtsat' mgnovenii vesny*, 1969). These writers insisted that the truth of the war belongs to their narratives because they were based on real archival research. By this assertion, these writers deny the truthfulness of the personal vision of the war in 'lieutenants' prose'.

Village prose: memory as nostalgia

Also begotten of the 'Thaw tradition', village prose was fundamentally driven by an attempt to explain the lost moral foundation of life, rather than by any quest for missing or distorted history. The writers who chose to write 'village prose' in the Thaw years undertook the theme of 'destructive acceleration of history' within the rural commune – Russia's most historic social model. As the result of the waves of urbanization that had taken place in Russia in the 1920s and then in the 1930s period of industrialization, the terrible consequences of collectivization (1929–1935), and the post-war destitution of the countryside, a new social type appeared – the 'interstitial' urbanites, who try to forget their rural roots as quickly as possible but nonetheless cannot fully assimilate into their new life. In 'village prose' these characters are contrasted to the righteous people in the countryside who, despite all the cataclysms of the times, have preserved their 'roots' and understand the individual's connection to history. This is 'native' history, however: not without reason, a new *topos* is cultivated in village literature, the 'native region' (*malaia rodina*). The solicitous attitude towards it – one's own village, or even one's own home in the village – becomes a metaphor for the attitude toward Russia as a whole.

Among the outstanding exponents of village prose are the writers Fedor Abramov (1920–1983), Vasilii Belov (b. 1932), Valentin Rasputin (b. 1937), Vasilii Shukshin (1927–1974), and Astafev who, as we have already seen, is notable for his war prose as well. The chief protagonist of their works is a simple man of the people, and the plots are often based on the writers' own recollections of childhood. Kathleen Parthé suggests that village prose 'has as its basis the genuine, long-term rural experiences and memories of the writer. It also drew upon his sense of the depth and beauty of rural traditions and language, as well as his awareness of the difficult history of the collectivized countryside.'[6]

In her study of nostalgia, Svetlana Boym suggests that 'two kinds of nostalgia characterize one's relationship to the past, to the imagined community, to home, to one's own self-perception: restorative and reflective.'[7] While restorative nostalgia deals primarily with the national past and future, reflective nostalgia is 'more about individual and cultural memory'.[8] In the work of one of the first village prose writers, Vasilii Belov, restorative nostalgia predominates, since Belov's quest looks to the inner life of the village in hopes of discovering the village-dweller's lost core of moral superiority over the 'interstitial' urbanite. The chief protagonist of Belov's novella *That's How Things are Done* (*Privychnoe delo*, 1966), Ivan Drynov, lives with his family in constant toil and hardship, but for them this is just 'how things are done'. Drynov is not portrayed as a 'model citizen' but, nonetheless, he is an organic part of the village's world that he nourishes, just as this world provides for him. Though not distinguished by good sense, Drynov has an incredible real-life tenacity that, the author is convinced, his own native soil gives him.

Belov brings to village prose the concepts of harmony and disharmony, through which he describes the lives of his protagonists. Harmony is expressed in unity with nature, in the honesty of one's actions, in living by the laws of ancestral memory. But disharmony intrudes when there is a break with the village's principles of living: most often, this disharmony is proof of the encroachment of an alien world that subjugates the wholesome world of the village. The disruption of the village's harmony is most often tied to the arrival of a regional authority, thanks to whom work – the foundation of village life – is turned into a sort of window dressing.

Belov continues this same theme in *The Carpenters' Tales* (*Plotnitskie rasskazy*, 1968), wherein he contrasts two types of village residents: the industrious master-craftsman Olesha Smolin and the do-nothing village demagogue Avenir Kozonkov; the latter, in Soviet times, has managed to become a boss. Avenir represents those who have destroyed their roots: he has thrown the bell down from the church, not to mention urinating from the bell tower, and has betrayed people. But, in the new life, it is Avenir who merits a personal pension, and Avenir who considers his own life to be honest. Olesha and Avenir are representatives of the same generation: but the meek Olesha does not betray the harmony of the village, while Avenir, the product of Soviet power in the countryside (which is exactly what brings disharmony in the peasants' life), has been transformed from a hardworking farmer into a dogmatist. Indeed, it would appear that Olesha is the one who preserves the lost harmony of village life. But at the end of the story, the author himself is surprised to see these two now-old men drinking together. The horror of the destructive force of the socialist order in the post-Revolutionary village is concentrated in this 'togetherness', in which the 'upright man' and the do-nothing dogmatist end up as equals.

Belov's discovery of discord in village life led him immediately to try to blame the city for this disharmony. His novella *Education, Doctor Spock's Way* (*Vospitanie po doktoru Spoku*, 1974) depicts the life of the 'interstitial' man Konstantin Zorin, who gladly left the village and settled in the city after finishing school. But life does not treat him kindly: his wife Antonina, who hastens to live by the city's rules and, as is the fashion, educates their daughter according to Doctor Spock's book instead of teaching her the native traditions, finally leaves him. The brief moment of togetherness that Konstantin has with his wife prior to their separation occurs in nature, far from the city; but it is violated by urban intellectuals who turn up and destroy the moment of sincere communion, replacing it with claptrap. Only upon his return to the village does Konstantin feel a sensation of harmony: in this place, the morally tortured hero is healed by his native soil.

Desiring to restore the ideal world of simple folk, Belov in his next works (*Harmony/Lad*, 1979–1981 and *The Best is Yet to Come/Vse vperedi*, 1986) seeks to resolve the conflict he finds in the pernicious influence on rural folk from foreigners, among whom he singles out Jews. The predominant anti-Semitic and anti-Western sentiments among the village prose writers associated with the journals *Nash sovremennik* and *Molodaia gvardiia*, and the newspaper *Literaturnaia Rossiia* in the late 1970s–1980s led to a crisis in this genre in the pre-*perestroika* years. The restorative nostalgia of many of these writers (Belov, Rasputin, Astafev) took on a tinge of Russian chauvinism, which reflected negatively on the quality of their prose. Historian Nikolai Mitrokhin has written about their active participation in the 'Russian Party' nationalist movement, which in Soviet times brought together russophile writers, critics, and Party leadership.[9] The well-intentioned principles of village prose, which were tied to preservation of the cultural heritage, the fight to save the environment, and respect for spirituality, took on an extremely nationalistic tone especially during Gorbachev's *glasnost'* period, which led to a sweeping negative appraisal of these authors' works, both among liberal audiences domestically and abroad. Sad though the turnaround in the position of these talented writers might be, one must not forget that they were the ones who restored the memory of the terrible trauma that the Revolution inflicted on the Russian countryside.

Thus, for the village prose writers, the guardians of the harmony of simple folk are the older generation who experienced all the ordeals of the Revolution, collectivization, and war but did not lose the real-life tenacity of the village. And it is this theme, the moral succession of generations, which concerns village prose authors like Abramov and Rasputin, who try to reveal where the rift in the transmission of moral principles begins. The old man Stavrov, for example, the hero of Abramov's tetralogy *The Priaslins* (*Priasliny*, 1958–1978), cannot understand his grandson Egorsha, who flees the village in pursuit of an easy life. But Abramov punishes the grandson, through his grandfather's own hands: the old man gives his house, which he has spent his whole life building, to Lizka, Egorsha's abandoned wife; in arranging matters thus it is as if Abramov is asserting that the succession has not died. But the novel does not offer the reader any possibility of an optimistic solution: Mikhail Priaslin, the character who most faithfully assimilates the rural ideals, constantly endures losses because he remains true to the village. Nevertheless, Abramov's 'desk drawer' stories that were written at the time leave no illusions as to the author's views about the destruction of the countryside – he blames the Soviet authorities. In the second part of the tetralogy, *Two Winters, Three Summers* (*Dve zimy i tri leta*, 1968), the family unity of the village community, restored temporarily during wartime, is replaced by discord in the ensuing peacetime. Vacuous chatterboxes like Egorsha, or state commissioners who rob the *kolkhoz* with their vouchers and party directives, triumph in the post-war village. Abramov demonstrates how disunited the village commune is as a world of mutual support: when Ivan Lukashin, a beloved and respected leader, is arrested in the usual 1950s Stalinist campaign, few people venture to sign a letter in his defence. All the peripeties of rural life in Soviet times have destroyed the world of the village as a community.

The writer Rasputin raises this very same issue in his story entitled 'Money for Mariia' ('Den´gi dlia Marii', 1967). The trusting village saleswoman Mariia, who has given everyone credit, comes up short by 1,000 rubles. To avoid prison, she must come up with this sum very quickly. But the villagers who have fed the hungry and the crippled and have always joined together to support orphans and to help during misfortunes, greet Mariia's husband Kuzma, who has come to ask for help, with closed doors.

The storehouse of memory, it turns out, is still in the village elders – Darya Pinegina in Rasputin's *Farewell to Matyora* (*Proshchanie s Materoi*, 1976), Anna in his *Borrowed Time* (*Poslednii srok*, 1970), and Vit´ka Potylitsyn's grandmother in Astafev's *The Last Bow* (*Poslednii poklon*, 1968). Their life-wisdom is contrasted to the contemporary hustle and bustle, to the pettiness of existence. Paradoxical though it seems, the destruction of the entire village milieu leads to the genesis of a new 'twist' within village prose: ecological prose, which tells the story of the annihilation of the most important Home – Nature, in harmony with which the countryside had always lived. In *Farewell to Matyora*, the village disappears under water in order to make way for the new hydroelectric power plant, and along with the village, the cemetery – a place for communion with ancestral memory – is lost. In Astafev's *King-Fish* (*Tsar´-ryba*, 1976), the militant attitude toward nature disrupts the life cycle itself and reveals the moral flaws in an 'interstitial' man who has failed to learn the ecological memory of the village commune. Despite its poetic language, this 'narrative in stories' is one of the most brutal texts of village prose. Its didacticism is evident: all the poachers who despoil the Enisei River are punished for their attitude toward nature. Nevertheless, the narrative ends with a general idyll and in harmony, a moral utopia in the form of a communal fish soup feast in the tiny village of Boganida. This soup is being cooked to celebrate the first catch, a ritual that is the very embodiment of harmony, a village prose writer's romantic daydream about a community of people living in fellowship with each other and with nature.

The characters in Shukshin's later short stories live in a world far removed from the utopian village commune. The village heroes in his first anthology, *Rural People* (*Sel´skie zhiteli*, 1963), are distinctive individuals, made strong by their ties to the land and the 'native region', but his 1970s short stories grapple with the image of the 'interstitial' character. Now his heroes can find no peace, lost in an 'interspace' between city and countryside. Even though they live on their native soil, these village characters constantly feel doubt about the 'rightness' of life; instead of helping them find 'harmony', the familiar walls only amplify their confusion. These characters are in a perpetual quest for something that lies elsewhere, the intangible meaning of their own existence. In the story 'I Believe' ('Veruiu'), Maksim Yarikov turns to the village priest for an answer about the meaning of life: none of the Soviet dogmas proclaimed on posters can lull the confusion that grips him every Sunday. Shukshin's simple heroes battle for their own dignity: in 'The Insult' ('Obida'), Sashka Ermolaev has been unjustly implicated in a drunken brawl, and tries to justify himself to the people queued in a store, but his callous listeners, wearied of constant waiting in queues, could not care less about the emotional state of Sashka, one of the Soviet era's 'little people'. Shukshin's 'interstitial' characters are most often 'oddballs' whose eccentricities lie in their constant attraction to the amazing and the beautiful. In 'The Microscope' ('Mikroskop'), Andrei Erin stands up to domestic squabbles in order to bring this amazing instrument into his house, so that he can discover the unknown world of microbes for himself. Vasilii Kniazev's sister-in-law in 'The Oddball' ('Chudik') drives him out of his brother's house because he has painted flowers and cranes on his nephew's baby carriage – in an attempt to make the dreary everyday world brighter and more beautiful.

But Shukshin comes nowhere near idealizing his characters. His negative characters are people who have lost the memory of village traditions. In 'Cut Down to Size' ('Srezal', 1970), the demagogue Gleb Kapustin has a voracious desire to 'punish' the educated city-dwellers who have come to the village. Devoid of the warmth and generosity of village folk, both traditional in the village prose that contrasts city and countryside, Shukshin's village greets its former inhabitants, now city-educated, with rudeness and a desire to humiliate them. The only thing alive in the foreman Shurygin's memory (in 'Tough Guy'/'Krepkii muzhik', 1970) is the destruction of tradition. For him, the ancient village church is only a sturdy brick building that he can use for a pigpen, and he is proud to have made himself the equal of revolutionary heroes who took the churches' crosses down. In distinction from his fellow village prose writers, Shukshin strives to depict the disharmony in the *soul* of the village inhabitant. The heroes of Belov, Astafev, and Abramov often maintain a spiritual faithfulness to tradition, but Shukshin's characters have lost the 'memory of the heart'.

Like war prose, village prose is a history of lost moral ideals that its writers try to resurrect from their own memories. The French anthropologist Pierre Nora writes, 'Memory is life... It remains in permanent evolution'.[10] The particularity of memory in village prose is that it is deprived of a dynamic: the village's ideals remain unshakable and do not submit to any correlation with time, since time can only destroy what has taken shape over the ages. And, for just this reason, village prose today is often perceived as the embodiment of a conservative (and sometimes aggressively traditional) moral utopia.

Urban prose: memory as the brushwood of history

The central hero of urban prose is the *intelligent*. By virtue of their education, the intelligentsia's connection with history is conditioned by knowledge of the intellectual traditions of their time; their life choice is not an intuitive whim, but the fully conscious choice of people who either accept or reject the compromises of their own times.

The leading light of urban prose was Iurii Trifonov (1925–1981), who opened his first historical narrative with these words: 'Every person has the reflection of history on him. On some it glows with a hot and fearsome light, and on others it is barely visible, barely warm; but it is there, on everyone. History blazes like a huge campfire, and each of us throws into it our own brushwood.'[11] The 'reflection of history's campfire' that glowed on the author himself was indicative of two great influences on his works: the experience of the Great Terror and the disillusionment of the Stagnation years.

Combined in Trifonov's creative work are an interest in describing everyday life and a profound and constant gravitation to Russia's history (more specifically, to its revolutionary past). As the author himself attested, his 'roots' were in history, from which he drew the material for his books. This might be the history of the 1917 Revolution as read from the history of his own family; the history of the 'People's Will' organization, presented as a densely populated dialogue – with Clio, the Muse of History, with the participants themselves, and with their opponents and sympathizers; the history of private lives in which earlier ideals disappear (his 'Muscovite' novellas); or, ultimately, his own biography as the son of a repressed Soviet party official, which became the basis for his later works. If for Trifonov-as-historian his main interest is in abused and manipulated memory, then for the texts of Trifonov-as-biographer, blocked memory is one of the most significant elements.

All of Trifonov's texts are tied to historical memory, from the broadest to the most intimate scope. Central to *The Campfire Glow* (*Otblesk kostra*, 1964) is his personal memory of his father Valentin, a prominent revolutionist who joined in the revolution at the age of seventeen, participated in the Civil War, and became a victim of Stalin's repressions. This novella is by no means a memoir, although the characters include several family members, notably Trifonov's uncle Evgeny, whose miraculously preserved diaries are included in the narrative. These real-life characters' lives are presented in the reflected 'glow' of the history surrounding them: thus Trifonov restores to the common historical memory the names of the cavalry commanders Boris Dumenko and Filipp Mironov, figures repressed during the Civil War and still forgotten by the Thaw's reconstruction of the past. The palimpsest modality continues to function when the partially 'repaired' history is covered with a new corrective layer. Trifonov's reference to the Revolutionary past is a quest for the lost revolutionary ideals for which his forebears had perished. Trifonov himself would shatter this typical Thaw mythology twice again, when he rewrote this plot: first, in *The Old Man* (*Starik*, 1978), and then in his posthumously published *Disappearance* (*Ischeznovenie*, 1987).

Impatience (*Neterpenie*, 1973), which is about the People's Will figure Andrei Zheliabov, belongs to this same series of works on history. Grounding himself in historical material, Trifonov attempts in this work to understand the sources of the Russian revolutionary movement, to decide for himself what the true significance (and possible necessity) of terror is to revolutionary struggle and to comprehend the prerequisite willingness to sacrifice oneself when getting involved in this movement. The novel ends by concluding that 'the enormous Russian ice flow did not cleave asunder, did not even crack or tremble' from the sacrifices that Zheliabov and his circle made: try as he might, Zheliabov cannot 'speed up history'. Written almost a decade after *The Campfire Glow*, the novel could justifiably serve as a preface to it, for both *The Old Man* and *Disappearance* are essentially responses to what an acceleration of history becomes. Zheliabov's 'impatience' is transformed into the intolerance of his successors.

Petr Letunov, the protagonist/narrator of *The Old Man*, combines two of Trifonov's favourite character types: he is both an old revolutionist and an historian. In *The Old Man*, Letunov reinstates historical memory by resuscitating the image of the falsely condemned Civil War hero Migulin. (Thus the author pulls features of the real-life heroes in *The Campfire Glow* – Dumenko and Mironov – into this fictional character.) Letunov was among those who had condemned Migulin, however, and thus he is driven not only by a noble impulse to reinstate the truth but also by his own guilt. In this way, Trifonov brings into his narratives an element of individuals' responsibility for the history they have themselves created. The admiration that Trifonov feels for the revolutionary zeal of his father and uncle gives way in *The Old Man* to circumspect analysis of three different types of revolutionists: the soulless doctrinaire Naum Orlik; Matvei Zaslavskii, a man full of hatred and the desire to avenge himself of personal insults; and the revolutionary ascetic Leontii Shigontsov. For all three, any manifestation of initiative or retreat from dogma is a betrayal of revolution. Letunov attempts to serve as an objective chronicler of history, restoring the truth but nonetheless preferring to block his own memory of betraying Migulin. Thus Trifonov combines the objectivity of history with the problem of personal responsibility for the past.

In *Disappearance*, Trifonov's most autobiographical novel, there is no place for revolutionary illusions and rosy ideals. The recollections of Igor Baiukov (nicknamed 'Gorik') about his repressed family are central to the narrative. An imposing figure is his father Nikolai, a famous Party functionary who sees and understands everything but prefers to explain the events of 1937 as a 'fascist conspiracy'. Nikolai's brother Mikhail, who holds an important military post, is right beside him. Both brothers know Stalin personally, but have arrived at a political compromise: they had supported Stalin's candidacy at the time only because of their dislike of Trotsky. In Trifonov's rendering, compromise always turns into personal tragedy. Sigrid McLaughlin remarks that '*Disappearance* is about the loss of home, home being a symbol for beliefs, ideals, justice, order, meaning and elementary well-being and belongingness. It is also about the mentality of conformism and obedience which produces the personality cult and was, in turn, reinforced by it.'[12] Thus a single multi-layered narrative arises from Trifonov's works which, when read sequentially from *The Campfire Glow* to *The Old Man*, and from thence to *Disappearance*, not only liberates pent-up memory but also restores the historical correlation between Stalinism and violence as components of revolution.

In her study of Trifonov, Natalia Ivanova writes about the social historicism of his creative work, which lies in the fact that he creates a social 'type' in his narratives.[13] One such type is the old revolutionist found in all his texts: Fedor Nikolaevich, the grandfather of the character Dmitriev in *The Exchange* (*Obmen*, 1969); Alexandra Prokofevna, mother of Sergei in *Another Life* (*Drugaia zhizn'*, 1969); and Ganchuk, an old man who is now a university professor in his new life (*The House on the Embankment/Dom na naberezhnoi*, 1976). These characters inhabit Trifonov's narratives as guardians of the noble revolutionary ideals lost by their children and grandchildren. But from the experience of interaction with history, Trifonov's 'old revolutionist' characters undergo a change and, due to faithfulness to high ideals, can appear dogmatic (Alexandra Prokofevna) or egotistical and cruel (Ganchuk). One might notice a parallel with village prose, since its old village women are somewhat like Trifonov's old revolutionists, with the latter's unshakable faith in revolutionary ideals and their disdain of the conformism and consumerism they see in the younger generations. But they are implacable enemies, since the old women revolutionaries destroyed just what the old village women nostalgically yearn for, and the former remember this destruction with pleasure. These Old Bolsheviks and village elders alike remain isolated, doomed to extinction: they have no one to whom they can pass their roots, nor any place in which this is possible. Trifonov also creates a type of conformist that is new to Soviet literature: one created by revolutionary history itself. Vadim Glebov (*The House on the Embankment*) is the hero that Stagnation culture needs, although his story unfolds in three different temporal layers: 1937, the peak of the Great Terror, when the inhabitants of the elite house on the embankment begin to disappear, one after another; 1947, during the new round of post-war repressions; and the stagnant 1970s, which the successful Glebov spends travelling abroad. Glebov deliberately betrays – in friendship, love, and in scholarship – but blames time itself for this: 'Whether you condemn me or not, you can't defy time; it twists whomever it wants.' Trifonov creates the story of a timeserver, on which he comments through his own recollections as the authorial guardian of memory. The author's nostalgic recollection of childhood is transformed into reflective nostalgia, in which both individual and cultural memory are subjected to scrupulous analysis.

At the heart of these two novellas lies the problem of moral choice, a challenge that all of Trifonov's heroes face. Antipov in *Time and Place* (*Vremia i mesto*, 1981) must choose between honest or dishonest behaviour when called upon to judge the authenticity of a literary text: though seduced by the potential 'blessing' of having his own book published in return for a favourable opinion, he is ultimately unable to complete this 'exchange' of his moral principles. By alternately combining and separating temporal layers (the cataclysms of the narrator's life constantly 'interrupt' the hero's life), the author shows how interconnected the insignificant and momentous events within a single human life are, and also how interwoven the lives of people around this individual are. In this novel, memory unfolds horizontally, not vertically, absorbing more and more personal histories that exist in parallel, and squeezing the larger history out to the periphery. Antipov recalls the date of Stalin's death not as a time of general mourning but as the date of an illegal abortion that he and his wife had scheduled, only at the last minute deciding to cancel it. Memory has no space for a hierarchy of events. History is just this type of memory, but in this case it is a history of human existence that goes beyond the bounds of a single life or a single geography and addresses the existential problems of good and evil.

History, be it remote or contemporary, is not simply a decorative background for the narratives of urban writers: their storytelling emerges from the connection between a person and history, between individual memory and historical memory. In Andrei Bitov's (b. 1937) novel *The Pushkin House* (*Pushkinskii dom*, 1978), Leva Odoevtsev is a keeper of the cultural memory of the past, a memory to which he is vitally connected (he is a scholar of literature, just as his father and grandfather before him were). Odoevtsev is a Stagnation-era hero: Bitov creates him as a talented man but of empty potential – and indeed, what else could Soviet history beget, with its vacillating moral principles, when a son (in this case Leva's father) has rejected his own father (a brilliant literary scholar and victim of Stalin's repressions) just to save his own job and prestige? But Leva, too, repeats his father's conduct when he sets out to meet his grandfather, returned from exile – to condemn his father for his shameful cowardice. Expecting praise from his grandfather, who has refused even to see his son, Leva is totally perplexed when the old man, enraged by this new betrayal, throws him out. As compared to his grandfather and 'Uncle Dickens', a family friend – both of whom, rooted in history, did not break the connection to cultural tradition in their lives – Leva is a person outside history, even though he is engaged with it (literary history) through his work. Just as Trifonov does, Bitov creates a *social type*: a person who, though talented, is without a foundation, without roots, the product of a cultural tradition torn apart and, because of this, doomed to inertia. Just as Trifonov does, Bitov engages in a quest for a new 'hero of our time', which he embodies in the careerist Mitishatev. Like Trifonov's Glebov, Mitishatev is an unprincipled man, constantly wavering according to surrounding circumstances; but Leva is incapable of opposing Mitishatev, since he has nothing to offer in the place of the latter's conformism. The climactic episode of the novel is telling: Leva, the failed heir of cultural tradition, and Mitishatev, a man outside tradition, both drunk, destroy the museum (the place where cultural memory is preserved) in the Pushkin House and then replace the ruined exhibit items with forgeries. Thus Bitov demonstrates how Leva, the urban man, not only cannot preserve a connection to history but also readily engages in the replacement of tradition with a simulacrum.[14] *The Pushkin House* is a metaphorical text about the destructive nature of a break with history, whether personal history (the Odoevtsev generations) or commonly held history.

In Bitov's novel, Leva becomes a tragic character who is incapable of restoring the connection to cultural history. The Sixtyists' generation, though 'awakened' by the changes of the Thaw, was ultimately incapable of defending the Thaw's ideals, and without a fight yielded its place to timeservers like Glebov and Mitishatev. In this context, being 'cast out of one's biography' becomes not a historical catastrophe but a manifestation of personal inadequacy, of voluntary capitulation. In urban prose, this is how the conflict of the intelligentsia hero with his time is resolved.

The literary phenomena of these differing kinds of prose brought to life by the Thaw's re-examination of history take unlocked memory as their very basis of construction. Their 'times and places' (to paraphrase Trifonov's title) do not coincide, since their authors' experiences are individualized, but these experiences belong to a single generation, nonetheless. But the boundaries between these trends are fluid: in urban prose, we often see as a protagonist a newly established city dweller who has not completely severed the ties with his childhood in the countryside; and seasoned village prose writers (Astafev, Rasputin) turn to writing war narratives. The high degree of individualization of memory in these works leads to the simultaneous existence within a single literary field of competing memories of the most significant historical landmarks in the country's cultural memory. *Homo sovieticus* acquires radically individual features and can no longer be perceived as an undifferentiated species and, following close on the heels of the split in the Soviet personality, the whole of Soviet history ceases to be understood as an unshakable monolith. It was just this type of literature that began the complex process of preparing for the new post-Soviet literature of the 1990s. The real achievement of the literary process that began to unlock memory in the Thaw period is the refusal to create a monopoly on memory; in doing so, it resurrected – however partially, as it constantly looked round for the censor – the complex experience of the Soviet *homo historicus*.

NOTES

1 Chudakova, Marietta, *Novye raboty. 2003–2005* (Moscow: Vremia, 2007), pp. 193–195.
2 Ricoeur, Paul, *Memory, History, Forgetting*, trans. Kathleen Blamey and David Pellauer (Chicago, IL: University of Chicago Press, 2004), p. 13.
3 Dubin, Boris, 'Pamiat´, voina, pamiat´ o voine. Konstruirovanie proshlogo v sotsial´noi praktike poslednikh desiatiletii', *Otechestvennye zapiski*, 4, no. 43 (2008), www.strana-oz.ru/?numid=45&article=1701 (last accessed 5 November 2008).
4 Chalmaev, Viktor A., *Na voine ostat´sia chelovekom. Frontovye stranisty russkoi prozy 60–90-kh godov* (Moscow: Moskovskii universitet, 2000), p. 36.
5 Director Larisa Shepit´ko adapted this novella in a 1976 Mosfilm studio film that she titled 'The Ascent' ('Voskhozhdenie'), by which she emphasized the existential significance of this story of betrayal.
6 Parthé, Kathleen F., *Russian Village Prose: The Radiant Past* (Princeton, NJ: Princeton University Press, 1992), p. 15.
7 Boym, Svetlana, *The Future of Nostalgia* (New York: Basic Books, 2001), p. 41.
8 *Ibid*. p. 49.
9 See Mitrokhin, Nikolai, *Russkaia partiia. Dvizhenie russkikh natsionalistov v SSSR 1953–1985* (Moscow: NLO, 2003).
10 Nora, Pierre, 'Between Memory and History: *Les Lieux de Mémoire*', *Representations*, no. 26, Special Issue: Memory and Counter-Memory (Spring 1989), p. 8.
11 Trifonov, Iurii, *Sobranie sochinenii v chetyrekh tomakh*, vol. 4 (Moscow: Khudozhestvennaia literatura, 1987), p. 7.
12 McLaughlin, Sigrid, 'A Moment in the History of Consciousness of the Soviet Intelligentsia: Trifonov's Novel *Disappearance*', *Studies in Comparative Communism*, 21, nos. 3/4 (Autumn/Winter 1988), pp. 303–311.

13 Ivanova, Natalia, *Proza Iuriia Trifonova* (Moscow: Sovetskii pisatel´, 1984), p. 98.
14 See Leiderman, N.L. and Lipovetskii, M.N., *Sovremennaia russkaia literatura. Kniga 2* (Moscow: URSS, 2001), pp. 260–266.

FURTHER READING

Belaia, Galina, *Literatura v zerkale kritiki. Sovremennye problemy* (Moscow: Sovetskii pisatel´, 1986).
Bocharov, Anatolii, *Chelovek i voina. Idei sotsialisticheskogo gumanizma v poslevoennoi proze o voine* (Moscow: Sovetskii pisatel´, 1978).
Chances, Ellen, *Andrei Bitov: The Ecology of Inspiration* (Cambridge: Cambridge University Press, 2006).
Ivanova, Natal´ia, *Proza Iuriia Trifonova* (Moscow: Sovetskii pisatel´, 1995).
Parthé, Kathleen, *Russian Village Prose: The Radiant Past* (Princeton, NJ: Princeton University Press, 1992).
  Russia's Dangerous Texts: History between the Lines (New Haven, CT: Yale University Press, 2004).
Surganov, Vsevolod, *Chelovek na zemle. Istoriko-literaturnyi ocherk* (Moscow: Sovetskii pisatel´, 1975).
Woll, Josephine, *Invented Truth: Soviet Reality and the Literary Imagination of Iurii Trifonov* (Durham, NC: Duke University Press, 1991).

10

MARK LIPOVETSKY

Post-Soviet Literature between Realism and Postmodernism

Perestroika in literature

The rapid revival of Russian literary life in the late 1980s and 1990s was a consequence of two significant events: the democratic reforms launched by Mikhail Gorbachev in 1987–1991, and especially the politics of *glasnost'* (openness), which created the opportunity for public critique of Soviet ideology and politics; the latter process, after the collapse of the Communist regime in 1991, led to the complete elimination of censorship. One of the most striking signs of this *perestroika* in literature was the return of numerous previously banned literary works. In this avalanche of masterpieces, artistically complex works such as the novels of Andrei Platonov, Vladimir Nabokov, Sasha Sokolov, Venedikt Erofeev, the poetry of Joseph Brodsky, along with classical texts of Russian, European, and American modernism, as well as émigré and underground literature, now became available to readers. It is significant, however, that the most heated critical discussion was triggered not by these works, but by more conventional novels that dealt with political issues and offered an anti-totalitarian vision of the Soviet past; these latter received the greatest critical attention and generated the most excitement among the reading public.

It comes as no surprise, then, that in the late 1980s and early 1990s literary journals engaged in ardent political discussions, which resulted in a drastic political polarization of the entire field of literary production. One group of journals, magazines, and literary newspapers were united by the critique of Stalinism and the Brezhnev 'Stagnation', attacks on Soviet ideology and its founders (including Lenin and Marx), Westernizing sentiment and intense opposition to nationalism; among this group, such 'thick journals' as *Novyi mir*, *Znamia*, *Oktiabr'*, and *Iunost'* played the most prominent role. On the other hand, such 'thick journals' as *Nash sovremennik*, *Molodaia gvardiia*, *Moskva*, and such newspapers as *Literaturnaia Rossiia*, and later *Zavtra*, were united in their advocacy of the Stalinist Empire, by their attacks on

'Russophobia' and 'rootless cosmopolitans' (euphemisms for Jews), their fierce defence of the Soviet past from liberal 'blackening' (which surprisingly co-existed with the cult of Russian monarchy and orthodoxy), and their hostility to Western liberalism. As a result of this 'war' between journals, even the Union of Soviet Writers split into opposing camps: the nationalistic Union of Writers of the Russian Federation and the liberal Union of Russia's Writers. It is also characteristic of this period of polarized political debates that the number of regular readers of the new literary publications grew substantially, and rapidly, too; the subscriptions for literary journals in 1987–1992 reached its absolute maximum – up to several million per journal.

The literary/political discussions of the *perestroika* period brought to the forefront discourses that had been developing in Russian culture since the 1960s. Nationalist discourse descended from the Stalin-period 'national bolshevism' and the ideology of an unofficial, yet quite powerful, 'Russian Party' which had existed since the late 1960s. The opposing liberal discourses had been formulated by Soviet dissidents; their writings had been published in émigré periodicals and circulated in the USSR through '*samizdat*' ('self-publication': typewritten and distributed through personal networks). After the failure of the pro-Communist coup in August 1991, when the seventy-year rule of the Communist party came to an end, the 'journal war' ceased almost completely. After the collapse of the one-party system of power, unified cultural politics vanished as well, and the struggle for influence on the political leadership lost its meaning.

In connection with these factors, perhaps, and also because of the economic crisis of the 1990s that impoverished and marginalized the intelligentsia (the main consumers of literary production), the role of 'thick journals', which had traditionally been the centres and organizers of literary life, rapidly declined in the mid-1990s. In 1997, cultural analyst Boris Dubin diagnosed 'the twilight of the civilization of thick journals': 'Neither events, nor reputations are created here [in 'thick journals'] anymore.'[1] The subsequent decentralization of literary life, which in its own way reflected the decentralization of political and cultural power, led to the growing importance of publishing houses and the rapid development of mass literature – both translated and home-grown – and resulted in a general atomization of readers' preferences, now that they were no longer defined by polarized discourses.

As a result, many critics and literati lamented the 'disappearance' in post-Soviet Russia of the 'literary process', which seemed to fragment into a multitude of disconnected individual phenomena, the success or failure of which was determined by accidental (and predominantly commercial) rather than aesthetic factors. The establishment of private literary awards, as opposed to the state-controlled and bureaucratically run system of literary prizes in the Soviet period, was a truly revolutionary step toward new forms of literary life. Ultimately, private (and generous) literary awards committees sought not only to support talented writers financially in a time of economic hardship but also attempted to assume the role of organizers of the literary process. Such awards as the Russian Booker Prize (established in 1991), the Anti-Booker Prize (1995–2001, established by *Nezavisimaia gazeta*), the Andrey Bely Award (established in 1978 as a non-commercial recognition among Leningrad underground writers), the Apollon Grigoriev Award (established by the Academy of Russian Writings in 1997, it lost its sponsor in 2003 but preserved its symbolic meaning), the National Bestseller Prize (established in 2001), 'The Big Book' Prize (established in 2006), and some others, initially managed to hold public attention. However, arbitrary or obviously mistaken decisions, the loss of sponsors – or, on the contrary, barely concealed state financing (as in the case of such heavyweight prizes as 'The Poet' and 'The Big Book') – in addition to the exponential growth in the number of competing literary awards (about 300 in 2006) – all this deprived the institution of literary prizes of the centralizing role that it had hoped to play.

Despite this, the literary process certainly did not vanish, but rather assumed new features indistinguishable through the critical lenses of the 'thick journals'. The complex interaction between postmodernist and realist tendencies constitutes one of these features: we will focus on the analysis of this interaction since, as it is driven by the problems tied to identity crisis and quests for identity, it reflects most perceptibly the process of innovation in Russian literature as the most crucial factor in the entire post-Soviet period.

The transformations of realism

Many post-Soviet critics interpreted the 'return' of formerly banned literature in the late 1980s and early 1990s as a sign of revival of the great tradition of Russian Realism. The anticipation of a new wave of realist writing that would finally refute the lies of Socialist Realism constituted an important facet of the literary atmosphere in the 1990s. Yet, the 'returned' literature (*vozvrashchennaia literatura*), especially works written in the 1970s and 1980s, such as *The Children of Arbat* by Anatolii Rybakov (1911–1998) or *White Robes* by Vladimir Dudintsev (1918–1998), hardly fulfilled this longing: the 'truth' of many 'returned' novels represented only an inverted version of the Socialist Realist myth and did not constitute a complete rejection of the paradigm.

Vladimir Dudintsev, for example, employs in his *White Robes* (1987) the 1930s–1950s models of the Soviet 'paranoid' novel. The novel depicts the clandestine struggle of a few true scientists who pretend to support the political campaign against genetics that was led by the infamous Trofim Lysenko in the 1950s, all the while secretly conducting genetic experiments and breeding a frost-resistant strain of potatoes. Those who in the 'classical' Soviet novel would be depicted as 'internal enemies', 'saboteurs', and 'agents of world imperialism', Dudintsev portrays with utmost sympathy as heroes and martyrs, as 'agent[s] of good sent into the camp of evil with the assignment of defeating them'. At the same time, their opponents – representatives of the Soviet scientific establishment – appear not just as cynics and crazed obscurantists, but as metaphysical rather than political enemies. Dudintsev's use of the Socialist Realist pattern is partially ironic, and his characters are aware of the stereotypical masks they are subverting; nonetheless, the logic of plot development in *White Robes* does not shake the fundamental opposition between 'good' and 'evil' heroes.

In a similar fashion, Anatolii Rybakov's highly acclaimed and wildly popular tetralogy *The Children of Arbat* (1987–1994) utilizes the structure and plot patterns of the Socialist Realist *Bildungsroman* (novel of education): its protagonist, Sasha Pankratov, evolves from a devoted Komsomol member to a conscientious opponent of the Soviet regime and its ideology. Although Sasha is surrounded by numerous fictional and historical personages, the system of the novel's characters is strictly binarist. Former idealists, such as Sasha and his close friends, find themselves either socially marginalized or arrested soon after the beginning of the Great Terror. The cynical conformists quickly reach high positions in the Party, the NKVD, or in 'ideological institutions', including the literary establishment. The same distribution of light and shadows is represented on the historical level in Rybakov's novel. Here the pole of cynicism is embodied by Stalin (whose inner monologues constitute a large part of the narrative) and his henchmen, while revolutionary idealism is manifested by various victims of terror.

This approach to Stalinism was deeply rooted in the culture of the Thaw, although Rybakov's novel suggests readings that transcend this paradigm. The literary critic Lev Anninsky noted that Rybakov believes that in Stalin's time the great revolutionary idea was appropriated by dirty-handed thugs, therefore 'it is necessary to retrieve the right idea into clean hands. But whose hands are clean?'[2] Rybakov's protagonist could have developed into an idealistic rather than cynical executor of the totalitarian violence, and only his arrest, when he was a university sophomore, has saved him from this path. Obviously, this scenario contradicts the Thaw vision of Stalinism, yet it remains underdeveloped in Rybakov's novel.

Similar disappointment was generated by the texts created in the post-Soviet period by former 'flagmen' of liberalism in literature such as Chingiz Aitmatov, Vasili Aksyonov, or Evgenii Evtushenko, among others. Their writings appeared to be outdated epilogues of the Thaw period's 'Socialist Realism with a human face' (as Sergei Dovlatov ironically described it) and, in a new cultural situation, the former intelligentsia's favourite authors suddenly found themselves marginalized and irrelevant.

The pejorative label 'chernukha' (from Russian 'chernyi' – black) signi-fied a new version of realism that emerged in the culture of *perestroika*, and which should be described more accurately as hyper-naturalist prose. Every-day cruelty and crime, tortures and humiliations of recruits in the army, the horror of prisons and other penitentiaries, the ordinary life of home-less derelicts and prostitutes, coupled with the interest of authors in the corporeal aspects of the everyday, especially sexuality (including the non-traditional) – these motifs were central for 'chernukha' and typically evoked anger and 'moral' indignation among critics and readers. This reaction sig-nified that hyper-naturalist prose did indeed address traumatic sensitivities of the collective Soviet/post-Soviet unconscious. Hyper-naturalist prose dis-covered the whole continent of horrible and ugly phenomena that had been artificially hidden from cultural view in Soviet literature.

Post-Soviet hyper-naturalism also revived the venerated tradition of respect for the 'little person', the 'humiliated and offended'. In Russian classical realism, this motif shaped the idealized martyr-image of the 'simple folk' exemplified by Nikolai Nekrasov's poetry and Dostoevsky's novels. But unlike nineteenth-century realism, post-Soviet hyper-naturalism represented the world of 'simple folk' as a concentration of social horrors; it exposed a bloody, never-ending war for survival that raged beneath the concealments of the stagnant 'peace' of Soviet life. Torture, humiliation, beatings, and murders – these and other scenes of everyday violence were typical subjects of hyper-naturalist prose. Tellingly, violence in this writing comes not from the authorities, but rather is inflicted by victims of social injustice upon each other, or those not much different from them and, most importantly, is accepted as a 'normal' social interaction. This approach to the depiction of the world of 'simple folk' dramatically undermined the idealization of the *narod* that constituted the 'sacred' values of such trends of late Soviet culture as 'village' and 'war' prose.

The new women's prose did not require an 'exotic' social background: its authors revealed nightmares within the ordinary and the everyday, espe-cially in love and family relationships. Helena Goscilo argues that this prose deconstructed idealistic notions of female modesty, faithfulness, and self-sacrificial behaviour which had been sacralized in Russo-Soviet cultural tradition, rather than recognized as signs of patriarchal repression: 'new women's prose fully and unjudgmentally acknowledges female pleasure as physical appetite; refers to it and to various other bodily processes, such as menstruation and birthing with calm explicitness; and allows that pleasure either to speak directly or through the mediation of another woman's vantage point.'[3] This profound shift in tone signified a deep problematization not just of social 'stability', but of existential and cultural 'normalcy' as well.

However, in hyper-naturalism the female body could not escape humiliation and violence. This is why in new women's prose the quest for pleasure was inseparable from physical suffering and sickness; one of the most frequent settings in this prose is the hospital – a chronotope which, in Goscilo's opinion, is analogous to the gulag in the works of a previous literary generations. As Marina Palei writes in the preface to her cycle of short stories about a provincial hospital: 'The existential nature of this institution [a hospital] with uncanny simplicity reveals a common foundation of life and death, and in this respect is similar to the nature of a boat, concentration camp's barracks, etcetera.'[4] At the same time, representatives of all social strata congregate in a hospital ward: 'a ward in a female hospital equals a microcosm of the entire women's segment of the society.'[5]

Liudmila Petrushevskaia (b. 1937) is one of the writers in whose works – which include numerous short stories, plays, two novels, fairy-tales and horror tales – the neo-naturalist poetics of women's prose reached the highest concentration and at the same time spawned a new level of conceptualization. One of Petrushevskaia's two novels, *The Time: Night* (1991), tells of a passionate and devastating maternal love possessing distinctly sadistic features. The perception of pain as a manifestation of love is precisely what in Petrushevskaia defines the relationship between mother and child and, above all, mother and daughter. A constant self-proclaimed proponent of love, Anna Andrianovna insists on its indivisibility from pain and suffering: 'Love them and they'll tear you to pieces.'[6] When her daughter Alena is taken to the maternity ward, Anna Andrianovna immediately concludes, 'he [Alena's husband – ML] has killed her', before realizing that 'she's started giving birth'.[7] The assumption of fatal consequences surfaces again at novel's end, when Anna Andrianovna returns to an empty apartment.

As noted by the critics, in the novel three generations of women – mother, daughter, and grandmother – are caught in a cycle of destructive repetition. Not one of the characters, however, learns any lesson from mistakes made earlier. Everything repeats itself without anyone's attempting to escape the circle of torment. This logic collapses three characters into one, at various stages of growth from the cradle to the grave. Extrapolating from experience here is impossible because distance between characters is non-existent: they merge smoothly with one another, belonging not to themselves but to the cyclical flow of time, which for them brings only losses, destruction, and waste.

The signals of repetition in the life of generations taking shape in this carcass form the internal rhythm of the novel as a whole. What is self-destructive for the family turns out to be the repetitious, cyclical form of its *stable* existence, an order of sorts. It is an illogical, 'maimed' order, but it is the only order they know. Petrushevskaia consciously erases the markers of time, history, and social structure, for this order is essentially timeless, eternal, and eventually *mythological*. This dimension of Petrushevskaia's novel is manifested through the thick, yet subtle network of mythological and cultural intertexts that connects the novel's protagonist, the mother, simultaneously with the Motherland, Baba Yaga, Hecate, and Anna Akhmatova.

The version of hyper-naturalist aesthetics represented by Petrushevskaia (and some other female writers – Svetlana Vasilenko employed similar methods in *A Little Fool* and *Shamara*, as did Liudmila Ulitskaia in *Kukotsky's Case*) comes close to the strategies of realist innovation, the opposite of hyper-naturalism. Writers following this trend – critic Naum Leiderman defines it as 'post-realism'[8] – in certain ways continued the artistic experiments of such modernists of the 1920s and 1930s as Evgenii Zamiatin, Isaac Babel, Boris Pilniak, and especially Andrei Platonov, who sought to hybridize realistic psychological analysis with modernist discourse and poetics. Similarly, writers of the 1990s inclined towards this trend hybridize the poetics of psychological analysis with the aesthetic arsenal of postmodernism, including (but not limited to) intertextuality, poly-stylistics, playful relationships between authors and characters, and the openness of texts to interpretations and variations.

A new development in 'post-realist' hybridization emerged in the prose of Sergei Dovlatov (1940–1990), one of the most popular writers of the 1990s. More than 150,000 copies of his collected works have been published, and this does not include numerous editions of his selected stories. Dovlatov began writing in the early 1970s, but, unable to publish his works in the USSR, he emigrated to the USA where, as an émigré author, he achieved considerable success. The first Russian writer since Nabokov and Brodsky to be published by *The New Yorker*, Dovlatov won the praise of such literary luminaries as Kurt Vonnegut and Joseph Heller. In the late 1980s and 1990s, his cycles of short stories (*A Suitcase, Ours, An Invisible Book, An Invisible Newspaper*), novellas (*The Zone, The Sanctuary, The Foreign Woman*), as well as his quasi-spontaneous *Notebooks* were published in

Russia, becoming instant classics, a status reinforced by his untimely death at the age of forty-nine. The most original aspect of Dovlatov's prose is his paradoxical hybridization of the epic and the absurd. Through various narrative devices such as repetition and ironic distancing, Dovlatov depicts absurdity as a foundation of the epic totality of the world and, furthermore, of the narrator's sense of kinship with the entire world: everything is connected by and through the absurd. Dovlatov's tragic-comic stories prove that any single absurd principle, when repeated throughout one and the same story, can generate a broad variety of plot situations. In the lives of Dovlatov's characters, absurdity is equivalent to an individual talent (and vice versa): both absurdity and talent shatter stereotypes and undermine the routine; both produce discomfort and even catastrophes. Though Dovlatov perceives absurdity as a danger, and seeks defence and shelter from it, it is in vain; he is secretly attracted to the absurdity of life as an aesthetic phenomenon.

The other version of 'post-realist' poetics – a more intellectually reflective than absurdist form – is represented by the prose of Vladimir Makanin (b. 1937). Makanin began publishing in the late 1960s, but his first major success occurred in the late 1970s, when his parable-like short stories and novellas about everyday life stimulated heated critical discussions and were considered programmatic for the entire 'generation of forty-year-old writers'. In Makanin's prose, one finds several recurrent motifs of a collectivist or 'hive' mentality: a village, a generation, a queue, or a mob. Each of these motifs possesses enormous metaphorical power as a model of the Soviet sense of community in general, and of *homo sovieticus* and *post-sovieticus* in particular. A new, recurrent image emerges in Makanin's novel, *Underground, or The Hero of Our Time* (1999), which represents the writer's perspective on the meaning of societal change in the post-Soviet period: the *obshchaga* (dormitory), which preserves the distinctive essence of the Soviet communal lifestyle. In the *obshchaga*, everything private becomes collective. The erasure of anything individual connects and likens the *obshchaga* to another extreme of Soviet 'communality', the *psikhushka* (mental hospital): in it, people are intentionally and forcibly turned into impersonal 'vegetables', indifferent to humiliation.

Petrovich, the protagonist of Makanin's *Underground*, is an apartment-sitter in the *obshchaga* and an unpublished Soviet underground author. Makanin proclaims Petrovich to be a 'hero of our time'. Petrovich, as a representative of the cultural underground ('UG-nik', as he calls himself), obtains his individual freedom in and through his reluctance to participate in any 'competition' for societal status and superiority. At the same time, he responds to any attempt to disrespect his ego, even an insignificant one, let alone an assault, with immediate physical aggression. His aggression violates all the unwritten rules of the *obshchaga* and, by putting him 'out of the game', saves him from accepting the *obshchaga* lifestyle. The 'tactic of a blow' leads Petrovich to commit two murders. First, he kills a man from the Caucasus who has robbed and humiliated him. Then he kills a KGB agent who had tried to use him as an informant and thus sought to disgrace and compromise him. After the second murder, Petrovich is committed to a *psikhushka*, where he realizes the uncanny similarity between the *obshchaga* and the *psikhushka*; more than that, he feels the parallelism between the sensations triggered by psychosis-inducing drugs and the paradigmatic themes of the Russian intelligentsia's cultural complexes (guilt, self-humiliation, an urge to repent, and the like).

Through the depiction of these murders and their effect on Petrovich, Makanin clearly displays the limits of his protagonist's freedom, limits that also constrain the entire underground, anti-totalitarian, non-conformist intelligentsia's culture. As a mirror-double of the *obshchaga*, Petrovich's underground freedom is not free enough, which is why the disintegration of the *obshchaga* leaves the 'hero of our time' with virtually nothing; it is also why, in the novel's finale, Petrovich is nostalgically eager to see the *obshchaga* as his spiritual motherland, as almost a paradise lost.

The severed (after *perestroika*) sense of belonging to the collective of the Soviet people that had been cemented by the shared mythologies of history and society comprises the foundation of the identity crisis that is one of the dominant themes in the culture of the 1990s. If Makanin sardonically objectifies the nostalgia for collective identities, many other representatives of post-Soviet realism try desperately to restore the sense of lost collective identity without any kind of problematization. This tendency is represented by many writers, both conservatives like Alexander Solzhenitsyn (who, in the 1990s published a cycle of two-part short stories and *April 1917*, the final novel of *The Red Wheel*, a historical tetralogy) and also liberal-minded writers like Viktor Astafev, author of the 1994 novel about the 'Great Patriotic War' (the Soviet term for the Second World War), *The Cursed and the Slain*; Georgii Vladimov, famous dissident writer and author of another war novel, *The General and His Army* (winner of the Booker Prize for the Best Russian Novel of 1994); and Zakhar Prilepin (b. 1975), whose novel about National-Bolshevik Party activists, *Sankia* (2006), attracted much critical attention. In aesthetic terms, this brand of post-Soviet Realism is oriented towards the revival of 'traditional realism' (which in each case is interpreted in its own manner). However, frequently what these writers perceive as 'traditional Realism' turns out to be just one or another variation of Socialist Realism. Thus, Astafev gravitates towards Mikhail Sholokhov's version of

Socialist Realism (*Quiet Flows the Don*), and Vladimov's poetics recalls the war prose of Konstantin Simonov, such as Simonov's Socialist Realist classic *The Living and the Dead*. And Prilepin's *Sankia* reminded many critics of the early versions of Socialist Realism exemplified by Maxim Gorky's novel *Mother* (1903). For many generations of post-Soviet readers and writers it is Socialist Realism that preserves the strongest imagery of collective identities; this is probably why the quest for a sense of unified identity frequently leads to the restoration of its models.

This process finds its most obvious manifestations in the post-Soviet mass literature that, within a decade, has developed from virtual non-existence into a multi-million-ruble industry. Its leading genres, such as the mystery novel, the action-thriller, the nationalism-tinged historical and/or fantasy narrative, as well as the novels about 'glamourous' *nouveau-riche* life, invariably combine strict realistic verisimilitude and typically Soviet models of personal/social identification as exemplified by their heroes and heroines. Cultural analyst Lev Gudkov defines this strategy of self-identification as 'negative identity': the self constantly needs the other, an enemy-figure, to define itself through confrontation. Unlike Soviet culture, in which the production of the 'enemy mythology' was controlled and organized by the state, in post-Soviet culture the concept of the enemy appears to be fluid and situational; nevertheless, it preserves its mythological power. In detective fiction, as well as in novels about the glamourous life, the other is frequently associated with former social winners, those who in late Soviet culture had possessed symbolic capital, especially the intelligentsia, who are depicted in new historical settings either as utter losers or cunning criminals (or as the latter pretending to be the former). In the action thrillers, patriotic historical fiction, and 'Slavic' fantasy novels, the others are typically outsiders 'who are alien in language, way of life, and faith. Human diversity, dissimilarity of individuals, nuances in social organization and gestures of autonomy by particular groups of people are treated in this type of novel – as in traditionalist and neo-traditionalist thinking more generally – as illegitimate and inexplicable. Any kind of difference is suspect: it always carries a threat and ends in catastrophe.'[9]

Thus, realism in the post-Soviet years comes full circle, beginning with the confrontation with Socialist Realism, undergoing a hybridization with modernism and postmodernism, and returning to Socialist Realist models, albeit frequently using them in a postmodernist manner, as 'emptied' (though quite popular) forms and recycling these forms as a matrix for collective identities – restored, recreated, or simulated. A different, although not completely contrasting logic, may be detected in the evolution of the main alternative to and opponent of realism in post-Soviet culture – postmodernism.

Postmodernism: from underground to mainstream

After the collapse of Party power in 1991, literary discussions gradually lost interest in political issues and focused instead on specifically aesthetic and cultural problems, especially those which emerged from the shadow of the *perestroika* period 'war of the journals'. In the late 1980s and early 1990s, several literary journals – central and regional alike – published special issues devoted to 'young', 'experimental', or 'underground' literature; in other words, to authors of different generations who embraced non-realist (more specifically, avant-garde and/or postmodernist) aesthetics. At the same time, leading critics – especially Sergei Chuprinin, Mikhail Epshtein, and Mikhail Aizenberg – mapped a hitherto unknown continent of Russian literature, one far removed from most readers and beyond 'commonly accepted' aesthetic paradigms.

In the Western European and North American cultural milieus, postmodernism typically emerged as a cultural reflection of a new level of modernity variously defined as 'late capitalism' (Fredric Jameson), a 'civilization of mass-media' (Jean Baudrillard), and as 'growing globalization' (Anthony Giddens). These categories are obviously inapplicable to the Soviet Union of the 1960s, when the first texts of Russian postmodernism appeared. Yet, although the word 'postmodernism' was introduced to Russian criticism only in the late 1980s, Russian postmodernism, paradoxically, arose within late Soviet culture as the transgression and undermining both of official discourses and of officially accepted forms of polemics with officialdom (such as, for example, the aforementioned 'Socialist Realism with a human face').

The *cynical* character of 'late socialist' culture served as a fertile ground for Soviet postmodernist discourse and cultural practices which, much like those of other countries, especially magnified and manifested 'incredulity towards meta-narratives' (Jean-François Lyotard). In Soviet culture, the grand narratives deconstructed by postmodernists were predominantly those of totalitarian/communist political mythology. In the post-Soviet period, the quasi-sacred 'meta-narratives' were recognized in the grand tradition of Russian 'literature-centrism', which envisioned literature as a secular religion and positioned writers as secular prophets engaged in transcendental quests for 'eternal' truth and beauty. To be sure, the postmodernist critique of meta-narratives was closely associated with the revival of the interrupted tradition of Russian modernism. However, it was not Vladimir Mayakovsky, Marina Tsvetaeva, Mikhail Bulgakov, Boris Pasternak, or Anna Akhmatova who were especially valued by Russian postmodernists, but rather Mikhail Kuzmin, Daniil Kharms, Konstantin Vaginov, Leonid Dobychin, and Vladimir Nabokov. The reason for this aesthetic 'discrimination' lies in the different attitudes of the aforementioned modernists towards the Russian 'literature-centric' tradition. Mayakovsky, Tsvetaeva, Bulgakov, Pasternak, and Akhmatova effectively employed this tradition as a means to elevate their individual positions; in this context, even their rebellions against the 'transcendental' authorities and values took on the import of a sacred ritual, a new myth construction. But late Soviet and post-Soviet postmodernists identified Kuzmin, Vaginov, Dobychin, and Nabokov as their closest predecessors and teachers, specifically because these modernists not only distanced themselves from Russian literature-centric discourses but also ironically deconstructed this venerated tradition.

For Russian postmodernists, the clear recognition of the repressive power inherent in any 'sacred' discourse that pretends to manifest Truth conflicts with their desire to find a 'true transcendental signified' instead of the 'sacred symbols' of Soviet culture and the stale 'spirituality' of the Russian classics. This is perhaps, *the* central problem of Russian postmodernism, one which first found adequate artistic expression in the prose poem *Moscow To the End of the Line* by Venedikt Erofeev (1938–1990). Written in 1969–1970, the poem was not published in the Soviet Union until 1989. However, it was well known to many readers thanks to its publication abroad, first in Israel in 1973, and then in other countries and by circulation in 'samizdat'. Since 1989, Erofeev's poem has truly attained cult status: a monument to two of its central characters was erected in the centre of Moscow, and annual re-enactments of the protagonist's round-trip from Moscow to Petushki station, accompanied by heavy drinking and the reading aloud of corresponding chapters from the poem, have become a popular youth ritual. In Erofeev's poem, the comical deconstruction of various sacred discourses (Biblical, romantic, Soviet–ideological) in a drunken monologue of the protagonist, who masterfully mixes explosive discursive (and not only discursive) cocktails, is coupled with his attempts to create a new sacred narrative capable of taming the surrounding chaos by means of the poetic word. This experiment ends with the tragic death of the narrator who, significantly, bears the same name as the poem's author; God's messengers kill Venichka by sticking an awl into his throat, thus aiming at his transgressive word or *logos*. The *logos* that Venichka creates – and for which he is killed – not only reveals the chaos of perceptible (social) reality but also painfully suggests doubt of *all* transcendental authorities and authoritative discourses.

The problematic interaction between the transcendental quest (frequently ironic and self-reflexive) and the deconstruction of repression stemming from transcendental signifieds generates two main strategies in Russian postmodernist literature: conceptualism and the neo-baroque. Conceptualism and the neo-baroque are in many respects opposites. Conceptualism gravitates towards avant-garde aesthetics and revives the traditions of OBERIU absurdist writers, as well as some other underground writers of the pre- and post-war periods. The neo-baroque leans towards the aesthetics of 'high modernism'. Conceptualism substitutes a system of impersonal discursive personas, rituals, clichés, stereotypical formulas, and gestures for the authorial face, while neo-baroque cultivates an authorial myth, although in a paradoxical or downplayed form, as in *Moscow To the End of the Line*. Conceptualism deconstructs and de-mythologizes authoritative cultural signifiers and entire languages of culture; the neo-baroque, by contrast, strives to re-mythologize the fragments and ruins of destroyed cultural entities.

Conceptualism developed as a powerful trend in Russian visual art, as represented by Ilia Kabakov, Erik Bulatov, Grisha Bruskin, Vitalii Komar, Alexander Melamid, and many other underground and émigré artists. Early literary versions of conceptualism can be detected in the poetry of the so-called Lianozovo group (named after a Moscow suburb where many of them resided), in the works of the young (pre-emigration) Eduard Limonov, and in that of the Leningrad underground poets Vladimir Ufliand and Oleg Grigorev. Further development of this aesthetic trend is evident in Dmitrii Prigov's and Lev Rubinshtein's poetry, Vladimir Sorokin's prose, in the various cultural activities of Prigov and Vagrich Bakhchanian, and in performative groups like 'Collective Actions' and 'Medical Hermeneutics'.

According to Prigov (1940–2007), the artistic consciousness of Moscow conceptualists was predominantly counter-cultural:

> [W]e criticized utopias, and the state institutions that were reproducing them; we aimed at the totality of any language that was associated with state discourses. We were allergic to any utopian discourse . . . including its reflection in so-called dissident art . . . We perceived Pushkin and Mayakovsky as ordinary representatives of Soviet power. Moreover, we believed that such moral idols of the previous generation as Akhmatova and Pasternak, after their publication [in the USSR], were also appropriated by the discourses of power.[10]

In accordance with this strategy, Prigov's own poetry simultaneously re-enacts and parodies the rhetorics of symbolic power integrated in various authorial discourses. In essence, in his thousands of poetic texts, Prigov tirelessly imitates and deconstructs what he defines as 'quasi-prophetic texts/personae':[11] from 'a great Russian poet' (ideally Pushkin) to the 'little man' (*malen'kii chelovek*) of Russian and Soviet classics, from the 'Soviet' poet to Japanese, Chinese, medieval, and gay poets (or rather their perception in the Russian collective imagination); from a flaming nationalist to a woman poet, etc. The paradox of Prigov's approach can be seen in the conflicting and mutually annihilating fusion of powerful cultural archetypes:

in his texts, the 'great Russian poet' acts like a 'little man', while the 'little man' lives the ambition of the 'great Russian poet'.

Vladimir Sorokin (b. 1955) continues Prigov's experiments, although in a divergent direction. By *creating* texts/personae – playful but convincing and recognizable models of various authoritative discourses – Sorokin uncovers the 'unconscious' of deconstructed discourse, the hitherto concealed secret of its sacredness, detecting a core and a source of the symbolic authority of any discourse in the brutal, bloody violence that harks back to archaic forms of authority. Once he began deconstructing Socialist Realist plots and characters, Sorokin soon realized that the same deconstruction was applicable to any other authoritative (and hence, sacralized) discourse. Although the objects of his artistic analysis in the 1980s and 1990s included Russian classics of the nineteenth century (*Roman/The Novel*), twentieth-century modernism (*A Month in Dachau*), and contemporary dissident discourse (*The Norm, The Thirties Love of Marina, The Queue*), Socialist Realism for him is still the ideal model for any authoritative discourse that strives to establish its power over the reader's mind and culture as a whole.

Each of Sorokin's texts exhibits a cascade of plot and stylistic devices that force the targeted discourse to 'spill out' its unconscious, to expose its methods of violence, its trademark models of sacrifice. Thus, in his scandalously famous novel *Blue Lard* (1998) Sorokin translates various narratives of the transcendental into corporeal imagery, a technique he customarily uses in his other texts. Hence, the central motif of the novel is blue lard, 'a substance whose entropy equals zero', a materialized harmony, and at the same time, a fat layer that the monstrous bodies of clones of great Russian writers generate in the process of writing: *Blue Lard* thus incorporates parodic texts written by clones of Tolstoy, Dostoevsky, Nabokov, and Platonov. Critic and prose writer Mikhail Berg interprets Sorokin's blue lard as 'the essence of sacredness and purity accumulated in Russian literature . . . the structural element of power in Russian culture – literature-centrism'.[12] The plot of *Blue Lard* relates the struggle for this substance between Stalin and Hitler, who are presented as figures in an 'alternative history' (they peacefully divide control over the world), and between past-oriented nationalists and characters from the globalized future. The novel comes to a close with a total collapse of the world, triggered by Stalin's injection of blue lard directly into his brain – an ironic metaphor for the merging of literature and dictatorial power.

A fusion of classical metaphors of the baroque ('the world as theatre', 'life as a dream') with characteristics of contemporary culture like the 'society of spectacle' (Guy Debord) and the 'hyper-reality of simulacra'

(Jean Baudrillard) shapes the poetics of the Russian neo-baroque in the prose of Andrei Bitov, Evgenii Kharitonov, Viktor Pelevin, Tatiana Tolstaia, Mikhail Shishkin, Sasha Sokolov, and in the poetry of the Nobel Prize Laureate Joseph Brodsky, Viktor Krivulin, Aleksei Parshchikov, Elena Shvarts, and many others. Unlike conceptualists, these postmodern writers – sometimes candidly, and with self-irony, and sometimes stoically – try to preserve connections with modernist aesthetics: in the neo-baroque, the quest for modernist sensibilities is valued as a self-sufficient, albeit usually fruitless, quest for 'the real' that lies hidden beneath endless layers of cultural simulacra and social spectacles.

To the same degree that Sorokin's works are emblematic of conceptualist prose, the neo-baroque is most fully manifested in the works of Viktor Pelevin (b. 1962). Unlike Sorokin, who desecrates authoritative discourses, Pelevin mythologizes (albeit ironically) the emptiness that follows as a result of the deconstruction of grand narratives, ideologies, and transcendental symbols. Thus Pelevin's novel *Generation P* (1999; *Babylon* in the British edition, *Homo Zapiens* in the American version) depicts the activities and rituals of post-Soviet copy-writers – creators and secular priests of the contemporary hyper-reality of simulacra. Clearly a postmodernist novel, it extends, in highly imaginative ways, the tradition of modernist myth-making. First, the novel's plot represents a protagonist's mythological quest (which, symptomatically, is similar to those in role-playing computer games). Second, *Generation P* is an adventure–industrial novel, in some ways similar to novels by Arthur Hailey (*Hotel*, *Airport*, *Wheels*, *The Moneychangers*, *The Evening News*), although its heroes do not run airports or hotels but instead produce addictive myths (also known as commercials) for the 'masses', myths on which the copy-writers themselves paradoxically appear to be hooked.

Third, the novel incorporates at least two extended mythological elucidations of contemporary society: one – pseudo-rationalistic – is delivered by the spirit of Che Guevara, and another – dialogical and performative – comes from Sirruf, an ancient dragon; both visit the protagonist, Vavilen Tatarsky, during his narcotic trips. Significantly, all three mythological structures – Tatarsky's quest, the 'professional' myth about the uncanny power of TV, and the mythological sermons of Guevara and Sirruf – are organized around an empty centre. In the story of Tatarsky, the empty centre is embodied by the personality of the protagonist, who does not deserve his ascension to the summit of mystical power for any other reason than his exotic name. In the stratum of the plot related to the technologies of mythological po⸱ the empty centre is formed by figures of supreme political and ⸱ authority who turn out to be computer animations; but eve⸱

as the novel's characters argue, by his/her very nature, 'is just a television broadcast'.[13] Finally, the philosophic narratives of Guevara and Sirruf disclose 'the experience of collective non-existence', 'a heaping of one unreality upon another, a castle constructed on air, the foundations of which stand upon a profound abyss'.[14]

Pelevin's *Generation P* holds a special place in the history of post-Soviet literature because it was the first postmodernist novel to succeed in attracting a wide readership, effecting the incursion of postmodernism into the mainstream of post-Soviet culture. Unlike Western postmodernists who, since the late 1960s, had been following Leslie Fiedler's advice to 'Cross the Border, Close that Gap' (in other words, to consistently seek the fusion between experimental and popular literature), Russian postmodernists until the mid-1990s evinced a typically underground contempt towards commercial success and mass readers' tastes. Such attitudes began to change in 1999 with the publication of *Generation P*, which was followed by other Pelevin novels and by the scandalous success of Sorokin's *Blue Lard*, when it was publicly burned and sued for 'pornography' by the pro-Kremlin youth group *Nashi* (Ours). Clearly postmodernist projects also appear, usually multi-layered and double-encoded, which are specifically designed to win mass readership and usually manage at least to become popular among the post-Soviet intelligentsia.

This popularization of the postmodern is vividly manifested in Boris Akunin's mystery novels; the new, post-Soviet version of 'gonzo' journalism by poet Lev Rubinshtein and Andrei Kolesnikov in *Kommersant*; Evgenii Grishkovets' quasi-autobiographical plays; Oleg Kuvaev's animated films about Masiania; and in other such works. However, postmodernism entered the mainstream of post-Soviet culture at an inauspicious moment. Since the late 1990s, Russia's social and cultural life has undergone dramatic change. Putin's period in Russian political history has been marked by 'restorative' tendencies, coupled with the rapid improvement of the country's economy thanks to high oil and gas prices. Cultural analysts Lev Gudkov and Boris Dubin identify the following as the foremost tendencies in Russian cultural and social life in the new millennium: the strengthening of 'neo-traditionalism, including the Orthodox Church's influence, the growth of isolationist tendencies and xenophobia directed both internally and externally (anti-Western and especially anti-American rhetoric); mythologization and "archaization" of national history both on the official level... and on the level of popular journalism, in mass cinematography and in TV programs'.[15] This cultural atmosphere embodies the acute state of an identity crisis, and its various manifestations are indicative of a hectic quest for new or renewed identities – collective and personal, colonial or post-colonial, national, imperial, ethnic, religious, etc. – that might fill the void left by the loss of Soviet identities.

Engaged in this process, post-Soviet (especially postmodernist) literature undergoes extraordinary mutations that draw postmodernism into a dialogue with various 'texts of identity'. These mutations recall Douwe Fokkema's characterizations of the 'late phase' in the development of Western culture which, in his rendering, focuses on feminist writing, historiographical fiction, post-colonial fiction, autobiographical writing, and 'fiction focusing on cultural identity'.[16] All these trends are present in the landscape of Russian postmodernism of the new millennium except, perhaps, for post-colonial fiction. But in the place of the latter, post-Soviet literature produced what might be labelled 'post-imperial' writing, which either deconstructs the lost imperial might or, more frequently, is nostalgic for it.

As part of this extensive process of identity renovation, postmodernist techniques, unfortunately, were employed to aestheticize the Soviet cultural heritage, effecting changes that many critics identify as the most visible sign of neo-traditionalism in the recent culture. Creation of a new hyper-reality of simulacra through the manipulation of Socialist Realist patterns and imagery was mainly reflected in visual genres – films and mini-series, television programmes, and mass celebrations such as, for instance, anniversaries of the victory in the 'Great Patriotic War' in 2000 and especially in 2005. In literature, a simulative restoration of Socialist Realist aesthetics is also perceptible, but less extensive than in visual culture, although the television and film industries employ many writers of the Soviet period who are still active. In literature, this tendency is illustrated by a telling episode when, in 2001, Ad Marginem, a press whose reputation was based on the publication of Russian postmodernist authors and translations of Western poststructuralist theorists, published *Mister Hexogen*, a novel by Alexander Prokhanov (b. 1938), a known ideologist of post-Soviet ultranationalism and the editor-in-chief of the ultranationalist newspaper *Zavtra* (Tomorrow). *Mister Hexogen* is typical of Prokhanov's poetics, based on the fusion of two hardly compatible elements: on the one hand, patterns borrowed from the late-Stalinist 'paranoid' novel that focus on the 'de-masking' of external and internal enemies and, on the other hand, an exalted and excessive metaphorism that recalls the imaginism and expressionism of the turn of the twentieth century. The involuntary postmodernist effect of this fusion contrasts, however, with the novel's heavily ideological content, exemplary for the post-Soviet negative identity, with its burning desire to locate 'national enemies' among ethnic, religious, and cultural 'others'. The publication of Prokhanov's novel by Ad Marginem was accompanied by a broad campaign of critical support, and effectively transformed Prokhanov into a 'fashionable' media persona,

MARK LIPOVETSKY

while his novel was hailed as a new departure in 'radical' and even 'experimental' literature. This campaign ended with Prokhanov's scandalous novel being awarded the National Bestseller Prize of 2001, causing yet another ideological split of the literary world.

For a writer of postmodernist orientation, close attention to neo-traditionalist and mass-oriented discourses of identity, including the discourses of negative identity, emerges in the twenty-first century as a prerequisite for active participation in post-Soviet culture. Furthermore, a postmodern hybridization of opposing discourses – discourses of Western versus Soviet modernity, for instance, or of post-modernity versus neo-traditionalism – animates the cultural mainstream and serves as its implicit engine. However, the hybridization in recent cultural practice of the (post)modern and neo-traditionalist discourses of identity is always tested by the problem of 'the other'. In neo-traditionalist discourse, 'the other' is defined in ethnic, religious, cultural or, more rarely, class terms; it is constantly demonized, while the mythology of 'otherness' is constantly absorbed into post-Soviet negative identities as a basis for aggressive self-definition and as a justification for violence. On the field of otherness, the process of discursive dialogue and hybridization frequently transforms into a heated conflict, and a virtual war of discourses not infrequently unfolds within one and the same text.

The denouement of this conflict's resolution, the shifting balance between hybridization of diverse discourses and discursive wars, will define the future direction of Russian literature – whether neo-traditionalist tendencies will subjugate postmodernist poetics and use it as a fashionable wrapper for their own ideological needs, or postmodernism will effectively deconstruct neo-traditionalist ideologies. Russian literature, as in the nineteenth century, is once again situated in the midst of a heated cultural debate about the strategies of self-identification. Although this situation is not altogether literature-centric, it certainly attributes a political, social, and historical urgency to literary poetics.

NOTES

1 Dubin, Boris, *Slovo – pis'mo – literatura. Ocherki po sotsiologii sovremennoi kul'tury* (Moscow: Novoe Literaturnoe Obozrenie, 2001), p. 181.
2 Anninskii, Lev, 'Ottsy i deti Arbata' in *Literatura i sovremennost'*, 1986–87 (Moscow: Khudozhestvennaia literatura, 1989), p. 328.
3 Goscilo, Helena, *Dehexing Sex: Russian Womanhood During and After Glasnost* (Ann Arbor, MI: University of Michigan Press, 1996), pp. 105–106.
4 Palei, Marina, *Otdelenie propashchikh* (Moscow: Moskovskii rabochii, 1991), p. 128.

5 Goscilo, *Dehexing Sex*, p. 122.
6 Petrushevskaya, Ludmilla, *The Time: Night*, trans. Sally Laird (Evanston, IL: Northwestern University Press, 2000), p. 51.
7 *Ibid.*, p. 48.
8 See Leiderman, Naum and Lipovetskii, Mark, *Sovremennaia russkaia literatura. 1950–1990-e gody, v dvukh tomakh* (Moscow: Academia, 2003–2006), vol. 2, pp. 583–667.
9 Dubin, Boris, 'Russian Historical Fiction' in Lovell, S. and Menzel, B., eds., *Reading for Entertainment in Contemporary Russia: Post-Soviet Popular Literature in Historical Perspective* (Munich: Otto Sagner, 2005), p. 188.
10 Prigov, Dmitrii and Shapoval, S., *Portretnaia galereia D.A.P.* (Moscow: Novoe Literaturnoe Obozrenie, 2003), pp. 93–95.
11 Prigov, Dmitrii, 'Kak vernut´sia v literaturu, ostavaias´ v nei, no vyidia iz nee sukhim! (Chto-to o Rubinshteine L´ve Semenoviche i cherez eto koe-chto o sebe)', *Indeks*, 1 (1990), pp. 211–212.
12 Berg, Mikhail, *Literaturokratiia* (Moscow: Novoe literaturnoe obozrenie, 2000), p. 113.
13 *Ibid.*, p. 166.
14 *Ibid.*, p. 80.
15 Dubin, Boris, 'Mezhdu kanonom i aktual´nost´iu, skandalom i modoi: Literatura i izdatel´skoe delo Rossii v izmenivshemsia sotsial´nom prostranstve' in his *Intellektual´nye gruppy i simvolicheskie formy* (Moscow: Novoe izdatel´stvo, 2004), p. 134.
16 Fokkema, Douwe, 'The Semiotics of Literary Postmodernism' in Bertens, H. and Fokkema, Douwe, eds., *International Postmodernism: Theory and Literary Practice* (Amsterdam and Philadelphia, PA: John Benjamins, 1997), pp. 30–33.

FURTHER READING

Baker, Adele, ed., *Consuming Russia: Popular Culture, Sex, and Society since Gorbachev* (Durham, NC: Duke University Press, 1999).
Balina, Marina and Lipovetsky, Mark, eds., *Dictionary of Literary Biography: Russian Writers Since 1980* (Detroit, MI: Gale Group, 2003).
Balina, Marina, Condee, Nancy, and Dobrenko, Evgeny, eds., *Endquote: Sots-Art Literature and Soviet Grand Style* (Evanston, IL: Northwestern University Press, 2000).
Borenstein, Eliot, *Overkill: Sex and Violence in Contemporary Russian Popular Culture* (Ithaca, NY: Cornell University Press, 2008).
Epstein, Mikhail, Genis, Alexander, and Vladiv-Glover, Slobodanka, *Russian Postmodernism: New Perspectives on Post-Soviet Culture* (New York: Berghahn Books, 1999).
Goscilo, Helena, *Dehexing Sex: Russian Womanhood During and After Glasnost* (Ann Arbor, MI: University of Michigan Press, 1996).
Lipovetsky, Mark, *Russian Postmodernist Fiction: Dialog with Chaos* (Armonk, NY: M.E. Sharpe, 1999).
Lovell, Stephen and Menzel, Birgit, eds., *Reading for Entertainment in Contemporary Russia: Post-Soviet Popular Literature in Historical Perspective* (Munich: Otto Sagner, 2005).

11

DAVID BETHEA AND SIGGY FRANK*

Exile and Russian Literature

The Russians seem to think they have a monopoly on exile.

(Anton Shammas)

Banishing writers in order to silence them is as old as the writing profession itself, and European literature is replete with examples of writers
who were exiled from their native country or city for their words or deeds.
The art of writers as diverse as Ovid, Dante, Rousseau, Mann, Joyce and
Kundera has been shaped by their experience of exile. Since the onset of
its modern period (i.e. from 1800 onwards) Russia has contributed more
than its fair share of writers in exile to world literature. The long list of
Russian writers who experienced exile at some point in their lives overlaps
to some extent with a list of Russian canonical authors, including Pushkin,
Lermontov, Turgenev, Dostoevsky, Bunin, Khodasevich, Tsvetaeva, Pasternak, Nabokov, Mandelshtam, Solzhenitsyn, and Brodsky. The large number
of exiled writers is testimony to the traditionally difficult and dangerous
relationship between the writer and the Russian state and the designation
of exile as an 'occupational hazard' for writers rings particularly true in the
Russian context.[1]

Exile as a theoretical concept, a psychological condition, or a concrete
experience is marked by duality. At the core of this duality lies the divided
identity of exiles, once they have been banished from a place of belonging
to a place that is perceived as other and foreign. Critics like Edward Said
and Michael Seidel have duly noted and analysed the exile's 'contrapuntal'
perception. Much has been made of this twofold exilic perception as being
conducive to the literary imagination in aiding the writer's simultaneous
perception of the real and the imaginary. This romantic concept of exile is,
however, challenged by the potential brutality of the experience itself. Exile
strikes at the heart of a writer's being, threatening to deprive the writer of
his or her very mode of expression, language. Linguistic barriers abroad and

publishing bans at home silence or at least muffle the writer's major tool, his or her voice. For writers, exile is therefore not only a foreign place. It is also a state of isolation from their readership and an act of resistance against the threat of losing their literary voice.

The notion of exile has become an integral part of the Russian literary tradition ever since Pushkin articulated his anxieties as a writer banished from the glittering capital in the North to the provincial backwaters of Southern Russia. In an ironic twist, it is a condition of disruption and fragmentation that has defined Russia's literary continuity and tradition in significant ways. Although other Russian writers before Pushkin (e.g. Radishchev) experienced persecution and exile at the hands of the state, it is only with Pushkin that the notions of 'genius' and 'national poet' become merged once and for all with the notion of physical displacement from home. The fact that subsequent generations of Russian writers have vigorously lighted upon and re-worked this connection to map their own exilic experience proves the point. In an interdependent relationship, exile and creative greatness have come to condition each other. Exile becomes significant because it produces great writers; writers become significant because they have been exiled. Exile has served to establish and affirm the elevated position writers in Russia enjoy. Whether a causal connection between exile and creativity can actually be posited is less important than the perception that this link is vital in the process of creating Russian literature. The humiliation of being outcast is compensated for by the implicit recognition of the Russian writer's significance in, and impact on, Russian society and culture. Vladislav Khodasevich memorably summed up this contradictory function of Russian writers:

> Of course we know of Dante's exile, Camões' poverty, André Chénier's scaffold, and much more, but, nonetheless, nowhere outside of Russia have people gone to such lengths, by whatever means possible, to destroy their writers. And yet, this is not a cause for our shame, but may even be a cause for our pride. That is because no other literature (I am speaking generally) has been as prophetic as Russian literature.[2]

The conversion of Russia's Imperial ambitions with its desire for dramatic territorial expansion dates to the reigns of Peter and Catherine in the eighteenth century. Russian writers sentenced to exile were henceforth typically banished from the country's political and cultural centres to such provincial peripheries as the Caucasus and Siberia. Given that 'exile' and 'home' are interdependent terms, the very concept of 'internal exile' implies that vast areas of the Russian empire have been perceived as 'other' or 'foreign' (*chuzhoi*). In a cultural tradition that tends to see literature as the social conscience of the nation and hence inextricably linked with the

Russian people (*narod*) and Russian soil (*pochva*), this perception of home-lessness within Russia has presented an acute challenge to writers' national and cultural identities. Similar questions of cultural and national belonging also faced the writers who joined the mass flight from the Bolshevik Revolution to Europe, America, and Manchuria as well as the many writers and intellectuals who stayed behind in the Soviet Union and withdrew into psychological isolation in response to their social ostracization. Contingent on the historical context, the strategies employed by writers to assert their identity as Russian writers have included both the dissociation of literature and geographical territory and the insistence on the close link between literature and native soil. In this chapter, we propose to sketch out the contours of a continuous discourse of exile in twentieth-century Russian literature by using the example of the literary practices of Russian writers in different historical situations: the *external exile* of writers of the Russian emigration in the interwar period in Europe, the *inner exile* of nonconformist Russian writers (as opposed to Soviet writers) in the Stalinist period, and the *linguistic exile* of Nabokov and Brodsky after their turn to English.

'Writing from afar': the first-wave Russian emigration

Following the Bolshevik Revolution, millions of Russians from all walks of life fled the country in an exodus of unprecedented proportions, establishing Russian settlements all over the world, with political and cultural centres in Prague, Berlin, Paris, and later New York. The 'first wave', as the Russian emigration of the interwar period came to be known, was quick to organize their cultural and political life abroad. Russians founded their own newspapers, publishing houses, educational establishments, theatres, Russian Orthodox churches, and countless political, artistic, professional, and social associations and organizations. The Russian émigrés in effect replicated fragments of their lost homeland, creating insular Russian communities which existed in separation from their host countries.

There were good reasons why Berlin was initially the most popular spot with émigré writers: the Weimar Republic was one of the first Western European governments to acknowledge the Soviet regime (thus writers with Soviet passports could visit there) and the weak German currency led to a mushrooming of publishing enterprises. By 1924 there were eighty-six Russian publishing houses and a substantial number of Russian book stores in Berlin, and throughout the 1920s numerous Russian newspapers, journals, and almanacs were published there, albeit many of them turned out to be short-lived. When in 1924 the Reichsmark stabilized and living expenses for émigrés increased, a large number of Russians, among them many émigré writers, moved on to Paris, which became during the mid-1920s the unrivalled centre of émigré cultural and literary life.

It is difficult to affix a precise moment when Russian literature 'split' into its Soviet and émigré factions. This process was certainly set in motion by the events of 1917, but after the Revolution there followed several years during which many Russian literary figures visiting the West had not yet firmly decided whether to cast their lot with those living 'here' or 'there'. While Berlin was still in its heyday as a Russian capital abroad, writers of various aesthetic and political stripes – Andrei Bely, Viktor Shklovsky, Marina Tsvetaeva, Boris Pasternak, Ilia Ehrenburg, Aleksei Tolstoi, Boris Zaitsev, Khodasevich, and Aleksei Remizov – intermingled there in a spirit of ferment and intense intellectual life. In the autumn of 1922 a large group of intellectuals, including a number of philosophers and religious thinkers (e.g. Nikolai Berdiaev, Nikolai Lossky, Fedor Stepun, Sergei Bulgakov), was expatriated. This last group especially would add a metaphysical element to émigré literature totally absent in the Soviet Union.

Although free of Soviet censorship, émigré literature never managed to develop free of political issues. Writers as aesthetically and politically different as Bunin, Zinaida Gippius, Khodasevich, Dmitrii Merezhkovsky, Ivan Shmelev, and Tsvetaeva were all inhibited, at various times and to varying degrees, by the politics of publishing. By the same token, the numerous skirmishes in print that punctuated the history of émigré literature were often inscribed with a political undercurrent. In Paris the politicization of the word could be seen in the character of Russian-language newspapers and journals: *Poslednie novosti* (The Latest News), the leading daily from the early 1920s until the Nazi occupation of Paris in 1940, bore the left-leaning imprint of its editor, the prominent pre-Revolutionary political figure and Constitutional Democrat (Kadet) Pavel Miliukov; *Vozrozhdenie* (The Renaissance), the chief rival of Miliukov's paper, was owned by A. O. Gukasov, an industrialist who enforced a right-wing editorial policy; *Sovremennye zapiski* (Contemporary Annals), the premier 'thick journal' of the emigration, reflected the views of its Socialist Revolutionary (SR) editors; and *Chisla* (Numbers), which became a haven for younger writers, apparently ignored the politics of the right and the left but not of 'age' – its very inception of studied aestheticism was polemically aimed at the old-guard atmosphere of *Sovremennye zapiski*. In addition, there were significant organs of émigré culture located in each city with a sizable émigré population: Berlin had *Rul'* (The Rudder); Warsaw had *Za svobodu* (For Freedom); Riga had *Segodnia* (Today), and Prague had *Volia Rossii* (The Will of Russia). Hence, as the representatives of the Russian press in Paris often polemicized with one another and the representatives of the 'provincial' press tended to vie with current opinion in the 'capital', what emerged was a picture of spirited factionalism.

Central to the self-definition of the Russian emigration were two notions, which could be summed up as 'agency' and 'national authenticity'. The Russians abroad referred to themselves as 'émigrés', a term which carried the distinct connotation of individual choice and deliberateness (vs. 'exiles' who have no choice in the matter) and also hinted at the future possibility of returning home. Although far removed from their geographical homeland, the majority of Russian émigrés regarded themselves as the keepers of an authentic Russian tradition and culture that was preserved and shielded from corrupting Soviet influences. Endless discussions about the role, function, and destiny of Russian émigré literature were shaped by these two concepts that lay at the heart of fierce battles over the legitimacy of Russian émigré letters.

Khodasevich, a leading poet and critic of the Russian emigration, took the view that there was nothing inherently anomalous in the existence of a national literature without a native territory; citing Dante, Mickiewicz, Bialik, and other representatives of traditions in exile, he argued eloquently that if Russian émigré literature failed to sustain itself, it was because it was not 'émigré enough' – that is, was not sufficiently conscious of its mission. Yes, the loss of homeland, of significance, of 'voice' (in his 1926 poem 'Petersburg', Khodasevich recalled how during the Revolutionary years people forgot their boiling teapots and felt boots drying on the stove to listen enthralled to his verse), the growing sense of isolation in a francophone environment – all these factors made life difficult, but not, the poet insisted, hopeless. The only hope was to find a way to bring to life the 'heavy lyre' that Khodasevich and others took into exile and thus continue the rich tradition of Russian literature. Some younger writers, among them Vladimir Nabokov-Sirin and Nina Berberova, followed Khodasevich's example.

On the other hand, Khodasevich's foil Adamovich felt that traditions (chiefly that of Pushkin) had been held up too long as icons and that it was time for younger writers to come to grips with the consequences of modern alienation. Lermontov the psychic exile was a better model for this current 'forgotten' generation than the formally impeccable and luminous Pushkin. Those that followed Adamovich were urged to turn inward in order to pour forth, in unmediated fashion, their feelings of anguish, uprootedness, and *accidie*. This essentially Modernist notion of man's spiritual homelessness in the twentieth century presented a suitable translation of the Russian émigrés' experience of geographical exile. The aesthetic expression of this mindset became in the early 1930s the so-called 'Parisian note' (*parizhskaia nota*) and 'human document' (*chelovecheskii dokument*): the former referred to the note of existential weariness and frustration accompanied by a polished poetic surface identifiable with the Adamovichians (especially Georgii Ivanov); the latter referred to the diaristic form of what today might be called 'confessional verse'. For Adamovich, the social and cultural fragmentation of exile and the separation from native soil and people was equal to a rupture in the Russian literary tradition. The only task left to émigré literature, in this view, was to 'retire, preserve the last values, keep them until better times. Or write down all that is most important for man, everything that is dearest, lofty, eternal.'[3] The very idea of an independent émigré literature as a continuation of Russian literature was seen as a betrayal of the national heritage: 'God forbid we should flourish here!'[4]

The precious memory of a lost Russia that was to be preserved without polluting 'foreign' influences of the host country became central to the distinct identity of the Russian emigration looking back at the lost homeland through the prism of collective nostalgia. This retrospection informed in particular the work of the older generation of émigré writers, who had established their reputation in pre-Revolutionary Russia (Mark Aldanov, Konstantin Balmont, Bunin, Gippius, Ivanov, Khodasevich, Merezhkovsky, Aleksei Remizov, Shmelev, N. A. Teffi [pseudonym of Nadezhda Lokhvitskaia], and Zaitsev). The older generation's insistence on the close link of their literature to the pre-Revolutionary culture of Russia served to maintain their significance and status as leading Russian writers as well as to secure the continuation of Russian literature. This sense of having to preserve an authentic Russian culture was summed up in the memorable phrase 'We are not in exile, but on a mission' ('ne v izgnanii, [a] v poslanii').[5]

The younger generation – those such as Berberova, Lydia Chervinskaia, Iurii Felzen, Gaito Gazdanov, Vasilii Ianovsky, Dovid Knut, Nabokov, Boris Poplavsky, Anatolii Shteiger, Vladimir Varshavsky – had come of age in exile. The further the homeland and any prospects of ever returning to it receded into the distance, the more these writers had to delineate their identity through their exile experience, steering a precarious course between continuing the Russian tradition (and risking a stagnant repetitive imitation of pre-Revolutionary literature) and engaging with the present situation and their host countries (with the frequently invoked threat of 'deracination'). In this sense the younger generation of Russian émigré writers could be defined not only by their age but also by their ability to write from a position somewhere between different countries, generations, and national literatures. Some notable works of the younger generation are equally obsessed with the memory of Russia and past experiences, yet the heroes of their works remain rooted in the here and now of émigré life (e.g. Nabokov's *Mary* and *The Gift*, Gazdanov's *Evening with Claire*). Many of the younger writers turned to their own present situation, using the world of Russia abroad as the setting for their (sometimes semi-autobiographical) novels and stories (Poplavsky's *Apollo the Ugly*; Felzen's *Deceit, Happiness*; Berberova's *Billancourt Tales*). For writers of the younger generation their exile experience tended to become integrated within a wider modernist context, especially French Modernism, with their own exile presenting a suitable outer manifestation of metaphysical and meta-fictional concerns.

What had started as a vibrant community of writers and thinkers involved in heated debates over questions of national and cultural identity and the preservation of cultural legacies turned gradually into a loose group of disparate men of letters who were forced to witness their own loss of relevance. With the exception of the work of Nabokov, who was by some hailed as the saviour of Russian émigré literature (Berberova called him a 'tremendous, mature, sophisticated modern writer … a great Russian writer, like a Phoenix … born from the fire and ashes of revolution and exile … All my generation were justified. We were saved'),[6] literary production appeared to be gradually replaced by literary feuds in which entrenched groups were arguing over something that did not exist. Gazdanov, for instance, declared in 1936 that émigré literature of the younger generation did not exist.[7] Few were able to overcome the language barriers that divided them from the potential readers of their host countries, and dwindling émigré communities with their ever-decreasing readerships turned the newly gained freedom from censorship into a lost opportunity. In short, Russian writers abroad experienced the loss of social and cultural significance that came with the absence of direct state persecution.

The first-wave Russian emigration entered a phase of disintegration with the onset of the Second World War. Alexander Kuprin returned to the Soviet Union in 1937; Khodasevich died of cancer in 1939; Tsvetaeva, ostracized by the émigré community because of her husband's involvement with the Soviet Secret Service, also returned to the Soviet Union in the summer of 1939; Aldanov and Nabokov emigrated to America; several writers and thinkers of the Russian emigration, including Ilia Bunakov-Fondaminsky, Felzen, Iu. Mandelshtam, and Mother Mary Skobtsova died in Nazi concentration camps. The literary community of Paris was further polarized by the politics of living in an occupied zone: Merezhkovsky (d. 1941) and Shmelev became tainted by their fascist sympathies, while Gazdanov was part of the French Resistance; Adamovich joined as an unlikely recruit in the war against Hitler and wrote the pro-Stalinist *L'autre patrie*; even Bunin, who was known in earlier decades of the century for his rabid anti-Bolshevism, had a brief flirtation with the idea of repatriation in the period following the liberation of Paris. In the post-war years Paris ceased to be the capital of the literary emigration and the first wave itself ceased to be a cultural entity united by a mission as well. New York gradually emerged as the new centre and home for the 'second wave' – those émigrés who arrived in the West in the wake of the Second World War.

'Moving my lips soundlessly at dawn': the inner exile of Russian writers in the Soviet Union

The persecution and marginalization of Russian writers who stubbornly insisted on writing literature in the modernist individualist tradition without any clear political orientation started in the 1920s in the Soviet Union and became all-encompassing from the 1930s onwards, when the Soviet state had consolidated its power. Beginning in 1934 and intensifying with the launch of Stalin's Great Terror, nightly raids and arrests, threats of imprisonment and torture, the sudden disappearance of friends and acquaintances, and publishing bans served to silence writers who stubbornly defied the state-imposed aesthetics and ethics of Socialist Realism. The strict separation of internal/private life and external/public life became a way of being not only for writers but for large parts of the population. The inner psychological exile of writers like Mikhail Bulgakov, Osip Mandelshtam, Anna Akhmatova, Isaac Babel, Iurii Olesha, or Boris Pasternak was by definition far less prominent than the noisy bickering displayed by émigré communities abroad, but the perception and conceptualization of their exile developed in a certain symmetry with that of the Russian emigration. Many writers remaining in Soviet Russia cast their experience of literary and political ostracization along the lines of a continuing tradition of exile in Russian culture. The antagonistic relationship between them and the state provided a firm link to the Russian literary tradition, with the result that their moral integrity in the face of the corruption of Soviet literature and its close ('un-Russian') collaboration with the state was quietly (most did not want to draw attention to themselves if they could help it) yet palpably asserted.

Unrelenting press campaigns, implicit and explicit threats and official and unofficial publishing bans muted many of Russia's finest writers. Akhmatova's work, for example, remained unpublished from 1925 to 1940. Mandelshtam did not see any of his work in print after 1933. And after 1929 Bulgakov's prose was published only posthumously and the large majority of his dramas remained unperformed. Writing throughout the 1930s for a readership far removed in space and time, Bulgakov equated his state-imposed silence explicitly with exile abroad, as a letter to an acquaintance in 1937 indicates: 'You say that writers fall silent in foreign countries, but does it matter to me where I fall silent – at home or abroad?'[8] The writer's voice was reduced to a whisper, softly reciting his works only to intimate friends, barely audible behind closed doors. Literature henceforth became a private affair. Manuscripts remained unprinted and were only circulated in *samizdat* handwritten copies and notebooks, while many poems were committed to memory, a throwback to the pre-Gutenberg era, as Nadezhda Mandelshtam noted.[9] In that climate of repression, Bulgakov's famously bold phrase 'manuscripts don't burn' must be seen as an expression of defiance and wishful thinking, rather than conviction.

The writer's isolation and silence became a dominant theme in the work of such marginalized writers as Bulgakov, Mandelshtam, and Akhmatova. The isolated artist, fictional and real, persecuted by society and the state, is the hero in the majority of Bulgakov's works during the last decade of the writer's life, when repeated press campaigns and rigid censorship prevented his work from being published (e.g. *The Cabal of Hypocrites*, *The Last Days (Pushkin)*, *The Master and Margarita*). For Mandelshtam, the sentence to three years of internal exile for his Stalin epigram ('We live not feeling the land beneath us/Our words cannot be heard beyond ten steps' [1933]) came, as it were, as the realization of many years of inner exile he had endured from the 1920s onwards. The theme of silence, especially the writer's silence, pervades Mandelshtam's work of the 1920s and 1930s ('Finder of a Horseshoe' [1923], 'The flat is quiet as paper' [1933], 'Yes, I am lying in the earth, my lips are moving' [1935], 'The theta and the iota of the Greek flute' [1937]), but it is the Stalin epigram which is probably Mandelshtam's fiercest insistence on his right to speak out, an attempt to summon poetry in the struggle against his own silence. Akhmatova's experience of her ostracization in Soviet society and culture was from the beginning closely allied with the persecution and imprisonment of people close to her (Nikolai Gumilev, Lev Gumilev, Punin, Mandelshtam). The theme of incarceration therefore appears to shade her perception of her own isolation, her 'civic death' as she called it elsewhere, and its related themes ('I know I cannot move from this place' [1939], 'And so in defiance' [1940]). Akhmatova asserts her poetic voice by speaking in place of others, implicitly as the voice of the Russian people in her *Requiem*, for instance, but also as the mourner of other poets' fates ('Voronezh' [1936], 'To the Memory of M. B[ulgakov]' [1940]).

The rapid and radical changes in Soviet society and culture left many writers, even those who initially welcomed the Bolshevik revolution, with a sense of being out of step with the time. In the case of Bulgakov and Mandelshtam this sense of standing outside history was heightened by the increasing isolation of Soviet culture from European culture. Spatial and temporal distances overlapped. Bulgakov and Mandelshtam felt cut off from pre-Revolutionary culture in time, and from the West in space. Mandelshtam, who had once defined Acmeism as 'nostalgia for world culture', longed for Italy, which he saw as a cornerstone in the development of Western civilization ('Do not Compare' [1937]). As if to resist the enforced movement further away from Western Europe to Cherdyn, Nadezhda Mandelshtam in her memoirs, themselves a fine piece of Russian literature, anchors the narrative of their exile firmly in the literary tradition of Europe and pre-Revolutionary Russia by linking Mandelshtam to Ovid and Pushkin:

> I had brought a small volume of Pushkin with me. [One of the guards, accompanying the Mandelshtams on the train to Cherdyn, also called] Osip was so taken by the story of the old gypsy [the old man's story about Ovid in Pushkin's verse drama *The Gypsies*] that he read it out loud to his bored comrades. 'Look at what those Roman Czars did to old men', Osip said to the others. 'It was for his poems they sent him away.' The description of Ovid's northern exile affected him greatly: he thought it was a terrible thing, and he decided to reassure me that we were not in for anything as bad as this.[10]

Bulgakov, whose brothers had chosen to go abroad after the Revolution, regretted his choice to remain in Russia even at the point when Stalin himself called him and seemed to offer him the option to leave. He would later refer to his choice as one of the five grave mistakes in his life: 'If it had not been for them . . . I should have been composing, not moving my lips soundlessly at dawn in my bed, but properly at a writing desk.'[11] Underlying Mandelshtam's and Bulgakov's desire to move beyond Russia's borders is a cultural cosmopolitanism, an assumption that literature can thrive independently and outside of its national territory. Indeed, a deterritorialized Russian literature promises cultural continuity and authenticity in comparison to the corruption of Soviet literature. By dissociating their work and themselves from the native country, these writers experience notions of inside and outside as reversed, with home becoming a place of exile despite its being 'within'.

Against this rejection of home, Akhmatova and Pasternak insisted on their rightful place in Russia. In the tradition that sees Russian literature as part of the social conscience, the inextricable link between the writer, the Russian people, and Russian soil is central to their identity as Russian writers despite their social and cultural marginalization. Already in 1922 Akhmatova declared that 'I am not with those, who have abandoned their land/To the lacerations of the enemy'.[12] Akhmatova defies her status as an outcast by invoking the powerful national myth of shared suffering and linking herself closely with the *narod*, or at least with the Russian women who are waiting in long lines in front of prisons. As the voice of the Russian people in her famous *Requiem* she articulates the close proximity to the Russian people and Russian soil as an exigency of her art:

> No, not under the vaults of alien skies,
> And not under the shelter of alien wings –
> I was with my people then,
> There, where my people, unfortunately, were.[13]
>
> (1961)

Pasternak, who had found the literary life of the émigré community in 1920s Berlin stale and trite, also insisted that Russian literature could not exist outside Russian territory. Following the scandal surrounding the foreign publication of *Dr Zhivago* (1957), Pasternak explained in an interview why he chose to return to the Soviet Union in 1923: 'everything would have been much more trivial. A person should live the life of his country. He should live an intense, natural life, and then his works will contain internal naturalness – and if a person is cut off from his native environment, then new creative juices will not come to him. You see, émigré literature has not created anything of significance.'[14] Pasternak poignantly reiterated this position in a public letter to Khrushchev in response to the threat of being stripped of his citizenship and expelled from the country: 'I am tied to Russia by birth, by life, and by work. I cannot imagine my fate separated from and outside of Russia.'[15] The letter (not all of which was written by Pasternak but which was signed by him) continued to drive this point home: 'leaving my native land would be equivalent to death.'[16]

In their focus on national and cultural authenticity the concerns of Russian writers inside the Soviet Union developed along fault-lines similar to those discussed and debated by the Russian diaspora abroad. Despite their diametrically opposed situations, Russian writers unwittingly converged in their attempts to preserve their Russian identity as writers and Russian literature as a national art and institution, whether from outside its homeland or within the country whose state had yet again turned against it. The symmetry of their responses to the threat posed to Russian literature indicates a continuation of the dialogue between the different concepts of a national literature and its place of belonging. Many of the books banned by Soviet censors, whether written by Russian authors in the Soviet Union or abroad, became accessible in their entirety to the Russian reader only in the era of '*glasnost*'. In the attempt to reclaim a whole complex of works hitherto ignored or forgotten in the Soviet Union, these works came to be known as 'returned' or 'restored' literature (*vozvrashchennaia literatura*), regardless of whether the works had been written within or outside of Russia, hinting at the idea of 'homecoming' and implying that there is a stable place, a true home where all Russian books belong.

Speaking in strange tongues: Nabokov's and Brodsky's linguistic versions of exile

Two exiled writers stand out in the Russian literary tradition of the twentieth century, in that they have not only traversed different countries and cultures, but have also performed breathtaking linguistic somersaults, switching from Russian to English in mid-career. Coming from divergent cultural and literary backgrounds, Vladimir Nabokov and Joseph (or Iosif) Brodsky moulded their exile experience to suit the exigencies of their individual art, constantly negotiating their positions between their status as 'Russian writers *in* exile' and 'American writers *of* exile'. Each used his specific experience of exile to determine his distinct identity as a writer with varying degrees of detachment from the Russian literary tradition of exile, thus illustrating the continuity and rupture of the Russian exile tradition in the second part of the twentieth century. The convergence and disparity of these two writers is to some extent encapsulated in descriptions of their own exile experience in terms of flying:

> I don't seem to belong to any clear-cut continent. I'm the shuttlecock above the Atlantic, and how bright and blue it is there, in my private sky, far from the pigeonholes and the clay pigeons.[17]

> Exile brings you overnight where it normally would take a lifetime to go . . . to be an exiled writer is like being a dog or a man hurtled into outer space in a capsule (more like the dog, of course, than a man, because they will never bother to retrieve you). And your capsule is your language . . . before long the passenger discovers that the capsule gravitates not earthward but outward in space.[18]

Their shared perception of exile as a state of isolation and suspension receives diametrically opposed interpretations. In his Romantic view of the solitary exile, Nabokov soars above such petty concerns as national identity, insisting on his individuality and freedom outside geographical or linguistic borders. For Nabokov, exile is an opportunity, an enabling condition which grants him an elevated position. Brodsky, on the other hand, admits the creative impulse exile can exert, but at the same time he underlines the painful experience of isolation, casting himself as the dog, an unspecified animal (one among many), insignificant and unable to communicate. In other words, Nabokov presents himself as an émigré in control of his own movement (he is the shuttlecock flying), while Brodsky sees himself as an exile, the passive object of the movement (the dog is being flown).

At the point when Nabokov changed to English, he had an established reputation as the leading Russian émigré writer under his penname 'Sirin'. His work of the Russian period had culminated in *The Gift*, which with its intricate patterns of allusions and references to Russian literature is both Nabokov's tribute and farewell to his native language and heritage. Perhaps it was his unrivalled position in Russian émigré literature at the age of forty together with his supposed multi-lingual upbringing ('I grew up a perfectly normal trilingual child'), which gave Nabokov the confidence to embark on another departure, this time from the Russian language, re-casting himself in the process into an English-speaking writer.[19] At the end of the 1930s in expectation of a move to an English-speaking country, Nabokov wrote *The Real Life of Sebastian Knight*, his first novel in English, about a writer caught somewhere between a Russian and an English cultural and linguistic legacy, one who remains ultimately unknown, with an uncertain identity and uncertain literary and biographical roots. With the switch in language, roughly coinciding with his departure from Europe to America in 1940, came a change in the writer's identity. Nabokov realized the absence of an exiled author in a vanishing act which in its boldness must be unique in Russian or any other literature. 'Across the dark sky of exile, Sirin passed, to use a simile of a more conservative nature, like a meteor, and disappeared, leaving nothing much else behind him than a vague sense of uneasiness', Nabokov noted in the English version of his autobiography, cancelling his former Russian self.[20] In place of Sirin, there appeared a hardly known author with an outlandish name, variously misspelled and mispronounced as 'No-bow-cough', 'Nabok*off*', '*N*abokov' or 'Na-bah-kov'.[21]

Through this linguistic switch Nabokov deeply inscribed the complex experience of exile into his art, pointing towards the lost voice and identity of an exiled writer but also writing his way out of exile into a different literary tradition and connecting with a new readership. If Nabokov were the man (and Nabokov is unthinkable as the submissive dog) in Brodsky's capsule, then this change to English would be his taking over the controls and steering the capsule back towards earth. Exile is controlled and reworked in his fiction and thus turned into a creative condition. In more pronounced fashion than in his Russian works, Nabokov's English novels translate the concrete experience of exile into meta-fictional and metaphysical concerns (e.g. the transition to a new metaphysical or meta-fictional reality at the end of *Bend Sinister*, the perception and invention of European and American spaces in *Lolita*, the mirror realities of *Pale Fire* and *Ada*). Novels like *King,*

Queen, Knave, Laughter in the Dark, or *Despair* undergo a distinct process of reworking in Nabokov's self-translations with specific Russian references being replaced by allusions to Western culture.[22] Nabokov therefore not only switched languages but also appeared to step out of the Russian literary tradition which relies on its own continuous renewal and reproduction in each new work. Nabokov, as it were, interrupted the chain of 'Chinese whispers', in which each writer both retains and transforms the voice of his Russian precursors.

There is, however, a strong sense of unease in Nabokov's apparently flippant cancelling of his 'Russianness'. Although the change in language was a matter of choice, on a personal level Nabokov perceived his self-imposed linguistic exile as a tragic loss: 'My private tragedy, which cannot, indeed should not, be anybody's concern, is that I had to abandon my natural language, my natural idiom, my rich, infinitely rich and docile Russian tongue, for a second-rate brand of English.'[23] This is a deeply intimate matter, yet its publication in the added postscript to his best-selling *Lolita* is anything but private. By openly lamenting his exile and loss, he manages to maintain a firm link with the Russian literary tradition, declaring his tender love for the 'softest of tongues'. Yet Nabokov's continuous engagement with Russian literature appears to remain firmly grounded in the past and in translation (the translation of his Russian novels into English and his famous translation of *Evgenii Onegin*) and does not encompass his English novels directly. At the same time, however, he repeatedly pointed to the continuity and development of his literary projects spanning both his Russian and American period (e.g. the Russian *Enchanter* is transformed into *Lolita*, the Russian 'Solus Rex' foreshadows *Pale Fire*). The ambiguity of his attitude becomes evident in an article he wrote after his arrival in America: 'The very term "émigré author" sounds somewhat tautological. Any genuine writer emigrates into his art and abides there. As for Russian writers, they have always loved their motherland nostalgically even without leaving it in reality. Not only Kishinev [Pushkin's place of exile] or the Caucasus but Nevsky Prospect seemed like a faraway exile to them.'[24] Here the exile experience becomes an abstract universal condition of writers, yet at the same time Russian literature is singled out as particularly 'exilic'. Nabokov thus integrates himself into a transnational community of writers in imaginary exile, yet at the same time he aligns his own exile with a specifically Russian sense of homelessness.

In his various reflections on his own situation as an exile, Nabokov keeps the Russian tradition of exile alive, fulfilling to some extent the duty of paying back what he had borrowed from his native literature. Nabokov manages at the same time to connect himself closely with his national heritage, which prevents his shuttlecock from being hurtled into outer space, and to maintain the distance from earth necessary for the creative writer. The meteor Sirin might have passed the planet without a trace to vanish into the depths of outer space, but the shuttlecock Nabokov remains both aloof from and firmly dependent on the impetus received from earth.

Being a poet in the first place, and a Russian poet who never made the shift to the Anglophone poetic idiom entirely successfully in the second, Joseph Brodsky is a different sort of exile than Nabokov. Both writers, to be sure, are the most vivid examples of what we are calling 'linguistic exile', yet the poetry/prose divide, and their different notions of the role of the writer in the Russian literary tradition, makes of their stories a study in contrasts. If Nabokov's pictorial genius finds expression as 'poetic prose', Brodsky's uniqueness as a wordsmith is above all 'choric', tied to the internal rhythms of different verse forms and prosodic effects, hence his inability to completely 'Americanize' his Russian verbal habits. Nabokov wielded his 'gift' in order to *transcend* the painful fact of exile on his famous 'magic carpet' of imagination, memory, and artistic form. Brodsky, by contrast, is more stoical, more 'existential', less inclined to the Symbolist act of transcendence. He does believe in a god-term – language – but this deity is severe and framed by 'Old Testament' thinking. The poet is exiled from humanity (his and others') by his service to his language. His lines of verse survive because, in Brodsky's eccentric theology, 'language is always older than the state and because prosody always survives history'.[25] Thus, Brodsky's heroes on the Russian side are decidedly not the artists who through their own acts of solipsistic prestidigitation rise above the pain around them, but rather those who write poetry in the face of, while fully acknowledging, great personal and national suffering: Akhmatova, Mandelshtam, Tsvetaeva.

Brodsky has always been both a native and a foreigner, no matter where his physical self happens to be located. In other words, he has perceived of himself by definition, existentially, as an exile within the world order, and this even before his troubles with authority began in Soviet Russia. Brodsky has always felt himself to be both European and something else – say, for lack of a better word, 'Eastern'. For Brodsky exile is too often connected in the public's mind to politics and ideology, which is why he will not have the word, unless metaphysically attenuated, applied to his poetry. When Brodsky was tried by the Soviet state for 'social parasitism' (*tuneiadstvo*) in February–March 1964 it was because, as the so-called crime suggested, he lived outside, or 'on', the host. He had held many odd jobs and gave the impression of hopping from one host's back to the other, of doing as he pleased; he was not, in a word, a solid citizen of Soviet letters. There is a kernel of truth here, since the state recognized rightly that it had an alien element in its midst. It was not that there was anything openly seditious or even political in Brodsky's early verse (although feelings of alienation and corrosive questioning were clearly present from the start), but rather that what was there could not be defined as belonging to the prevailing idiom.

Brodsky, then, will not allow us to write him into the scenario of the tragic exile. What was left behind for Brodsky in the Soviet era was not a Silver but rather an Iron – or, better, Stone – Age, and what was acquired in America was not only loss but also the freedom to be alone with time, eternity, and his ever-attenuating notions of poetic discourse. There is, then, little left of the Russian literary myth of the exiled writer's special status in Brodsky's thinking:

> Whether we like it or not, Gastarbeiters and refugees of any stripe effectively pluck the carnation out of an exiled writer's lapel. Displacement and mis-placement are this century's commonplace. And what our exiled writer has in common with a Gastarbeiter or a political refugee is that in either case a man is running away from the worse toward the better. The truth of the matter is that from tyranny one can be exiled only to a democracy.[26]

Brodsky addresses the moral bind of the contemporary expatriate writer, who if he lives in a place other than his homeland has to contend with the competing categories of 'exile' (someone who is banished against his or her will), 'émigré' (someone who lives elsewhere but chooses to do so), and 'tourist' (a modern avatar of the romantic traveller of nineteenth-century fame who journeys to a foreign country to experience its otherness in a safe, 'consumerist' manner).[27]

Brodsky's pre-1972 poems on a travel theme couch those works in tradi-tional exilic terms.[28] Lyric verses conceived within a 'proper' exilic frame-work – i.e. those poems whose settings evoke the northern banishment to Norenskaia (1964–1966) – appear to 'contaminate' the settings of other pieces linked with travel, since the perception is, and this was something Brodsky seems to have played upon, the speaker's relationship to the 'powers at the centre' (as he writes from the periphery) is always already problematic if not clearly dangerous. By situating his speaker in Lithuania or on the Black Sea coast, the poet writes himself into mythological situations (say, that of Ovid) that have a subtext of 'banishment to the margins of the Empire'. Being an exile still has something of the martyr's aureole about it (if laden with heavy doses of irony) and automatically inserts Brodsky into a tradi-tion that goes back to Pushkin. Embedded in Brodsky's caustic treatment of a Soviet Empire in decline is an elegiac longing for the high modernist values (Mandelshtam's and Akhmatova's in the first instance) of an earlier

Silver Age that was perceived as 'Russian' and authentic. Once abroad, however, Brodsky through his speaker would test his nostalgic notions against reality. Istanbul is not the place of Yeats' singing birds that keep drowsy Emperors awake, but the place of Islamic *kosnost'* (stagnation), disregard for the individual, architectural chaos ('Flight from Byzantium'). Likewise, since the Petersburg/Leningrad palimpsest of Brodsky's youth ('Guide to a Renamed City') cannot be recaptured (here Brodsky resembles Nabokov by fearing the loss of memory that goes with return), Venice becomes the ever-decaying, ever-reconstituted city of watery reflections, ghostly shimmerings, necropolis inside petropolis inside the floating identity of a speaker whose home is everywhere and nowhere (*Watermark*).

In the final analysis, then, Brodsky is an exile among exiles. In this respect his closest predecessor in the Russian poetic tradition is probably Tsvetaeva. In his poetry, exile is explored more as a metaphysical problem, more as the inevitable departure of the soul from the body, than as the political expulsion of the citizen from the state. By making language 'older than the state' and by asserting that prosody 'survives history', Brodsky constructed an exemplary poetic life (even after becoming a celebrated American man of letters) by always framing existential concerns in terms (*a priori*) of linguistic ones. Therefore, the pain and dislocation that inevitably went with physical banishment ('history'), and which Brodsky was willing to acknowledge if only stoically, could never be defined for the poet in terms outside his linguistic ones.

By frequently banishing writers beyond narrowly defined geographical, social, cultural, and national boundaries, the Russian state has continuously created a powerful foil – an 'other' – against which a collective identity of Russian writers could be effectively defined. In this way, an integral measure of state persecution has been turned on its head. Exile has proven an effective tool for constructing the myth of the martyred Russian writer. Exile has become the common denominator for writers divided by such opposite fates as Nabokov's success story and Mandelshtam's tragic end, or Brodsky's Nobel Prize award and Khodasevich's artistic eclipse. Writers as different in temperament and thinking as Bulgakov and Akhmatova, or Tsvetaeva and Bunin, participated in what constitutes a continuous dialogue about Russian writing in exile, elevating Russian literature to the rank of a national institution.

Against the threat of silence and eventual oblivion which exile poses to writers, Russian literature has evolved an intricate system of cross- and self-referencing, a peculiar national intertextuality, in which writers have integrated the words of their predecessors and contemporaries into their own work (*preemstvennost'*). The awareness of a particular national tradition and heritage inscribed in the canonical texts of Russian literature has become a collective literary memory which has subverted the state's attempts to silence its writers and sought to ensure the continued existence of Russian writers posthumously and *in absentia*. Constant attempts at silencing writers have been ironically counter-productive, as writers invariably responded by making themselves more audible than they might otherwise have been without the threat of exile. The voices of Russian writers have overcome spatial and temporal distances to create a theme which pervades and continuously creates Russian literature.

NOTES

* Frank would like to acknowledge the support of the Leverhulme Trust through the award of an Early Career Development Fellowship.
1 Levin, Harry, 'Literature and Exile' in *Refractions: Essays in Comparative Literature* (New York: Oxford University Press, 1966), p. 68.
2 Khodasevich, Vladislav, 'Krovavaia pishcha' in *Literaturnye stat'i i vospominaniia* (New York: Chekhov, 1954), p. 285.
3 Adamovich, Georgii, 'O literature v emigratsii', *Sovremennye zapiski*, 50 (1932), p. 339.
4 *Ibid.*, p. 333.
5 Gippius, Zinaida, *Pis'ma k Berberovoi i Khodasevichu*, ed. Erika Freiberger Sheikholeslami (Ann Arbor, MI: Ardis, 1978), p. 14. Berberova claimed to have coined the phrase in an earlier poem.
6 Berberova, Nina, *The Italics are Mine*, trans. Philippe Radley (New York: Harcourt, Brace & World, 1969), p. 319.
7 Gazdanov, Gaito, 'O molodoi emigrantskoi literature', *Sovremennye zapiski*, 60 (1936), pp. 404–408, p. 407.
8 '"Ne vse li ravno, gde byt' nemym . . . ": pis'ma M. A. Bulgakova bratu, N. A. Bulgakovu', ed. V. V. Gudkova, *Druzhba narodov*, 2 (1989), p. 201.
9 Mandelshtam, Nadezhda, *Hope against Hope: A Memoir* (New York: Atheneum, 1970), p. 192.
10 *Ibid.*, p. 52.
11 Milne, Lesley, *Mikhail Bulgakov: A Critical Biography* (Cambridge: Cambridge University Press, 1990), p. 186.
12 Akhmatova, Anna, *Polnoe sobranie stikhotvorenii/The Complete Poems of Anna Akhmatova*, trans. Judith Hemschemeyer, 2 vols. (Somerville, MA: Zephyr Press, 1990), vol. 1, p. 547.
13 *Ibid.*, vol. 2, p. 95.
14 Fleishman, Lazar, *Boris Pasternak: The Poet and His Politics* (Cambridge, MA and London: Harvard University Press, 1990), p. 293.
15 *Ibid.*, p. 297.
16 *Ibid.*
17 Nabokov, Vladimir, *Strong Opinions* (London: Weidenfeld & Nicolson, 1973), p. 117.
18 Brodsky, Joseph, 'The Condition We Call Exile', *The New York Review of Books*, January 21 1988, p. 18.

19 Nabokov, *Strong Opinions*, p. 43.
20 Nabokov, Vladimir, *Conclusive Evidence* (New York: Harper & Brothers, 1951), p. 217.
21 Nabokov, *Strong Opinions*, pp. 51–52.
22 For Nabokov's method of self-translation, see Grayson, Jane, *Nabokov Translated: A Comparison of Nabokov's Russian and English Prose* (Oxford: Oxford University Press, 1977).
23 Nabokov, Vladimir, 'On a Book Entitled *Lolita*' in *The Annotated Lolita* (New York: Vintage, 1991), pp. 316–317.
24 Quoted in Dolinin, Alexander, 'Nabokov as a Russian Writer' in Connolly, Julian W., ed., *The Cambridge Companion to Nabokov* (Cambridge: Cambridge University Press, 2005), p. 57.
25 Brodsky, Joseph, *Less Than One: Selected Essays* (New York: Farrar, Straus & Giroux, 1986), p. 52.
26 Brodsky, 'The Condition', p. 16.
27 See Turoma, Sanna, *Brodsky Abroad: Empire, Tourism, Nostalgia* (Madison, WI: University of Wisconsin Press, 2010).
28 *Ibid.*, pp. 16–44.

FURTHER READING

Aciman, André, ed., *Letters of Transit: Reflections on Exile, Identity, Language and Loss* (New York: New Press and London: I. B. Tauris, 1999).

Bethea, David M., *Joseph Brodsky and the Creation of Exile* (Princeton, NJ: Princeton University Press, 1994).

Boym, Svetlana, *The Future of Nostalgia* (New York: Basic Books, 2001).

Cavanagh, Clare, 'The Death of the Book à la russe: The Acmeists under Stalin', *Slavic Review*, 55, no. 1 (1996), pp. 125–135.

Johnston, Robert H., *New Mecca, New Babylon: Paris and the Russian Exiles, 1920–1945* (Kingston, Montreal: McGill–Queen's University Press, 1988).

Kristeva, Julia, *Strangers to Ourselves*, trans. Leon S. Roudiez (New York: Columbia University Press, 1991).

Livak, Leonid, *How It Was Done in Paris: Russian Émigré Literature and French Modernism* (Madison, WI: University of Wisconsin Press, 2003).

Raeff, Marc, *Russia Abroad. A Cultural History of the Russian Emigration* (New York and Oxford: Oxford University Press, 1990).

Robinson, Marc, ed., *Altogether Elsewhere: Writers on Exile* (Boston, MA and London: Faber & Faber, 1994).

Seidel, Michael, *Exile and the Narrative Imagination* (New Haven, CT: Yale University Press, 1986).

Struve, Gleb, *Russkaia literatura v izgnanii* (Paris: YMCA Press, 1984).

Tabori, Paul, *The Anatomy of Exile: A Semantic and Historical Study* (London: Harrap, 1972).

12

BIRGIT BEUMERS

Drama and Theatre

Russian drama in the twentieth century is inextricably linked to the theatrical performance: after the Duke of Saxe-Meiningen (1826–1914) introduced the concept of the director at the Meiningen Company in Germany in the 1870s, the way in which a play was represented on stage became a skill in its own right: the art of directing was born. Therefore, this chapter links developments in dramatic writing to innovations in theatre art, and vice versa.

We will explore the emergence of a director's theatre in Russia in the 1890s, which brought on to the stage the plays of a new generation of playwrights by relying on psychological realism. This approach met resistance in the 1910s, when the Symbolist theatre proposed instead a return to archaic forms such as rituals. The Revolution created a new impetus for artistic innovation combined with political commitment, and throughout the 1920s Russian theatre and drama thrived: satires exposed the bourgeois resistance to the Revolution, while theatre directors collaborated with artists from the visual arts, architecture, and cinema. The 'great experiment' – not only in theatre, but also in literature, film, and visual arts – came to an end with the imposition of Socialist Realism in the 1930s, which forced theatres into quasi-psychological realism and dramatists to write politically engaged and ideologically sound plays. Reacting to this, theatres innovated production techniques and staged contemporary readings of the classics, which offered a means for social and political criticism in a veiled form. Only a few playwrights gained prominence in the post-war era, and their work is linked to certain theatres. For much of the second half of the twentieth century, theatres and directors were more influential than the plays and dramatists themselves: therefore, from the Thaw onwards, our emphasis shifts also to theatres and the writers associated with them. The *glasnost'* era liberated playwrights from formal and thematic fetters, and theatres and playwrights looked back to the interrupted avant-garde traditions of the 1920s and the forbidden pages of the country's history. This excitement was short-lived, although many playwrights were translated and staged outside Russia. The chapter concludes with a brief discussion of a new generation of playwrights who have conquered theatres both at home and abroad – by now in the twenty-first century.

Before the Revolution

Although it is arguable whether the dramatist Chekhov (1860–1904) belongs to the nineteenth or the twentieth century, it is doubtless impossible to begin a discussion of twentieth-century Russian drama and theatre without at least a short mention of Chekhov and the theatre director Konstantin Stanislavsky (1863–1938).

Chekhov's major plays – *The Seagull* (*Chaika*, 1896), *Uncle Vania* (*Diadia Vania*, 1897), *Three Sisters* (*Tri sestry*, 1901), and *The Cherry Orchard* (*Vishnevyi sad*, 1903) – were truly innovative: Russian theatres at the time operated in a declamatory style highly unsuitable for Chekhov's atmospheric dramas. Chekhov also broke away from the classical five-act structure (exposition, rising action, climax, falling action, denouement) to a four-act composition that, it appears, fills the gaps: instead of showing action on stage, Chekhov focuses on the characters' emotional responses to events that happen between the acts. Moreover, Chekhov's protagonists face social change, but they are unwilling to act or to take the initiative to adapt their lives accordingly; instead, they remain passive and merely cope with the consequences of their own inactivity. Yet while Chekhov scrutinizes the lethargy of his gentry and intelligentsia characters, he portrays them with sympathy and irony. Not shown as 'victims' of social change, they laugh at their own ineptitudes and unfitness for the new way of life: slapstick and vaudeville are frequently employed in Chekhov's major plays, especially in *The Cherry Orchard*, although these elements have often been ignored in twentieth-century productions. Chekhov's characters require a delicate and subtle psychological approach; they challenge the director to treat the text not as an expression of feelings but as a cover-up for emotions.

This quality of Chekhov's plays was fully appreciated by Konstantin Stanislavsky, who in 1896 opened the Moscow Art Theatre[1] – the first theatre that was accessible to the general public without class distinction – with *The Seagull*. Largely on the basis of Chekhov's plays, Stanislavsky developed an approach to the actor's work that involved a close identification with the character in order to facilitate an understanding of the 'subtext' that lay hidden behind the words; that stressed the role of an elaborate stage set to create the atmosphere necessary for the audience to fully identify with a situation; and that separated the world on the stage from the audience through the so-called 'fourth wall', imitating the real world on stage while allowing the audience emotional, but no physical, contact with that world. Stanislavsky's theatre relied on the actors to capture the characters' psychology in order to make the audience share the characters' emotional experiences (*perezhivanie*).

After Chekhov's premature death in 1904, the Moscow Art Theatre continued to play an important role in the development of drama in the first decades of the twentieth century. A playwright with different concerns but a similar approach to drama, and an admirer of Chekhov, was Maxim Gorky (real name Aleksei Peshkov, 1868–1936). From a petit-bourgeois background and engaged with revolutionary groups from 1888 onwards, Gorky, like Chekhov, portrayed people who were bored with their old way of life but unwilling to accept the signs of social and political change that appeared on the horizon with the revolutionary movements in the 1890s. In contrast to Chekhov's plays, Gorky's are devoid of humour: at the play's end, the characters are still frustrated, but they are politically more aware and committed. They need to work for the improvement of life and society, but have no real hope. For Gorky the dramatic conflict lay in a clash not of characters but of ideas; hence his plays are usually static and lack stage action, because confrontations are enacted verbally.

The Lower Depths (*Na dne*, 1902), perhaps Gorky's best-known play, explores an ideological conflict: the inhabitants of a doss house (a setting that emphasizes the sense of physical entrapment) are comforted by Luka, who offers them a faith that involves the acceptance of suffering and requires fortitude and patience. Whilst Gorky refrains from denying Luka his belief in God as a way of coping with life, he uses another character, Satin, to expose its falsity: the treacherous faith in the future or another life is exposed as the 'religion of slaves and masters'. Through Satin, Gorky asserts that the recognition of lies is the first step towards change, while hope remains beyond the scope of *The Lower Depths* – and most of Gorky's other plays.

Gorky's characters are social types rather than individuals: they represent the attitudes and demeanours of entire classes. His plays take their subject matter from life in the provinces and their characters from the bourgeoisie and the merchant classes, which are shown as lacking spiritual values, leading a debauched life, and having neither hope nor interest in the future. *The Petty Bourgeoisie* (*Meshchane*, also translated as *Philistines*, 1902) and *Summer Folk* (*Dachniki*, 1905), for example, both expose the emotional traumas of a society ripe for revolution, as well as the generational conflict that lies at the heart of the stifling atmosphere captured in the plays. *The Lower Depths* for the first time brings onto the stage the lower classes of society, criminals and prostitutes, who are discontented with their lot. *Vassa*

Zheleznova (first version, 1910) centres around a mother, Vassa, who tries to keep her family together even at the price of corrupting their moral values. Her behaviour destroys her family and literally cripples her son Pavel, who is deformed; he is reminiscent of Osvald in Henrik Ibsen's *Ghosts* (1881), who suffers from syphilis as a symbolic burden for his mother's hypocrisy and as a result of his father's philandering. This theme ties both Ibsen and Gorky to the naturalist tradition that permeated nineteenth-century literature.

In the first two decades of the century, psychological realism reigned in the theatres, because playwrights were concerned with the passing of a social order. The dramatic form remained largely conventional, dwelling on states of mind rather than actions, and offering diagnoses rather than solutions. Such conventional structures and themes would remain prominent in the years following the 1917 Bolshevik Revolution.

However, a second trend of theatre and drama developed simultaneously to psychological realism, opposing the Moscow Art Theatre's approach. Russian Symbolists took an interest in theatre, aware of its potential for a synthesis of art forms from music to set design, as in the Wagnerian *Gesamtkunstwerk*. They took their inspiration from the Belgian playwright Maurice Maeterlinck (1862–1949), a translation of whose *Blue Bird* (*L'oiseau bleu*, 1908) enjoyed great popularity in Russia after Stanislavsky produced it for the Moscow Art Theatre. The Symbolists urged the theatre to turn away from external reality towards the inner life of the human soul, dwelling on philosophical content; these plays, however, were difficult to stage. Leonid Andreev (1871–1919) is the most accessible exponent of this movement. In his dramas he portrays the disintegration of the bourgeois world; however, he does not follow Gorky's example of insisting on the necessity for social change. Instead, he focuses on the destructive force of human (mostly female) passion to the petty-bourgeois world, as is evident in his 1912 play *Ekaterina Ivanovna*. In *The Life of Man* (*Zhizn´ cheloveka*, 1906) he sets the cycle of human life against a metaphysical backdrop: the cyclical structure of eternity is undermined by the linearity of time. Andreev is preoccupied with the impact of metaphysical ideas on human fate; and without departing from realism, he makes powerful use of colour and light for the creation of atmosphere.

Alexander Blok's (1880–1921) *The Fairground Booth* (*Balaganchik*, 1906) is perhaps the best-known Symbolist play; his other works include *The Stranger* (*Neznakomka*, 1908) and *The Rose and the Cross* (*Roza i krest*, 1912). *The Fairground Booth* combined folk motifs and the popular *commedia dell'arte*, involving the stock characters Pierrot, Harlequin, and Columbine in a melodramatic triangle that was peppered with references to the literary circles of the time. The Symbolist poet and theorist

Viacheslav Ivanov (1866–1949) argued that theatre should return to the medieval mystery play and embed the performance in a ritual that would place equal emphasis on text, music, song and word.[2] Thus, modern theatre would place life rather than a hero at centre stage, and offer no denouement but pose a question. Ivanov's comments were in part a reaction to the Moscow Art Theatre's realism, and they echo the preoccupation manifested in Sergei Diaghilev's art magazine *World of Art* (*Mir iskusstva*, 1909), which insisted that art should stop fabricating reality and called for conventionality (*uslovnost'*) instead of verisimilitude (*dostovernost'*).

A synthesis of art forms was achieved in the work of a key figure in Russian theatre, the director Vsevolod Meyerhold (1874–1940). At the Komissarzhevsky Theatre in St Petersburg, he nurtured his interest in the Symbolists' new drama: the concepts of conventionality and the use of *commedia dell'arte* elements are both evident in his post-Revolutionary work. Between 1908 and 1917 Meyerhold was the director of the Imperial (Alexandrinsky) Theatre in St Petersburg, where he staged grand-scale productions of classical drama, intensifying his collaboration with composers and set designers to create a 'synthetic theatre' by bringing together different art forms.

From the Revolution to Socialist Realism

When the October Revolution occurred in 1917, the theatre was ripe for change: both the new regime and artists were quick to realize opportunities. Many theatre directors welcomed the Revolution and offered to put their art at the service of the new regime, and they were supported by the new Commissar of Enlightenment, Anatolii Lunacharsky (1875–1933). In August 1919 the theatres were nationalized; in 1922 the Central Repertoire Committee (*Glavrepertkom*) was established to oversee repertoire policy and ensure that a sufficient proportion of Soviet and revolutionary plays would be staged. Meyerhold left the Alexandrinsky and dedicated his art to the Revolution; from 1918 to 1921 he was in charge of the Moscow Theatre Section of the Commissariat of Enlightenment. During this time, commonly known as the 'Theatrical October', he demanded a complete break with theatrical traditions: the theatre, he insisted, should become exclusively a tool for state and party propaganda. Along with other young directors, Meyerhold sought to organize mass theatrical spectacles, an example of which is Nikolai Yevreinov's *Storming of the Winter Palace* (*Vziatie zimnego dvortsa*), performed on the square of the Winter Palace on 7 November 1920 by 8,000 participants for over 100,000 spectators. A celebration of the Revolution, the spectacle emphasized the theatricalization of real life and history while also politicizing art.

While Stanislavsky had aimed for an illusion of reality on stage in the Moscow Art Theatre, Meyerhold sought to break with this 'illusionism': his sets were created by constructivist artists, who left the building mechanisms visible, and the costumes resembled factory wear. Aspiring, like the Symbolists, to a synthesis of the arts, he involved a variety of art forms. Meyerhold collaborated with renowned visual artists such as Liubov Popova, Alexander Rodchenko, and Varvara Stepanova in his productions of plays like Fernand Crommelynck's *The Magnanimous Cuckold* (*Le Cocu magnifique*, 1922) or Alexander Sukhovo-Kobylin's *Tarelkin's Death* (*Smert' Tarelkina*, 1922). Meyerhold thought of theatre as a magnifying glass that would enhance certain aspects of reality. Thus he preferred episodic structures, and would often adapt classical plays by breaking them up into fragments. Theatre also had a social function: Meyerhold went to factories to perform plays (e.g. Sergei Tretiakov's *Gas Masks* [*Protivogazy*, 1924], performed in a gas factory), in order to bring art to the working class. On stage, he used placards to indicate location (a device also found in Brecht's epic theatre); documentary footage and cinematic devices such as screens, slogans, and projections further enhanced the parallels to real life, making the spectator aware of being in a theatre. Meyerhold's actors were trained in biomechanics: stage movements were choreographed and paced, rather than psychologically motivated. Words were of secondary importance, since the characters were 'types' with little psychological depth: Meyerhold practised a theatre of demonstration (*predstavlenie*) rather than one of emotional experience.

Though theatre directors had long experimented with performance methods, the first Soviet play had yet to be written: this was Vladimir Mayakovsky's *Mystery-Bouffe* (*Misteriia-Buff*, 1918, 1921), which showed the triumph of the proletariat. This play was prefaced with a scathing attack on Stanislavsky's realism, calling for the 'fourth wall' (the imagined barrier between the stage and the auditorium) to be broken: however, realism continued to prevail in the dramatic writing of the 1920s, especially in the treatment of historical themes such as the Revolution and the Civil War. During these early years, recent history was largely presented in foreign settings, as in Tretiakov's *Roar, China!* (*Rychi, Kitai!*, 1924) and *Are you Listening, Moscow?!* (*Slyshish', Moskva?!*, 1923) – the latter set in Germany. *Roar, China!*, staged at Meyerhold's theatre in 1926, dealt with the injustice of the British colonizers in China, who demanded the execution of two boatmen to redeem the drowning of a British agent on the Yangtze river; but the people's solidarity ultimately opposed and triumphed over the exploiters. Tretiakov draws on the agitational skit (*agitka*) for his subject matter, but his characters are emotionally moving. Similar examples of exotic revolutionary settings include Vladimir Bill-Belotserkovsky's

Echo (1922), which explores the impact of the Russian Revolution on America.

Satire was a prominent genre of the 1920s, inspired largely by the absurdities of life created during the New Economic Policy (NEP, 1921–1928), which Lenin introduced to alleviate the economic crisis in the aftermath of the wars and revolutions. The most prominent figures of NEP satire are, without doubt, Mikhail Bulgakov (1891–1940), Nikolai Erdman (1900–1970), and Vladimir Mayakovsky (1893–1930). Bulgakov's *Zoya's Apartment* (*Zoikina kvartira*, 1926) indirectly addresses the housing crisis: Zoya bribes a housing official in order to keep her large apartment, claiming that she runs a sewing workshop there; in reality, this is a guise for a brothel that she runs to entertain, among others, a rich entrepreneur. The whole of society is subversive: bribery, drug addiction, prostitution, violence, and murder pervade everyday life and turn it into a phantasmagoric experience. *Zoya's Apartment* had the most successful stage interpretation at the Vakhtangov Theatre, which had developed a style of fantastic realism that was highly suited to Bulgakov's play.

Erdman's two satires *The Warrant* (or *The Mandate*; *Mandat*, 1925) and *The Suicide* (*Samoubiitsa*, 1928) both use an episodic structure, disrupting character development in favour of showing types created by a certain – absurd, Soviet – way of life, and both plays were directed by Meyerhold. *The Warrant* is full of slapstick and verbal humour: it deals with the Guliachkin household, which maintains a bourgeois lifestyle while superficially accepting Soviet values as its head Pavel joins the Party for the sake of personal gain. The false belief in the possibility of a return to the old order is parodied in the figure of the cook, Nastia, who wears a dress believed to have belonged to the empress, whilst the abuse of power in the Soviet lifestyle is highlighted in the theme of Party membership as a vital tool for survival in the new society. In *The Suicide*, the unemployed Podsekalnikov surely must be depressed: when he ventures into the kitchen at night to get some sausage, his wife suspects that he intends to commit suicide. The wife alerts a neighbour, and soon, the representatives of a whole range of organizations want Podsekalnikov to commit suicide for a political or social cause – but, in fact, he had not wanted to end his life at all. The play, with numerous puns, exposes the new regime that, despite its verbosity, has nothing to do with life. Mayakovsky's *The Bedbug* (*Klop*, 1928) and *The Bathhouse* (*Bania*, 1930) are anti-utopian satires. They portray life in the NEP era as chaotic and subversive, while the perspective of the future ambiguously oscillates between a controlled and regulated life and idealized perfection. Thus *The Bedbug* involves time travel into a future that is sterile and regulated, deprived of real life, love, and all the things that make life imperfect. Yet this future is also technically perfect, bright, and stable. The play enjoyed a much-acclaimed stage production by Meyerhold in 1929 with constructivist sets for the second, futuristic act designed by Alexander Rodchenko.

Censorship prevented this genre from flourishing in the 1920s. However, Evgeny Shvarts (1897–1958) used fairy tales and legends to disguise his satirical portrayal of totalitarianism in the 1930s and 1940s in his plays *The Naked King* (*Golyi korol'*, 1934) and *The Shadow* (*Ten'*, 1940), both of which drew on Andersen's fairy tales. They were staged, however, only after the Thaw, at the Sovremennik Theatre.

The work of the Association of Real Art, OBERIU (Ob˝edinenie real'nogo iskusstva), offers aesthetic resistance to the realist mainstream of the 1920s, collapsing both dramatic form and character. Daniil Kharms' *Elizaveta Bam* (1928) is a play that best fits into the relatively short-lived tradition of the absurd: Elizaveta Bam is visited by two men, Petr Nikolaevich and Ivan Ivanovich, who come to arrest her for a murder she has yet to commit: this is the murder of Petr Nikolaevich at the play's end. Kharms deliberately blurs the borders between theatre and life: realities shift, and the sequence of events, both temporal and logical, is disrupted. The play exhibits a distortion of reality and turns the theatre into a place that *creates* reality rather than representing it. Another OBERIU play, Alexander Vvedensky's *Christmas at the Ivanovs* (*Elka u Ivanovykh*, 1938), which mocks Christmas as a celebration that covers up domestic violence, creates episodes that are surreal and (for stage representation) impossible.

In the late 1920s realism was preferred to formal innovation and by 1932 was established as 'the only true form of artistic expression', when Socialist Realism became state policy and thus the Soviet standard for all the arts. Plays with revolutionary themes now set their action in Russia, as for example in Konstantin Trenev's *Liubov Yarovaya* (1926), which sets a melodramatic plot – that of the eponymous heroine and her husband Mikhail – against an epic revolutionary backdrop, making problems on the human scale appear trivial in comparison to the grand movements of the Red and White armies. Trenev represents both factions by a large number of different characters and types, such as the aristocracy and the clergy among the Whites, but he refrains from a black-and-white attribution of good and evil characters to the conflicting armies: a White officer (Mikhail Yarovoi) is good until he betrays his best friend and fails to keep his word to release Red captives, and there is a negative Red in the figure of a thief, who is later shot by his fellow-soldiers. The play develops the melodrama between Liubov and her husband, who has fled and whom she eventually turns in. The political thus triumphs over the personal; but, more importantly, good prevails over bad and right over wrong – and this humanistic message guaranteed the play's stage success: it premiered at the Maly Theatre, where it is still part of the stock repertoire, even today.

The conflict between the Whites and the Bolsheviks also informed Bulgakov's play *The Days of the Turbins* (*Dni Turbinykh*, 1926), which he had himself adapted from his novel *The White Guard* (*Belaia gvardiia*, 1925). *The Days of the Turbins* shows the effect of the turmoil during the Civil War on a Kievan family. The Turbins belong to the old humanist intelligentsia and face political and personal choices when, between 1918 and 1919, Kiev is first under a hetmanate supported by the occupying German army, then is defended by the Whites against the threat of Symon Petlyura's army that is fighting for independence, and is finally taken by the Bolsheviks. The Turbins' sympathies are with the Whites, who are portrayed with psychological depth and shown in a positive light – capable of risking their lives to protect others. However, Bulgakov ensures a balanced portrayal by also showing instances of the Whites' immoral and unethical conduct – abandoning comrades, friends, and family to save their own lives. *The Days of the Turbins* may not be the most important play in Bulgakov's dramatic oeuvre, but it was immensely influential at the time, largely for two reasons: first, it allowed the Moscow Art Theatre actors to play characters that, unlike the flatly drawn Bolsheviks of the new revolutionary plays, possessed a certain depth; second, Stalin's personal support for the production (he saw it fifteen times, and it was brought back into the repertoire in 1932 at his request).

Vsevolod Ivanov's *Armoured Train 14–69* (*Bronepoezd 14–69*, 1927–1931), also set in the Civil War, deals with the peasant Vershinin, who has recently joined the Bolshevik ranks. Despite all odds, Vershinin seizes a train harbouring Whites who are about to leave the country, showing his commitment to the cause. In contrast to Bulgakov's protagonists, Vershinin shows no compassion: the cause is most important. Vsevolod Vishnevsky's *Optimistic Tragedy* (*Optimisticheskaia tragediia*, 1933) deals with a female commander who brings order into a unit of sailors. Dramatic characters were portrayed as placing the political above the personal, and plays became a way of rewriting the official 'historical truth'. Both of these features fitted well within the parameters of Socialist Realism.

Socialist Realism dominated dramatic writing during the 1930s and 1940s. Alexander Afinogenov's (1904–1941) *Fear* (*Strakh*, 1931) offers a good example of a Socialist Realist hero: Ivan Borodin is a scientist who leads a research institute, but his background is the old intelligentsia, which stops him from accepting the new Soviet people. He has to admit defeat, however: after being dismissed, he recants and is returned to the institute as a fully integrated member of the collective. The development of his social consciousness from half-hearted to fully committed Communist culminates in a happy ending, but the play also draws attention to the downside of the good-to-better development in Socialist Realist drama – the reliance on the text and ideas rather than on situations and life. Nikolai Pogodin was a popular playwright of his time: in *Kremlin Chimes* (*Kremlevskie kuranty*, 1940), he shows how Lenin convinces a reluctant engineer to work for the new regime. The appearance of Lenin on both screen and stage was frequent in the 1930s, and served to emphasize his proximity to the people. Another play by Pogodin, *Aristocrats* (*Aristokraty*, 1935), explored the building of the White Sea canal by prisoners and their resultant reform into productive and conscientious labourers. Thus industrial achievements and ideological conversions became the subject matter for drama in the 1930s.

Alexei Arbuzov's *Tania* (1938) chooses a more interesting approach but remains stereotypical in structure. Tania leaves medical school when she gets married, but her husband perceives this as lack of devotion to socialism, and eventually leaves her for another woman who participates in the transformation of society. Tania changes: she finishes her studies and becomes a doctor, and ultimately she is allowed to find personal happiness. The play is rife with coincidences, and the symmetrical structure makes it appear contrived; but the characters are psychologically convincing. Arbuzov made another important contribution to theatre when, in 1938, he organized a studio for young actors and dramatists wherein he employed a collaborative-writing method to create a play: the result was the play *City of the Dawn* (*Gorod na zare*, 1941), about the construction of the city of Komsomolsk-on-Amur. The studio's activities came to a halt with the war. During these years only a few plays were written, and they were largely about the war experience.

The purges of the late 1930s had a tragic and devastating effect on the diversity of the arts: Mayakovsky committed suicide in 1930; Kharms was imprisoned from 1931 to 1932 and again in 1941, meeting his death in captivity; Erdman was arrested for anti-Soviet writing in 1933; Tretiakov was arrested and shot in 1939; Meyerhold's theatre was closed in 1938, and he was arrested and shot in 1940; his wife, the actress Zinaida Raikh, was brutally murdered in the same year. Stanislavsky's theory was 'canonized' after his death in 1938 and psychological realism was elevated to Stanislavsky's 'method': this meant that theatres were to treat the stage as a closed space from whence no communication with the audience was possible. Therefore, not only did experiments with acting methods come to a halt, but theatre also became stale and detached from life.

The immediate post-war years saw another clamp-down in the arts, which culminated in Andrei Zhdanov's appointment in the Central Committee as the supervisor for cultural policy from 1946 to 1948, a period thus usually referred to as *Zhdanovshchina*. It was during this period that the so-called theory of conflictlessness (*bezkonfliktnost'*) in drama was promoted. Whereas 'the tension between good and better' had thitherto been acceptable, this theory proclaimed that Socialist Realist drama cannot contain a conflict – thus removing the most essential premise for dramatic structure. This led to a stagnation of dramatic writing, and consequently to a crisis in the theatre arts, given the absence of good contemporary plays.

The Thaw and afterwards

The Thaw alleviated this crisis somewhat. First, an editorial in the newspaper *Pravda* on 7 April 1952 attacked the drama-without-conflict theory and called for playwrights to express the truth and speak out against any negative aspects of Soviet life. Second, theatre arts were affected when a 1955 editorial in the Party's leading theoretical journal *Kommunist* advocated diversity and deprecated the levelling and uniformity in the arts due to psychological realism. Third, the rehabilitation of Meyerhold led to a revival of some of his productions. Finally, the creation of the Ministry of Culture in 1953 led to changes in the control over theatres that appeared to signal a relaxation.

The Thaw influenced the theatre in a variety of ways: first, a new generation of playwrights emerged with Leonid Zorin (b. 1924), Viktor Rozov (1913–2004), and Alexander Shtein (1906–1993) – even though the first harbingers of the Thaw, Zorin's *The Guests* (*Gosti*, 1954) and Shtein's *A Personal Matter* (*Personal'noe delo*, 1954), both about corrupt party officials and the misuse of authority, did not elicit a positive response from the authorities. Second, young and promising directors were appointed to head prestigious theatres, among them Georgii Tovstonogov (1913–1989) to the Bolshoi Drama Theatre (BDT) in Leningrad; Anatolii Efros (1925–1987) to the Lenin Komsomol (Lenkom) Theatre in Moscow; and Iurii Liubimov (b. 1917) to the Taganka Theatre in Moscow. Third, for the first time in many years, a new theatre was founded: the Sovremennik (Contemporary) in Moscow, which was headed by the young actor Oleg Efremov (1927–2000). Playwrights and directors alike sought innovation and a break with the stale psychological realism that had made experiments with style impossible.

Rozov's plays provided an impulse for directors to push the limits of psychological realism. These plays focus on the passage of young boys to adulthood, thus appealing to a young generation. The Sovremennik opened in 1957 with a production of Rozov's *Alive Forever* (*Vechno zhivye*, 1943–1956) staged by Efremov, who combined a stylized, abstract set with an authentic approach to life. *Alive Forever* explores Veronika's loss of her fiancé in the war and her inability to come to terms with that loss. In *In Search of Joy* (*V poiskakh radosti*, 1957), the hero demolishes a piece of furniture, a symbol of the petty bourgeoisie, with his father's sabre; the gesture accompanying this act became symbolic of the break with tradition. In Efros' production of Rozov's *On the Day of the Wedding* (*V den´svad´by*, 1964) at the Lenkom, the heroine's last-minute withdrawal from an unsuitable marriage was formally represented by her breaking free from the set, which consisted of tables and chairs arranged for a wedding party. Rozov's plays deal with personal relationships in the modern world, the impossibility of heroism, the incompatibility of ambition and reality, and the need to come to terms with whatever life holds in store while remaining truthful to oneself.

These are also the concerns of Arbuzov's post-war work, as manifested in *My Poor Marat* (also *The Promise*; *Moi bednyi Marat*, 1964): the play is about a woman choosing her husband out of duty rather than love (marrying him after he has been injured during the Leningrad siege), but love triumphs at the end. Arbuzov makes characters face up to their real feelings despite appearances.

The Sovremennik discovered Alexander Volodin (1919–2001), who exposes the world of façades in his plays: *The Factory Girl* (*Fabrichnaia devchonka*, 1956) is set in a factory that is to be featured in a film and which therefore attempts to pretend that work conditions are perfect. The worker Zhenka criticizes the masking of problems, and is ultimately supported by her peers. Volodin innovated dramatic composition by using cinematic devices such as flashbacks and parallel action. Many of Volodin's plays have served as film scripts, such as *Five Evenings* (*Piat´ vecherov*, 1957; film by Nikita Mikhalkov, 1978). Volodin is interested in the personal life of ordinary people, and often treats relationships and failed romances with a touch of irony: the individual alone can find happiness, despite social and ideological constraints.

Efros' productions of Chekhov's *The Seagull* in 1966 and *The Three Sisters* in 1967 aroused huge controversy, since Efros interpreted the plays in terms of the 'lack of communication' that is characteristic of the theatre of the absurd, another taboo in Soviet theatre. This led to his dismissal from the Lenkom and his transfer to the position of staff director at the Malaya Bronnaya Theatre. Here he directed classical dramas and developed both his method of structural analysis for the exploration of character psychology and his concept of 'psycho-physics' – the psychological motivation of movement.

Liubimov had noticed a dangerous uniformity in Soviet theatre, and he abhorred the use of make-up, costumes, and decorative props. With his students, he staged Brecht's *The Good Person of Szechwan* in 1963 and successfully applied the concept of epic theatre to the production. The play was set on a bare stage; posters decorated the sides, and panels indicated locations; songs were used for commentary, and a musical rhythm set the pace of the production; choreographed movement replaced verbal action. These elements, drawn from Brecht and Meyerhold, characterized Liubimov's style at the Taganka, as well as a thematic focus on the individual in solidarity with the people as a means of ensuring success; this enhanced the strong socio-political stance of the theatre. The range of theatrical devices was fully explored in the Taganka's repertoire, but especially vividly in *Ten Days that Shook the World* (1965), which was based on John Reed's eponymous account of the revolution.

In the 1960s Liubimov, as well as other directors in the major theatres, focused on classical texts and novels rather than on new plays, manifesting a shift away from the text towards visual interpretation. This period was driven by a fascination with the possibilities of theatre, which contrasted with the dearth of dramatic writing that could match the theatrical experiment. Moreover, censorship interfered heavily in theatre repertoires in the late 1960s, when several productions critical of the authorities or otherwise controversial were banned. The Party once again promoted the production theme in drama (especially forcefully during the Twenty-Fifth Party Congress in 1976), compelling playwrights to portray heroes in the workplace. The plays of Alexander Gelman (b. 1933) were among the more successful attempts to meet this challenge. In his 'production dramas' the psychological scrutiny of characters is set against an industrial theme: he deals with the conflicts of modern men that resulted from work, and he sets the ethics of work against the individual's conscience. *Minutes of a Meeting* (*Protokol odnogo zasedaniia*, 1976, based on his script for the film *The Award* [*Premiia*, 1974]) investigates a factory's refusal to accept a bonus after having falsified their figures. *Alone with Everyone* (or *A Man with Connections*; *Naedine so vsemi*, 1982) explores the crisis between a husband and wife that follows an industrial accident, in which their son lost both hands, and for which the father is held responsible: the façade of their achievements, social and personal, breaks apart.

In 1970 Efremov left the Sovremennik to become Chief Artistic Director at the Moscow Art Theatre, where he introduced yet another generation of playwrights into the repertoire, such as Alexander Vampilov (1937–1972). Vampilov was without doubt the most popular playwright in the Soviet Union during the 1970s. Vampilov challenges a social type that manifests its presence in the post-Thaw world: an egoist and materialist, lacking any moral values, who – in exceptional circumstances – reveals his true self.

Farewell in June (*Proshchanie v iiune*, 1966) investigates the theme of corruption: the student Kolesov is bribed by the dean, Repnikov, to break off his relationship with the latter's daughter in exchange for a good degree. Although Kolesov agrees, he later tears up the degree certificate: his career is the price paid for his belated sincerity. In *The Elder Son* (*Starshii syn*, 1968), the self-betrayal is of a materialistic nature: the medical student Busygin pretends to be the illegitimate son of Sarafanov. Busygin compromises his honesty and sincerity when he falls in love with Sarafanov's daughter but fails to abandon his false identity. *Duck-Hunting* (*Utinaia okhota*, 1970) relies on flashbacks as the protagonist, Zilov, recalls the events that have led up to the present: after a night of drinking, he finds that his friends have played a joke on him and sent him a wreath for his own funeral. While Zilov sits in his room making telephone calls, he brings to life the memory of the past, remembering things that have gone wrong at work and in his personal life; then he invites his friends to the funeral wake as he prepares to kill himself – but then he instead decides to go duck-hunting. Zilov has no sense of remorse for the past, or any responsibility for the present; in the history of Soviet drama, his character has become known as the type of modern man who is indifferent and uninterested without, however, being repulsive. Zilov suffers from an 'invalidity of the soul' and is an outsider or a 'chudak', a typical feature of Vampilov's characters.[3]

Gorbachev's reforms had an immediate effect on the arts, and Russian theatre benefited greatly from new opportunities. By granting theatres partial independence from state control and allowing them to stage productions that had been banned or for which approval was pending, Gorbachev hoped to inspire support for his reforms among the intelligentsia. Theatres responded to the cause of *glasnost'* by staging new plays and implementing organizational reforms.

Organizational reforms affected the management of theatres, initiating a gradual transition to cultural organizations that were financially and (mostly) administratively independent. An experiment allowing theatres to run their own budgets proved beneficial to the studio theatres, which obtained official status and subsidies; consequently, their number grew rapidly. Some later turned into professional theatres. These studios staged both new plays and the previously forbidden plays of the theatre of the absurd or of the Russian OBERIU figures Kharms and Vvedensky.

Another important playwright of the period is Viktor Slavkin (b. 1935), who treated genuinely new themes (the sub-culture of the Stagnation) in a new form (a collage of various sources). His plays are inextricably linked to theatre director Anatolii Vasiliev (b. 1942), who used improvisation to tackle the reminiscence-driven text by Slavkin without stifling it. Vasiliev directed Slavkin's *A Young Man's Grown-Up Daughter* (*Vzroslaia doch' molodogo cheloveka*, 1979), which caused a stir for its use of jazz music, earlier condemned as decadent. On the small stage of the Taganka Theatre, Vasiliev directed Slavkin's *Cerceau* (*Serso*, 1985), which was acclaimed as a landmark in Soviet theatre history. In it, the forty-year old Petushok ('Rooster') invites colleagues, neighbours, and accidental acquaintances for a weekend at a dacha. The characters talk, but without revealing their true feelings. After a series of excursions into the past, the tragic isolation of each of them becomes apparent, but still they are incapable of sharing more of their lives with each other. This conclusion would hold true for many relationships, professional and other, that had been formed during the Soviet era.

Other playwrights were discovered, like Nina Sadur (b. 1950), Liudmila Petrushevskaia (b. 1938), and Alexander Galin (b. 1946), and their plays were quickly absorbed into the repertoire. Many playwrights made an impact with only a few plays, and others just held their places in repertoires: the period has no real leading dramatist. Galin's *Stars in the Morning Sky* (*Zvezdy na utrennom nebe*, 1987) caused a stir both at home and abroad as the first play to address prostitution: it deals with the evacuation of prostitutes from Moscow during the 1980 Olympics in order to show a 'clean' city to foreign visitors.

Petrushevskaia's *Cinzano*, although written in 1973, was first staged and published during *perestroika*, when it won international acclaim in a studio production. The play portrays the squalor of everyday life and alcoholism. Petrushevskaia's plays are glimpses of everyday existence, spoofs at best; they are devoid of any development. Petrushevskaia uses gossipy, but not vulgar language. Beyond the witty and ironic discourse lies the bleakness of Soviet life: the ordinary problems of women in *Three Girls in Blue* (*Tri devushki v golubom*, written 1983); the drunkenness of the three men in *Cinzano*; and the shortage of living space and its crippling effect on human relations in her short play *Love* (*Liubov'*, 1974).

Sadur's first play, *The Weird Peasant Woman* (*Chudnaia baba*, 1982), actually consists of two shorter plays. In the first, Lidiia encounters an old woman in the field, who plays a game with her that sends her down a dark hole, from which she is re-born. Returning to the real world in the second play, Lidiia is unable to discern this world from the other world. *Drive On* (*Ekhai*, 1983) deals with a peasant intent upon commiting suicide on the rails and the train driver who tries to stop him – but then the peasant simply walks away with an old woman who appears. Sadur combines Soviet reality with the surrealism of Russian folklore and folk belief, using a poetic rhythm for the language of her folksy characters. Her plays recall the surreal and phantasmagorical atmosphere of Kharms, while her use of Russian folklore and fairy tale themes remains idiosyncratic.

The established theatres were slower than the studios in their response to new playwrights: in the first instance, they drew on the work of established playwrights who wrote politically engaged plays. The Lenkom, for example, distinguished itself with its productions of Mikhail Shatrov (1932–2010), well known for his plays about Lenin, such as *The Sixth of July* (*Shestoe iiulia*, 1966) and *The Bolsheviks* (*Bolsheviki*, 1966), as well as *Blue Horses on the Red Grass* (*Sinie koni na krasnoi trave*, 1979), which was about the Third Youth League Congress. During *glasnost'* Shatrov moved into the limelight with *The Dictatorship of Conscience* (*Diktatura sovesti*, 1985), which for the first time mentioned figures such as Bukharin and Trotsky that had been blotted out of Soviet history books. *The Dictatorship* marked the turning point in repertoire politics under Gorbachev when it opened at the Lenkom Theatre in 1985. Indeed, the Lenkom's artistic director at the time, Mark Zakharov (b. 1933), had already made a name for himself at the theatre by developing a wide-ranging repertoire, including the first Soviet rock opera, *Perchance* (*Iunona i Avos'*, 1981), by Andrei Voznesensky and Anatolii Rybnikov. During the Gorbachev years Zakharov was politically engaged, penning articles that challenged the interference of bureaucrats in the theatrical process.

The post-Soviet scene

After the collapse of the Soviet Union and the reorganization of theatres, with studios acquiring a permanent status, established theatres being forced to find external funding, and commercial enterprises thriving on mediocre productions with a star-studded cast, many playwrights disappeared from the stage: Petrushevskaia and Sadur turned to prose; Galin spent several years in the United States; Slavkin turned away from writing full-length plays; and Alexei Kazantsev and Mikhail Roshchin founded a journal and later the 'Centre of Dramaturgy and Directing', which became instrumental in the discovery of new plays in the late 1990s. The theatre scene of the 1990s was desperately searching for genuinely new voices and new forms, echoing Treplev's call in *The Seagull* (Act I): 'We need new forms.'

In the 1990s several playwrights contributed to the development of the dramatic genre both with their plays and by facilitating the emergence of new playwrights. Nikolai Koliada (b. 1957), probably one of the most prolific and widely staged playwrights of the 1990s, ran a small theatre in Ekaterinburg and taught young dramatists. Roman Viktiuk directed several of his plays, including *The Catapult* (*Rogatka*, staged 1993) and *Oginski's*

Polonaise (*Polonez Oginskogo*, 1994). *The Catapult* is about the development of a homosexual relationship between two young men. Beyond the surface of reality lurks a dream world, in which the characters admit their true feelings. The dream sequences free the characters from the restrictions of the everyday and of social reality by means of displacement into another world. This juxtaposition of two worlds, the beautiful dream world and the grim reality, separate and irreconcilable though one nevertheless enriches the other, forms an underlying principle of Koliada's plays and stage productions.

Another recent phenomenon is Evgenii Grishkovets (b. 1967), whose texts include *How I Ate a Dog* (*Kak ia s´el sobaku*, 1998) and *Simultaneously* (*Odnovremenno*, 1999). Grishkovets is a stand-up comedian who performs his own monologues, based on reminiscences of his Soviet childhood. His episodic plays for the theatre (and not performed by himself), such as *Notes of a Russian Traveller* (*Zapiski russkogo puteshestvennika*, 1999), *Winter* (*Zima*, 2000), and *The Siege* (*Osada*, 2003), quickly found their way into theatre repertoires. Here, too, Grishkovets parodies Soviet reality by drawing on associations and experiences shared with his audience.

In the 1990s Russian theatre and drama managed to recoup the past and reconnect to lost avant-garde traditions, then to part from these and move on. It took, however, several years of adaptation to commercialization (in at least part of the theatres) until a new trend in theatre and drama would emerge. Theatres and playwrights had to come to terms with the past, but also adapt to globalization and its effects and compete with Western playwrights for stage productions, and they had to adapt to the virtual worlds and the significance of alternative realities.

In lieu of a conclusion: 'New Drama' in the new millennium

In the twenty-first century a genuine surge of new dramatic writing has taken place, exhibiting a vitality comparable to that of drama at the turn of the twentieth century. 'New Drama' is a loose movement of playwrights that emerged from a festival organized in 2002 by the Moscow Art Theatre and the Golden Mask Festival's director Eduard Boiakov.[4] New Drama also makes use of documentary theatre, shown in the off-venue teatr.doc theatre and using the 'verbatim' technique that was brought to Russia notably through Royal Court/British Council seminars in 1999. 'Verbatim' – the recording of interviews to capture contemporary speech – is used to explore marginal social groups and to define an alternative discourse to that of the establishment, that of the commercial and glamourous language of boulevard theatres. New Drama has no manifesto, but promotes playwrights like Ivan Vyrypaev, who wrote, directed, and performed *Oxygen* (*Kislorod*, 2002) and *Genesis No. 2* (*Bytie No. 2*, 2004), both of which frame the indifference and violence of everyday life in a religious structure. The director Kirill Serebrennikov became famous for his productions of new Russian and British plays, in which he refrains from illustrating the violence inherent in the plays' texts. He directed the plays of Oleg and Vladimir Presniakov, *Terrorism* (2002) and *Playing the Victim* (*Izobrazhaia zhertvu*, 2003) at the Moscow Art Theatre.

This new wave of plays dealing with themes of violence and indifference in a non-psychological manner will without doubt characterize dramatic writing of the twenty-first century in a no less powerful manner than Chekhov influenced drama at the turn of the last century.

NOTES

1 Moskovskii khudozhestvennyi teatr (MKhT), until 1919 when it became the Moscow Academic Art Theatre – Moskovskii khudozhestvennyi akademicheskii teatr (MKhAT); in 2004 the original name was restored. For the sake of consistency, 'Moscow Art Theatre' has been used throughout this chapter.
2 Ivanov, Viacheslav, 'Presentiments and Portents: The New Organic Era and the Theater of the Future' (1906) in his *Selected Essays*, trans. and ed. Robert Bird and Michael Wachtel (Evanston IL: Northwestern University Press, 2001), pp. 95–110.
3 Maiia Turovskaia highlights these features in her article 'Vampilov i ego kritiki' [Vampilov and his critics], *Sibir'*, 1 (1976), pp. 102–115.
4 The festival was held at the Moscow Art Theatre in 2003, in St Petersburg's Lensovet Theatre in 2004, at the Meierhold Centre, Moscow, in 2005, and at the Praktika Theatre, Moscow, in 2006 and 2007.

FURTHER READING

Beumers, Birgit, *Yury Lyubimov at the Taganka Theatre 1964–1994* (Amsterdam: Harwood, 1997).
Beumers, Birgit and Mark Lipovetsky, *Performing Violence: Literary and Theatrical Experiments of New Russian Drama* (Bristol and Chicago: intellect books, 2009).
Braun, Edward, *Meyerhold: A Revolution in Theatre* (London: Methuen, 1995).
Farber, Vreneli, *The Playwright Alexander Vampilov: An Ironic Observer* (New York: Lang, 2001).
Freedman, John, *Silence's Roar: The Life and Drama of Nikolai Erdman* (Oakville, ON and London: Mosaic, 1992).
Golub, Spencer, *The Recurrence of Fate: Theatre and Memory in Twentieth-Century Russia* (Iowa City, IA: University of Iowa Press, 1994).
Leach, Robert, *Vsevolod Meyerhold* (Cambridge: Cambridge University Press, 1989).
Revolutionary Theatre (London: Routledge, 1994).

Leach, Robert and Viktor Borovsky, eds., *A History of Russian Theatre* (Cambridge: Cambridge University Press, 1999).

Russell, Robert, *Russian Drama of the Revolutionary Period* (Basingstoke: Macmillan, 1988).

Rzhevsky Nicholas, *The Modern Russian Theater* (Armonk, NY: M.E. Sharpe, 2009).

Segel, Harold B., *Twentieth-Century Russian Drama: From Gorky to the Present* (Baltimore, MD: Johns Hopkins University Press, 1993).

Smeliansky, Anatoly, *The Russian Theatre After Stalin* (Cambridge: Cambridge University Press, 1999).

Worrall, Nick, *Modernism to Realism on the Soviet Stage: Tairov–Vakhtangov–Okhlopkov* (Cambridge: Cambridge University Press, 1989).

The Moscow Art Theatre (London: Routledge, 1996).

13

JULIAN GRAFFY

Literature and Film

The story of film in Russia begins on 4 May 1896 in St Petersburg, with a showing by the Lumière Brothers of their 'cinematograph', just over four months after they had first exhibited it to paying customers in Paris. The earliest Russian films were newsreels, the first of them footage shot by a French cameraman nine days later of celebrations to mark the coronation of Nicholas II. For over a decade the cinematic diet offered to Russian audiences consisted of foreign fiction films and Russian newsreels, but by 1907 early Russian entrepreneurs were anxious to make fictional films from Russian subjects. Since a new Russian art form had to be invented, these pioneers naturally turned to the existing arts for inspiration, to theatre, painting, and photography for the visual resolution of their works, to literature, theatre, and song for their initially minimal narratives. In 1907 Alexander Drankov shot a version (now lost) of scenes from Pushkin's tragedy *Boris Godunov*. A year later his studio produced *Stenka Razin*, directed by Vladimir Romashkov. Released on 15 October 1908, and now conventionally known as the first Russian film, it was based upon a popular song about the rebel hero, which audiences were encouraged to sing while watching it. Thus literary sources gave film-makers their plots and gave audiences stories with which they were already familiar. In 1909 Petr Chardynin filmed Chekhov's story 'Surgery' (*Khirurgiia*) and then turned to Gogol's *Dead Souls* (*Mertvye dushi*). His approach to a work of this length was to stage and film two episodes from the novel, in which Chichikov visits Sobakevich and Pliushkin. After this other characters from the novel were presented, without any connection with the plot, and the film concluded with the appearance on stage of several other figures from the writer's work, posed around a bust of the writer in a picturesque group. Chardynin based the visual aspect of his work on the illustrations produced by Petr Boklevsky in the 1860s. In short, in the words of Semen Ginzburg, 'the film helped the viewer who knew *Dead Souls* to visualize the heroes of the novel'. Chardynin's approach was not so much creative as illustrative: he produced a twenty-one-minute version of Dostoevsky's novel *The Idiot* (*Idiot*) in 1910 and a thirty-minute version of Tolstoy's *The Kreuzer Sonata* (*Kreitserova sonata*) the following year, while Vasilii Goncharov's *The Life and Death of Alexander Pushkin* (*Zhizn´ i smert´ A.S. Pushkina*, 1910), played out the most familiar moments of the poet's life, from his early readings at the lycée to his duel and death, once again relying upon the audience's knowledge of the subject to excuse the breakneck speed of the narrative. Of course the large percentage of the audience who were illiterate could read neither the intertitles nor the literary sources, but even they were deemed likely to have some familiarity with the plot of *Anna Karenina*, which was filmed in both 1911 and 1914. In his 'selective list' of literary works brought to the screen in the years before the Russian Revolution, Veniamin Vishnevsky counts forty-eight adaptations of Pushkin, forty-three of Chekhov, twenty-five of Gogol and twenty-four of Tolstoy.[1] Several leading contemporary writers, from Maxim Gorky to the Symbolists Alexander Blok, Andrei Bely, and Fedor Sologub, were fascinated by the cinema and Iurii Tsivian tells us that the literariness of pre-Revolutionary films was sometimes enhanced by calling reels 'chapters' or by having the pages of the source text appear on screen, a practice which remained popular for decades.[2]

Within a few years, however, considerably more subtle engagements with Russian literature began to appear. As Rachel Morley has shown, *Child of the Big City* (*Ditia bol´shogo goroda*, 1914), by the leading pre-Revolutionary director, Evgenii Bauer, re-works elements of the plots and the characters of Pushkin, Gogol, and Dostoevsky in order to show their inadequacy in a harsh new century, in which the relationships between men and women were undergoing rapid change.[3] Two years later, Iakov Protazanov drew upon the increasing technical sophistication of the industry to make a remarkably atmospheric version of Pushkin's story *The Queen of Spades* (*Pikovaia dama*).

The debate about film and literature in the post-Revolutionary years

Bauer's death in June 1917 can be seen in retrospect as marking the end of an era in Russian cinema. The Bolshevik leaders who came to power five months later had strong views about the use of cinema for ideological purposes. The People's Commissar for Enlightenment, Anatolii Lunacharsky, suggested in October 1919, two months after the cinema had been nationalized, that 'it is impossible to imagine a richer source for cinema than the cultural history of mankind as a whole', but added that 'we must concentrate only on moments that are important for agitation and propaganda'.[4] Lenin famously said that 'of all the arts the most important for us is cinema', while Trotsky called it 'the most important weapon' and 'an instrument which we must secure at all costs!'[5]

Overall, however, the Bolshevik leaders held conservative views about art (Lenin described himself as a 'barbarian' with regard to the new artistic movements), and this led to tensions between them and the new cinematic avant-garde. Though the key figures who emerged in these years all proclaimed their allegiance to the new ideology, they did not share the politicians' enthusiasm for films based in 'cultural history', and were scathing in their attacks on cinema's 'literary' heritage.

The first of the wave of young directors to articulate a theory of cinema in print was Lev Kuleshov, who had begun his career before the Revolution as an assistant to Bauer. In a series of articles published between 1917 and 1922, he repeatedly stressed the difference between cinema on the one hand and literature and theatre on the other, and cheerfully embraced a new term which had been used to disparage his ideas:

> Our art is abused for its cinema specificity (*kinematografichnost'*): 'You are not always literary! You are not theatrical!' The whole point of cinema lies in its great degree of cinematic specificity. Actors, directors, artists, inscribe your banner in clear letters: the idea of cinema is the cinematic idea.[6]

Kuleshov insisted that 'there is no doubt that theatre and theatre workers bring nothing but harm to cinema', learning instead the lessons of the American films which were so popular among 'the people who sit in the cheap seats', and concluding that the essence of cinema lay in montage and 'Americanism' (*amerikanshchina*).[7] His first full-length feature, *The Extraordinary Adventures of Mr West in the Land of the Bolsheviks* (*Neobychainye prikliucheniia mistera Vesta v strane bol'shevikov*, 1924), which he described as a verification of his theory, values dynamic action and stunts over the psychological approach to character of his pre-Revolutionary predecessors. Kuleshov's treatment of his literary source is significant. The original 'literary script', by the writer Nikolai Aseev, based the gang who trick Mr West when he arrives in Moscow on characters in *Oliver Twist*, but subsequent re-workings by members of Kuleshov's film collective weakened the Dickens connection, causing Aseev to describe his involvement as a 'sad experience'.[8] Nevertheless, Kuleshov's break with the literary heritage was never complete, and during the next ten years he would film both Jack London and O Henry.

Vsevolod Pudovkin, who began his career as an actor for Kuleshov, was another avant-garde director ready to make literary adaptations. His first full-length film was a version of Maxim Gorky's novel *Mother* (*Mat'*, 1926), though the plot was re-worked to stress the social analysis of a working-class family. He also turned to literary sources for his second film *The End of St Petersburg* (*Konets Sankt Peterburga*, 1927), the script of which drew upon both Pushkin's 'The Bronze Horseman' and Andrei Bely's novel *Petersburg*. And in both cases, Pudovkin found inspiration in Tolstoy, whom he described as 'the only writer absolutely identical to reality', re-reading Tolstoy's novel *Resurrection*, while working on the trial scene in *Mother* and the representation of the countryside in *The End of St Petersburg*.[9]

On 22 July 1922 a group of young artists who styled themselves the FEKS (*Fabrika ekstsentricheskogo aktera*, *The Factory of the Eccentric Actor*) published in Petrograd, which they re-named Eccentropolis, the manifesto of *Eccentrism*, which they had patented in December of the previous year. They saw the future of art as lying in the circus, the cinema, the music-hall, and detective novels. Their attitude to the high cultural heritage was as dismissive as Kuleshov's, and expressed with greater vigour. They insisted that 'all the two hundred tomes of the philosophy of German Expressionism are not as expressive as a circus poster'. They thought that the place for conventional reviews of theatrical productions was 'down the toilet', and pined for a production of Othello in which he would be shot by a 'wild Brazilian'. In short 'we prefer Charlie [Chaplin]'s backside to Eleonora Duse's hands!'[10] In this context, the decision of two of their number, Grigorii Kozintsev and Leonid Trauberg, to film Nikolai Gogol's story 'The Overcoat' caused alarm and bewilderment in some quarters.

The film was scripted by the Formalist literary theorist and prose writer Iurii Tynianov, who explained his unconventional approach to filming Gogol in a polemical introduction to the published script:

> The film story *The Overcoat* is not a film illustration of Gogol's famous story. Illustrating literature for the cinema is an arduous and inauspicious task, since the cinema has its own methods and devices, which are not the same as those of literature. The cinema can only try to reincarnate and reinterpret literary heroes and literary style in its own way. That is why we have before us not a Gogol tale, but a film tale *in the manner* of Gogol, where the story is made more complicated, and the hero is dramatized in a plane which is not given by Gogol, but which is as it were suggested by Gogol's manner.[11]

The first half of the film is based mainly on another of Gogol's Petersburg tales, 'Nevsky Prospect', and the hero, Bashmachkin, is still a young man. All in all, according to the calculations of Iurii Tsivian, Tynianov used 'at least ten' other Gogol sources, as well as alluding to works by Pushkin and Dostoevsky.[12] The finished work was styled a 'Film-Piece in the Manner of Gogol'. Thus although the Bashmachkin of the film is a character who, strictly speaking, did not exist in Gogol's work, the radically innovative approach to adaptation, combined with the use of light and shadows and grotesque, distorting angles, produces a brilliant evocation not just of the world of Gogol but of the whole 'Petersburg text' of nineteenth-century Russian literature. But the film-makers also saw their film as provoked by contemporary experience. Kozintsev and Trauberg had mused of casting Charlie Chaplin in the role of the 'little man' hero,[13] and Kozintsev insisted that it was the 'cruel' St Petersburg winter of 1920–1921 and the sense of disorientation evoked by the Revolution that led them to the weirdness and nightmare in Gogol's writings.[14] The finished work was proclaimed a masterpiece by some and excoriated by others. As Tynianov noted in a 1929 memoir of his work with the FEKS:

> One critic called me an insolent illiterate and, if I am not mistaken, proposed cleaning up the FEKS with an iron broom... Another's reasoning was as follows: the classics are national property; the scriptwriter and the directors have distorted a classic – the Public Prosecutor's Office should try them for plundering national property.[15]

The most extreme position in the debate was taken by Dziga Vertov and the members of his Kino Eye group. In their August 1922 publication 'We. A Version of a Manifesto' they pronounced 'psychological Russo-German film-drama' 'absurd', and deemed all 'romantic' and 'theatricalized' old films 'leprous', 'mortally dangerous', 'contagious'. They called for the acceleration of the death of the old cinematography so that a new cinema, purged of 'the poison of the psychological novel', could come into being. A year later, in 'The Kino Eye. A Revolution', they described all existing films as 'a literary skeleton plus cine-illustrations', complained that pre-Revolutionary fictional models were still hanging over film-makers like icons, and reiterated the death sentence they had pronounced on 'all films without exception'. They proclaimed that 'from today', neither psychological nor detective dramas, neither theatrical productions, nor Dostoevsky could be of any use to film-makers, and greeted the new hegemony of the film newsreel.[16] This led to polemics with film-makers whom Vertov considered less radical in their approach to plot and narrative, such as Sergei Eisenstein, yet it is worth noting that even at his most extreme, in his 1928 master-work *The Man with the Movie-Camera* (*Chelovek s kinoapparatom*), Vertov was forced to resort to such 'literary' devices as a plot, which told of the film's own making, and a structure based in a day in its protagonist's life.

Eisenstein's position was more nuanced. In his famous 1923 article 'The Montage of Attractions', he spoke of freeing theatrical productions from reverence to the literary tradition and in 'The Montage of Film Attractions', written the following year, he insisted that his approach 'liberates film from the plot-based script'. His 1925 discussion of his first feature film *Strike* (*Stachka*, 1924), contended that 'the absence of plot and hero' made the film's form more revolutionary than its content, 'an ideological victory in the field of form'.[17] None of Eisenstein's feature films is a literary adaptation, yet the list of his unrealized projects contains many such, starting with a version of Babel's *Red Cavalry* stories in 1924. And in his response to a January 1928 questionnaire on the relationship of literature and cinema, he described literature as 'an 'inexhaustible fund' for cinema, 'a storehouse of materials'. While proclaiming the 'process of purging cinema' of literature and theatre as complete, he nevertheless felt that 'in beginning to discover its own particular paths cinema is now displaying once more a curious conjunction with literature, but . . . with literature's formal side', concluding that the link between them was likely to be 'a platonic one'.[18]

But while these debates raged, literary adaptations continued to be made, and to find box office success. Iakov Protazanov, who had filmed Pushkin before the revolution, made versions of Tolstoy's *Father Sergius* (*Otets Sergii*) in 1918, and of three Chekhov stories, as *Chiny i liudi* (*Ranks and People*), in 1929. He also contributed to a new and officially encouraged sub-genre of literary adaptation, of works set in or after the revolutionary period. His *Aelita*, 1924, moved the emphasis of Alexei Tolstoi's novel from Mars to the mundanity of NEP Moscow, but his 1927 version of Boris Lavrenev's story about the love affair between a White officer and a Red Army woman sniper, *The Forty First* (*Sorok pervyi*) was imbued with revolutionary romanticism: at its end the heroine prefers ideological duty and martyrdom to the fulfilment of personal desires.

The 1930s: sound comes to Soviet cinema

The Cultural Revolution of the late 1920s led to an increase in censorship and in consequence to the production and release of fewer new films. The ensuing situation was often referred to as a 'script crisis', and part of the solution proposed in the 'Resolution' of the First All-Union Party Conference on Cinema, in March 1928, was to draw upon 'the sufficiently rich resources' of workers in literature and theatre, since 'as a younger art form, cinema can utilize all the best achievements of literature'. This position was reiterated at the Conference of Sovkino Workers in December of the same year, where it was proposed that 'the best literary resources be grouped around the film studios and they be used to devise plots'. This return to the hegemony of the written word alarmed the avant-garde. Leonid Trauberg complained of 'crude attempts at a transition to literature' and insisted on the continuation of 'experiment' in cinema. Nevertheless, technical developments would soon combine with the drive for increased ideological control to create a climate in the industry that was conducive to the making of literary adaptations.[19] Though the first Soviet sound feature film was not released until June 1931, the debate around what sound would do to Soviet cinema had been raging since the publication of the so called 'Statement on Sound' on 5 August 1928. What the writers of the statement, Eisenstein, Pudovkin, and Grigorii Alexandrov, feared was that the unimaginative use of sound would result in a cinema of '"dramas of high culture" and other photographed presentations of a theatrical order', fears which were partially borne out.[20] In Soviet cinema, as elsewhere, the move to sound required the use of actors who had 'good voices', and the natural place in which to look for such actors was the theatre. They, in turn, were ideally suited for films drawn from the classics, which led to the flourishing of a conservative repertoire in 1930s Soviet cinema, including costume dramas of the plays of Ostrovsky and the minor prose of Pushkin, Dostoevsky, and Chekhov.

The supporters of an ideological role for Soviet cinema, on the other hand, saw that sound could offer greater naturalism, more complex plots, and far more extensive dialogue, thus enhancing a film's didactic power. The early 1930s saw sound versions of prose set during the Revolution and Civil War, including Iakov Protazanov's 1931 film *Tommi*. Based on an episode in Vsevolod Ivanov's 1921 story 'Armoured Train 14–69', it uses the resources of sound cinema to show the lack of understanding (in all senses) of its British soldier hero, a member of the Intervention forces. Eventually, however, he proves malleable to indoctrination, in a scene that culminates in his exultant reaction to hearing the word 'Lenin'. Other such adaptations followed, including *Chapaev* (1934), directed by the Vasilev Brothers, the most successful and popular film of the Stalin era. Dmitrii Furmanov's autobiographical 1923 novel openly questioned Chapaev's heroic status and was equally concerned with recording his own maturation as a Red Commissar. The film, by contrast, relegates Furmanov to the role of wise-but-dull mentor, attempting to bring Chapaev to ideological consciousness, and constructs Chapaev as a hero of myth, whose very faults contribute to his legendary status. By 1934 the Civil War could be treated as a historical adventure story, with elements drawn from American westerns, and with a touching, doomed love story (invented by the Brothers) added to the mix. There are stirring battle scenes, jokes, and songs, and the film ends with Chapaev's heroic death under White attack in the Ural River, enabling audiences to luxuriate in shared grief for a lost hero and a lost heroic time.

The adaptations of Maxim Gorky's autobiographical trilogy, describing his childhood and youth in late-nineteenth-century Russia, were among the most influential films of the late 1930s. Gorky was already a major figure when the books were published, in 1913–1922, but by the time the films appeared he had become the most famous of all Russian writers, particularly through his central role in the emergence of the doctrine of Socialist Realism in 1934. So Mark Donskoi's films, *The Childhood of Maxim Gorky* (*Detstvo Gor'kogo*, 1938), *My Apprenticeship* (*V liudiakh*, 1938) and *My Universities* (*Moi universitety*, 1939), functioned as a testament to a canonic figure (Gorky had died in 1936) and played a crucial part in the dissemination of the Gorky myth. By their combination and development of key episodes from the literary sources, they attempt to tell a coherent story of how the young Aleksei Peshkov became the great writer Maxim Gorky. Thus he is repeatedly shown writing poetry, or encountering classic works by Pushkin, Gogol, or Lermontov for the first time. Violence and oppression are rife in the urban settings of the films, and everyone he meets enjoins Peshkov to 'endure'. But his exceptional qualities are already apparent as he repeatedly inspires others to stand up for themselves and fight for change. The stories are punctuated by shots of the majestic River Volga, and each film ends with Peshkov's leaving the city and walking out 'into Russia'.

Other directors turned to adaptations of classic French writers. Mikhail Romm filmed Maupassant in *Boule de Suif* (*Pyshka*, 1934), and there were versions of Balzac's *Gobseck* and Hugo's *Les Misérables*. Of course these source texts were partly chosen because they addressed the poverty, exploitation, and class division of nineteenth-century French society, but they also served the paradoxical purpose of taking Soviet audiences, who of course had no possibility of travelling abroad, into a France of the imagination.

An explicitly escapist role was played by a number of adaptations of Western children's stories. Jules Verne's tales of adventure and heroism in an exotic setting had been popular in Tsarist Russia, a success matched among Soviet audiences by three films made from his work, *The Children of Captain Grant* (*Deti kapitana Granta*, 1936), directed by Vladimir Vainshtok, its sequel, *The Mysterious Island* (*Tainstvennyi ostrov*, 1941), directed by Eduard Pentslin, and Vasilii Zhuravlev's *A Captain at Fifteen* (*Piatnadtsatiletnii kapitan*, 1945). *The Children of Captain Grant* begins in Scotland, already represented as picturesquely exotic, in July 1864, but this exoticism is quickly doubled and re-doubled, as the children sail off in search of their father to Patagonia and then to Australia (all of course evoked on studio sets or on Soviet locations). In the Andean cordillera they are cast into a crevasse by an erupting volcano, and Captain Grant's son is carried off by an enormous vulture, only to be saved by a noble Native American Brave, who shoots the baleful bird dead. In Australia they encounter convicts and shipwreck. Eventually, on an island off New Zealand, the children are re-united with their father. *The Children of Captain Grant* has charming songs, with music by Isaak Dunaevsky and words by Vasilii Lebedev-Kumach, the men who provided the music for Grigorii Alexandrov's 1930s musicals; it has a love story; it has distant locations, re-iterated by repeated shots of maps or revolving globes; and for Soviet audiences it has minor changes to Verne's original, bringing a dose of anti-imperialist politics, with references to the English oppression of the Scots and the harsh lives of Australian convicts. Thus Vainshtok's adaptation seasons gripping entertainment with a pinch of ideology, a formula that was repeated in the later Verne films.

Ideological changes were also made to classic British works. Vainshtok's next film, *Treasure Island* (*Ostrov sokrovishch*, 1937) retains the adventure plot of Robert Louis Stevenson's classic story, but motivates the hunt for the treasure by the need to fund an Irish rebellion against British rule. Jim Hawkins becomes a young woman, Jenny Hawkins, who cross-dresses as a ship's boy in order not to be parted from Dr Livesey, whom she has nursed after he was wounded in the uprising, and with whom she is in love. At the end of the film she is congratulated for proving that 'young female patriots can do their duty to their mother-land'. Elated, she shouts 'Long live freedom!' and leads a rendition of one of the songs which Lebedev-Kumach wrote for the film, 'Beat, Drum!', which ties the film's heroics to the rhetoric of the Stalinist 1930s by speaking of defending the motherland in battle to the end and concludes, as does the film, with the repeated words 'who is not with us is a coward and an enemy'.

The addition of ideology is even more striking in Alexander Ptushko's *The New Gulliver* (*Novyi Gulliver*, 1935), which combines live action with animation in the tale of Petia, a Young Pioneer who is given a copy of *Gulliver's Travels*. He dreams of becoming Gulliver and of being shipwrecked in a Lilliputia which is represented as a heavily militarized state, riddled with police and police spies, in a way both visually and socially reminiscent of the representation of fascist Germany in the Soviet films of the 1930s.

The Second World War and late Stalinism

During the Great Patriotic War, 1941–1945, the Soviet film industry was entirely at the service of the war effort, and the overwhelming majority of films made during these years were set during the war itself, while many of the others looked at figures from Russian history to provide models of exemplary heroism. This left little scope for literary adaptations (though Sergei Gerasimov's film of Lermontov's play *The Masquerade*, which was being made at the Lenfilm studios at the time of the German invasion, was completed and released in September 1941). Writers were involved in the war effort as combatants, as war correspondents and, of course, providing scripts. Three films were made from the work of Konstantin Simonov, notably *Wait for Me* (*Zhdi menia*, 1943), directed by Alexander Stolper and Boris Ivanov, based on a play and a famous lyric, which examined the contribution of women to the war effort, both in taking over men's jobs and, more crucially, in providing a model of stoic endurance and hope. And the 'mobilization' also embraced popular literary personages. One of the first responses to the German invasion, released on 31 July 1941, was the short film *Chapaev is with Us* (*Chapaev s nami*), directed by Vladimir Petrov, in which the legendary commander, instead of drowning in the Ural river, swims to the other side and inspires Red Army fighters to continue the fight against Hitlerite Germany. Another character brought back to spur on the war effort was Timur, the hugely popular Pioneer hero of Arkadii Gaidar's story 'Timur and his Gang' and the 1940 film of the same name. In Lev Kuleshov's *Timur's Vow* (*Kliatva Timura*, 1942), Timur and his fellows learn how to deal with incendiary bombs and vow to help their older comrades in their struggle against the fascist enemy. And in Sergei Iutkevich's *The New Adventures of Švejk* (*Novye pokhozhdeniia Shveika*, 1943) Jaroslav Hašek's First World War soldier Josef Švejk, mobilized into Hitler's army in the Balkans, does everything he can to help the partisans and dreams of exacting ever more gruesome punishment on Hitler himself.

Unsurprisingly, post-war Soviet film-makers continued to be preoccupied by the Second World War. While some films celebrated the brilliance of Comrade Stalin as military strategist others, including several literary adaptations, were devoted to the individual heroism of ordinary Russians. The most dramatic of these, *The Young Guard* (*Molodaia gvardiia*, 1948), taken from a novel by Alexander Fadeev, describes the heroic resistance to German occupation by a group of Komsomol members in the Donbas mining town of Krasnodon. The novel won a Stalin Prize in 1946 and Sergei Gerasimov filmed several scenes from it with his students at the State Film Institute. When the novel came under unexpected attack the following year for underplaying the leading role of the Party and Fadeev was forced to embark upon a re-write, Gerasimov had already started work on a feature film. The epic two-part film, re-edited in the light of the criticism of Fadeev, appeared in 1948. It begins with evocative scenes of the chaotic evacuation of the town in the face of German invasion, following them with the emergence of the underground resistance group. Though the film's effect is marred by its failure to distinguish more than half a dozen of its characters, and it softens the scenes of their torture and death, it is enlivened by the acting of its young cast, many of whom would be stars of Soviet cinema for decades to come.

The disruption caused by the evacuation of the film industry during the war, combined with a heavy increase of censorship in the Cold War years, led to a dramatic drop in the number of films being made in Soviet studios, and the era became known as the *malokartin´e*, the time of few films. Unsurprisingly, in these circumstances, desperate studios took to filming theatrical productions. By the early 1950s Soviet film-goers were subsisting mainly on an unpalatable diet of the plays of Griboedov, Gogol, Ostrovsky, Turgenev, Tolstoy, Shchedrin and other nineteenth-century classic writers. In 1953 alone, there were four films of plays by Maxim Gorky.

Thaw cinema

If, at the end of the Stalin period, recourse to literary and theatrical works was a sign of the exhaustion of cinematic imagination, in the Thaw years it represented renewal. The desire to return to the sources of Communist enthusiasm, before the disaster of Stalinism, led to a number of adaptations of novels and stories of the 1920s set during the Civil War period, many of them already adapted during the Stalin years. The original adaptation of Boris Lavrenev's story *The Forty First*, was a black-and-white silent film. Grigorii Chukhrai's 1956 re-make is a lush technicolour melodrama. The sands of the Karakum desert and a storm on the Caspian Sea are visually stunning, and the love affair on a deserted island between the sniper, Mariutka and her White officer captive is rendered with such erotic force that her final assertion of revolutionary duty has enormous tragic power. It prompted attacks on the film as a 'foul White concoction', but the film's negotiation of the tension between feeling and duty, between the search for individual happiness and commitment to a Soviet ideal, encapsulated the mood of the Thaw and it achieved great success, both in the Soviet Union and abroad.

A similar clash between private desires and the demands of society lay at the heart of the most powerful of the several adaptations of nineteenth-century Russian literature that appeared in the Thaw years, Iosif Kheifits's adaptation of Chekhov's story *The Lady with the Little Dog* (*Dama s sobachkoi*). The film was released in January 1960, for the centenary of Chekhov's birth, but it transcended the predictability of the 'anniversary' genre. It expanded a seventeen-page story, with little direct speech, into a full-length film, compellingly rendering the lethargy and boredom of out-of-season Yalta, the provincialism of Saratov (which Kheifits makes Anna Sergeevna's home), the crassness of Gurov's Moscow friends, and the smugness of his cigarette-smoking wife. The scene in which Gurov chases Anna Sergeevna up and down the stairs of the Saratov theatre is shot with a particularly poignant urgency.

Shakespeare, too, spoke directly to the moods of the time. The Khrushchev years opened with films of *Othello* and *Twelfth Night* and ended with a remarkable *Hamlet* (1964), directed by Grigorii Kozintsev, which uses Boris Pasternak's translation, has music by Dmitrii Shostakovich, and is graced by a compelling performance by Innokentii Smoktunovsky, one of the leading actors of his generation, in the title role. Shot in black and white, the film jettisons large parts of the text, instead using the majestic natural setting to dramatic effect. It opens and closes with shots of the sea, and moves several scenes, including Hamlet's 'To be or not to be' speech, into the open air, thus emphasizing the role of the castle as dark prison. Two years earlier Kozintsev had published a book entitled *William Shakespeare Our Contemporary*, and his reading of the play is apparent from an article of 1964: 'It goes without saying that *Hamlet* for us is not a tragedy of vacillation, of *Hamletism*, not a tragedy of reflection. *Hamlet* is a tragedy of conscience.'[21] Smoktunovsky's Hamlet is noble, thoughtful, an energetic battler against injustice.

But among the most eagerly awaited films of the Khrushchev years were the cinematic adaptations of works that described the hopes and sensibilities of post-war Soviet youth. The first two novels of Vasilii Aksenov, a key member of the 'Young Prose' movement centred on the new literary monthly *Youth* (*Iunost´*), were both filmed in 1962, *Colleagues* (*Kollegi*, 1960) by Aleksei Sakharov and *A Ticket to the Stars*, (*Zvezdnyi bilet*, 1961) as *My Younger Brother* (*Moi mladshii brat*) by the veteran director Alexander Zarkhi. Both films portrayed the confused desires of their heroes with sympathy but both, and especially *My Younger Brother*, are flawed by the changes they make to Aksenov's plots and the compromises they deem necessary to bring his work to the screen. In this way, too, they are emblematic of a time of a contradiction.

Late Soviet cinema

In the period leading up to the fiftieth anniversary of the October Revolution, in 1967, Soviet studios were enjoined to make commemorative films on early Soviet history. Some young film-makers embraced the challenge to address this conventional subject matter without the dull piety that had accrued over decades, among them Alexander Askoldov, whose *The Commissar* (*Komissar*, 1967) is taken from Vasilii Grossman's story 'In the Town of Berdichev'. This tale of a pregnant female commissar who is billeted on the family of a Jewish tinsmith during the Civil War, with its premonitions of the fate of these Jews in the Holocaust, was far from the usual evocations of revolutionary heroism, and the cinematic authorities found the unvarnished representation of the harshness of the Revolutionary period unpalatable.

They complained that the film was 'deheroicized', too tragic, too full of religious allusion and metaphor. The film was shelved, and emerged only in 1988, when it detonated like a long-hidden bomb.

Overall, the Brezhnev years are conventionally regarded as a period of 'Stagnation', and conservatism, and other adventurous literary adaptations shared the fate of *The Commissar*. Among the most thoughtful of the films that *were* released were adaptations of 'village prose', though their blunt portrayals of life in the Soviet countryside made their path to the screen far from easy. The writer and director Vasilii Shukshin made five films of his stories, beginning with *There is a Fellow* (*Zhivet takoi paren'*), in 1964, and culminating with *Snowball Cherry Red* (*Kalina krasnaia*), in 1973, the tragic story of a peasant who, after twenty years in prison, attempts to make a new life on a collective farm. Everything about the film – its criminal hero, its tragic view of life, its sense of the destruction of the old Russian village, its persistent religious symbolism, its failure to refer to the Communist party or the Soviet authorities – would seem to have made its banning inevitable. And yet, almost miraculously, the film was suddenly passed for exhibition, allegedly because it had reduced Leonid Brezhnev to tears. In its first year of release it was seen by 62,500,000 viewers, making it the second most successful film of the year.

One of the most popular Russian directors of the late twentieth century, Nikita Mikhalkov, turned repeatedly to literary sources in his early career, to Chekhov, to the Soviet playwright Alexander Volodin and, in 1979, to Goncharov, for his *Several Days in the Life of I.I. Oblomov* (*Neskol'ko dnei iz zhizni I.I. Oblomova*). Both Goncharov and Lenin were born in the town of Simbirsk, and this may have exacerbated Lenin's sense of the lethal power of *oblomovshchina*, a preference of torpor to action, which he repeatedly excoriated as a remnant of the old Russia. That the town was re-named (and remains) Ulianovsk (and not Goncharovsk), might seem to be a victory for the Leninist (and Stoltzian) value of practical action. In this sense Mikhalkov's film, with its idealization of the Russian landscape, of childhood, of the past, represents a radical reaffirmation of the sensibility of Oblomov, and it sets an agenda for the cult of pre-Revolutionary Russia in Mikhalkov's later career. But though he captures Oblomov's nostalgia and sentimental energy, Mikhalkov elides the heady moral and intellectual scepticism of Goncharov's original.

Recent developments

One of the key manifestations of *glasnost'* in Soviet culture had been the belated publication of banned texts by Soviet writers, some of which, such as Mikhail Bulgakov's 'Heart of a Dog', soon found their way to the screen (*Sobach'e serdtse*, 1988, directed by Vladimir Bortko). The new freedom also made it possible to make more adventurous versions of nineteenth-century classics, and in a 1989 article the critic Maiia Turovskaia insisted that making a screen adaptation involves not 'following a classic author, but struggling with him from new aesthetic positions',[22] a suggestion borne out by one of the most ambitious and imaginative literary adaptations of the post-Soviet period, Kira Muratova's *Chekhovian motifs* (*Chekhovskie motivy*, 2002). Muratova yokes together two little-known works from Chekhov's early years, a short story and a one-act drama, to produce a film which fearlessly changes the original texts, interpreting them through the prism of her own concerns, and yet, paradoxically, manages to provide subtle and illuminating readings of the Chekhovian source material.

The dangers of excessive fidelity, by contrast, are apparent in a television adaptation of Mikhail Bulgakov's *The Master and Margarita*, probably the most popular of all twentieth-century Russian novels among Russian audiences. Alas, the 'literariness' of Vladimir Bortko's 2005 film, which lasts eight hours and quotes whole sections of the novel verbatim, and the illustrative nature of its visual imagination, perform the dubious and almost unprecedented feat of calling into question the reputation of the source material. Despite this misfire, Russian television companies continue to be committed to the filming of classic Russian literature: in recent years there have been versions of *The Idiot*, *A Hero of Our Time*, *Doctor Zhivago*, *The First Circle*, and many other major works of the past two centuries. Literature and cinema, adversaries and allies, will continue their symbiotic relationship. It is remarkable in this context that the greatest of contemporary Russian film-makers, Alexander Sokurov, himself the director of staggering and original film versions of the work of Platonov, Shaw, the Strugatsky Brothers, and Flaubert, contended in 2006 that 'ultimately, cinema is nothing but the product' of existing forms of art, of literature, music and painting. 'For a great cinema...one needs...great literature.'[23]

NOTES

1 Vishnevskii, V., *Khudozhestvennye fil'my dorevoliutsionnoi Rossii (Fil'mograficheskoe opisanie)* (Moscow: Goskinoizdat, 1945), pp. 157–160.
2 Tsivian, Yuri, 'Early Russian Cinema: Some Observations', in Taylor, R. and Christie, I., eds., *Inside the Film Factory: New Approaches to Russian and Soviet Cinema* (London and New York: Routledge, 1991), p. 18.

3 Morley, Rachel, '"Crime without Punishment": Reworkings of Nineteenth-Century Russian Literary Sources in Evgenii Bauer's *Child of the Big City*', in Hutchings, S. and Vernitski, A., eds., *Russian and Soviet Film Adaptations of Literature, 1900–2001: Screening the Word* (London and New York: RoutledgeCurzon, 2005), pp. 27–43.

4 Lunacharsky is quoted from Taylor, R. and Christie, I., eds., *The Film Factory: Russian and Soviet Cinema in Documents 1896–1939* (London and New York: Routledge, 1988), p. 47.

5 Lenin (1922) and Trotsky (1923) are quoted from Taylor and Christie, eds., *The Film Factory*, pp. 57, 95, 97.

6 Kuleshov (1918) is quoted from Taylor and Christie, eds., *The Film Factory*, p. 45.

7 Kuleshov (1922) is quoted from Taylor and Christie, eds., *The Film Factory*, pp. 66, 72, 73.

8 Iangirov, R.M., 'K istorii "Mistera Vesta . . . "', in Chudakova, M.O., ed., *Shestye tynianovskie chteniia. Tezisy dokladov i materialy dlia obsuzhdeniia* (Riga and Moscow, 1992), pp. 217–222 (pp. 218–219).

9 Pudovkin, V., 'Kak ia rabotaiu s Tolstym' (1928) in his *Sobranie sochinenii v trekh tomakh* (Moscow: Iskusstvo, 1974–1976), vol. 2 (1975), pp. 58–59 (p. 58).

10 The Eccentric Manifesto is quoted from Taylor and Christie, eds., *The Film Factory*, pp. 58–64 (translations modified).

11 Tynianov, Iu., 'Libretto kinofil'ma "Shinel'"', *Iz istorii Lenfil'ma* (Leningrad: Iskusstvo, 1973), vol. 3, pp. 78–91 (p. 78).

12 Tsiv'ian, Iu., 'Paleogrammy v fil'me "Shinel'"' in Chudakova, M.O., ed., *Tynianovskii sbornik. Vtorye tynianovskie chteniia* (Riga: Zinatne, 1986), pp. 14–27 (p. 15).

13 Kozintsev (1973) is quoted from his *Sobranie sochinenii v piati tomakh* (Leningrad: Iskusstvo, 1982–1986), vol. 4 (1984), p. 109.

14 Kozintsev (1966), is quoted from Christie, I. and Gillett, J., eds., *Futurism. Formalism. Feks: 'Eccentrism' and Soviet Cinema 1918–36* (London: BFI, 1978), pp. 26–27.

15 Tynianov, Iu. N., *Poetika. Istoriia literatury. Kino* (Moscow: Nauka, 1977), p. 347.

16 Vertov's articles are quoted from Taylor and Christie, eds., *The Film Factory*, pp. 69, 90, 91, 94.

17 Eisenstein's articles are quoted from Eisenstein, S., *Selected Works: Volume 1. Writings, 1922–34*, ed. and trans. Richard Taylor (London and Bloomington, IN: BFI and Indiana University Press, 1988), pp. 35, 40, 59.

18 Eisenstein, *Selected Works: Volume 1*, pp. 96, 97, 98.

19 References to the script crisis are quoted from Taylor and Christie, eds., *The Film Factory*, pp. 212, 243, 251.

20 The 'Statement on Sound' is quoted from Taylor and Christie, eds., *The Film Factory*, p. 234.

21 Quoted from Kozintsev, Grigorii, *Sobranie sochinenii v piati tomakh* (Leningrad: Iskusstvo, 1982–1986), vol. 1 (1982), p. 494.

22 Turovskaia, M., 'Ob ekranizatsii Chekhova. Predvaritel'nye zametki', *Kinovedcheskie zapiski*, 5 (1989), pp. 25–40 (p. 31).

23 'Interview with Alexander Sokurov', cond. and trans. Jeremi Szaniawski, *Critical Inquiry*, 33 (2006), pp. 13–27 (p. 23).

FURTHER READING

Dobrenko, Evgeny, *Stalinist Cinema and the Production of History: Museum of the Revolution* (Edinburgh: Edinburgh University Press and New Haven, CT: Yale University Press, 2008).

Gillett, I. and J., eds., *Futurism. Formalism. Feks: 'Eccentrism' and Soviet Cinema 1918–36* (London: BFI, 1978, reprinted, 1987).

Hutchings, Stephen, *Russian Literary Culture in the Camera Age: The Word as Image* (London: RoutledgeCurzon, 2004).

Hutchings, Stephen and Vernitski, Anat, eds., *Russian and Soviet Film Adaptations of Literature, 1900–2001: Screening the Word* (London and New York: RoutledgeCurzon, 2005).

Taylor, Richard, and Christie, Ian, eds., *The Film Factory: Russian and Soviet Cinema in Documents 1896–1939* (London and New York: Routledge, 1988).

Inside the Film Factory: New Approaches to Russian and Soviet Cinema (London and New York: Routledge, 1991).

Woll, Josephine, *Real Images: Soviet Cinema and the Thaw* (London: I.B. Tauris, 2000).

Youngblood, Denise, *The Magic Mirror: Moviemaking in Russia 1908–1918* (Madison, WI: University of Wisconsin Press, 1999).

Russian War Films: On the Cinema Front, 1914–2005 (Lawrence, KS: University Press of Kansas, 2007).

14

MARIA ZALAMBANI

Literary Policies and Institutions

Literature as an institution and the institutions of literature

Literature always played a central role in Russian culture, since the time when, having undergone a process of secularization, it sanctioned a sacralized relationship towards the Word, replacing the role of the Church with that of the state. Secularization took place at the time of Peter I, when the word of the church was delegitimized and replaced by that of the state, although the same institutional system and the same mechanisms of sacralization of the writer's image were maintained. Literature became a dominant cultural institution, and a literature-centric system began to take shape. This system dominated Russian culture throughout the eighteenth, nineteenth, and early twentieth centuries, and in Soviet times it was consolidated, making literature an overtly politicized and ideologized institution. The writer, who ever since his sacralization had been considered a prophet, messiah, and holder of the truth (*istina*), and had exercised a dominant influence on the masses, was the focus of this literature-centric system. S/he had always played a superior part as compared to other artists, beginning in the eighteenth century when classicism conferred an educational role upon the writer; this continued throughout the nineteenth century, with the writer becoming the source of a 'sacred', 'magical' Word, as represented by Pushkin in his poem *The Prophet* (*Prorok*, 1826). Retaining this function in Soviet times, the writer was charged by the state to play a leading role in the making of *homo sovieticus*. Thus literature, becoming the basis of the whole Soviet cultural system, exploited its secular literature-centric experience and conveyed the values and directives of the Soviet state until the latter's collapse in 1991.

The peculiarity of Soviet literature lay in the fact that it was a complex sociopolitical institution completely governed by the field of power (the Party, the state). As such, it managed a network of other hierarchically organized minor institutions. The set of specific institutions on which the functioning of the economy of cultural goods was based – institutions of consecration (literary prizes, the Union of Writers, the Academy of Sciences), institutions of reproduction of producers (universities, higher education institutes, the Gorky Literary Institute), and institutions for distribution and circulation of culture (editorial market, mass media) – in the Soviet era became ever more effective and rigid.

Within this system, literary journals played a predominant role, particularly the 'thick journals'. Typical Russian periodicals, these latter were characterized by their volume and by the eclecticism of the themes covered, and from the time of Nikolai Karamzin had dominated the journalistic market. After a brief disruption of the literature-centric structure of culture beginning in 1905, the 1917 Bolshevik Revolution restored this structure, and 'thick journals' regained their leading role. For this reason, it is mainly through the development of literary journals, which always prismatically refracted the events of every external cultural and political movement, that we shall try to depict the literary arena of the twentieth century. In their pages theoretical debates developed, the process of creating a new writer was completed, and a new literature and literary criticism arose.

Other institutions, whose functions were closely tied to those of journals and newspapers, were created alongside the literary journals. Thus, a new publishing system supported the literary journals' policies. The State Publishing House (*Gosizdat*), a global state institution for administering publishing activities, controlling distribution all over the country, and developing strong censorship functions, was founded in 1919. This cultural system was completed by another important institution, literary prizes: these sanctioned the authority of recognized writers and edged non-conformist authors to the fringes of the literary field.

The literary centrism of the system brought about a tightening of censorship. In the Soviet era, the state established strict control over the written word through its main censorial institution, the Chief Administration of Literary and Publishing Affairs (*Glavlit*, 1922) which, in collaboration with the secret service organizations, ensured that Party *dicta* were not violated. Soviet censorship exercised a double function: the first operated as a procedure of exclusion, by the possibilities it excluded *a priori* (self-censorship and 'preliminary censorship');[1] the second limited the means of expression, pre-establishing the possibilities of invention that were available. The result was the long-lasting domination of Socialist Realism.

Thus the Soviet cultural system maintained a literature-centric structure till its end, conferring a sacral value to the written word, which was charged to 'debate' theoretical issues in 'thick journals', to spread Party directives through daily newspapers, and to provide a representation of Soviet life through literature (Socialist Realism).

With *perestroika* (restructuring), this complex institutional system began to change: autonomy in the literary field increased, while institutionalization in both publishing and censorship decreased. The Soviet state's subsequent breakdown precipitated the collapse of literature as a higher cultural institution; the written word definitively lost its sacral, prescriptive power, and literature became primarily an entertainment activity. The literature-centric system collapsed along with the Soviet Union.

Cultural policy and literary institutions in pre-Revolutionary Russia

Russian literature had played a central role in nineteenth-century culture: debating problems of national identity, presenting the intelligentsia/people and Slavophilism/Occidentalism dichotomies, and treating many other themes (such as the messianic role of Russia) that were not merely literary. But as the twentieth century dawned, the physiognomy of the literary field radically changed. Economic development, the 1890s industrialization, and the increase in the level of popular culture because of more widespread literacy, all affected it significantly.[2] The 1905 Revolution led to the abolition of preliminary censorship and freed the written word from centuries-old slavery. In this atmosphere of freedom of the press, many new authors appeared, giving rise to a new status for the writer from about 1900 to 1917. Thanks to the flourishing of journalism, the book industry, and public debates, Russian writers grew in fame and prosperity and, sacrificing the 'prophet' status they had always held, acquired a new social status: now they were professionals, members of an autonomous intelligentsia, and financially independent.

This situation created a new interchange with the reader: the orientation on the reader, the process of bringing literacy to the masses, and the development of the media and the press, led to the rise of popular writers and commercial literature. New authors, publishers, and distributors emerged from the lower classes. The literary field was shaken up by these changes affecting the production, distribution, and reception of literature. An important link in this chain was, of course, the new readers (coming from the rural class or from among lower-class urban residents), whose increasing numbers stimulated a more active market for popular literature. These transformations in the production and circulation of literary products affected journals and newspapers as well. 'Thick journals', oriented to the educated reader, enormously increased their distribution. Illustrated weekly magazines ('thin magazines') and popular daily newspapers, intended for a wider and more diverse reading public, also flourished.

The results of these changes were astonishing. On the eve of the 1917 Revolution, the literary field in Russia had finally gained an unprecedented autonomy. The existence of two cultures – one popular, one elitist – was due to the fact that an extraordinary metamorphosis had taken place in attitudes and beliefs, raising social awareness among ordinary people. Literacy had shaken up the literary and social fields: new agents from lower social classes had appeared, with new attitudes and interests, clearing the way for the fall of the old regime; they could have opened a way to a new kind of cultural economy as well, had not the Bolshevik Revolution intervened.

The first years of the Soviet regime

The Bolshevik Revolution radically changed the Russian literary arena, causing a serious decline in professionalism among Russian writers and restoring literary centrism. Literature became a political tribune, as Lenin had predicted in his 1905 article 'Party Organization and Party Literature', in which he had asserted that 'literature must become *part* of the common cause of the proletariat, "a cog and a screw" of one single great Social-Democratic mechanism'.[3] Assigning a predominantly enlightening political role to literature, Lenin had predicted the future course of Soviet literature: a literature under the aegis of the Party, a Party-minded literature *(partiinaia literatura)*, interpreting and promulgating its representation of what Soviet life should be.

In any case, the earliest years of the Soviet regime were a period of ferment, when the pursuit of a new revolutionary aesthetic was under way. It was a period of aesthetic manifestos – evidence of the polychromatic multiplicity of existing literary groups, but also of the struggle among aesthetic currents to affirm their leading role in the literary arena.

Immediately after the October Revolution, almost all the 'bourgeois' groups were erased from the cultural scene; only *poputchiki* (fellow-travellers) remained, those who neither accepted nor rejected the revolutionary slogans. But they, too, were very soon defeated, so that the conflict mainly affected the groups that had embraced the revolutionary slogans: Proletkult, VAPP (the All-Russian Association of Proletarian Writers – later RAPP, the Russian Association of Proletarian Writers), and LEF (the Left Front of Arts). Within this struggle, aesthetic manifestos were a powerful instrument: through them, each group presented its literary programme in order to gain the legitimacy necessary to bridge the gap of literature, which was fading away after October.

Once again, literary journals became the arena for struggle. Alexander Bogdanov, the leader of Proletkult, found his tribune in his group's journal, *Proletarskaia kul'tura* (proletarian culture),[4] wherein he published articles about an art meant to be the organizer of life: a collective proletarian art built on 'comradely co-operation'. Despite the fact that Proletkult's programme was rejected (Lenin raised objections), the stress on art as an important element in the forging of life remained in all subsequent proletarian programmes. LEF defended the idea of art as construction of life in the pages of its eponymous journal. LEFist intellectuals tried to reject the idea of 'art for art's sake' in favour of a collective, impersonal creativity, meant as an art derived from labour processes, but their programme was defeated by the emerging VAPP, the tribunes of which were the journals *Na postu* (On guard) and *Na literaturnom postu* (On literary guard). VAPP appropriated many elements of the prior aesthetic programmes but, following the Party's new line, they brought literature into the bosom of the state and garnered Party support. The evolution of the different proletarian organizations reveals how the struggle to lead new cultural policy was more political than aesthetic: RAPP, for example, in fact syncretized many elements from the different aesthetic manifestos when formulating its own programme under the aegis of the Party. Nevertheless, the aesthetic–political foundation of Soviet literature was laid: literature had to be the product of an anonymous (collective) writer who thought of art as a life-building process, embodying the mind of the Party.

Within the domain of VAPP/RAPP, a fundamental principle was established: the complete dependence of the literary field on the field of power. This was sanctioned by a 1925 Party resolution, its publication affirming the Party's first open interference in the artistic field. The tribunes from which this document was issued were the most peremptory Party voices: *Pravda* (Truth), on 1 July 1 1925, and *Izvestiia* (News), in no. 25–26, 1925. The resolution resulted from a request made by the proletarian journal *Na postu*, clamouring for more Party support and for a dominant position for proletarian writers in Soviet cultural life. The Party answered by refusing to ally itself with any specific group; but the publication of a document concerning literary politics was a political act that started a new chapter in Soviet cultural life, which would thereafter see the Party as a main source of creative inspiration.

Understanding the importance that literary journals had always had as a cultural institution, Lenin had consented to the founding of two 'thick journals' in 1921: *Pechat' i revoliutsiia* (The Press and Revolution), headed by Viacheslav Polonsky, and *Krasnaia nov'* (Red Virgin Soil), founded by Alexander Voronsky. Following the pattern of traditional Russian 'thick journals', they were supposed to cover all scientific and artistic themes; but *Krasnaia Nov'* soon abdicated this role and became a mere literary journal, and *Pechat' i revoliutsiia* narrowed its scope, mainly covering literary criticism, literature, and art. The evolution of these journals shows the increasing loss of autonomy of the literary field: 'thick journals', initially conceived to give voice to different literary debates, became periodicals that institutionalized the *dicta* of the Party. Initially, *Krasnaia nov'* advocated a conciliatory policy toward the *poputchiki*; but when in 1927 Voronsky was forced to leave and was replaced by Fedor Raskolnikov from RAPP, the journal's politics radically veered toward a more Party-aligned policy. Polonsky, engaged in a polemic with proletarian writers, was similarly forced in 1929 to leave *Pechat' i revoliutsiia*, and in 1930 the journal was suppressed. Thus, in the second half of the 1920s, when proletarian writers prevailed, 'thick journals' became the tribune of the Party.

While literary journals and newspapers proclaimed the Party's voice, another institution was commissioned to defend it: censorship. Some forms of censorship had appeared immediately after the October Revolution, but they were institutionalized only in 1922, with the foundation of Glavlit. In fact, when the market of the New Economic Policy (NEP) allowed the rise of new publishers, and the availability of books was rich and flourishing (and thus dangerous and unforeseeable), the Soviet state resorted to time-tested means and, following the tsarist pattern, restored censorship. According to the document that defined the roles and aims of Glavlit, published on 2 December 1922, the main characteristics of Soviet censorship were the following: (1) control over *every* (national and foreign) printed work, with the right to adopt heavy sanctions; (2) prohibition to contradict Soviet ideology; (3) constant participation of the secret police in censorship interventions; (4) professionalism of censors; (5) political evaluation of works being reviewed; (6) compilation of a list of banned books.[5]

Soviet censorship generated another important institution: *spetskhrany* ('special holdings'), areas where prohibited books were confined. *Spetskhrany* were instituted in the 1920s – following a tsarist pattern – to hold all anti-Soviet literature, and were associated with all the country's most important libraries. When a book was censored, it could be mutilated, destroyed, or sent to *spetskhrany*. Access to these areas was restricted to a very limited number of readers, exclusively Party members. So, while the Party established control over libraries, purging books and determining the readers' choices, a great number of works migrated to the 'book gulag'; these migratory waves became ever more frequent after the consolidation of Socialist Realism.

The Stalinist period

The Stalinist era was characterized by the consolidation of Socialist Realism, the aesthetic of which had been synthesized from the various artistic manifestos of the previous two decades. Writers became the anonymous executors of the 'social command' (*sotsial'nyi zakaz*), working under the aegis of the Party. Socialist Realism operated as an institutional practice, since literary criticism and theory in the Soviet Union functioned not only *a posteriori* but – and above all – *a priori*, exercising both descriptive and prescriptive functions, establishing norms and injunctions that regulated the system of culture. As a result, the theoretical discourse concerning art and literature from the mid-1930s to the mid-1950s was dominated by the 'life–work paradigm': life and work had to be described as a public matter, against the background of comradely Soviet life developing under the protection of Stalin and the Party.[6]

The new Socialist Realist canon needed a new collective, mass author – the product of a process of balancing pressure from above (the demands of the State) and requests from below (the taste of the masses). One of the main channels for recruiting writers was the 'call of shock-workers[7] into literature'. Beginning in 1930, RAPP successfully initiated the 'bolshevization of literature'; literary journals were the means through which this project was realized. Journals and newspapers such as *Pravda, Udarnik literatury* (The Shock-worker of literature), *Oktiabr'* (October), *Na literaturnom postu, Literaturnaia gazeta* (Literary newspaper), and *Literaturnaia ucheba* (Literary training) played a central role: they realized the call, recruiting writers among the working class and teaching them to write. Literary journals offered the shock-workers a lively medium wherein they could publish their copious works, organized 'lit consultancies' (*lit-konsul'tatsii*) for those who sent their works to the press 'on their own' (*samotek*), and provided 'lit training' (*lit-ucheba*). The reaction was huge, and lit consultancies, which had to explain to an author what was required for artistic writing, were organized by many journals, most notably *Literaturnaia ucheba*, whose lit consultancy section was headed by Maxim Gorky. Gorky was the foremost leader in 'producing' Soviet writers: he organized literary training and promoted 'literary brigades' – among which was the well-known brigade that wrote *Belomorsko-Baltiiskii kanal. Istoriia stroitel'stva* (History of the Construction of the White Sea–Baltic Canal), the apogee of collective creativity and representation of Soviet reality. He became the leader of Socialist Realism, endowing it with the aesthetic base that Stalin's political project needed.

After 1934, literary training was based on teaching of the classics, and was taught by the masters of Soviet literature (Demian Bednyi, Marietta Shaginian, Alexander Fadeev, Fedor Gladkov, and many others), who published new handbooks about how to write. In 1937, Pushkin was completely rehabilitated, and Socialist Realism found further legitimization in the classics and in folklore. The process of producing the Soviet writer was nearing completion: the advancement of a new generation of writers who had interiorized control, the 'social command', and Socialist Realist slogans, had been accomplished. This new Soviet intelligentsia, 'built from zero', replaced the old one and re-populated the Soviet literary arena. This was the most tangible result of the effective Stalinist institutional system. What was happening on the repressive side – purges and open repressions – was only a means to clear the literary field of 'undesirable effects'.

Through the 'call of shock-workers into literature', the Party achieved not only the 'bolshevization of literature' but also complete control over the masses' questionable feelings and thoughts (frequent solicitation of letters from readers was a means to learn about and thus control the 'spontaneity' [stikhiinost'] of the people, which was perceived as inherently anarchic), at the same time ridding the field of fellow-travellers. The last act of the drama could take place: 'writers were freed from RAPP by joining the Union of Writers that was being created, but now under conditions *imposed by authority*.'[8] The 'shock-worker of literature' model was adopted for moulding the working-class author at the beginning of the 1930s; but after 1934, when the Party wanted professional 'engineers of human souls', the dilettantism of this model was replaced by the 'craftsmanship of artistic production' that Fadeev proclaimed in 1937.[9]

In the meantime, the Union of Writers, an organization that would play a central role in literary policy, had been founded. It arose in 1932, after the publication of the Party resolution stating that all existing artistic organizations were abolished and were to be replaced by artistic unions supportive of the Soviet state's policies. The union brought the Party's cultural policy into the literary field, and had the power to define the status of 'writer'; it also exercised censorial functions, since it decided what could be published, and where. The union was organized in the Party's own 'image and likeness', and admission to it depended more on political reliability than on professional talent. By approving a work, the union assured it and its author a definitive 'consecration', which allowed the writer a series of material privileges. This was why admittance to the union required a complex ritual, while expulsion was used as a punishment for 'disloyal members': exclusion meant the end of every privilege intrinsic to the writer's status and, above all, the impossibility of engaging in any artistic activity. One of the most famous cases involved Anna Akhmatova and Mikhail Zoshchenko, expelled from the union in 1946 after a Party resolution condemned them as 'extraneous to Soviet literature'.[10]

The process of producing new writers required a place wherein they could be 'forged', so another fundamental institution was created in 1933: the Gorky Literary Institute. As described and shaped by Gorky himself, this was the place where writers learned the language, culture, and ideology that they were to perpetuate. After the 1920s struggles between the popular and revolutionary models for a new language and a new literature, the 1930s were the years in which the popular model triumphed, with a return to the national roots of Russian literature. Having its origins in the Russian classics and in a return to folklore, this model helped to imbue the new Soviet culture (and state) with authority, thus consolidating a new national identity. Gorky's writings suggested that Russian traditional culture would play this legitimizing and consolidating role, thanks to the authority of the classics and of pre-Revolutionary realism; since his ideas won out, he became the leader in this transformative process.[11]

The coronation of the Soviet writer took place in 1934, when the First Congress of the Union of Soviet Writers was convened. The Congress sanctioned the literary course for the future, opening with Andrei Zhdanov's speech, which proclaimed Socialist Realism as the artistic method to be adopted for Soviet literature. Stalinism turned from the institutionalization of cultural organs to that of minds and souls, as suggested by Stalin's formula (cited by Zhdanov at the Congress), according to which writers were to be 'engineers of human souls' and Socialist Realism was to be the method adopted to realize this aim.[12] If before it had been an 'external' censor who decided what to expunge from a text, from then on it was to be the authors' 'inner censor' who must suggest to them what they should write, and how they should write it.

As usual, the literary journals were the primary milieus for organizing the literary process: they guided literary debates and recruited the new class of writers. The Union of Writers controlled fourteen literary newspapers and eighty-six literary and social journals; its main organ, *Literaturnaia gazeta*, became the 'holy writ' of Soviet literature.

The organization of the literary process followed two main directions. On the one hand, literary journals promulgated the Party's *dicta* on cultural policy; on the other, they removed undesirable influences and people from the literary field. The results of these campaigns of denigration are well known; but much more important are the performative effects of the press language of these years. At the same time that the most authoritative newspapers were launching the new Soviet political slogans in their editorials and publishing

Party resolutions, they were also featuring extracts of the First Congress of the Union of Soviet Writers, thus consolidating the aesthetic of Socialist Realism.

Then, having hybridized Stalin's political project with the new mass-writers' aesthetic, Socialist Realism sought a theoretical foundation. A promising forum for this search in the 1930s was the journal *Literaturnyi kritik* (The Literary critic) where, in 1933, a debate about Marxist–Leninist aesthetics began. Its main theoreticians were the Marxist critics Mikhail Lifshits and Georg Lukács, who tried to legitimize Socialist Realism by giving it a philosophical base derived from Hegel's and Marx's theories and by condemning RAPPist 'vulgar Marxism'. But, very soon, Socialist Realism developed into a literary practice that was subject to the political necessities of the State and built around the genealogy of the 'positive heroes' who embodied the abstractions against which Marx and Engels had written; accordingly, *Literaturnyi kritik* was no longer necessary, and was closed in 1940 after campaigns against it were waged in *Liternaturnaia gazeta* (in 1939) and in *Krasnaia nov'* (in 1940).

Literary journals and newspapers also led campaigns against non-aligned writers. These campaigns had already started by the end of the 1920s (as evidenced by the cases of Mikhail Bulgakov, Boris Pilniak, and Evgenii Zamiatin in 1929), and in the following decades became a common practice. In 1936 the 'campaign against formalism' began with an article in *Pravda* denouncing formalism and 'naturalism' in Dmitrii Shostakovich's music. This led to a debate concerning all the forms of art that were produced in collaboration with the artistic unions. As far as literature was concerned, the goals of the campaign were to destroy formalism in literary criticism once and for all, and to expel the last remaining fellow-travellers still working in the field. A milestone of this discussion was the debate that took place in the Union of Writers (13 March 1936), the conclusions of which were published in *Literaturnyi kritik* (1936, no. 5). This was the prologue to the large-scale repressions of writers in 1937–1938 when, of the 597 delegates to the First Congress, 180 were repressed.[13] After a wartime reprieve, in which the state, the cultural elites, and the people had drawn together against the common enemy, the next period of severe repressions took place in 1946.

On 21 August 1946, *Pravda* published a Party resolution against the literary journals *Zvezda* (Star) and *Leningrad*, both of which had published works by Zoshchenko and Akhmatova. As usual, the Party directive was disseminated through the most influential newspaper, and it gave instructions for how the cultural policy was to be implemented in literary journals. Obligingly, these journals carried out Zhdanov's policy,[14] resulting in a ferocious ideological struggle that was fought in the philosophical, scientific, literary, and musical fields, raising waves of ideological terror. Writers were first demolished through the press and then arrested. Many were denounced by articles appearing in *Literaturnaia gazeta*, which played a leading role as the mouthpiece of the Union of Writers.

In parallel with the Union of Writers and literary journals, yet another institution – Glavlit – was called upon to eliminate undesirable influences from the literary field. Glavlit was reorganized in the 1930s at the request of the Party Central Committee, which wanted better control over state and war secrets. Purges inside the organization itself resulted in a requirement for new recruitments. The first criterion for enlisting censors became ideological reliability, and thus the level of education diminished considerably. Then, in 1941, all forms of censorship came under a new head, the Chief War Censor. This gave Glavlit a militarized character, producing a model of war censorship that would persist beyond the end of the war, when first *zhdanovshchina* and then Cold War would impose a climate of maximum control. The requirement was to punish non-aligned writers, as Glavlit head Pavel Lebedev-Polianskii had proclaimed in 1931.[15] Purges also involved books: widespread 'bibliocide' in the 1930s and 1940s destroyed an incredible number of books, and many others were 'interned' in the *spetskhrany*.[16]

Thus Stalinist cultural policy had cleared the field of the old literature and had created a new literature supported by a powerful, institutionalized system.

The Thaw and Stagnation

The Stalinist era had consolidated the Socialist Realist canon and created an effective system of cultural institutions. However, Stalin's legacy became particularly burdensome, leading the new Soviet leader Nikita Khrushchev to partially deny this legacy in the Twentieth Party Congress (1956); nevertheless, neither he nor his successors (until Mikhail Gorbachev) discarded the practices and institutions established during Stalinism.

It is usually recognized that the Thaw meant a real change in Soviet cultural life; but, in reality, only superficial changes were made in these years, never affecting the essence of Stalinist cultural policies. Even the easing of censorship that immediately followed Stalin's death rapidly dissolved.

Censorship was accused of not having promptly carried out the tasks that the Twentieth Congress had assigned; consequently, Glavlit was again reorganized. Restructuring within Glavlit led to its complete submission to the Party, in particular to the Central Committee's Ideological Commission (*Ideologicheskaia komissiia TsK*) which, guided by Mikhail Suslov from 1958 to 1964, became the heart of cultural policy. As a period of transition, the Thaw represented a time of adjustment characterized by continuous oscillations, like a pendulum swinging from one extreme to the other. This allowed a shift toward a stricter policy during post-Thaw Stagnation, leading to the trials of Joseph Brodsky in 1964 and of Andrei Siniavsky and Iulii Daniel in 1966.

Characteristic of Khrushchev's era was the ambivalence of the Party's cultural policy: on the one hand, Khrushchev needed the support of the intelligentsia for his anti-Stalinist policies; on the other, he did not trust them and often came into conflict with them. When wooing the co-operation of the intellectual community, Khrushchev reduced the pressure of censorship and permitted the publication of many innovative literary and scientific works; nevertheless, he on several occasions attacked artists (such as Ernst Neizvestnyi and Boris Zhutovsky) and writers (Andrei Voznesensky, Evgenii Evtushenko, Robert Rozhdestvensky, and others).

A shift in Party policy occurred under Leonid Brezhnev in 1969, when Stalin was finally rehabilitated and direct Party control over the cultural elites was re-established. This process had started in 1968, when intellectuals' protests (such as those in support of the Prague Spring protests) were spreading widely and the Party accordingly reacted with a secret January 1969 decree asking for a stricter ideological control.[17] Glavlit in 1966 had regained its role as the main censorial institution, and now reinforced its position in the struggle against these first protests by intellectuals.

An example of this policy shift can be illustrated by the campaign initiated against Alexander Solzhenitsyn, after his 1967 letter to the Union of Writers asking for the abolition of censorship. In reaction to this letter, attacks against the author began in the press; he was subsequently expelled from the Union of Writers in 1969, and finally deprived of Soviet citizenship in 1974.

Nevertheless, new feelings were spreading among the cultural elites, giving rise to dissent which acquired different colours ranging from liberal, to nationalistic, to neo-Stalinist sentiments. Literary journals again became the arena of struggle among the different trends. If we observe the development of Oktiabr´, Novyi mir (The New world), and Molodaia gvardiia (The Young guard), we can see how neo-Stalinist, liberal, and nationalistic feelings (respectively) were developing in Russian society and how the Party used a flexible policy of alliances to steer a middle course. At first an alliance among the Party, Oktiabr´, and Novyi mir led to the defeat of Molodaia gvardiia; but later the Party elites would attack Novyi mir for its liberalism and Oktiabr´ for its (neo-) Stalinism.[18] In 1969–1970, Novyi mir, the liberal journal that had played a major role under Alexander Tvardovsky's direction (1950–1954, 1958–1970) was 'neutralized', and social criticism disappeared from the Soviet media. *Novyi mir* had been a symbol of liberal and anti-Stalinist literature in the 1950s and 1960s: its publication of Solzhenitsyn's *Odin den´ Ivana Denisovicha* (One Day in the Life of Ivan Denisovich, 1962) had been a turning point in Soviet policy toward the press, raising new hopes for a different cultural life. But in 1970, when Tvardovskii was removed and his editorial group abandoned *Novyi mir*, this heralded a significant conservative change in Soviet cultural policy.

The Party manipulated the press on three different levels: removing representatives of the progressive movement from literary journals (in 1969, Vasilii Aksenov, Andrei Voznesenskii, and Evgenii Evtushenko were expelled from the editorial board of *Iunost´* [Youth], and Tvardovskii's removal followed shortly afterward); leading attacks against liberals (above all in *Literaturnaia gazeta*); and excluding all extremist factions from literary debates. Literary criticism was thus transformed into an effective literary institution, as evidenced by the 1972 Party resolution that defined literary criticism as the regulator and censor of the literary field.

One result of this policy was the rise of the counter-institution called *samizdat*, which literally means 'self-published'. When the official publishing houses rejected their works, authors themselves printed and distributed them among acquaintances, thus developing a counter-cultural market (consisting mainly of intelligentsia). *Samizdat* products first appeared in the form of open letters (from Solzhenitsyn, Arkadii Belinkov, and Georgii Vladimov) ostensibly addressed to the Union of Writers and to the Congress of Soviet Writers but in reality directed to Soviet and Western intellectuals, and then in the form of *samizdat* journals. By the end of the 1950s, *samizdat* became the main means of disseminating non-official culture; it turned into an important sociocultural institution that gave the human rights and dissident movements a voice. *Samizdat* had its Western counterpart in *tamizdat* ('published there') – censored Soviet literature published abroad (often in Russian), which was then brought back to the Soviet Union and secretly circulated among the intelligentsia. Authors like Solzhenitsyn, Brodsky, Akhmatova, Marina Tsvetaeva, and Boris Pasternak became known through *samizdat* and/or *tamizdat*.

Samizdat was a symptom of the struggle fought by non-official culture against official institutions: it was the struggle of heretics and 'pretenders' against the orthodox and the 'rulers' of the literary field; the former enacted subversive strategies aiming at challenging the established rules of the literary field, while the latter adopted strategies of self-preservation. In this phase, the convergence between the intentions of non-official culture and those of civil society was fundamental: non-conformist movements and dissidents had widespread social support (whether implicit or explicit) and thus acquired the necessary strength to bring 'disorder' into the cultural field. This disorder was the basis of the inevitable future implosion of the system.

Non-official culture was supported in the West, where not only did *tamizdat* publish non-recognized authors, but also Nobel Prizes brought prestige to this culture, when awarded to non-legitimized Soviet writers (Pasternak in 1958, Solzhenitsyn in 1970, and Brodsky in 1987). At the same time that the Soviet system was legitimizing its Party-*apparatchik* authors by awarding them Lenin and Stalin Prizes, the rejected culture was being brought out from the shadows and into the international arena. The institution of Soviet literary prizes (beginning in 1941, the most important of which was the 'Stalin Prize') had started in the 1920s with the conferring of state honours, as a system to set boundaries by identifying and rewarding insiders while expelling outsiders from the literary field; Stalin simply reinforced this system by making these lines of division deeper and more definite. The award of the Lenin Prize to Brezhnev in 1979 definitively sanctioned a system which implied the total identity between culture and politics and which had established a literary model totally independent of aesthetic judgement.

In an attempt to counter the effect of Western policy, the Soviet press waged libellous campaigns against authors who had succeeded in the Western arena: Pasternak's case is a good example. When Party-supported candidate for the Nobel Prize Mikhail Sholokhov was passed over in favour of Pasternak, the Party issued a resolution (23 October 1958) in which it not only denigrated Pasternak's novel but also tasked the Union of Writers and the press with a campaign against the author. On 28 October, the union expelled Pasternak, and the following day Pasternak wrote a telegram to the Swedish Academy refusing the prize. In the days following, a huge Soviet press campaign in the press painted the author as anti-Soviet.[19]

The new international dimension of the problem, the fear of losing a national identity so dearly won during wartime, and the need to face Western society – all these considerations made Soviet cultural policy more prudent in subsequent years, preferring prevention over punishment. Undesirable writers were invited to 'choose emigration of their own free will' (Brodsky, in 1972) or else they were deprived of Soviet citizenship, thus providing the same result (Solzhenitsyn, in 1974).

The rift between the two cultures was so wide, however, that it was destined to become an unbridgeable abyss, as *perestroika* would demonstrate.

Perestroika and post-Soviet Russia

The Soviet system carried within itself an enormous contradiction, revealed in the gap between a rapidly developing civil society and a static, bureaucratic, and pyramid-like state, which led to the implosion of the system itself. Begun during the Stagnation period, this process became manifest under Gorbachev, who through *glasnost'* tried to co-opt civil society as a way of renovating the system. But even before the new institutions that might have been able to reconstitute the state could appear, the system began to fall apart.[20] The policy of *glasnost'* itself hastened the fall of the over-centralized Soviet state and, contemporaneously, produced wide-ranging effects on the cultural field. The weakening of ideological control helped to ease censorship: this led to the rehabilitation of many writers and to the publication of previously censored authors such as Akhmatova, Bulgakov, Pasternak, Pilniak, Zamiatin, Nina Berberova, Vladislav Khodasevich, and Andrei Platonov.

When Gorbachev broke the monopoly on information, Soviet public culture began to disintegrate. Gorbachev relied on the cultural elites (and media) to realize his reforms, and they in fact did play a significant role both in delegitimizing Brezhnev's regime and in supporting Gorbachev's reforms. Liberal intellectuals were appointed as editors of certain publications (such as *Ogonek* [Flame], *Znamia* [The Banner], *Moskovskie novosti* [The Moscow news], and *Novyi mir*), which enormously increased the average growth coefficient of these periodicals. Mass media radically changed the cultural atmosphere in the country.

Alongside criticism of the present (its bureaucracy and corruption, and malfunctioning of the system), the revision of official Soviet history took its first steps: the October Revolution and the concept of socialism were reassessed, Stalin's regime overtly condemned, and the Party's role in Soviet society revised, thus beginning to erode the role of the country's main cultural institution.

The press regained its social role, not only attacking the old system but also revealing the deep schism occurring in the intellectual community between liberals and nationalists (as shown by the polemics between the publications inspired by liberal ideas – *Ogonek*, *Znamia*, and *Moskovskie novosti* – and those that supported Russophile positions – *Nash sovremennik* [Our contemporary], *Molodaia gvardiia*, and *Moskva* [Moscow]). This struggle continued throughout *perestroika* and culminated in the liberals' victory; but the amazing result of this victory was that, by causing the disintegration of literary centrism, it led to the decline of 'high literature' in favour of mass culture, and the voice of the cultural elites lost its 'prophetic' dimension.

The end of the literature-centric system is well reflected in the evolution of literary journals. Symbolic of the change in the status of literature was the drop in circulation of 'thick' literary monthlies: today's printings constitute less than 1 per cent of the millions of copies that were still being printed in 1989–1990.[21]

The abolition of censorship (on 27 December 1991) and the lifting of many taboos also contributed to the change in literature's status in post-Soviet society. Socialist Realism had not only sacralized the work of art and its producer but also established the rules of social behaviour according to norms of morality and etiquette. Therefore, its disappearance from the literary arena – together with censorship – eliminated boundaries and limits in the choice of topics (including erotic and sexual themes), thus depriving literature of its inner secret, the secret of 'fiction' that established contact between the reader and reality through a convention. Now this secret has been stolen by the media, which affirm a new representation of reality. Audio-visual culture deprives literature of its status as a privileged cultural channel, and cinema and videos are now the intermediaries between written culture and consumers: they play the role of interpreting the Word.

The rules of the game have dramatically changed, and thus claimants to the status of writer now have to face different obstacles: not the judgement of Party-run cultural institutions but the recognition of the public, which makes them viable in the market. In Soviet society, the importance of social status was very high; but in post-Soviet society, the value of money is surpassing that of social status, aggressively invading the cultural field and influencing all its forms of existence.

The change in literature's status, the end of literary centrism in Russian culture, and literature's loss of power as the holder of the Word: all these changes make literature less fearful to the state, which can often, therefore, ignore the literary process. However, the field of information is still heavily conditioned by political power. Therefore, in the Putin era, the price the writer has to pay for an apparent autonomy is that of living as far as possible from the field of power, bowing more and more to the power of the market.

In the early years of the twentieth century, Russia passed through a peculiar historical crossroads when it began to edge away from the *ancien régime*. The period of relative liberalization characterized by the abolition of preliminary censorship in 1905 and the subsequent flowering of the cultural market was a time in which Russia could aspire to modernization after the Western model. The Bolshevik Revolution was a sort of Restoration, a return to the ancestral slavery of the Word which had characterized the old order; it marked a turn from the dizzying period of liberalization of the Word to a completely ideologized and politicized use of it, wherein the state employed literature to exercise the performative effects of the Word, relying upon a strong literature-centric system. The fall of the Soviet Union completed the parabola of the twentieth century, a graphic moving from 'the power of the market' in pre-Revolutionary Russia to 'the market of power' in Soviet Russia, and then back to 'the power of the market' again after 1991 – this final shift the verdict of a market economics dominated by mass culture and temporal success.

NOTES

1 'Preliminary' (predvaritel'naia) censorship was applied in editorial offices to manuscripts or typescripts before publishing; 'subsequent' (posleduiushchaia) censorship dealt with already published works.

2 See Brooks, Jeffrey, *When Russia Learned to Read* (Evanston, IL: Northwestern University Press, 2003).

3 Lenin, Vladimir, *Collected Works* (Moscow: Progress Publishers, 1965), vol. 10, pp. 44–49.

4 Bogdanov, Alexander, 'Proletariat i iskusstvo', *Proletarskaia kul'tura*, 5 (1918), p. 32.

5 'Prava i funktsii Glavlita i ego mestnykh organov' (1922) in Blium, Arlen, ed., *Tsenzura v Sovetskom Soiuze 1917–1991* (Moscow: ROSSPEN, 2004), pp. 36–37.

6 Guldberg, Jørn, 'Socialist Realism as Institutional Practice' in Günther, Hans, ed., *The Culture of the Stalin Period* (New York: St Martin's Press, 1990), p. 162.

7 The term *udarnik* (shock-worker) appeared in the 1930s to designate advanced (*peredovye*) workers in socialist production.

8 Dobrenko, Evgeny, *The Making of the State Writer* (Stanford, CA: Stanford University Press, 2001), p. 226.

9 Fadeev, Alexander, 'O trebovatel'nosti v masterstve' in his *Za tridtsat' let* (Moscow: Sovetskii pisatel', 1957), pp. 151–155.

10 'Postanovlenie Orgbiuro TsK VKP(b) o zhurnalakh "Zvezda" i "Leningrad"' in *Vlast i khudozhestvennaia intelligentsiia* (Moscow: Materik-Al'fa, 2002), pp. 587–591.

11 Gorham, Michael S., *Speaking in Soviet Tongues* (DeKalb, IL: Northern Illinois University Press, 2003).

12 *Pervyi Vsesoiuznyi S˝ezd sovetskikh pisatelei* (Moscow: Sovetskii pisatel', 1990), p. 4.

13 Babichenko, Denis, '*Schast'e literatury'. Gosudarstvo i pisateli 1925–1938* (Moscow: ROSSPEN, 1997), p. 126.

14 Andrei Zhdanov (1896–1948) was the Communist party Central Committee secretary responsible from 1944 to 1948 for the implementation of Stalin's policy in ideology and culture. Hence the term 'Zhdanovism' (*zhdanovshchina*), a period of cultural repression starting in 1946.

15 'O politiko-ideologicheskom kontrole nad literaturoi v period rekonstruktsii' (1931) in Arlen, ed., *Tsenzura v Sovetskom Soiuze 1917–1991* (Moscow: Rossiiskaia Politicheskaia Entsiklopediia, 2004), pp. 190–191.

16 Blium, Arlen, *Sovetskaia tsenzura v epokhu total'nogo terrora* (St Petersburg: Akademicheskii Proekt, 2000), pp. 94–123.

17 'Postanovlenie sekretariata TsK KPSS' (1969) in *Istoriia sovetskoi politicheskoi tsenzury* (Moscow: ROSSPEN, 1997), pp. 188–191.

18 Krechmar, Dirk, *Politika i kul'tura pri Brezhneve, Andropove, Chernenko 1970–1985 gg.* (Moscow: AIRO-XX, 1997), pp. 37–57.

19 *Boris Pasternak i vlast'. Dokumenty* (Moscow: ROSSPEN), 2001, pp. 143–144, 155–159, 161–163, 349–379.

20 Lewin, Moshe, *Russia/URSS/Russia* (New York: The New Press, 1995), pp. 300–305.

21 Ivanova, Natal'ia, 'Triumfatory, ili novye literaturnye nravy v kontekste novogo vremeni', *Zvezda*, 4 (1995), p. 179; see also data in Boris Dubin, *Slovo-pis'mo-literatura*, pp. 135–147.

FURTHER READING

Berg, Mikhail, *Literaturokratiia* (Moscow: NLO, 2000).

Blium, Arlen, *Za kulisami 'Ministerstva pravdy'* (St Petersburg: Akademicheskii proekt, 1994).

  Sovetskaia tsenzura v epokhu total'nogo terrora (St Petersburg: Akademicheskii proekt, 2000).

  Kak eto delalos' v Leningrade. Tsenzura v gody ottepeli, zastoia i perestroiki, 1953–1991 (St Petersburg: Akademicheskii proekt, 2005).

Brooks, Jeffrey, *Thank You, Comrade Stalin!* (Princeton, NJ: Princeton University Press, 2000).

  When Russia Learned to Read (Evanston, IL: Northwestern University Press, 2003).

Clark, Katerina, *The Soviet Novel* (Bloomington, IN: Indiana University Press, 2000).

Dobrenko, Evgeny, *The Making of the State Reader* (Stanford, CA: Stanford University Press, 1997).

  The Making of the State Writer (Stanford, CA: Stanford University Press, 2001).

Dubin, Boris, *Slovo-pis'mo-literatura* (Moscow: Novoe literaturnoe obozrenie, 2001).

Garrard, John and Garrard, Carol, *Inside the Soviet Writers' Union* (New York: Free Press, 1990).

Gudkov, Lev and Dubin, Boris, *Literatura kak sotsial'nyi institut* (Moscow: NLO, 1994).

Günter, Hans and Dobrenko, Evgeny, eds., *Sotsrealisticheskii kanon* (St Petersburg: Akademicheskii proekt, 2000).

Günter, Hans and Khensgen, Sabina, eds., *Sovetskaia vlast' i media* (St Petersburg: Akademicheskii proekt, 2006).

Instituty upravleniia kul'turoi v period stanovleniia. 1917–1930-e gg. (Moscow: ROSSPEN, 2004).

Shlapentokh, Vladimir, *Soviet Intellectuals and Political Power: The Post-Stalin Era* (Princeton, NJ: Princeton University Press, 1990).

15

CARYL EMERSON

Russian Critical Theory

There is a curious shape to twentieth-century Russian writing on literary creativity. It swings between a bold revolutionary modernism – materialistic, mechanistic, impersonal, poised to dissolve the bourgeois subject together with the socioeconomic class that nourished it – and a naive idealism relying on archaic categories of spiritual epiphany and unconditional emotional commitment. From 1934 until well into the 1960s, the spiritual extreme dominated the USSR's official theory of art: although deeply conservative and faith-based, the doctrine of Socialist Realism played a radical role in the pragmatic modernization of the Stalinist–Soviet state. As that state decayed and finally collapsed in the late 1980s, the Soviet Union at last 'caught up with and surpassed' the West – at least on the artistic front. With some justification, although also with that hint of cultural supremacy so congenial to Russian critical thought, the émigré theorist Mikhail Epstein claimed that postmodernism itself was born in Russia during the Brezhnev Stagnation.[1] Not in French academies but in shabby post-Stalinist space, strewn with the (literal) ruins of the Socialist Realist fantasy, did all truth claims become preposterous, all mega-narratives lead nowhere, all speaking subjects (and all objects spoken of) become mere simulacra, and all explanatory systems begin to feel faked. If symbolism in search of a mystical totality accommodated itself to revolutionary modernism in the 1920s, then the closing years of the century in Russia were positively postmodern in their cynical sophistication at manipulating the cliché and fragment.

Can anything like an organic whole be found in this fascinating twentieth-century trajectory? Debate still rages over the degree of ideological continuity: avant-garde in the 1920s, 'medievalized' during the Stalinist period, and then, after two decades of timid thaw, proto-postmodernist up to and through the new millennium. In this sequence, attention at times has focused on the fate of the authorial function (the agent), at times on the form (structure) of the artifact, at yet other times on the needs or fantasies of the audience (the 'New Soviet Person'). Here too one notes a polar oscillation.

The Formalists of the 1910s–1920s were constructive, concerned with poetic autonomy and thus with how an artwork 'was made' (and less with the face of the maker). The most creative final Soviet generations were satiric and *de*constructive, focusing on how works were unmade (again, the face of the author was elusive: collective, cartooned, or debased). In between the making and unmaking of artifacts, the strangely disembodied doctrine of Socialist Realism made its debut: on one hand utopian, on the other punitive, it served as a policing function that mercilessly weeded out the wrong image while promising the Soviet public some as-yet-unseen perfected version of humanity immune to parody and decay. In this environment, unsurprisingly, literary thinkers and genre theorists such as Mikhail Bakhtin (1895–1975) or Lidiia Ginzburg (1902–1990), for whom the idiosyncratic face and the doubting voice always took precedence over ideal prototypes or impersonal structures, entered mainstream critical discourse only marginally.

The logic of this critical trajectory is often obscured by the fact that it was so capriciously unfree. Terms that possessed technical meaning during one decade (say, 'formalist') could later become lethal floating signifiers of official abuse. In the legally atheist state that emerged victorious from the Civil War (1918–1921), a religious or metaphysical movement might be tolerated if it adjusted its apocalyptic rhetoric to accord with visionary Bolshevism; such was the path taken by some second-generation Symbolists. A school of criticism might begin rebelliously, then be housed in state institutions, then later be expelled and ritually shamed (as were the Formalists in the 1910s–1920s) – or, alternatively, might nurture itself in unofficial study groups only to be dissipated later by arrest or exile (the experience of the Bakhtin Circle in the 1920s–1930s). The present chapter does not aim to provide an institutional history of those bewildering, often belligerent acronyms that dot the age: OPOYAZ, Proletkult, Pereval, *The Smithy*, RAPP, LEF, New LEF, and the various 'deviations' from orthodox Socialist Realism. Excellent accounts of these groupings already exist. It also excludes Russian critics in emigration, from Vladimir Nabokov and Andrey Siniavsky to the many energetic bi-cultural theorists at work in the USA and Europe since the mid-1980s. Here we sample only the more durable figures and methodologies on Russian soil. This domestic pool is rich, for Russian criticism, like Russian politics, has traditionally nurtured global ambitions. However local or politically conditioned, debates over literature were seen as timelessly relevant – not only for analysing artistic texts but also for organizing life-experience in every other domain. Russian theories of art (from Tolstoy through Mikhail Bakhtin to Iurii Lotman) generated guidelines for life, blueprints for the human psyche, and 'secondary modelling systems' that promised to crack codes of public behaviour, reigns of tsars, and myths of cities. During the

Stalinist years, the nation's greatest writers were cleansed and re-canonized in manic, state-sponsored 'Jubilees' (the centennial of Tolstoy's birth in 1928, of Pushkin's death in 1937). Such cults could also develop around Russian critics. When Roman Jakobson (1896–1982), in voluntary exile since 1920, was permitted to re-visit his birthplace in 1956, he was received rapturously – as a structural linguist, certainly, but even more as a celebrity, a thinker who had returned to Russia from the land of the dead, proving that Russia was not dead to the rest of the world.

This confidence in the 'critic as cultural seer' – first for Russia, then for the world – is shared by all five representative approaches to literature discussed here. Formalism in the 1910s–1920s is followed by its nemesis, the 'psychological' critics (of whom the Freudians are the loudest but the least interesting). Next come the 'Bakhtinians', institutionally invisible in their own time, who were recognized as a school and an adjective only posthumously. Marxist–sociological orientations, of which Socialist Realism was the ultimate state-approved expression, control the middle third of the century, survive into the 1990s, and range from naive to inspirational to savagely repressive. Finally, semiotic approaches to literary culture emerge in the 1960s, chipping away at ossified 'SocRealism' with new terminology and tools. To focus our juxtaposition of these approaches, we will ask the same three questions of each.

First, how much autonomy should art (or the 'aesthetic function') enjoy among other human strivings and social tasks? Second, does each method-ology presume one particular material, medium, genre, or mode as opti-mal – poetic word, prose word, visual image (static, dynamic), gestural or social sign, parodic or ironic intonation – and if so, how does this preference (or prejudice) limit the range of its application? And, finally, how does each critical approach justify the production of cultural arti-facts? Struggles over the purpose of art were bitter during this century, but rarely was it suggested that art had *no* purpose, that it satisfied only its author's need for disinterested patterning, private expression, or mere play. We open with the school most insistent on literary autonomy, Russian Formalism, where art was thought to serve life best by looking at itself in a mirror.

Russian Formalism

Formalism was born during the First World War, inspired by the avant-garde movements of Futurism and Constructivism as well as by the immediacy of battlefield violence. Unlike the 'art for life's sake' criticism associated with Russia's moralist–realist novelists, but also unlike the Symbolist critics who resisted this realist ethic with their otherworldly visions ('art for the sake of a spiritual life'), the rigorously secular Formalists sought to verify art by its craftsmanship, autonomy, and intensity of shock effect. The author was reduced to one among several 'functions'. Heroic biographical criticism was defiantly set aside. Interiority became suspect. Literary signs had referential and communicative value, of course – but not to the soul. A creative act or image qualified as a 'literary fact' only if artistic technique was identified as its 'dominant' function. When devices of 'literariness' were isolated, poetic language could be separated from practical (everyday) language and a professional *science* of literature could be born.

Viktor Shklovsky (1893–1984) was Formalism's most aggressive 'scientist' in this sense. He did not preach art for art's sake; on the contrary, art should serve life as its stimulant and irritant. His provocative pre-Revolutionary essay 'Art as Device' (1916) argued that art is obliged to 'make everyday objects strange' so that habitual perception is jolted awake. This 'estrangement' [*ostranenie*] from the realm of the ordinary or predictable is what guarantees the palpability and worthiness of artistic effort. Although life's routine inevitably 'automatizes' and deadens us, art (like revolution) has a cutting edge that can revive feeling – and thus restore meaning. This pursuit of the 'hard edge' was characteristic of Formalist critics. Technique, not sentiment, was the mark of artistry. Thus Formalists sought repeating patterns, grammatical as well as phonic, which could be heard, measured, and juxtaposed (most conveniently in binary oppositions). In meticulous statistical studies of Russian poetry, Boris Eikhenbaum (1886–1959), Iurii Tynianov (1894–1943), and Boris Tomashevsky (1890–1957) raised versification to a quantified science. In their analyses of prose fiction, a cool and cerebral voice predominated. Eikhenbaum, for example, read Gogol's 1842 story 'The Overcoat' not as the author's lament for a victimized Petersburg clerk but as an experiment in *skaz* (artificed, eccentric storytelling), a grotesque woven of *zvukovye zhesty* (sound gestures) and *zvukorech´* (sound-based speech) in which a contrived sentimentality alternates with an equally contrived parody of that sentiment. Such vacillating intonation, Eikhenbaum argued, could never generate mimetic images or plausible personalities, for the reader's inner eye remains blank and sympathies unengaged. The Formalists' favoured tactic of detecting 'mechanisms' that could keep psychology out of the picture explains in part their attraction to formulaic literature. In his *Morphology of the Folktale* (1928), for example, Vladimir Propp (1895–1970) broke down all fairy tales into thirty-one discrete plot-events or 'narratemes' that unfolded in a fixed sequence, with all necessary activity distributed among seven types of agents. Motivation or meaning outside this rubric was simply unreadable.

In his whimsical and anecdotal style, Shklovsky produced a series of polemical treatises on detective fiction (Sherlock Holmes), the picaresque (*Don Quixote*), the mystery novel (Dickens), and the self-parodying narrator (Sterne). In each, a successful prose narrative was shown to depend neither on inner moral prompts nor on life's outer challenges but on familiar units of literary plot organized in a new, shocking way. Eikhenbaum, in his study *The Young Tolstoy* (1922), even claimed that Tolstoy's periodic condemnations of his own behaviour and his elaborately public confessions later in life were tasks more intrinsic to 'literariness' (that is, to experiments in genres of punitive self-exposure) than to bad conscience or any intent to reform. What Formalists claimed for individual works and authors they also claimed for entire evolving historical periods. Tynianov maintained that literary history was driven not by emerging social or ethical concerns but by rival competing genres, which were successively automatized, estranged, and re-integrated. To progress, literature looked first of all at its *own* face.

As Formalism itself evolved, ingenious attempts were made to get out of the mirror – to accommodate more 'extra-literary material' in the form of affections, pressures, and real-life events. Still, even at its most flexible, a Formalist lens rendered a great deal unreadable. With its emphasis on newness and shock as central to aesthetic perception and value, parody remained its preferred mode. Narrative forms such as epic, legend, or holy writ were scantily appreciated, since their 'prior-ness' was not merely a prerequisite for later parody: it was a source of reverence and respect in its own right. And if a complicated past was mostly uninteresting to the Formalists, their view of the future was motivated by equally simplistic criteria; it needed only to differ from the present. By and large, the deeper psychology of creators and receivers remained outside a Formalist purview. Precisely the issues surrounding this psychology were raised by the next three groups of critics, although the treatment in each is governed by a different dominant. For the psychologists, the starting-point was '*intra*-personal relations'; for Bakhtin it was '*inter*-personal relations'; for the Marxists-sociologists it was 'societal relations' based (more or less rigidly) on socio-economic determinants.

The psychological critics

Psychological criticism on Russian soil must not be reduced to the psychoanalytic, although that ideological import was by far the best organized as a school. Freud's major writings were quickly translated into Russian, and their secular, materialist view of artistic creativity found sympathizers in the atheist Bolshevik state, including Trotsky. Disciples sought out dialectical relations between Freud and Marx, and between Pavlovian reflexology and consciousness (in a synthesis called 'reactology'). In 1910 one early convert, the psychiatrist Nikolai Osipov, published a psychotherapeutic study of Tolstoy's heroines. Osipov diagnosed Natasha Rostova (from *War and Peace*) and Kitty Shcherbatskaia (from *Anna Karenina*) as traumatized hysterics, claiming that Tolstoy's disgust for doctors masked this fact from the reader.[2] With more justification, Ivan Yermakov (1875–1943), director of the State Psychoanalytic Institute and editor of its book series, published on the 'repressed–aggressive' psychic profile of Nikolai Gogol (1923) as revealed in 'The Nose' – which was, according to Yermakov, a masterpiece of anal erotics and castration anxiety by a writer with the courage to compel his readers to confront the reality of both.[3]

Orthodox Freudian literary interpretation enriched the discourse of the era, but on balance did not persuade beyond its own circle of committed believers. In 1927, Bakhtin's Marxist associate Valentin Voloshinov (1895–1936) published his *Freudianism: A Critical Sketch*, explaining the 'ideological dominant' of Freudian doctrine as the natural product of a disillusioned social class, the European bourgeoisie, which sensed the end of its role in history and thus had defaulted in desperation to the passive criteria of sex and age within a single, abstract biological organism. Earlier in the decade, the genre theorist Boris Griftsov (1885–1950) included a section in his 1924 book *The Psychology of the Writer* titled 'Freud's Method and Dostoevsky'.[4] Measuring Griftsov's verdict against our three concerns (art's autonomy, the critic's preferred mode, and justification for the literary work), we see that a Freudian framework fails Dostoevsky on all counts. It must fail, Griftsov notes, because the two aims of psychoanalytic criticism are incompatible. As a therapy it is devoted to healing what is pathological, but as an aesthetics it reduces the poet to a dreamer–neurotic – which can only result in a hybrid method that would 'cure the world of creativity' (38). Psychoanalytic readings treat all genres as personal confessions rather than as aesthetic constructs (246–247). And not only does this method permit art little autonomy from life, but the life it does reflect is pre-scripted, impoverished, a simpleminded world of infantile sexuality that 'drastically narrows the [critic's] field of observation' (242).

In the tradition of Russian Naturalist readings from the 1860s, Griftsov puts forward another psychology of the creative act, which recalls John Dewey's *Art and Experience* (1934). Art's primary nutrient is everyday life, Griftsov argues. But since 'experiences are endlessly varied', shapeless, flowing, a work of art can be born only when events coalesce into a whole for the writer (53). Constraints are real, since in a given historical period, 'types of creativity are *not* endlessly varied'; every available genre filters some things out and favours others. The novella emerged as a byproduct of busy people temporarily safe or in hiding, telling stories to pass the time – thus its mood is one of relief and pleasure; the Greek novel was a charmed form, a unique mix of lyric and wandering impulses (66–85). Cervantes might have begun his novel *Don Quixote* as a parody of worn-out devices, as Shklovsky claimed, but most likely he did not assemble it mechanically; while getting to know his hero, the author's goals changed, and the novel's end can be read as a complex, original 'justification of chivalry' (47–48). Griftsov insists that the conscious process of creativity always involves a slow growth of personality out of the living word, which affects the writer and the writer's product far more profoundly than any unconscious complexes.

This conviction was shared by the developmental psychologist Lev Vygotsky (1896–1934), whose 1925 study *The Psychology of Art* juxtaposes to both Freudian and Formalist methods a more objective quest for the 'psychology of form'.[5] If Shklovsky's *ostranenie* demoted the aesthetic reaction to mere invigorated sense perception ('sensualistic one-sidedness' [57]), then Freudian critics had failed to explain the positive social tasks of aesthetic emotion (for trash literature and pornography would suffice to release a tabooed sexual drive [79]). Through analyses of Bunin's prose, Pushkin's *Eugene Onegin*, and Shakespeare's *Hamlet*, Vygotsky offers his alternative, 'art as catharsis'. By this term he means something other than a safety-valve for pathogenic impulses or a sudden discharge of nervous energy in the final scene. Vygotsky, as did Aristotle himself, understood catharsis as a matter of cumulative thick description. It does not reside solely in the subject's body but in the artwork too; 'the very texture of aesthetic objects is threaded with psychological elements'.[6] This texture/text produces a prolonged aesthetic reaction by organizing contradictory feelings ('irritants') so that each reader is *transformed* (not merely woken up or pleasured) in the nervous–psychical sphere. For Vygotsky, faith that the literary word could transfigure the body neurophysiologically and 'prepare the organism for action' (248) was part of his enlightened materialism, a specifically human behaviourism that he saw as the only possible creative answer to Pavlovian reflexology. Because language originates outside our psyche but reshapes us internally, 'art is the social within us' (249).

Our final two exemplars of psychological criticism also endorse the 'social within us' as the starting point for literary value, although with varying degrees of anxiety and dread. Lidiia Ginzburg (1902–1990), Tynianov's most gifted student, illustrates the integration possible among Formalist ideas, 'psychologism', and structuralism. Her key text, *On Psychological Prose*, appeared only in the 1970s. Like Griftsov an adept at French literature, Ginzburg specialized in memoirs, confessions, diaries, work-ing notebooks of creative writers, and epistolary correspondence – all warm, quasi-fictive genres belonging to a category she called 'the human document'.[7] Her Formalist training prompted her to seek impersonal rules. But because such 'in-between' narratives are not autonomous from life (in Ginzburg's own prose they are straightforward attempts to survive one's life), a subtle bifurcation of authorial perspective is required, both protective and pitiless. Drawing on her own private torment as a lonely, unemployed academic, a Jew, a lesbian, and a resident of Leningrad during the Block-ade of 1941–1944, Ginzburg devised literary mechanisms for self-distancing [samootstranenie] that permitted unprecedented access to the self while for-malizing, and thus containing, the resultant pain and vulnerability.[8]

Ginzburg's books on Lermontov (1940), the lyric (1964), and the literary hero (1979) were traditional Soviet-era genre studies, in which every form is expected to gravitate toward that vaguely defined virtue, Realism. Only with her volume on 'psychological prose' (1972–1977) did Ginzburg emerge as a pathbreaking scholar of Tolstoy. She too considers Tolstoy a moral realist, but not for the usual reasons (Tolstoy as epic singer of life, or depicter of a 'dialectic of the soul', or, in Bakhtin's curmudgeonly image of him, as isolated, self-absorbed 'monologist'). Quite the contrary: Tolstoy's realism derives from his excruciating attention to outer convention, social norms, collapses in our everyday attempts at communication, failures to fit in, all of which are under pressures so contradictory that individual behaviour seems unexpected and unpredictable. The hero feels unfree – but does not know why. This unfreedom cannot be reduced to a simple tragic dichotomy between desire and duty. Tolstoy perfects his tools of logical analysis, all the while knowing that the direct causality of any act will never be demonstrated; and his mastery of this tension-filled literary procedure proves the multi-faceted 'conditionedness' [obuslovlennost'] of all human experience.

Similar to Bakhtin but more uncompromisingly secular, Ginzburg insists that art has a cognitive, formal, and moral function. Only through the word can the threat of the 'social outside us' be tamed. Her hyper-conditioned Tolstoyan-style hero, desperate to discover the causes of his distress, needy of public recognition and useful service, is an outgrowth of her own notebooks, experimental prose fiction, and wholly non-Freudian analyses of erotic love. For Ginzburg as for her beloved subject Tolstoy, the power of the 'social within us' could at times be more crippling than enabling.

Such was not the view of Mikhail Bakhtin. In the 1920s, Bakhtin devised a tripartite model of the psyche – socially conditioned, benign, gender-neutral – that would become the bedrock of his literary dynamics. The psyche is trusting, like Vygotsky's child in the world, and unrelated to Freud's triad of punitive Superego, enlightened but fragile Ego, and unteachable Id.[9] At its core we find not sex and authority, but the relationship of a curious self to a loving other. The Bakhtinian model provides for three perspectives: an *I-for-myself* (how I feel from inside to my own consciousness), an *I-for-the-other* (how I look from the outside to someone else), and its converse, *the-other-for-me*. In this new variant on the 'social within us', we work ineluctably with other individuals' views of us. *I-for-myself* is mute and in flux, because its identity is the product of bits of 'finished surface' that others see and project back on to it. As Bakhtin expressed the matter in a fragment from the mid-1940s, 'it is not me who looks out on the world with my own eyes . . . [but] out of my eyes, someone else's eyes gaze forth'.[10] For Bakhtin, both the creation and reception of art are responsible, life-affirming, interpersonal acts. If the Formalists, in search of artistic autonomy, turned a mirror on literature and harvested the expected symmetries and systems, then Bakhtin, in search of parallels between the authoring of selves and the authoring of literature, discredited all mirror relations and celebrated all loopholes out of them. Replication and symmetry, he believed, trap us hopelessly within a single-consciousness loop that can create nothing strange, hopeful, or new.

The Bakhtinians

Bakhtin was a maverick Kantian, an innovative philosopher of language, a Russian Orthodox believer and a student of German phenomenology who insisted on working with the materials of his time: Einstein's relativity, Max Scheler's views on sympathy, Ernst Cassirer's modelling of the Renaissance cosmos, and Maxim Gorky on the reflection theory of art. Bakhtin adjusted every twentieth-century idea he touched upon to his own purpose, and yet applied none of these ideas in any depth to twentieth-century literature. He helped his friends Pavel Medvedev and Valentin Voloshinov write Marxist-inflected books on social linguistics and against Formalism and Freud – but his own debate with Formalism is couched as an old-fashioned neo-Kantian critique of 'materialist aesthetics' in favour of an artistic realm of freedom between cognition and ethics. Sources for Bakhtin's messianic carnival utopia are multiple, but that vision is realized most gloriously in the sixteenth-century novels of François Rabelais; after that, the vigour of laughter progressively declines. Except for the application of a collective carnival body to Stalinist culture – a terrifying exercise only implicit in his texts – Bakhtin appears depressingly silent on the creative literary possibilities of the twentieth century. The organic weight and self-evident value of history, stretching back thousands of years and projecting into an unfinalizable future that Bakhtin called 'Great Time' (where all our neglected or orphaned utterances will be heard) is felt more profoundly in Bakhtin than in any other theorist of the century, including even his gifted Hegelian–Marxist rival Georg Lukács. Three major ideas from Bakhtin's arsenal have become classic tools in literary criticism: dialogue, carnival, and his version of the time–space matrix, the chronotope. We discuss the first two in relation to the novel, Bakhtin's preferred literary genre, and only insofar as they justify aesthetic activity in ways distinct from our earlier schools.

By *dialogue* (or dialogic energy), Bakhtin means the reciprocity, addressivity, and open-endedness of all relations – both among utterances and within the word. The dialogic self is largely a voice, or series of voices. Among its strengths is that it differentiates, remembers, and is extremely difficult to kill off. It can hear a dozen voices embedded in every utterance, with a personality behind each one. Dialogic processes always increase the amount of consciousness in the world, since their primary obligation is to console and supplement others by seeing or hearing what these others cannot perceive for themselves. In Bakhtin's mature, deeply Romantic thought, dialogue and heteroglossia become trademarks of the novel, the most freedom-bearing, consciousness-proliferating, and interactive genre on earth. In the form of that extreme dialogism Bakhtin called 'polyphony', authors design characters who potentially know as much about themselves as their authors do, and this knowledge permits them to develop autonomously, surprising even their creator. Bakhtin acknowledges that some utterances – the Homeric epic as well as certain novels, such as Tolstoy's – are not designed to foreground open-ended interaction; such verbal works he labels monologic, 'authoritative' rather than 'internally persuasive' utterances.[11]

By contrast, *carnival* (or carnival energy) is not a word but a *body* – and specifically, a robust, fertile, grotesque body 'on holiday'. It seeks pleasure and play; it can communicate without having to learn a complex verbal language; it is free from shame and embarrassment; it is open to new experience; it is full of appetite and is not under a deadline to get anything done. The carnival self is easy to affirm because it requires no discipline to maintain. And – crucially for Bakhtin – it laughs. Carnival laughter released from the mouth is fearless and indifferent to death. As a route to well-being it is more foolproof than *words* released from the mouth (carnival words are mostly obscene). Laughter is arguably even more efficient than loving gazes from the eyes, which inevitably personalize and thus can cause pain. In fact the carnival self barely has eyes; it is all lips, cheeks, breasts, buttocks. These body parts are not discussed in their sexual function, however, which Bakhtin shrugs off (together with sexual desire) in a casual way that would astonish the Freudians. Body protuberances are outward- and other-oriented because they want to eat.

Since the carnival self remembers so little and regrets nothing, it is difficult to say exactly why it needs any specific other at all. Although it welcomes an endless stream of *others-for-me*, it doesn't do much with them; other bodies pass through my body, or gestate in it, because the carnival body is above all a conduit. As authors and readers in the carnival mode, therefore, we are left with a swollen but still somehow impoverished *I-for-myself*, a mass of interchangeable impulses that neither learns nor ages. Unsurprisingly, Bakhtin's book on Rabelais's world scarcely discusses its learned author and cursorily dismisses Renaissance humanism. Carnival energy can be faceless, violent, tedious. But Bakhtin was enamoured of this energy and worldview throughout his life, considering it compatible with dialogue and valuing its courage, perseverance, optimism, and lack of acquisitive ego. In times of terror and famine – the Stalinist 1930s–1940s – such an open-ended, well-fed model of collective abundance and fearlessness must have been inspirational. The ideology of carnival remains the most contested aspect of Bakhtin's legacy. Is it subversive, destabilizing, dialogically egalitarian in its reaching-out and casting-down, or is it collaborationist, tyrannical, silencing, vampiric, monologic? Books are sooner burned than read on a carnival square. For Bakhtin, however, a carnival attitude toward death and the body is always affirmative.

Bakhtin and Ginzburg survived the Stalinist period, although on the periphery, without professional security, and with little published presence. For most of the century, the approved approaches to literature and art favoured other dominants: materialist in the Marxist sense (that is, 'dialectically materialist' rather than carnivalesque or grotesque) and tied to the politics of class struggle. These insiderly approaches – sociological and socialist–realist – constitute the official frame, or background noise, of the Soviet period. Through them, art was justified by very different criteria and its autonomy categorically denied.

The Marxists and Socialist Realists

In 1924 Trotsky passed his judgement on the Formalist school. While certainly 'arrogant, immature, superficial and reactionary' in many of their overstatements, nevertheless the Formalists had 'raised the theory of art from alchemy to chemistry'.[12] He appreciated their Futurist boldness as revolutionary and their quantified studies of organized poetic language as useful 'preparatory work'. In the end, however, Trotsky declared Formalism a retrograde 'abortive idealism' that worshipped the Word rather than the Deed as its primary reality. The status of the *deed* – both the acts and objects that art reflects, as well as the heroic deeds that a Marxist artwork should inspire – will organize our comments about this powerful, but ultimately repressive, critical orientation.

Among the paradoxes of Marxist literary criticism worldwide is its distinguished history out of power and its far shabbier record once it becomes official doctrine. Some of the 'Old Bolshevik' generation – Anatolii Lunacharsky (1873–1933), Nikolai Bukharin (1888–1938), Alexander Voronsky (1884–1943) – bravely resisted the full politicization of literature while still insisting on its social and class function. Others, such as Vladimir Friche (1870–1929) and Vladimir Pereverzev (1882–1968), created a school of 'sociological poetics' so rigidly governed by economic determinism that its trivializations (of Tolstoy as landlord writer or of Dostoevsky as split between bourgeois and mystic) were eventually condemned as 'vulgar sociologism' even within the system. In 1934, literary theory became a branch of state policy, the ideological wing of 'artistic production' within the Second Five-Year Plan. As enunciated by Maxim Gorky at the First Congress of the Union of Soviet Writers, literature's task was to transmit a 'truthful, historically concrete representation of reality in its revolutionary development'. The method, 'Socialist Realism', would supplant both the 'critical' and 'romantic' realisms of the nineteenth century. This overtly pedagogical doctrine begins not with an exemplary literary artifact nor even with a clear-cut set of devices or psychological models, but as a plan for the ideal provisioning of the Soviet consumer of literature. First the desired literary profile of the Stalinist subject would be determined, and then the writer who could realize it would be summoned into being.[13]

What was that profile? The New Soviet Reader would willingly reject bourgeois narratives of personal love and private material accumulation in favour of sterner stuff: industrial productivity, construction of a metro or canal, sacrifice in war, heroic high-risk deeds of discovery or rescue. Since these plots already promised a good deal of suffering and deprivation, authors were not to dwell on the perverse sides of human nature nor on any perceived inadequacies in today's material existence. Those were relics: real enough, perhaps, on the bodies of the heroes – but not reality in its 'revolutionary development'. Whereas the old realisms were critical, pragmatic, and objective (a mirror held up to the world), revolutionary truth would develop through a new type of transformational dialogic feedback, in an energy field surrounding and infusing the subject. Immersed in the proper collective milieu and nourished by it, any person could become 'conscious' and begin to see. Four paired principles eventually governed the vision of a conscious subject. 'Party-mindedness' (submission to general Party ideals) was co-ordinated with 'idea-mindedness', the current leading priority of the Party. 'Class-mindedness' (portraying a struggle that the proletariat must win) was linked with 'people- or folk-mindedness', the mandate that art be accessible and attractive to the masses by drawing on their traditions, melodies, rhythms, and language. A fifth concern was 'art-ness' [*khudozhestvennost´*], but the artist did not control this virtue: it was realized automatically once the other four principles were in place.

Recent work on Socialist Realism as a theoretical canon has highlighted some unnerving features. Beginning with the early pugnacious Formalists up through the carnival grotesque of mid-career Bakhtin, dismemberment and the rhetoric of cheerful annihilating violence were common metaphors. Into this discourse, Marxist class struggle fit effortlessly. But as the 1930s matured, and especially after 1936 when socialism was declared accomplished and domestic class warfare abolished, the requirement of 'conflictlessness' (*non*-antagonistic social contradictions) made plot construction difficult. A mass readership desires action, risk, suspense – but outcomes were now invariably positive, even if on the surface tragic. Since values were fixed, friends were either vacuous or revealed suddenly as treacherous; enemies had to be displaced as cartoons beyond the nation's borders and then re-imported as spies or saboteurs. The reflection theory of art could be sustained only through the patent falsehood that life was already ideal.[14] Any parody of the Communist purpose was taboo. Historical optimism was mandatory – but how was it to be grounded? God had been discredited, and history, which had not delivered up the expected world-wide proletarian victory, was unreliable. The old utopias were hopelessly pastoral, the modernist industrial ones impossibly distant. Since there were no appropriate models, the new (and often newly literate) Soviet Reader was expected to cultivate 'the ability to take pleasure in the aesthetic contemplation of not-yet-created objects'.[15] This assignment, essential for the morale of the working class but problematic even for a practised myth-making Symbolist, became the primary justification for aesthetic production.

Socialist Realism did not originate as a repressive device tailored for the Stalinist 1930s–1940s. It was the legacy of the founding fathers (Marx, Engels, Plekhanov, Lenin), reworked from guidelines into 'controlling mechanisms'.[16] External censorship was indispensable to it, of course, but subjects were also 're-forged' internally; 'idea-mindedness' [*ideinost´*] would become the inner censor in the writer's own creative process' (368). Ambivalent or neutral narration, as well as failure to imbed a tendentious idea in a work of art [*bezydeinost´*], was a criminal offence, for 'party-mindedness meant not just sympathizing with the proletariat but fusing with it' (369). Arguments like these owe more to psychological criticism than to either socialism or realism. But in fact, Socialist Realism produced literature only as a byproduct. Its primary product was power: an often arbitrary power to dictate paths to the truth. Significantly, its official spokesman in 1934, Maxim Gorky, explained his decision to return to Soviet Russia in 1928 as due in part to his 'hatred for truth that was an abomination and lie'; 'people need a different truth', he insisted, 'one which would not depress but rouse their working and creative energy'.[17] By the 1960s this energy was gone, although the lie lazily remained in force. The Thaw became the Stagnation and the social command for art lost its faith- and terror-driven mandate.

The Tartu School Semioticians

After Stalin's death in 1953, literary theory in the Soviet Union was paralysed. Although individual academic figures won devoted local followings – emerging often from the relatively sheltered field of Classics, such as the philosopher of myth Aleksei Losev (1893–1988) – institutionally, it took a decade for the literary profession to revive and speak to a broader public. The innovators included a group of young, high-technology philologists grouped around Iurii Lotman (1922–1993) at the University of Tartu in Soviet Estonia, and their mathematically minded linguistic colleagues at Moscow State University. Hoping to re-invest literary study with some professional autonomy, these scholars saw the future of their discipline – and its escape from the dead weight of Marxist cliché – in the new fields of cybernetics, computer modelling, information theory, machine translation, and semiotics or 'sign systems'. Paradoxically, the very impersonality of these processes promised to be liberating. Models for studying literature that had focused around the 'ethical person in an ethical society' – that code-phrase of old-fashioned Marxist–Leninist humanism – had all too easily been co-opted by the state. In 1961, a Thaw year, the Party officially endorsed cybernetics as a 'major tool for the creation of a communist society'. Cybernetics sounded upbeat, modernizing, untainted, quantified, too esoteric to be dissident. Although eventually Lotman too would have his apartment raided for subversive anti-Soviet materials, overall the 'Tartu Linguistics Summer School' baffled Party watchdogs. They neither sponsored nor outlawed it. Thus was Soviet semiotics born: within a secular, materialist framework, cautiously speaking of 'processes' and 'functions' rather than of economic evils or moral universals, it was perceived not as antagonistic to Marxism–Leninism but as somehow off to the side of it.

In 1962, Viacheslav Ivanov introduced semiotics at its first Moscow symposium. This new cultural discipline, he intimated, was the perfect Russian synthesis: it improved on Pavlovian reflexology as well as its humanized successor, reactology, and also on Vygotsky's psychology of art and the

Formalists' hard-edged device, all within a reassuringly progressive Hegelian framework. Cybernetically, 'the human being may be described as a mechanism that carries out operations on semiotic systems and sequences... A human individual's potential can be evaluated by describing all the sign systems he is competent to use'.[18] The potential of a collective could be measured in just the same way. Humanity was destined to evolve toward ever-greater complexity in the number and intricacy of its programmes. Thus semiotics held out the promise of formalist precision but without any embarrassing neglect of motivation, content, or social context. It would be a formalism that had matured into structuralism after acquiring a proper human face.

The Lotman group of the 1960s–1970s were 'quantifiers', whose interest in computer modelling mimicked the binary thinking of early Formalists. But the differences are crucial. Semiotics was less sensuous, less psychologistic, more norm-based and neutrally scientific. In the communication model elaborated by Roman Jakobson in the 1950s (with its parameters of context, message, contact, and code), semioticians cared most about the last. But this was no Morse code. The Tartu scholars had been raised and trained in a socialist–Marxist ethos. It was second nature to them that any sensible structuralist approach to art should attend to 'content' (to plot- and social-dimensions), and to real communication between real people within a cultural continuum filled with value. Lotman's *Structure of the Artistic Text* (1971) expanded the Formalist idea of a self-sufficient aesthetic object acting via devices into a broader vision of art understood as 'a form of cognition', a 'magnificently organized generator of languages', 'the most economical compact method for storing and transmitting information'.[19] A work of art was an authored message in its own right, of course, but it was also a 'secondary modelling system', a dynamic interplay of signs linking author and readers over time through shared codes. And because a great artwork is such a richly compact and efficient message, it can, and does, produce new codes out of itself.

The Tartu School soon expanded its concept of 'artistic text' to the whole of culture, beginning to read behavioural norms as codes and individual actions as messages. Among the most controversial were two studies from the late 1970s organized around a perennial binary, Russia's difference from the West, although safely displaced to pre-Petrine Russian culture.[20] The first (1977) argues that traditional Russian culture knew no progress in the Enlightened, gradualist sense of the term, no 'open tomorrows' or neutral zones with value as yet unassigned, and thus posited no purgatory; heaven became hell instantaneously and on the same spot. This mental set (it was implied) is conducive to reaction and utopian revolution, but not

CARYL EMERSON

to hybridization, pragmatic compromise, or the incrementally new. In the second (1980), Lotman emphasizes the traditional Russian preference for a Christ-like sacrifice (one-sided, voluntary, an unconditional offering up of the self) over commercial transactions or mutual bargaining, seen as demonic and unclean. The West, on the contrary, intuitively believes in contracts (reciprocity, compulsion, equivalent obligations, conditioned agreement), which to the true-believing Russian resembles more pagan magic than religious morality. The essays were fastidiously annotated, but the fearful simplicity of their conclusions, as well as their evocation of an undifferentiated 'West', has since made non-semiotic historians nervous on both sides of the Atlantic. In another celebrated essay treating the early-eighteenth-century Russian populace collectively as 'decoders', Boris Uspensky argues that Peter the Great consciously designed his massive revolution from above to be read as blasphemous – which is to say, to be read at all, since a religiously inflected sign system was the only language available to the receivers of his message.[21] Bold studies such as these catapulted the Tartu theorists to fame at a time when structural anthropology was a rising field world-wide.

In his final decade, Lotman complicated his binary grids with more flexible organic images: the 'semiosphere', partial overlaps in translatability, and the random products of cultural 'explosion'. In 1984 he remarked (with some overzealous expropriation but also with much sobriety) on his own School's relationship to Bakhtin, claimed as a predecessor.[22] His stock-taking can serve to sum up this chapter, since it circles round to Russian Formalist concerns.

How is semiotics different from dialogics? Lotman notes that Bakhtin, too, emerged out of the great Saussurean revolution in linguistics in the 1910s, but had added two crucial aspects to the debate: 'dialogism', and the dynamic character of the sign. Bakhtin knew that a perfect mechanism could produce only *in*variants, not variants, and that a perfect system (or 'system of systems'), where decoding is identical with encoding (no noise, no slack, no misinformation, no evolution), is closer to a nightmare or a prison cell than a science. Some semiotic systems require absolute precision in decoding and stasis over time (say, road signs), but creative human culture does not. Individuals can never be reliable encoders or decoders; personal experience gets in the way. This is proper, Lotman insists, because (in an echo of Formalist *ostranenie*) 'the entire mechanism of culture strives to make more difficult the reception of what is sent' (150). Culture always benefits when codes are multiplied and understanding is complicated. Bakhtin predated the communication revolution and thus (according to Lotman) he thought somewhat 'impressionistically' about artistic matters, never defining 'dialogue' or 'dialogic'. The potential of these terms was refined by semioticians, who identify dialogue as 'a means for transmitting information between different coding systems' (153). This information need not be verbal and need not be naked fact, but whoever possesses it must desire to communicate it. Thus Lotman offers a corollary to Bakhtinian dialogue: it is a 'mechanism for the assimilation of new information that arose in the process of establishing contact' (154). Bakhtin would have disputed these emendations, although doubtless with a smile. Until the end of his life he believed that 'semiotics deals primarily with the transmission of ready-made communication using a ready-made code'.[23] But in the same jotting from his final notebooks (1970–1971), Bakhtin prefigures Lotman precisely: in live speech, he notes, 'communication is first created in the process of transmission'. It would appear that these two powerful approaches to cultural theory were finding a common language.

Russian theory at the end of the millennium

In 2004, Galin Tihanov published an essay provocatively titled: 'Why did Modern Literary Theory Originate in Central and Eastern Europe? (And Why Is It Now Dead?)'.[24] His answer: from its narrow professional goals under the Formalists of the 1920s, Russian literary theory had swollen to embrace a global theory of culture by the 1990s – and this ambition collapsed as did all mega-narratives during that decade, 'the last stage in the protracted demise of literary theory as an autonomous branch of the humanities'.[25] The Russian sociologist Dina Khapaeva concurs, noting that Tartu semiotics dissipated as a school around the time the Soviet Union itself dissipated, its place filled with a passion for translating critical terms from other national traditions (an activity that enriched Russian culture but did not explain it).[26] The post-communist watershed is still too recent to predict the future shape of Russian critical thought, if indeed national boundaries survive at all in the now-fluid worlds of theory.

What can be said in sum about our trajectory? Since societal relevance and miraculous rebirth are among the guiding themes of this chapter, it is appropriate that Socialist Realism occupied a prominent place in it. Leading up to that artificially created, officially mandated doctrine were three far more cosmopolitan schools, each of which posed a radically different task for literature: the Formalist, the Psychological–psychoanalytic, and the Bakhtin Circle. Leading down off the socialist–realist slope was the Tartu School, which revived certain Formalist methodologies while striving mightily near the end to integrate semiotics with dialogism. Off to the side without a 'school' are the unclassifiable loners and witnesses, still being recuperated together with their age. Paradoxically, for all its profligate violence and censorship, the Russian twentieth century demonstrates the truth of Bakhtin's counter-intuitively optimistic claim near the end of his life that 'nothing is absolutely dead: every meaning will have its festival of rebirth'.[27]

NOTES

1 Epstein, Mikhail N., 'Postmodernism, Communism, and Sots-Art' in *Endquote: Sots-Art Literature and Soviet Grand Style*, trans. John Meredig, ed. Marina Balina, Nancy Condee, and Evgeny Dobrenko (Evanston, IL: Northwestern University Press, 2000), pp. 3–31.
2 Miller, Martin A., *Freud and the Bolsheviks: Psychoanalysis in Imperial Russia and the Soviet Union* (New Haven, CT: Yale University Press, 1998), p. 37.
3 See Yermakov, Ivan, 'The Nose' [edited and compressed] in Maguire, Robert A., *Gogol from the Twentieth Century* (Princeton. NJ: Princeton University Press, 1974), pp. 156–198.
4 Griftsov, B. A., *Psikhologiia pisatelia*, completed 1924, first published 1988 (Moscow: Khudozhestvennaia literatura, 1988). Further page references in text.
5 Vygotsky, Lev, *The Psychology of Art*, trans. (unreliably) Scripta Technica (Cambridge, MA: MIT Press, 1971). Further page references in text.
6 Yaroshevsky, Mikhail, *Lev Vygotsky*, trans. Sergei Syrovatkin (Moscow: Progress Publishers, 1989), p. 140.
7 Ginzburg, Lydia *On Psychological Prose* (1977), trans. and ed. Judson Rosengrant (Princeton, NJ: Princeton University Press, 1991).
8 Van Buskirk, Emily, 'Samoootstranenie' kak eticheskii i esteticheskii printsip v proze L. Ia. Ginzburg', *Novoe literaturnoe obozrenie (NLO)*, 81 (2006), pp. 261–280.
9 For a bold interpretation of Bakhtin, 'the first Russian postmodernist', in the context of Freud, Dostoevsky, Vygotsky, Stalin, Lacan, and the 'philosopher at the mirror', see chapter 10 of Etkind, Alexander, *Eros nevozmozhnogo. Istoriia psikhoanaliza v Rossii* (St Petersburg: Meduza, 1993), pp. 388–412.
10 'Chelovek u zerkala' [The person at the mirror] in *M. M. Bakhtin: Sobranie sochinenii*, vol. 5 (Moscow: Russkie slovari, 1996), p. 71.
11 See 'Discourse in the Novel' (1930s) in *The Dialogic Imagination: Four Essays by M. M. Bakhtin*, trans. Caryl Emerson and Michael Holquist (Austin, TX: University of Texas Press, 1981), pp. 341–343.
12 Trotsky, Leon, *Literature and Revolution*, chapter 5, 'The Formalist School of Poetry and Marxism' (Ann Arbor, MI: University of Michigan Press, 1971), p. 162; later quote on p. 183.
13 See Evgeny Dobrenko's two-volume study, *The Making of the State Reader* (Stanford, CA: Stanford University Press, 1997) and *The Making of the State Writer* (Stanford, CA: Stanford University Press, 2001). Stalinist-era writers were obliged to *follow*, not to facilitate in forming, the mass lowbrow readership that was ideologically sanctioned to receive them.
14 Dobrenko, Evgeny, 'Sotsrealisticheskii mimesis, ili "zhizn'" v ee revoliutsionnom razvitii' in Günther, H. and Dobrenko, E., eds., *Sotsrealisticheskii kanon* (St Petersburg: Akademicheskii proekt, 2000), pp. 459–471, esp. pp. 461–463. This

indispensable one-thousand-page volume of critical essays is referred to hereafter as *SK*.

15 Postoutenko, Kirill, 'Istoricheskii optimizm kak modus stalinskoi kul'tury' in *SK* pp. 481–491, esp. p. 483.

16 Balina, Marina, 'Ideinost' – klassovost' – partiinost' ' in *SK* pp. 362–375. Further page references in text.

17 Quoted by Donald Fanger in Fanger, Donald, trans. and ed., *Gorky's Tolstoy and other Reminiscences: Key Writings by and about Maxim Gorky* (New Haven, CT: Yale University Press, 2008), p. 9.

18 Translated text (adjusted) from later version, Ivanov, Vyacheslav Vs., 'The Role of Semiotics in the Cybernetic Study of Man' in Lucid, Daniel P., ed. and trans., *Soviet Semiotics* (Baltimore, MD: Johns Hopkins University Press, 1977), pp. 27–44, esp. pp. 28, 36–37.

19 Lotman, Jurij, *The Structure of the Artistic Text*, trans. Ronald Vroon (Ann Arbor, MI: Michigan Slavic Studies, 1977), pp. 2, 4, 23.

20 Both in Shukman, Ann, ed., *The Semiotics of Russian Culture* (Ann Arbor, MI: Michigan Slavic Publications, 1984): Lotman, Ju. M. and Uspenskij, Boris A., 'The Role of Dual Models in the Dynamics of Russian Culture' (1977), pp. 33–35; and Lotman, Ju. M., '"Agreement" [Contract] and "Self-Giving" [Handing over oneself] as Archtypal Models of Culture' (1980), pp. 125–140.

21 Uspenskij, B. A., 'Historia sub specie semioticae' (1974), in Lucid, ed. and trans., *Soviet Semiotics*, pp. 107–115.

22 'Nasledie Bakhtina i aktual'nye problemy semiotiki', Russian translation of a paper by Lotman delivered in German in Jena, Germany (1984), at the conference 'Roman und Gesellschaft', published in *Iu. M. Lotman, Istoriia i tipologiia russkoi kul'tury* (St Petersburg: Iskusstvo, 2002), pp. 147–155. Further page references in text.

23 'From Notes Made in 1970–71' in Bakhtin, M. M., *Speech Genres and Other Late Essays*, trans. Vern W. McGee (Austin, TX: University of Texas Press, 1986), p. 147.

24 Tihanov, Galin, 'Why did Modern Literary Theory Originate in Central and Eastern Europe? (And Why Is It Now Dead?)', *Common Knowledge* 10, no. 1 (2004), pp. 61–81.

25 *Ibid.*, p. 63.

26 Khapaeva, Dina, *Gertsogi respubliki v epokhu perevodov. Gumanitarnye nauki i revoliutsiia poniatii* (Moscow: Novoe literatunoe obozrenie, 2005), p. 126.

27 'Toward a Methodology of the Human Sciences' in Bakhtin, M. M., *Speech Genres and Other Late Essays*, trans. Vern W. McGee (Austin, TX: University of Texas Press, 1986), p. 170.

FURTHER READING

Bakhtin, Mikhail, *The Dialogic Imagination: Four Essays by M. M. Bakhtin*, trans. Caryl Emerson and Michael Holquist (Austin, TX: University of Texas Press, 1981).
  Rabelais and his World, trans. Hélène Iswolsky (Bloomington, IN: Indiana University Press, 1984).

Brandist, Craig, *The Bakhtin Circle: Philosophy, Culture and Politics* (London: Pluto Press, 2002).

Erlich, Victor, *Russian Formalism: History – Doctrine*, 3rd edn. (New Haven, CT: Yale University Press, 1955/1981).

Ginzburg, Lydia, *On Psychological Prose*, trans. and ed. Judson Rosengrant (Princeton, NJ: Princeton University Press, 1991).

Jakobson, Roman, *Language in Literature*, ed. Kristina Pomorska and Stephen Rudy (Cambridge, MA: Harvard University Press, 1987).

Lipovetsky, Mark, ed. Eliot Borenstein, *Russian Postmodernist Fiction: Dialogue with Chaos* (Armonk, NY: M. E. Sharpe, 1999).

Lotman, Ju. M. and Uspenskij, B. A., *The Semiotics of Russian Culture*, ed. Ann Shukman (Ann Arbor, MI: University of Michigan, 1984).

Lotman, Yuri M., *Universe of the Mind: A Semiotic Theory of Culture*, trans. Ann Shukman (Bloomington, IN: Indiana University Press, 1990).

Lucid, Daniel P., trans. and ed., *Soviet Semiotics: An Anthology* (Baltimore, MD: Johns Hopkins University, 1977).

Matejka, Ladislav and Pomorska, Krystyna, eds., *Readings in Russian Poetics: Formalist and Structuralist Views* (Normal, IL: Dalkey Archive Press, 2002).

Robin, Régine, *Socialist Realism: An Impossible Aesthetic*, trans. Catherine Porter (Stanford, CA: Stanford University Press, 1992).

Shklovsky, Viktor, *Theory of Prose*, trans. Benjamin Sher (Normal, IL: Dalkey Archive Press, 1991).

Trotsky, Leon, *Literature and Revolution*, chapter 5, 'The Formalist School of Poetry and Marxism' (Ann Arbor, MI: University of Michigan Press, 1971).

Vygotsky, Lev, *The Psychology of Art*, trans. Scripta Technica (Cambridge, MA: MIT Press, 1971).

INDEX

Cambridge Companions to. . .

AUTHORS

Edward Albee edited by Stephen J. Bottoms

Margaret Atwood edited by
Coral Ann Howells

W. H. Auden edited by Stan Smith

Jane Austen edited by Edward Copeland and
Juliet McMaster (second edition)

Beckett edited by John Pilling

Bede edited by Scott DeGregorio

Aphra Behn edited by Derek Hughes and
Janet Todd

Walter Benjamin edited by David S. Ferris

William Blake edited by Morris Eaves

Brecht edited by Peter Thomson and Glendyr
Sacks (second edition)

The Brontës edited by Heather Glen

Frances Burney edited by Peter Sabor

Byron edited by Drummond Bone

Albert Camus edited by Edward J. Hughes

Willa Cather edited by Marilee Lindemann

Cervantes edited by Anthony J. Cascardi

Chaucer edited by Piero Boitani and Jill Mann
(second edition)

Chekhov edited by Vera Gottlieb and
Paul Allain

Kate Chopin edited by Janet Beer

Caryl Churchill edited by Elaine Aston and
Elin Diamond

Coleridge edited by Lucy Newlyn

Wilkie Collins edited by Jenny Bourne Taylor

Joseph Conrad edited by J. H. Stape

Dante edited by Rachel Jacoff
(second edition)

Daniel Defoe edited by John Richetti

Don DeLillo edited by John N. Duvall

Charles Dickens edited by John O. Jordan

Emily Dickinson edited by Wendy Martin

John Donne edited by Achsah Guibbory

Dostoevskii edited by W. J. Leatherbarrow

Theodore Dreiser edited by Leonard Cassuto
and Claire Virginia Eby

John Dryden edited by Steven N. Zwicker

W. E. B. Du Bois edited by Shamoon Zamir

George Eliot edited by George Levine

T. S. Eliot edited by A. David Moody

Ralph Ellison edited by Ross Posnock

Ralph Waldo Emerson edited by Joel Porte
and Saundra Morris

William Faulkner edited by
Philip M. Weinstein

Henry Fielding edited by Claude Rawson

F. Scott Fitzgerald edited by Ruth Prigozy

Flaubert edited by Timothy Unwin

E. M. Forster edited by David Bradshaw

Benjamin Franklin edited by Carla Mulford

Brian Friel edited by Anthony Roche

Robert Frost edited by Robert Faggen

Gabriel García Márquez edited by
Philip Swanson

Elizabeth Gaskell edited by Jill L. Matus

Goethe edited by Lesley Sharpe

Günter Grass edited by Stuart Taberner

Thomas Hardy edited by Dale Kramer

David Hare edited by Richard Boon

Nathaniel Hawthorne edited by
Richard Millington

Seamus Heaney edited by
Bernard O'Donoghue

Ernest Hemingway edited by Scott Donaldson

Homer edited by Robert Fowler

Horace edited by Stephen Harrison

Ibsen edited by James McFarlane

Henry James edited by Jonathan Freedman

Samuel Johnson edited by Greg Clingham

Ben Jonson edited by Richard Harp and
Stanley Stewart

James Joyce edited by Derek Attridge
(second edition)

Kafka edited by Julian Preece

Keats edited by Susan J. Wolfson

Lacan edited by Jean-Michel Rabaté

D. H. Lawrence edited by Anne Fernihough

Primo Levi edited by Robert Gordon

Lucretius edited by Stuart Gillespie and
Philip Hardie

Machiavelli edited by John M. Najemy

David Mamet edited by Christopher Bigsby

Thomas Mann edited by Ritchie Robertson

Christopher Marlowe edited by Patrick Cheney

Andrew Marvell edited by Derek Hirst and
Steven N. Zwicker